Black
Political
Mobilization

SUNY series in Afro-American Studies
John Howard and Robert C. Smith, Editors

Black Political Mobilization

Leadership, Power, and Mass Behavior

MINION K.C. MORRISON

State University of New York Press

Cover photo by Fred Ward, Courtesy of Black Star.

Published by
State University of New York Press, Albany

© 1987 State University of New York

All rights reserved

Printed in the United States of America

No part of this book may be used or reproduced
in any manner whatsoever without written permission
except in the case of brief quotations embodied in
critical articles and reviews.

For information, address State University of New York
Press, State University Plaza, Albany, N.Y., 12246

Library of Congress Cataloging-in-Publication Data

Morrison, Minion K. C., 1946-
    Black political mobilization, leadership, and power.

    (SUNY series in Afro-American studies)
    Bibliography: p.
    Includes index.
    1. Afro-Americans—Mississippi—Politics and
government.   2. Afro-American leadership—Mississippi.
3. Mississippi—Politics and government—1951-
I. Title.   II. Series.
E185.93.M6M67   1987   323.1'196073'0762   86-30051
ISBN 0-88706-515-5
ISBN 0-88706-516-3 (pbk.)

10 9 8 7 6 5 4 3 2 1

For Johnetta and Iyabo
and
B.G.T.

Contents

List of Figures and Tables — *ix*

Preface — *xiii*

1. The American Political System and Mobilization Politics — *1*
2. Black and White in the Southern Regional Context — *23*
3. Neo-Populism in Bolton — *53*
4. Heroine in Mayersville — *95*
5. Agrarian Townsman in Tchula — *123*
6. The Electorates: Politics, Economics and Ideology — *163*
7. The Political Economy of Rural Black-American Mobilization — *209*
8. Conclusion — *243*

Notes — *255*

Bibliography — *281*

Index — *293*

List of Figures and Tables

FIGURES

1.1	Mississippi Counties, ca. 1980	2
2.1	Black Concentration in Mississippi	37
3.1	Town of Bolton, Mississippi, ca. 1980	54
3.2	Center of Early Black Political Participation	57
4.1	Town of Mayersville, Mississippi, ca. 1980	96
5.1	Town of Tchula, Mississippi, ca. 1980	124
6.1	Median Percentage of Voting-Age Negroes Registered to Vote, by Percentage of County Population Negro in 1950, in 11 Southern States	172
6.2	Information on Organizations and Indirect Local Leaders in the Three Towns	189
6.3	Information on Organizations and Indirect Local Leaders, by Town	189
6.4	Preferences for Integration	200
6.5	Opposition to Power Sharing, by Education and Income	202

TABLES

2.1	Black Legislative Representation (Lower House), 1870-1890	40
2.2	Black Registration, 1867-1955	44
2.3	Black Voter Registration 1962-1967 in Selected Counties	49
2.4	Black Elected Officials in Mississippi, 1967-1970	50
3.1	Hinds County Population 1840-1860	55
3.2	1973 Election Returns, Bolton	89
4.1	Population in Issaquena County	97

6.1	Percent of Eligible Voter Participation, 1952-1976	165
6.2	Relations of State Restrictions on Voting to Past Frequency of Voting	166
6.3	Population in Standard Metropolitan Areas (SMAs), by Regions: 1900, 1930, and 1950 (in thousands)	169
6.4	Racial Population Distribution, 1940-1980	171
6.5	Socioeconomic Characteristics	176
6.6	Voter Registration and Length of Registration in Three Mississippi Towns, Post-1977	179
6.7	Voting for State and National Executives, 1972-1976	180
6.8	Voting in Local Elections, Post-1967	182
6.9	Political Information: Local, State, and National (1972-1980)	185
6.10	Electoral Participation: Gubernatorial and Presidential	186
6.11	Correct Knowledge of Elected Officials: Local, National and State	187
6.12	Knowledge of Issues/Leaders in African and Foreign Affairs	191
6.13	Pearson's Correlations (SES) with Africa Knowledge	193
6.14	Zero-Order Correlations/Knowledge and Opinion Variables	194
6.15	Interactions with Local Government, Old Regime	195
6.16	Interactions with Local Government, New Regime	196
6.17	Percentage in Bolton and Tchula who Believed They Could Influence What the Government Did	197
6.18	Opinions on Racism in South Africa	204
6.19	Pearson's Correlations (SES) With Africa Opinion Variables	204
6.20	Zero-Order Correlations and Opinion Variables	206
7.1	County Population Migration, 1960-1975	215
7.2	County Farm Ownership (A) and Operation (B) among AfroAmericans, 1940-1978, by Number	216
7.3	County Farm Ownership (A) and Operation (B) among Whites, 1940-1978, by Number	216
7.4	Sources of Income for Two Counties	219
7.5	Taxes on Certain Classes of Personal Property (1978), by County ($ millions)	220

7.6	Sales Taxes in the Towns, 1969-1980 ($ thousands)	*221*
7.7	Gross Sales ($ millions) by Category, 1970, 1974, 1978, 1980	*223*
7.8	General Fund and Water Utility Revenues, 1970-1976, Bolton	*224*
7.9	Chief Sources of Bolton Revenue, Post-1973	*225*
7.10	Revenue in Bolton 1973-1974 ($ thousands)	*228*
7.11	Federal Support (by Agency, Type and Town)	*232*
7.12	Phase Two Projects	*235*

Preface

> Since 1954 we have been presented with an uninterrupted stream of Negro race-advancement activity: school integration suits, bus boycotts, voter registration drives, freedom rides, 'package' integration demands, and the 'ins'—sit-ins, kneel-ins, wade-ins, and finally sleep-ins. Negro Americans are attaining 'firsts' on literally a daily basis: Leroy Johnson became in 1962 the first Negro to be elected to the Georgia Senate since Reconstruction, Henry Frye the first Negro Assistant U.S. District Attorney in North Carolina. Stores hire their first nonwhite clerks, schools take in their first nonwhite pupils and a deep-South governor for the first time invites the Negro constituents to an inaugural barbecue. And quietly the Negro and white pastors of a deep-South city dine together for the first time as members of an integrated ministerial fellowship.
>
> Negro political leadership necessarily has been caught up in this revolution in race relations, for the structure of race relations has always defined the essential features of race leadership.[1]

> The great crusade in Montgomery inspired black leaders throughout the South to attempt to project the style and charisma of Martin Luther King. But while no one quite managed to walk in the footsteps of the master, his movement was fittingly apotheosized in the sit-ins crusade, which was launched by black students early in 1960. To young black people in the South, the Montgomery boycott was the only important social action ever brought off by blacks in the nation's history. To them, King became an instant hero—something of a black superman. At the very least, he was for them a new father figure, a welcome substitute for the obsequious, ingratiating, and cowardly image historically portrayed by adult black males in the region.[2]

These two evaluations largely sum up the period of black political mobilization that is the focus of this analysis. Though the cases herein are about Mississippi, they are merely representative of a broader phenomenon of political change that sustains a new leadership class in electoral power in the southern region. Electoral power, however, is but the end product of a process that begins with an emphasis on moral rights and symbols, sometimes apparently oblivious to welfare goals. Yet the earlier focus was probably necessary in order to develop skills for the material welfare phase denoted by control of political institutions.

For our purposes it is most useful to think of the Montgomery boycott as the catalyst, and Martin Luther King as the symbol of the evolving mobilization campaign. Shortly after Montgomery, the general confidence and perception of improved social and political prospects on the part of blacks were obvious. This set off a plethora of activities that culminated in the occupation of institutional positions by blacks today in the South.

Voter registration was one of the prime examples. The Voter Education Project (VEP) in Atlanta reported in 1964 that registration success after 1960 was remarkable: "Between 1952 and 1962, Negro registration increased from 1,008,614 to only 1,286,654." But after the broad activation of students and other black leaders around King-style actions, this registration figure rose by more than 100 percent to 2,164,200.[3] Ladd has already shown that a state legislator was elected by these voters in Georgia in 1962. And there were other visible signs of success. For example, the VEP illustrated that Blacks had a major impact in certain states on the outcome of the Johnson and Goldwater presidential election. They show that the improved registration of blacks and their significant turnout in Florida, Tennessee, Arkansas and Virginia made the difference for Democratic victories in these states.[4]

The greatest impact down through the 1960s was to be realized at the local level, in rural places. In a catalog of political success, Mack Jones has shown that blacks won a good portion of the available local offices: on school boards, as aldermen and women and council members; election commissioners, clerks, constables and sheriffs; and as town and municipal mayors. At the state level the most frequent positions held were in state houses, though in most states the numbers were small.[5]

With the continued movement and the passage of the Voting Rights Act in 1965, the registration of blacks and their electoral success improved even more dramatically: by 1968 there was not a single former confederate state with a registration level below 50 percent.[6] These changes were occurring even in Mississippi, where in 1967 the first black was elected to the state legislature, and in 1969, Charles Evers was the first small town (Fayette, population 1,700-plus) mayor to be so elected.[7]

In the long struggle for human and political rights, few groups have been as systematically repulsed as blacks. The intensity of the struggle for political rights has hardly been greater than that period in the 1960s when everywhere highly mobilized blocs of blacks sought political office as a means of destroying racial exclusion and hatred. Mississippi, a state where the racial division in public life was so sharp, underwent a transformation, insofar as the election of blacks was concerned. The successful and varied nature of the mobilization there makes the state a good illustrative case for exploring this period of political change in American life.

To this end, this analysis explores three Mississippi towns where blacks controlled institutional politics after 1973—Bolton, Tchula, and Mayersville. Each municipality, under 2,000 in population, had a black mayor and a set of circumstances that made it possible to explore a range of problems attendant to 'black power,' or to the further refinement of American democracy.

Mississippi politics has been greatly affected by the presence of a large black population almost from the beginning in the early 19th century. Indeed, in some measure the large fertile delta region provided not just opportunity, but a justification for the importation of a large African laborer class.

At the time it was no dishonor that these laborers were brought in as slaves; this was a common and accepted practice elsewhere in the South. Yet it was this massive African presence that gave the state its personality. As so many Africans were brought in, maintenance of the white owner class was always an issue. The laborers were perceived as a threat, not just because of the competition they presented whites, but for other reasons of assumed African inferiority. In this context, problems were thought to arise from the unbridled character of a near-majority black population, and/or the potential for 'inappropriate' interactions between 'inferiors' and 'superiors.' Subsequently, racial interactions and the social structure were designed to guarantee the political hegemony and reasonable 'purity' of the white group.

Mississippi became the most calculatedly segregated of the southern states. Its philosophical justification for white supremacy was as strong as the material character of everyday life.

The struggle for power by blacks in Mississippi, even in the best of times, has been first and foremost about their inherent right to participate in the allocation of public resources. The struggle in Mississippi probably only differs from that of many other places in the United States because of the depth of racial division. Yet this is what makes the present cases of black electoral success in the state so interesting. Despite the sustained historical racial division, today the success of formal black participation in Mississippi compares more than favorably with that in most other states. This study of the black mayors is but illustrative of much broader phenomenon occurring in the state. For now, this pattern is consistent with what is happening elsewhere in the nation.

Blacks have been contenders in only two periods in Mississippi state history—roughly between 1869–1876, and about 1967 through the present. Ironically, in both periods Mississippi was on the cutting edge of black electoral power. In the first period many Blacks had offices, but nowhere near the range of those in the present period.

Much of the difference is related to the independent resources and the ideas that blacks brought to the new period. As contenders in 1967, blacks had a wealth of organizational and human resources committed to social and political change. From the churches, the 'streets,' and the campuses emerged a class of leaders that sought to capitalize upon the new spirit. Rapid mobilization followed, and so did an entirely new national coalition of support that resulted in the contending forces in Mississippi and elsewhere achieving unprecedented power. Thus at the same time that Cleveland could boast of electing Carl Stokes as mayor, Mississippians in black-belt Holmes County could boast of electing the first black (Robert Clark) in modern times to the state legislature. This was followed in 1969 with the election of a black as mayor in the biracial town of Fayette (Charles Evers). This began a cycle of successes in highly mobilized communities all over the state, despite national attention to more visible urban places, such as Cleveland.

The significance of these 1967 events was that they represented the culmination of an intensified campaign against racial segregation and discrimination. Though the elected leaders were practical, cautious and traditional politicians, they symbolized success for previously disfranchised blacks. Many new voters had taken great risks to even seek change. They had dared to confront "mean white folks" and to stimulate risk-taking on the part of friends and neighbors. They had been instrumental in mobilizing outside support and using it judiciously to bring about change. Indeed, this period that culminated in winning political office was itself often not about formal officeholding. It is more properly thought of as a form of social mobilization whereby education brought changes in attitudes and created conditions conducive to seeking institutional political power.

The indigenous leaders, however, rapidly turned their attention to institutional politics. Some of the younger leaders felt redeemed, but also catalyzed or revitalized by Clark and Evers. Now that the taboo of blacks in formal electoral positions had been broken, other posts were sought.

While many other aspects of common human rights of blacks in the state were unsettled, the focus now shifted to the electoral arena. Many would-be office holders even began to perceive other unsettled racial issues as subject to resolution via institutional positions. They developed rapid strategies for seeking the "political kingdom," particularly where a black majority existed. The voting legislation for which most had fought so diligently was a major tool of this mobilization.

In Mississippi, this strategy saw black candidates emerge for the state legislative, state executive and local municipal positions. Initially, hardly any of these were successful in the state legislature; Robert Clark remained the sole black there until reapportionment in the mid-1970s. Elsewhere, however, blacks enjoyed remarkable success. They were elected to school boards, aldermanic posts, various local judiciary posts, and county clerkships. One of the most successful areas, however, was that of municipal executives. It was not long after 1970 that Mississippi had over ten small towns with a black mayor. The numbers of such towns with aldermen and women was much greater still. Moreover, it was also not long after the Joint Center for Political Studies (JCPS) started its recordkeeping (1970) that Mississippi became the state with the most elected black officials.

Such shifts in political realities are of note anywhere, and political scientists scramble to find ways of accounting for the circumstances. My motivations have been similar. How do we explain what has happened to blacks in politics in Mississippi, and other southern states, under circumstances of population concentration and mobilization? There are also subsidiary questions—such as who are the leaders that fill the positions and how do they come to fill them; what are the attributes of the people they represent (aside from their being black)? In other words, there is a broad need for description and documentation of such occurrences.

In the following analysis, all of these areas are explored in accounting for the political role of blacks in the contemporary rural South. The towns of Bolton, Mayersville and Tchula in rural Mississippi provide the cases for this study. Each elected a black mayor in the 1970s, and in individual ways each provided a broad spectrum of events and leadership styles for analysis. As such, they provide a window on the more general process of black electoral politics, in the area where blacks have enjoyed the broadest success.

While much of the change in the late 1960s and 1970s was symbolic, the active focus was the redress of past racial exclusion. Therefore, the focus in this analysis is on the extent of fundamental change in black leadership and its constituency that led to the assumption of power. It is argued that consistent with a mobilization that began in the 1960s in the rural South, blacks not only acquired the trappings of political office, they also sought to redefine the task of governance and to create an essentially new kind of community. This means that virtually a new leadership class emerged without debts or deference to the old ways of the South; that a collective purpose was adopted by the newly-franchised electorates; and that actual resources were acquired through which power could be exercised.

In this context, the assumption of political power was not merely that of "equals" trading spoils; it was rather a highly mobilized group displacing what was seen as an oppressor class. This distinction is important because of what it reveals about the effort to restructure the allocation of routine political resources in the rural South. It makes it possible to account for the political shifts and to draw guidelines for measuring them.

The theoretical focus that is adopted here is that of mobilization understood as the combination of certain resources, the activation of which make it possible for the assumption of power or control of government. This process dictates certain preconditions that when met sustain the new leadership class, including the election to office, an ideology of social change and a purposive welfare program. There are, of course, some other preconditions that also play a vital role in the quest for power: charisma and youth. At the same time, a variety of factors characteristic of the mobilization process—attitudes and behaviors consistent with group solidarity toward the ends of social change—create a constituency supportive of power acquisition. Hence the purpose of this exploration is not merely to describe the process by which the power shift occurred, but also to elaborate how the terms of order were defined, essentially by the independent efforts of black people.

In answering these questions about a grossly understudied area, an unusually vast and complex number of procedures were required and utilized. First, even before any research questions were formulated, I followed the electoral campaigns of the earliest leaders in the 1960s and gained familiarity with their loci of operation. From time to time, I was also actively exploring local issues around which constituents were mobilized. In the formal preparation of the study after the three towns were selected, research methods included the following: archival survey of historical documents; review of local government records; multiple and substantive interviews of mayoral leaders; a reputational survey of local leaders; and a household survey of each town's citizens. The initial work (which also served the function of a pretest) took place at Bolton in 1977. Then over the three years of 1979–82, the tasks noted above were completed in Bolton and also carried out in Mayersville and Tchula.

Much of the discussion of mobilization as the overriding theoretical focus, and that of the preconditions for leadership, are taken up in the first chapter, which is then followed (Chapter Two) by an exploration of southern history as it created conditions for mobilization. The succeeding three chapters provide case studies of the individual towns and their leaders. Chapters Six and Seven are concerned with the constituency and its linkage to leadership. First, in Chapter Six, the electorates are described together with an analysis of behaviors and attitudes in the period of intense mobilization. Chapter Seven then seeks to determine the success of the political leadership in meeting its own goals and those of the immediate constituency. In this presentation it will be seen that while there are benefits and drawbacks, overall the immediate consequence of this shift for black betterment has been remarkably successful. And finally, Chapter Eight draws together some conclusions and offers prospects for these areas.

As is usually the case, I have acquired many debts in thinking through this topic and in preparing the manuscript. I suppose I owe the greatest debt to so many of those (whose names I never knew and/or cannot remember, or those whose modesty would not allow them to take credit), who like me dared to raise troubling questions about political and social change in the 1960s. It was they with whom I communed for days on end, and from whom I garnered great inspiration. Many of these individuals, like me, had found their way as students and professors to a small Mississippi college which served as a nurturing ground for ideas about change for black life. Though much of the curriculum of the small college was not itself related to the "movement," the activist orientation of some of the faculty, and the now-old-fashioned tradition of urging students to think about broad questions regarding human nature and science, were important. This learning environment inevitably led students to seriously question contemporary realities. I was fortunate to have enjoyed the benefits of such an environment.

It was under these circumstances that an interest in explaining the political changes in the South emerged. I maintained an interest in the problem long after an early field research project in Fayette, Mississippi, completed with my colleague and friend, Joe Huang. The form that the work would take only crystallized in 1977, when the National Science Foundation funded a pilot project to be conducted in Bolton. Further work was funded by the National Endowment for the Humanities.

Naturally, I also acquired many other debts to colleagues and student assistants. Gordon Henderson provided much technical assistance in the early part, while Stephen Rozman provided encouragement (both then in Tougaloo College). Later, David Stamps, then at Syracuse University, provided good technical assistance and encouragement. The student interviewers are too many to mention, but their work was very ably managed by my research assistant at the time, Walter O'Meally. Though he had apprehensions about the first visit to Mississippi, his enthusiasm and companionship in the field never waned.

In the course of the field work itself, very little could have been accomplished without the assistance of the three mayors. Each took time from their busy schedules to submit to long interviews, to take me on town tours, and to arrange situations for my comfort and exploration. They also made their staffs and records available; and went out of their way to be open about their business, without any apparent regard for areas that might reflect negatively upon themselves.

During the preparation of the manuscript, I enjoyed the good fellowship of my colleagues at Syracuse University, who encouraged this work and listened over time, with much patience, to one other aspect of the "mayors book." One of these colleagues, Randolph Hawkins, also provided occasional technical assistance toward the end. Others at Syracuse contributed much, including Gershon Vincow (then dean of the College of Arts and Sciences), who provided additional financial support, and Mike Kirchoff and the staff at the cartographic lab. I enjoyed the remarkable research assistance of Pieter Kiwiet, who though dizzied by the figures got through them all. To this end he provided superb aggregations of data for charts and graphs. Lionel André, an excellent undergraduate student, also assisted with some content analyses of newspapers. Of course many typists have turned their hand at the Department of Afro-American Studies at Syracuse: Sondra Tranen, Roxanne Raicht, Dora Peterson, Sheila Hicks, Deborah Bussey, Paula Webster, and Carolyn Wright. Their untiring efforts have been essential and are much appreciated.

Other individuals, libraries and librarians have been most useful. The Bird Library at Syracuse provided many resources from its own collections; while the interlibrary loan librarian, Mrs. Dorcas MacDonald, sometimes worked miracles in acquiring almost anything I requested. Virgia Brocks-Shedd at the Coleman Library (Tougaloo) was helpful, as was the staff of the Schomberg Library in New York City. Fred Cooper, formerly of Jackson, Mississippi, sent many useful packages, as did various Mississippi state offices.

My family has endured this project, as others, with the same degree of confidence and good spirit. Johnetta, my wife, has read parts that interested her; and Iyabo, my daughter, occasionally answered the phone and unexpectedly spoke of informants with glee.

Minion K.C. Morrison
Syracuse, September 1986

1

The American Political System and Mobilization Politics

Blacks in the South experienced a virtual revolution in status and participation by 1970. This was all a part of a long process of resistance to abject racism most often effected in social segregation and political disfranchisement. Mississippi's policies of this nature were broader and more visible than most other southern states. Though Blacks were disfranchised *defacto* by 1880 and *dejure* by 1890, a culmination of forces only 40 or so years later set in motion the process of group mobilization for independent acquisition of social and political resources. This mobilization became more self-consciously trained on the goals of social integration and collective group power in the mid-1950s. By this time, a sufficiently large number of local organizations and leaders forged ongoing relationships and synchronized goals that yielded solidarity. The effectiveness of this effort created conditions for a more strategic mobilization of blacks for political purposes. The objective in this analysis is to theoretically account for this process of mobilization in southern politics and to use three cases in Mississippi to illustrate this phenomenon.

The three towns of Bolton, Tchula and Mayersville are a part of this revolution. They emerged in the mid-1960s from a period of white rule and

Figure 1.1 Mississippi Counties, ca. 1980.

sociocultural domination just short of one hundred years. The civil rights movement touched each town in direct ways, producing a new variety of aggressive black leaders and constituents that would fundamentally alter institutional political arrangements. This rapid change was the product of mobilization that saw the citizens consciously organize for political action and then take up the mantle of public demonstrations and voter education and registration. Such activation resulted in electoral victories for black leaders as early as 1969 in Bolton. In 1973 a black mayor, Bennie Thompson, was elected, followed by similar mayoral successes in Tchula and Mayersville in 1977. The mobilization activity and consequence in these three places are the objects of this exploration.

Mobilization is defined as the collective activation and application of community or group resources toward the acquisition of social and political goods. These social and political goods are regarded (at least theoretically) as legitimate, though the fact of mobilization suggests that the collectivity in question is isolated from such goods. This condition of isolation was prevalent for blacks in the form of disfranchisement all over the southern region in the 1950s, though legitimate citizenship status was intact. As such, the objective circumstances of black exclusion and the activation to acquire such assets invites analysis via a scheme of mobilization.

Prior to fully exploring mobilization, it is useful to look at other possible explanatory models for understanding black political life in American society. There are several very prominent theories for explaining American political phenomena, especially pluralism and elitism. But how useful are they in explaining the status of black people and the political mobilization that characterized the period of this analysis? Pluralism is perhaps the most widely used of these models, but is probably the least practical in accounting for the status of blacks in the system.

The thesis of the pluralists is that the political system is open and routinely accessible to members of the body politic. Though first feared by the "founding fathers,"[1] group organization became the most desired means for securing political goods. David B. Truman described how pluralism works.[2] He assumed, as do most other pluralists, that in a democracy there is bound to be a plethora of groups, where a premium is placed on their identification and organization as such; virtually everyone employs such a strategy for achieving political goals. The ends of democracy are met because everyone can and does bid. The benefits one receives depend on what one puts in.

Dahl's pathbreaking analysis of New Haven illustrated the idea. According to him, over a period of 150 years New Haven went from "cumulative inequalities" to "non-cumulative or dispersed inequalities." That is, the possession of degrees of influence in New Haven came to be highly disperse and variable; citizens were therefore rarely locked into position. He found this hypothesis to be sustained by six characteristics, many of which form the basis of pluralist theory today: (1) different citizens possess a wide range of different resources for influence; (2) such resources are unequally distributed; (3) rarely does one possess a high capability of influence in all resource areas; (4) no single resource dominates the influence sector, or (5) the decision process; and (6) no sizable group is without "influence resources."[3]

Despite the broad acceptance of the pluralist scheme, it has been found wanting by elite theorists. They argue that the American political system is far less open than the ideology of the revolution suggests. A careful analysis of those with influence and power, they say, reveals a small group generally enjoying very high socioeconomic status. This group owns, has access to, or influences all the significant resources, yielding a monopoly on public policy in virtually every sphere. Dolbeare and Edelman trace the roots back to the earliest days:

> Beard argu(ed) that the Framers were men who had acquired vast holdings of bonds and scrip (issued by the Continental Congress during the Revolutionary War) at low values, to which they had fallen because of the inability of the Congress to pay its debts. He implied that they then constructed a powerful government that could raise revenue and pay off the bonds at full value—to their great profit.[4]

They conclude, as have others, that the Framers did indeed share an "upper-class ethos"[5] shaping a pattern that characterizes contemporary American politics. "The basic character and workings of the American political economy are shaped by wealthy, service-demanding, and often multinational corporations." When the financial institutions are added that control credit (large banks), one uncovers a small network of interlocking interests that dominate political and economic resources. For example, "only 220 banks account for practically all lending in the United States." And since such a large proportion of their loans are made to the corporations, this "contributes to both greater influence and shared interests and to dependence on conditions that facilitate repayment of such loans." Moreover, the insurance and investment concerns dominate "the economy's sales, assets, and profits," and thereby "create the context and establish the lending priorities for all actions by major American institutions." The government participates in this because it is often infused with members from corporate structure who oversee the advance of public policies favorable to such big businesses. Otherwise the government is simply too fragmented to effectively thwart corporate influence.[6]

One of the best-known studies of elite power was done at the local level. In this study of Atlanta, contrary to Dahl's findings in New Haven, Floyd Hunter found a power elite. Indeed, "the exercise of power was limited and directed by the formulation and extension of social policy within a framework of socially sanctioned authority." Therefore, "a smaller number of individuals [were] found [to] be formulating and extending policy than those exercising power." "They form cliques or crowds . . . [and are] held together by common interests, mutual obligations, money, habit, delegated responsibilities, and in some cases by coercion and force."[7] Subsequently, Michael Parenti is led to the conclusion that circumstances like those cited above constitute impediments to open participation.[8]

Elite analysis does provide a kind of explanation for Afro-American status insofar as blacks are outside of the small elite group. This does not account for the virtual absence of them in an elite structure which is theoretically open however. It has been left to black scholars in combination with some elite theorists to concentrate upon racism as a significant other variable that determines the exclusion of blacks. Together they show how the dynamics of elitism and racism are linked to the mobilization that led to black political empowerment. They illustrate how the "group" base of politics has not really worked for blacks. While some other ethnic groups have gradually moved from exclusion to (more or less) independence of movement and systemic involvement, blacks have consistently remained largely excluded. Marguerite Ross Barnett explains this differential within the structural dynamics of racism. On the one hand, she shows how pluralism works for some. These white groups are "politically integrated in the American system, [and] . . . find a congruence (at the structural level) [sic] between American political ideology (individualism and egalitarianism) and their day-to-day existence."[9] But the same is not true for blacks, who in a theoretically non-hierarchically ranked society, are consistently subject to such ranking. "(R)acism is a pervasive ideology that ranks Blacks as a group below all others because it assumes the inherent genetic inferiority of Blacks."[10]

That considerations are made on the assumption of genetic inferiority is taken up time and again by scholars. Even in our own time, Mack Jones refers to this lingering notion.[11] Dolbeare and Edelman refer to the "long-lived and pervasive . . . value of white supremacy. . . . [As] an animating feature of Americans and their governmental policies throughout our history."[12] Morris has said that racism has come to constitute a "set of attitudes and beliefs that affect virtually all aspects of social relations," whose pervasiveness "can be viewed as a part of a larger 'disease' of cultural chauvinism which the colonists brought with them from Europe." It has "creat[ed] and maintain[s] . . . the subordinate-superordinate structure of the society, . . . [with] continuing consequences for the place accorded Blacks in the political system, [and] the distribution of goods and services by the system."[13] This racial ranking, notwithstanding other restrictive elements, has a devastating effect on individual black political participation. Blacks, more often than not, do not have the option to act individually, since the assertion of inferiority is collective. Barker and McCorry sum this up:

> The status of blacks in American society has largely been determined, as Chief Justice Taney said in *Dred Scott*, by the "indelible marks" of race and color. And for the most part, these are the same "indelible marks" that continue to shape the everyday life of blacks and other minorities in this country. For example, whites have no worry about whether they will be harrassed by police. Longhairs as longhairs might be, but not whites as whites. Whites have no worry as to whether they can buy a house where they choose. . . .

But blacks in America have to be very much aware and alert to such concerns. Indeed, despite massive civil rights legislation, black Americans can never be sure. With respect to blacks, the dominant cutting edge in America remains very much one of race and color, not one of class and status.[14]

In light of the weaknesses of pluralist theories and the relative incompleteness of elitist theories in accounting for racial exclusion, another model has been more successfully adopted. Variously referred to as the "colonial" model or "institutionalized racism," these ideas focus on the importance of racist practices that isolate blacks, and thus create all the conditions conducive to mobilization for systemic change. This approach "begins with a delineation of the status of blacks in the society and proceeds to an explication of the conditions essential to the achievement of change. (There) is a conviction that black America constitutes a distinct national entity existing in a colonial type relationship to white America."[15]

This "colonialism" is "institutionalized" insofar as it "relies on the active and pervasive operation of anti-black attitudes and practices (that) permeate the society, on both the individual and institutional level, covertly and overtly."[16] The domination of blacks in this case is not unlike that experienced by the colonies of Africa and Asia: blacks entered the relationship involuntarily; whites "carry out a policy which constrains, transforms or destroys indigenous values, orientations, and ways of life"; blacks tend to be administered by representatives of the dominant group, where "assumed racial inferiority forms the basis for exploitation, control and psychic oppression."[17]

The virtue of such an approach to an understanding of black life is that it directs us to the question of how else black citizens may move toward the goal of democratic inclusion. It has been seen that the broad exclusion of blacks is not explained by pluralism, nor does the theoretically open system of elite rule nullify the racial standard. Besides, neither of these schemes provide for a degree of transformation sufficient to rectify the powerlessness historically experienced by blacks. Neither can account for the mobilization analyzed in Southern towns like Bolton, Tchula and Mayersville. However, "the colonized people approach suggests the orientation of such change as the acquisition of a substantial measure of autonomy, and—for some elements of the black community—the eventual emergence of a separate political community."[18] Thus there is fairly close linkage between this thesis and the behaviors of black southerners beginning in the 1950s that focused on the mobilization of the racial community constituency through which political goods would be sought. It was this racial organization and solidarity that undergirded the civil rights campaign and later the drive for electoral office.

Mobilization as a theory has been much utilized by scholars concerned with the decolonizing world where wholesale transformation was occurring. Largely this results from generic aspects of the term having to do with massive movement of some kind in a social or political context; usually where democracy is the form of political community. Deutsch has called this general thrust social mobilization:

> ... overall process of change, which happens to substantial parts of the population in countries which are moving from *traditional* to *modern* ways of life. It denotes a concept which brackets together a number of more specific processes of change, such as changes of residence, of occupation of social setting, of face-to-face associates, of institutions, roles, and ways of acting, of experiences and expectations, and finally of personal memories, habits and needs, including the need for new patterns of group affiliation and new images of personal identity. Singly, and even more in their cumulative impact, these changes tend to influence and sometimes to transform political behavior.[19]

Few scholars, however, considered that social mobilization was the end of the process; it was merely a beginning for a broader effort at expanding the articulate body politic. This combination of forces was referred to as the process of modernization. David Apter defined it almost exclusively as the effort to achieve democratization, defined as late-nineteenth century European political forms. Modernization "[s]o altered . . . the character of western society that it became a model . . . for the comparison of countries elsewhere. [The] emphasis [in] the new nations [is] development of national forms of polity, the objects of which are to increase the social product with fair shares for all."[20] That is, these tendencies to modernize and mobilize are set in motion after some threshold is reached that leads to a sequential and unilinear process of "fundamental democratization."[21] Some authors even equate the colonial experience with this inexorable drift toward "democratization." "Because commercial and some industrial enterprises established in the colonial territories had their markets and main source of investment in their home countries, there is a correlation between the rising economic status of the metropole and the increase in commercialization and modernization of the overseas territory."[22]

But this is only one side of what would seem to be the thrust of this mass movement of peoples to new activities and identities. The other side is political mobilization. Not only were the countries of Asia and Africa attempting to alter and reform their traditional patterns of existence, they were also raising some fundamental questions about their relationship to the system of colonial domination. The great sweep of changes that started after World War I, and reached a fever pitch around World War II, were indicative of complex phenomena designed to achieve redistribution of social and political resources in these societies. The complexity of the process resulted from the fact that even as some elements were intensively engaged in the "transition" from traditional roles, others were concerned with the transfer of administrative power from the colonialists. Even though the actors in the latter case were quite set apart from the mass of the indigenous, the entire society was nevertheless engaged by the proposition for power transfer.

The thinking of the comparativists has been instructive in clarifying the concept of political mobilization. They focus on the development of new loyalties, leadership, solidarity and activism on the part of those seeking massive changes. Those who sought to replace the colonialists did so by demonstrating that mobilization of the masses was possible in a variety of ways. One author has defined it as "a process by which significant numbers of previously quiescent persons are brought to perform relatively deliberate and concerted political acts . . . voting, joining a political organization, . . . political strike or demonstration, armed rebellion *inter alia*."[23] In this case the onus is placed upon the masses to act to achieve political change.

Other scholars emphasize the same factors, but include leadership. Hence, J.P. Nettl has said that mobilization is "the notion of substantial changes in defining new referents for different sections of the population, *as well as to the success of an elite in forcing acceptance of its new reference groups* (emphasis added).[24] For him this process is attitudinal. He speaks of the "commitment to action," and having the means to "translate" such commitment "into action or observed behavior." By this he means that a combination of forces must be at work in order to produce Kearney's "deliberate political acts"; they occur in several stages that are presumably sequential. Those that are especially relevant to this study are:

(a) the existence of values and goals requiring mobilization;
(b) action on the part of leaders, elites or institutions seeking to mobilize individuals and groups;
(c) the institutional and collective means of achieving this mobilization;
(d) the symbols and references by which values, goals and norms are communicated to, and understood as internalized by, the individuals involved in mobilization.[25]

These theories were useful in explaining a variety of third world political behavior similar to that to be explained in the American South. Following World War II, the colonized territories began a campaign for independence, albeit under the terms set by and within the context of the colonizing western democracies. Like the southern blacks that followed them, mobilization occurred on two broad fronts. First, there was horizontal mobilization "involv[ing] the marshalling of popular political support by class or community leaders and their specialized organizations. Ignoring the leaders and members of natural associations or little platoons, they made direct ideological appeals to classes or communities." Second, there was differential mobilization, or organized appeals to "internally differentiated communities through parallel appeals to ideology, sentiment, and interest."[26] What emerged was a broad campaign for self-determination, increased participation, broadened leadership and fundamentally altered social relations.

Though the third world experience and comparative theory is useful, there are certain obvious problems. While defining the process of mobilization, the comparativists tend to lose sight of the complex factors underlying the assumption of new commitments and the willingness to act. A part of the problem is the acceptance of an assumed unilinear process of modernization, heavily imbued with psychological components: clashes between traditional (usually ethnic) ties and the looser social arrangements of modern life. This obscures the prominence of political resource factors like resource transfer and redistribution, and the attendant antagonisms between the powerful and the powerless.[27]

One other obvious problem is the material differences between the United States and the poor nations of the third world. The "social mobilization" described by Deutsch is clearly inappropriate for the United States, one of the most highly democratized and industrialized societies in the world. For example, in the social sphere there is little in the way of a traditional society to be transformed; America is highly urbanized. Media technology is among the most sophisticated in the world, and political participation of the variety suggested by Kearney is very broad in the United States. So the phenomenon to be explained about black mobilization begins at another point or stage: that where the focus is on harnessing known and widely available resources to others in the political community.

Notwithstanding the disclaimers, the outsider status of blacks in the political community provides circumstances that can sustain a political mobilization movement quite like that experienced among third world nationalists several decades ago. It has already been argued that institutionalized racial exclusion is critical to this isolation. The ideology of racism (often in conflict with other ideas such as egalitarianism) has created a lag in black political development of great magnitude. This "stable unrepresentation" yields a consequence whereby "some groups are described as occupying a status outside the arena of decision-making on a more or less permanent basis."[28] Blacks were therefore susceptible to mobilization around new commitments and to take actions not unlike those described for Africa and Asia.

It will be recalled that the definition utilized for mobilization in the present study specifically focuses on resource acquisition as a product of community activation. This perspective is consistent with the particular efforts of blacks to gain and institutionalize control of Deutsch's "aspects of modern life," and not merely "exposure"[29] to them; and their efforts to capture a fair and legitimate share of power and economic resources for community use. In this regard a small but significant body of theory has guided this approach and is much more appropriate for the American environment.

Emitai Etzioni was one of the earliest scholars to try and account for mobilization in the context of the western democracies. In his definition one sees an immediate concern for resource control. For him, mobilization is "the process by which a unit gains significantly in the control of assets it previously did not control." Therefore, "(a) mere increase in the assets of members, of subunits, or even of the unit itself does not mean that mobilization has occurred, though it increases the mobilization potential. The change in the capacity to control and to use assets is what is significant." His classification of these assets is as follows: "*coercive* (e.g., weapons, armed forces, manipulative technologies), *utilitarian* (e.g., goods, information services, money); *normative* (e.g., loyalties, obligations)."[30]

Charles Tilly has been even more highly directed toward the resource perspective. He says, "mobilization refers to the acquisition of collective control over resources"[31] for which there are several components. A mobilizing entity must be concerned with "accumulating resources" and then with "increasing collective claims on the resources." The latter is achieved "by reducing competing claims; by altering the program of collective action, [and] by changing the satisfaction due to participation in the group as such."[32]

What is missing from this stripped-down definition is some attention to the "collective activation" aspect of mobilization. This aspect has been well-noted by some contemporaries of Tilly. Their ideas aggregate around organization and some particular accompanying activities (often modest) for mobilizing constituents. Hence Doug McAdam discusses "insurgency" within social movements instead of mobilization. "Social movements would appear to be collective phenomena arising first among segments of the aggrieved population that are sufficiently organized and possessed of resources needed to sustain a protest campaign."[33] Therefore "protest activity is the result of a combination of expanding political opportunities and indigenous organization, as mediated through a crucial process of collective attribution."[34] Gamson also pinpoints organization, even to the extent of de-emphasizing activation: "Mobilization is a process of increasing the readiness to act collectively by building the loyalty of a constituency to an organization or a group of leaders. Activation is part of an influence attempt, mobilization is part of an organizing process that precedes specific efforts at influence."[35] Similarly, in Oberschall's conflict model mobilization is defined as "the process of forming crowds, groups, associations, and organizations for the pursuit of collective goals."[36] Moreover, each of these authors use social protest as the most significant means of activation.

An important underlying theme in these and earlier theories is loyalty and the "creation of community." Just as Deutsch alluded to the "modern community," later theorists refer to "networks of communal relations,"[37] "interactional networks,"[38] or the "creation of commitment."[39] These may all be summed up in Kanter's notion of the moral community that sustains any drive toward mobilization, seen as activation for resource acquisition.

> The community represents an attempt to establish an ideal social order within the larger society, [and] it must vie with the outside members for loyalties. It must ensure high member involvement despite external competition without sacrificing its distinctiveness or ideals. It must often contravene the earlier socialization of its members in securing obedience to new demands. It must calm internal dissention in order to present a united front to the world. The problem of securing total and complete commitment is central.[40]

This variety of mobilization raises certain questions about those susceptible to it and about how the process starts. It would seem to apply to a wide variety of circumstances, but is more limited to those individuals (like southern blacks) who mobilize on their internal strengths to seek institutional benefits. As Tilly reminds us, though we may speak of the rich and powerful mobilizing, such is merely an "offensive" or "preparatory" tactic for marshalling or redeploying existing resources. It is only when "defensive" tactics are used that collective activation for resource acquisition can be seen. This "defensive mobilization [occurs when] a threat from outside induces the members of a group to pool their resources to fight off the enemy."[41] Tilly even concedes that we may be limited in this regard to the powerless poor, whose conditions of daily life require such defensive tactics.

If the above is true, then it may be allowed that these behaviors tend to sustain the proposition that it is protest activity that marks the early mobilization campaign. The forces behind such activity are usually noninstitutionalized and have few of the *accoutrements* of traditional power sources. What they have are "shared targets and objects of hostility held responsible for grievances, hardship, and suffering."[42] According to McAdam it is a long and cumulative process to "insurgency" or collective activation. The group must be poised to take advantage of and create opportunities, on the strength of its indigenous organization and leadership.[43] The latter sustain group consciousness and generate pressures that produce flexibilities in the opposition. Eventually there is the realization of the moral community and sustained collective actions that yield substantive power resources for the mobilizers.

The general poverty and powerlessness of black Americans, until the mid-1960s, made them especially susceptible to the type of mobilization described above. As has been noted, the continuance of a virtual racial caste in the United States left few options to blacks for seeking political benefits. Though the nation was effectively democratic for most and possessive of remarkable material resources, racial discrimination prevented black inclusion. Nowhere was this more apparent than in the South, where political exclusion was coupled with a virulent hatred and social isolation for blacks. This disfranchisement following the Civil War also included social segregation in the form of Jim Crow laws and virtual peonage.

Black resistance to this status was always prevalent, but culminated in the 1940s and '50s with a much more strategic and broader community organization and activation. Not surprisingly this took place largely in the South, where the most susceptible of the black population remained. With remarkable consistency to the dictates of mobilization, these black southerners first revitalized their local organizations by creating regional networks. Though these regional networks did not initially have central secretariats, they responded to common interests and problems and fostered regular communication. Their actions ranged from lobbying and litigation by the National Association for the Advancement of Colored People (NAACP) to public protests by the Congress of

Racial Equality (CORE). At the same time, regional leaders such as Martin Luther King, Jr. and numerous local ones from among clergy, students, and professionals emerged. In a way not particularly indicative of the past, these activities were highly organized around general themes of political and social integration for black betterment. And the leadership exhibited a high degree of commitment in articulating these issues, and in furthering community solidarity. For many, civil rights activity became full-time employment, yielding a salient campaign of national scope.

A new moral community emerged from this. In time, new symbols and a language accompanied this mobilization that were articulated among constituents. This is recognizable in the independent public ways blacks began to identify and assert themselves in dress, speech and self-definition. In short, political mobilization was underway. The broad activation for resource acquisition resulted in a clear set of values and goals; actions by leaders and constituents appropriate to these values; the development of institutional means; and finally the development of the outward signs of a new political commitments.

That this process was long since underway has been noted by some scholars, though few have fully explored the benefits of the mobilization theoretical scheme. Many focus on merely one or another aspect of activism as the driving force of contemporary black political developments. Everett Carll Ladd describes the impact of a mobilization system in two Southern cities where the increased demands of blacks and the pressures from those aligned with blacks were creating new expectations, goals and black leadership in North and South Carolina.[44] Matthews and Prothro concentrate on similar issues in what they refer to as the "revolution" that was occurring in the 1960s as a result of activism in the black community.[45] Still others concentrated on sheer mobilization, but without identifying it as such. Carmichael and Hamilton actually adopted the concept of modernization to show how old values of the old South were challenged by expanded participation for blacks.[46] William J. Wilson has called this era that of "lower-class based politics," when southern civil rights activism and ghetto riots increased the visibility of issues such as "unemployment, underemployment, inferior education, inadequate housing, and police brutality."[47] Later, the War on Poverty programs that were designed as correctives aided political mobilization. "These programs were often transformed from community service agencies into local political structures staffed and directed by lower-class militants."[48] Robert Brisbane has also used an essentially mobilization theme in his work on the subject, though he sees the process as merely one of a cycle of ebbs and flows for the last two centuries.[49]

However, two recent analyses of the South have focused squarely on mobilization as a process that accounts for the activation of the black community and its successful acquisition of political resources. Doug McAdam and Aldon Morris are both concerned with the development of the civil rights movement and how it converted powerlessness into relative degrees of power in the South. They each show that what emerged in the form of street demonstrations in the 1960s was neither spontaneous nor ad hoc. These acts were but the culmination of a highly organized campaign by blacks to acquire political resources. McAdam presents a substantive analysis of how the activities of black churches, colleges, and the NAACP converged into a campaign for change. This assemblage of forces created communications networks, provided leaders, and broadly contrived or took advantage of opportunities. This was all achieved within the context of "collective attribution," meaning conscious group acceptance of the mission of the campaign. In supporting his arguments, McAdam offers a preponderance of aggregate evidence showing both how organizations and leadership developed, and how the symbiotic relationship enjoyed with the masses produced insurgency.[50]

Subsequently it was left to Aldon Morris to analyze detailed cases to show the patterns and structures that led to the political successes in places like Bolton, Tchula and Mayersville. He utilizes an "indigenous perspective" to document the rise of the civil rights movement. "A well-developed indigenous base includes the institutions, organizations, leaders, communication networks, money, and organized masses within a dominated group. . . . [This] also encompasses cultural elements—music, oratory, and so on." By the 1950s such a base was available in the South and used by its "organizers [to] transform indigenous resources into power resources and marshal them in conflict situations to accomplish political ends."[51]

Like McAdam, Morris agrees that the churches, the NAACP, students, and local organizers were at the forefront of this mobilization. He argues that the earliest institutional center of the movement, in the form of leadership, physical facilities, and economic independence, was the church. Moreover, it provided "collective enthusiasm generated through a rich culture consisting of songs, testimonies, oratory and prayers that spoke directly to the needs of an oppressed group." This was all cemented by the charismatic or magnetic personality of the minister.[52] This organizational advance was buttressed by and often fused with the local NAACP branches. Together these forces started a confrontation that resulted in manifold organizations, but for the movement, a more complex organizational structure. The manifold organizations could be found in towns like Mayersville or Tchula (Morris discusses Baton Rouge, Montgomery, and Tallahassee). But the critical factor was the way these coalesced for "collective attribution." There were mergers, confederations or ad hoc agreements that linked local and regional groups into networks whereby they undergirded collective activation for acquisition of political resources.

The importance of strategic organization and leadership to successful mobilization is described by Morris with consummate skill. He focuses on how Martin Luther King, Jr. largely managed the early portion of the mobilization via the Southern Christian Leadership Conference (SCLC). In the first place, King was the quintessence of the traditional black leader: a clergyman, organizer of independent Baptist congregations, and extraordinarily charismatic. After the Montgomery boycott, King was literally in contact with all of the mobilizing efforts in the South and highly influential upon them. The SCLC ultimately became the glue (albeit decentralized) for the manifold organizations, including the NAACP and CORE. Even the later student movement kicked off under King's gaze and the assistance of SCLC staff. Moreover, King virtually managed or exerted untold influence upon allied external groups that were of considerable import to the mobilization.[53]

The recent political experiences of the towns of Bolton, Tchula and Mayersville are at the heart of the type of mobilization identified here. They are southern towns in which a consensus of will (or base for collective attribution) occurred that led to activation for acquisition of political goods. This took the form of a civil rights ideology in the spirit of Martin Luther King, Jr.—a program for broad human rights and welfare development based on social, political, and economic redistribution. In the process the black masses became intensely politicized and sophisticated in differentiating ideas, issues, and policies. Their campaign was highly organized, as noted by Morris, first in seeking basic human rights in mass civil rights actions. Later this took the form of voter registration, community organization, voting, and working for political parties. The mobilization culminated in the 1970s in virtually a complete transfer of institutional power to blacks.

It would readily be seen that the descriptions of these towns reveals an active process of mobilization. Already the organization and consensus within the community have yielded some results. Therefore, in applying the mobilization scheme, the focus is not so much on the generation of process, but its motion and the benefits it produces. If the view of McAdam and Morris is accepted that indigenous leadership, mass organization, and collective attribution are the cornerstones of mobilization, then how do we characterize these phenomena as they emerged in the three towns in Mississippi?

In the treatment of mobilization in this study, it has been instructive to focus on the nexus between local leadership, the local social and political experiences during the civil rights campaign, and the ideology of the constituents. It is argued that when these factors combine in a certain way they yield mobilization for political change. Clearly, in the 1960s blacks responded to similar systems of racial exclusion in Mississippi towns, though individual town racial histories somewhat differed. In spite of the fact that these systems were sustained with much violence, opportunities arose and were created by blacks through which a will to change was institutionalized. All along, leaders were of particular importance in this—structuring the agenda, organizing activities, and establishing network linkages. Their functions, however, were only as good as the constituents who stood behind them, ready to act and maintain pressure on the leaders and the opposition. This analysis explores this symbiotic relationship in operation, and the results it achieved, by analyzing leaders and constituents in their turn.

The towns in which these leaders and constituents mobilized were like so many other southern towns in their small overall population, ruralness, heavy black population, economic impoverishment, and (until the late 1960s) in the near total disfranchisement of black citizens. The largest of these towns is Tchula with a population of 1739; Bolton has 816, and Mayersville, 500. Tchula and Mayersville are located in the heart of the Mississippi delta where "cotton was king" and plantation operation demanded a large enslaved class. They have, therefore, almost always had a majority Afro-American population. The setting is dominated by recurring plantation flatlands, merging one into another for hundreds of acres. Bolton differs in that it is just outside the fertile delta and is closer to a city of considerable activity.[54] Yet it is not so far removed as to be devoid of elements of plantation society. Bolton's fertile land makes it a significant agricultural area, and once it also had a large number of slaves.

Today there are considerable socioeconomic differences between Bolton and the other two towns. These result largely from Bolton's location in Hinds, the largest and most prosperous of Mississippi's 82 counties. Bolton's per capita income (about $3,500) is lower that that of Hinds County ($4,181) and the nation ($4,164), but it is higher than that of Issaquena County ($3,114) where Mayersville is located, and much higher than that of Holmes County ($1,916) where Tchula is. Proximity to urban Jackson (30 miles away) provides advantages for Bolton. Sixty-five percent of the townsmen are employed in manufacturing; median school years are close to the county's 12.3, and there is ready access to health care (333 doctors and 1,019.2 hospital beds per 100,000 residents). Little of this is available in either of the other towns. There are only small industries in Holmes County, and none in Issaquena. Median school years in both counties are just above eight years. Health care access in Issaquena County is naught and little better in Holmes, where there are 22 doctors and 354 hospital beds per 100,000 residents. Thus, only Bolton compares in any way favorably with general statistics for the poor state of Mississippi.[55]

Notwithstanding the problems of leadership study in general the nature of mobilization in these towns helps to narrow the focus for this study. Since the activation that occurred in these small places was for the acquisition of political goods, electoral office was a prominent concern. Virtually all of those who assisted in organizing their communities in the 1960s campaigns went on to seek public office. In fact, there were few other institutional positions available through which political goods could be allocated. Thus we may limit ourselves to this group in the discussion of the mobilization of black leadership.

The leaders that buttressed and accelerated the mobilization in the three towns may be characterized as follows: (a) as already noted, each holds a formal public office (in this case mayor) and each is ubiquitous in other organizational outlets for leadership. In these positions they are new in that they were never part of the old guard of influentials anointed by the white power structure; (b) they, like most American leaders, come from a socioeconomic status well above that of the mass of their constituents; (c) all are relatively young and possess charisma; (d) each subscribes to the ideology of, and participated in, the civil rights movement of the 1960s; and, (e) each has a purposive approach to political action that emphasizes welfare benefits earmarked for the express "needs" of the black community.

Formal office-holding and other organizational positions were revealed as significant via a modified reputational survey.[56] In general the findings confirm the proposition that emergent leadership in these rural towns consists largely of elected officials. This finding is consonant with a major shift in black participation in southern politics. Since 1967, black elected officials have considerably grown in number, and have been replacing the previously anointed ministers and teachers.[57] Many of them are also the local notables and, as such, tend to belong to almost every public and private organization within the constituency—the church, local NAACP, local poverty and social welfare organizations (Headstart, sundry health, et alia), ad hoc political groups, educational associations, and even purely social groups (for example, citizens' band radio and motorcycle clubs). Often they are founding members and/or office-holders in these local organizations.

Mayors, the most clearly identified of the group, also have affiliations far beyond the local arena. They are members and hold offices in the regional and national organizations of mayors, serve on national and regional boards, and in international groups and organizations. Few others come even close to matching the reputation of the formal leaders. In Bolton this is evident from the systematic survey of the community when only the mayor and one or two aldermen were mentioned with any frequency; in Mayersville it was the mayor, aldermen and women, and a resident county supervisor; in Tchula it was the mayor, aldermen and women, and a state legislator. It is noteworthy that the leaders from pre-civil rights days, who owed their influence to acceptance by whites, are no longer visible. The shift to elected leaders thus signals basically new terms for leadership recruitment that have been defined by the black community itself.

The status of these leaders (mayoral and aldermanic) being studied here is far above that of their black constituents. Indeed, their achievements and potential exceed those of the local whites. Virtually all have education above high school, and in two of the towns the educational level goes beyond the first college degree. Two of three mayors (Thompson and Carthan) have college degrees and a considerable degree of advanced training. Thompson has a master's degree in education and is working on a dissertation for a doctorate; Carthan has an advanced degree in administration and also studied law. The aldermen and women are equally well-educated. In Mayersville, one member is college-educated, and the others have high school and/or some advanced technical training. The educational training represented in Bolton is much higher, where all four black members of the board have college degrees. It is clear that in the matter of educational achievement the emergent elected leadership class is as distinguished as most public officials in being set apart from its constituency, whose median educational level in the 1970 Census was 9.3 years.

Social background and economic status (earnings and employment) are not much different. All of the leaders are, relative to local circumstances, in a higher economic class. The two mayors with postgraduate educational training are also from family backgrounds of economic means. Thompson, whose deceased father had been a mechanic, was brought up alone by his mother, a school teacher, whose steady income provided considerable status in the broader community. Young Thompson himself initially was to go into teaching.

Carthan, on the other hand, came from a family whose economic well-being derived from agriculture and business investments. His father (recently deceased) owned land, was a profitable farmer, and provided advantages to his growing children not generally available in the area. Young Carthan followed his father into business after a stint in education. When he became mayor, Carthan owned productive farms, one of the largest grocery stores in Tchula, several rental properties, and entertainment spots. In the absence of mayoral duties, he could have been in a position to dominate a major part of the town's economy. Mrs. Blackwell does not have the family background support or the liquid economic potential. But she is seen as having access to individuals of means and as possessing considerable expertise on civil rights, women's rights, and rural issues. For these she receives fees, and thereby advances her economic position.

Charisma is also very prevalent among these three mayoral leaders. As compared to their constituents, they do have extraordinary qualities and powers even if these are not "superhuman" or "supernatural" as Max Weber might expect.[58] It is not merely the moral authority the Mississippi leaders can invoke that bestows legitimacy upon them. Rather, it is the "social validation" of the local community that sustains them as charismatic figures. As John Friedland noted, "It is only when the message conveyed by charismatics to social groups is relevant and meaningful within the social context that authority emerges."[59] Circumstances in the Mississippi towns are propitious for the exercise of charismatic leadership. The leaders ultimately lend only centrality and intensity to the broad demands of the masses. Indeed, some scholars define the charismatic only as an idealized "projection" of the apparently "passive" masses who are "the true instigators" of the charismatic image.[60]

Another aspect of charisma is especially important among blacks. It has long been noted by scholars of Africa and Afro-America that one's effectiveness as a leader depends largely upon how one frames an argument, the words one chooses to use, and the strength of one's speech inflections and nuances in moving an audience. Our Mississippi leaders do have these capabilities. Each leader is spellbinding as an orator before large audiences and captivating in more personal settings. This is recognizable both experientially and in content. In speech, the rhythmic flow and lyrical quality, and an intensity of tone, are at work to arouse the audience.[61] This "romantic" cast is strengthened by content which corresponds to the views and sentiments of the audience. In short, one who is regarded as wrong-headed on the interests of the black community cannot attain leadership status under present conditions.

Youth is also prominent, particularly in combination with charisma. Thompson and Carthan were accepted as leaders while still in their twenties; Blackwell achieved prominence in her thirties. This is in sharp contrast to an earlier state of affairs when most black leaders did not achieve acceptability until they were quite old. In the past, whites endorsed blacks as leaders only after an extended period of surveillance. Today, most of the leaders are much younger because they build their bases of power within the black constituency.

Youth appears to aid in sustaining the charismatic figure, where substantial energy and mastery of modern ideas and communications technology are required. It is significant that these new mayors have made no alignments with traditional interests that would limit their policy choices or direction. They owe local allegiance only to the masses, who have everything to gain from social change.

A civil rights ideology, one that disdains actions and policies that in any way suggest unequal black status, or an incremental approach to social change, is also important. These leaders are committed to the complete incorporation of black political interests into the political system. They reject paternal relationships with whites based on the assumption that "the present status of blacks [is] marked by a lack of education, industrial skills, cultural refinements, and experience in government," and that they must yet undergo a certain amount of training before taking up the full responsibilities of citizenship.[62] In this regard, it works to the leaders' advantage that they participated in the civil rights movement of the 1960s, joined its public protests and community organization efforts, and took a firm, uncompromising stand on the moral imperative of equality. Each leader had a very strong ideological posture along these lines, though the record of Mrs. Blackwell is relatively stronger because of her earlier participation in civil rights mobilization.

The last characteristic of mobilization leadership is the purposive and interventionist political program, quite naturally a product of civil rights ideology. The leaders each develop a program that seeks to directly improve the marginal material circumstances of their constituents. Beyond this, however, the leaders seek to make a fundamental break with former resource distribution patterns that sustained white control. The purported nature of their programs directs efforts at the new black constituents. Three stages of this progress are already evident, though these should not be seen as exclusive or terminal. The first emphasizes basic necessities, the second involves social service delivery, and the third seeks infrastructural projects.[63]

Notwithstanding the general characteristics, mobilization was carried out somewhat differently in the three towns, being affected by idiosyncratic and situational factors. Personal traits, background, and experience in gaining public prominence constitute the idiosyncratic factors; while circumstances of each town, including its economic position, its special approach to race relations, and the like, constitute the situational factors. Such factors have brought forth three styles of operation that may be described as the radical populist, hero(ine) inventor, and the agrarian townsman.

The radical populist style is denoted by the uncompromising assertion of political ideals opposed to the status quo; a variety of progressivism and intellectualism with roots in social democracy. This yields a concern for and focus upon the masses that are without power and other resources for exerting influence. The leader utilizing this style will exhibit a concern for the "grassroots" people (the idealized man in the streets), whose interests are pursued aggressively. All this is done with a view to correcting the imbalance between those of privilege and those without. The radical populist is best represented by Bennie Thompson of Bolton. He is inwardly-oriented, grassroots-based, but ultimately intellectually inspired. This leader is single-minded, even abrasive, about issues of racial discrimination and protection of the interests of the poor, excluded masses. He derives his bearing, in most cases, from civil rights experiences: direct confrontation in the streets and/or community organization activities of the post-1965 movement. On this score Thompson has been labeled variously as militant[64] or "race-man,"[65] though he has exhibited a willingness to negotiate within the traditional political system.

The heroine inventor style is denoted by the singularly important public figure who uses the traits of personal drive, independence and goals of social change to forge a new community. In this regard the outstanding leader has the added responsibility of creating a literal "new" institutional framework for doing public business, based on the same ideas about social change. Such a figure usually emerges in an inchoate, isolated community that is catalyzed by a strong symbolic public personality. This makes a safe place, therefore, for the daring, highly individually creative leader to thrive.

Unita Blackwell of Mayersville is most representative of the hero(ine)/inventor type, who often becomes such in the American rural political environment by sheer independence of spirit. Considering that black constituents in rural places were disfranchised until quite recently, the resulting powerlessness makes the heroic figure attractive. In the face of fear, apathy and a tradition of exclusion, a strong and independent personality becomes the symbol necessary to inspire mass participation. Blackwell has become that symbol. In matters of race relations, she has been irrepressible, bold and tenacious. In the process she has created an entirely new framework on the ground—town incorporation—for the exercise of power. An ostensibly democratic framework of politics enables her to mobilize her constituents to greater participation, and thus expand her influence. At the same time, it restrains the propensity to excess or indiscretion.

The agrarian townsman style is based on a mixture of sentiments that emanate from southern rural and town life. In the rural South there are certain known elements in the relations of the masses to authority—powerlessness and economic dependency, but with high appeals to ethics. The town, on the other hand, is a place with a quicker pace and broader communications that create the bases for a cosmopolitan outlook. In this particular context of mobilization and social change the agrarian townsman is the one who seeks to maximize the best aspects of both world views—the principles from rural life and the broad diverse strategies available from the town. The latter is then subject to use in alleviating rural powerlessness. Insofar as the agrarian townsman is a product of both worlds, this combination of seeming opposites is facilitated. In ways akin to the populist, then, this leader can strengthen the rural masses against the elites. Cosmopolitan ideas such as social integration, political participation and independent individual expression are popularized as means to the goals of principled politics in a mostly rural, but highly mobilized community.

Eddie Carthan of Tchula is the agrarian townsman. He is a product of the regional, historical development of the South, long the most rural part of the country with its abundance of plantations surrounding small towns. Often the small town centers, with a few general stores and a post office, are about all the contact rural folks have with mass society. As the agrarian townsman he serves as a middleman between town and farm in his agriculturally-based area. Carthan is indeed involved in both rural agriculture and town business, and enjoys access to the town and farm in other ways because of present or former residence in both areas. This arrangement allows him to maintain connections throughout the rural region and to seek to meld the two communities.

Leadership is but one critical factor to successful mobilization. The constituents constitute the other. It is they who give legitimacy to the new ideals by expressing commitment and then acting in concert for the acquisition of goods. Their importance is first understood in the way they may be defined. These constituents are the entirely new group of electors who were disfranchised until 1965–67. The act of registration was for many the signal of the commitment to new ideals. This act by large numbers of individuals was combined with the bolder acts of leaders in public demonstrations and other protest campaigns. They were the footsoldiers whose presence inspired the leaders. This will be seen in the individual studies of the mobilization campaigns undertaken by the leader in each town.

Later, the constituents' complete assimilation of the ideals and strategies of mobilization helped the leaders in further elaborating the goals to be achieved. The independent role of the constituency will be analyzed with reference to four variables where the critical factor of mass activation will be seen. In the first instance, the sheer incidence of activation and commitment is measured, showing the remarkably high degree of voter participation. This is compared with several other variables—ideology, efficacy and political information—in order to postulate the depth of mobilization. On all these the empirical results indicate a strong combination of positive indicators for activation and application toward resource acquisition.

Finally these two elements, leaders and constituents, came together to create optimal conditions for acquisition of the new political resources. Among the constituents there was solidarity of purpose and new commitment for social change. The guiding principles also served to sustain protests, voter registration, and electoral participation. The function of the leaders was to organize a program to achieve the highly-directed goals of their constituents. In short order, this amounted to marshalling resources to respond to basic welfare needs, and channeling the energies of highly mobilized black constituents toward takeover of local political institutions. It was in the dynamic of action between the two forces, therefore, that mobilization—defined as resource acquisition—was achieved.

In teasing out the process of mobilizing for political resources in these three Mississippi towns, I have been guided by the following questions. First, notwithstanding the mobilization construct, how can we describe the occurrence of rapid social and political changes in the southern region since the 1950s? What are blacks now doing that they did not do before? Who are the key leaders in this and their terms of reference?

Then there are a series of historical questions. What is the nature of local history and how does it account for contemporary issues of participation, and indeed structure the present debate? Is there a particular way, perhaps through mobilization, of analyzing the complex political landscape in the South, especially the three towns in Mississippi? Are there characteristics about their ruralness, their leaders and their constituents that are revelatory about the democratic process? In light of whatever theory is proposed, again such as mobilization, what assessment can be made of actual practice? And finally, how does what we see square with what we know about American politics? Are there new rules, or merely new ones for negotiating the political process? The following chapters seek to answer some of these questions, and merely open up discussion of others.

2

Black and White in the Southern Regional Context

How does the South fit into the great universe of American politics, and what are the implications of this for mobilization politics? Is this region historically imbued with the same general ideals of democracy, aggressive spirit and sense of destiny that inspired the "founding fathers"? If so, what of the contradictory status of blacks? Answers to these questions are sought by evaluating several periods in southern and Mississippi political history from the era of enslavement. The discussion begins by taking up the problems of aristocracy, materialism, and white intragroup cleavage as a means of understanding the southern past. An analysis is made of certain avowed appeals to an aristocratic ethos *vis-à-vis* the material realities of southern life. Then the importance of a major cleavage within the white community that separated the planters and the yeoman farmers of the hills is taken up.

Of course, none of this can be entirely understood without analyzing the importance of the enslaved; although not legitimate members of the community at first, their presence structured the debate about public affairs. Even after enslavement, the status and function of blacks continued to be seen as something less than legitimate. Therefore, how did blacks figure in this universe, especially in light of the planter-hill cleavage?

These relationships are elaborated in reference to the organization of the political community in several periods. The analysis begins with enslavement, and takes up (in their turn) reconstruction, disfranchisement, and contemporary mobilization. It will be seen that white racism and ambivalence has caused nonparticipation by blacks, while at the same time laying the foundation for mobilization. On the strength of independent community structures and activities in a basically segregated society, blacks moved toward mobilization for the acquisition of political resources. Though our focus in this chapter is historical, the development of this mobilization will be documented from about 1950. This is when revitalized community organization and a broad range of opportunities to oppose segregation presented themselves.

Aristocracy and Materialism in the Old South

Notwithstanding the contradictions of the "founding fathers," it is evident that the Southern United States was fated to pursue some rather different interests than the North. The southern dependence upon agriculture and enslavement were two of the most important variables in this regard. There were also several other related variables. One of these was an element of social class, perhaps of a precapitalist nature, that often yielded extreme intragroup cleavage among whites—aristocrats versus a plethora of working poor. Then, all these were overlaid with a contradictory sense of solidarity that was based on a well-wrought concept of caucasian destiny. In these parts, there was never any overwhelming challenge to live by the dictates of democracy and capitalist ideals that theoretically inspired the North. Therefore the answer to how the South fit into the American polity is that the ideological fit was always imperfect. The consequences of this have been significant for all southerners, but particularly for blacks who were never deemed to be legitimate members of the community.

In reading historical tracks and interpretations of the region, southerners repeatedly make allusions to an "old world" past. The characterization of all manner of human interactions was reminiscent of feudal paternalism, where the landowner (patron) and his charges (clients) made certain formal exchanges in an interdependent relationship. Some scholars have referred to this charitably as a kind of aristocratic regime:

> Theirs was an aristocratic, antibourgeois spirit with values and mores emphasizing family and status, a strong code of honor, and aspirations to luxury, ease, and accomplishment. In the planters' community, paternalism provided the standard of human relationships, and responsibilities of gentlemen. The gentleman lived for politics, not, like the bourgeois politician, off politics.[1]

John C. Calhoun, however, is seen by many southerners as having given the definitive philosophical view of aristocracy in the South. He framed his arguments on the basis of reading ancient western political philosophy. After all, Aristotle had looked upon Africans as "naturally" susceptible to slavery, an institution that made "a noble life possible for the master."[2] Calhoun reasoned that these ancient circumstances were present in the South of his day. He argued that the basis for any successful society was the existence of two classes—one to rule, and the other to serve the rulers. It was assumed, contrary to the view of Thomas Jefferson, that all men were not created equal, insofar as the capacity to achieve was concerned. Blacks and whites "are united to a certain extent, . . . and . . . equality of citizens, in the eyes of the law, is essential to liberty in a popular government." But there is no equality, he continues, in the manner ("conditions") that individuals take advantage of liberty. Thus liberty is only of importance for those who have superior "intelligence, sagacity, energy, perseverance, skill, habits of industry and economy, physical power, position and opportunity." This leads to a quite natural state of "inequality of conditions," which is nevertheless the driving force of "progress."[3]

These and similar ideas allowed Calhoun and the southern political elites to develop a political philosophy that was aristocratic and essentially antidemocratic. These "gentlemen" perceived themselves to be ordained to rule because of natural superior qualities. Thus all but a small number of southerners, of any color, were excluded from public affairs. Aside from natural selection this small group maintained itself by the cultivation of its talents—a fact that required the existence of a massive servant class. Following the ideals of Plato and Aristotle, these elites believed that the higher arts of governance and society required time for training. Therefore, slavery was necessary so that those select few (as in Greece) would have the "leisure to cultivate their minds, define their city and help guide its policies." Likewise, both Plato and Aristotle had noted the importance of time for training in the higher arts of governance and society.[4]

Like the rulers in the city states, the southern "statesmen" propounded a thesis that they were required to look after the "security" of those enslaved and less well-endowed. That is, they would look after their own "security" and the propagation of higher civilization, but would be equally attentive to the "security" of those unable to exercise liberty with benefit. The higher class had an obligation to provide for the "survival" of the inferior because Calhoun believed "preservation and perpetuation" of the human species to be far more important than the potential for "progress and improvement."[5] For him, the elite was benevolent, and for essentially moral reasons. Or as Genovose has suggested, the planters were more gentlemanly than materially inclined.

But for the status of the African and the racial ideology that sustained it, the aristocratic pretensions of the southern ruling class might be plausible. However, the evidence leaves grave questions about the moral concerns of the white planters for the human "security" of the enslaved Africans. The moral choice made in the end seemed only designed to denigrate African humanity *vis-*

à-vis Europeans. Notwithstanding Calhoun's assertion of morality, the historical record is replete with European efforts to document African inferiority and the policies adopted therefrom. First there was the curse of skin color; later came the assertion that these "near men" were the missing link in evolution;[6] and finally the quintessential truth of science was used to "prove" that Africans possessed smaller brains and other deficient physical traits.[7] The policies that emanated from these used Africans more as instruments to enoble the Europeans and their material desires, and not to improve the moral turpitude of the enslaved.

Consequently, the southern planter class and regime maintained its economic and political hegemony on this racial standard. The blacks were inferior, and because they were it was possible to relegate them to the instrumental position of a laboring class. They could be called upon for this purpose without guilt, or without any procedures like indenture to improve the status of enslavement. Their function was purely to further the material conditions for planter hegemony. As for the question of benignity, this also seemed but a product of the material interest. The planters looked upon their efficient slave property as an investment that had to be protected. A minimum of goods were provided for this purpose of keeping "the tools" operable. Nevertheless, according to Calhoun, it was "bondage" that harnessed the natural base proclivities of Africans so that they would be productive.[8]

Moral benignity and the aristocratic claim are made less credible because of the role and function of the poor whites. Though they were not subject to enslavement and did not wear the badge of inferiority, this was their only advantage, which in the labor market could be a curse. They had to endure the "stigma upon manual labor which developed in the slaveholding states. Free labor could have no social standing in a society where labor was considered degrading and unworthy of a white man."[9] This yielded high unemployment rates for whites, or a status but one step above that for the enslaved.[10] As prevalent was competition with blacks, where planters squeezed poor whites with the threat of replacement. This not only thwarted black-white alliances but prevented collective action by the white poor for job security.[11] Blacks could always be brought in to drive down the cost of this paid labor.[12] Poor whites had a degree of vulnerabilty not as great as that for blacks, but more complicated. Their position was tenuous and ultimately dispensable. This gives even less credence to the idea of the southerner's aristocratic obligation to protect labor. White laborers were protected only insofar as they contributed to the maintenance of the political regime, including its economic hegemony.

White Intragroup Factionalism in Mississippi

Notwithstanding whether aristocracy or some variant thereof characterized the historical South, it is evident that intragroup factionalism was a pattern that made the racial standard all the more important to public organization in many southern states. Racial solidarity masked many other conflicts in the white community: elements of class, philosophical differences about the organization of society and the distribution of power, and certain geopolitical variations. V. O. Key characterized the entire South as a faction-ridden, non-party region in his classic study. He argued that, at least for local purposes, "the political battle has to be carried on by transient and amorphous political factions within the Democratic Party." The consequence of these highly factionalized circumstances was little permanent political organization through which local government could routinely be staffed. The "congeries of transient squabbling factions" yielded the following:

> In the conduct of campaigns for the control of legislatures, for the control of governorships, and for representatives in the national Congress, the South must depend for political leadership, not on political parties, but on lone-wolf operators, on fortuitous groupings of individuals usually of a transient nature, on spectacular demagogues odd enough to command the attention of considerable numbers of voters, on men who have become persons of political consequence in their own little bailiwicks, and on other types of leaders whose methods to attract electoral attention serve as substitutes for leadership of a party organization.[13]

This pattern was common in a number of the former confederate states and was very prominent in Mississippi. In Alabama, Key has shown that personal followings were supremely important to electoral success for candidates of ideological similarity, who might otherwise have had general appeal. In the absence of a party mechanism to capitalize on such general appeal, the factions held the day.[14] South Carolina at the time Key wrote was even more indicative of the factionalized pattern—so much so that its politics were labeled that of "friends and neighbors;" providing a localism so intense that it bordered on "sectionalism." Mississippi too was highly factionalized with leadership developing around discrete bases of support. Here, ideological similarity left only demagoguery as the tool for creating appeal. The names of Bilbo and Vardaman easily come to mind as the best case examples in Mississippi history. These governors (later United States Senators), gained notoriety by their race-baiting campaigns for control of the otherwise factionalized landscape.[15]

The longstanding local political cleavage within the white Mississippi constituency can be reduced to that of the hills versus the delta. The former is a hilly region in the eastern part of the state with less fertile land and, consequently, an economy made up of less well-off small farmers. The area includes the Tennessee River Hills (with altitude as high as 700 feet and "thin, red sandy and pebbly loams"); adjacent Pontotoc Ridge (with broken surfaces and "soil too sterile for successful agriculture"); the Flatwoods just south of the preceding areas (with "grey sticky clay that is very retentive of water, difficult to cultivate, and . . . not highly productive"); and the North Central Plateau, a large strip extending from the Tennessee border to the eastern midsection of the state (with "yellowish brown loam containing . . . silt and [highly erosive] clay. . . ."[16]

Livelihood in the hills was based on small farms and lifestyles were individualistic. These yeomen, so to speak, "because of the poorness of the soil on which they dwelt or the great inaccessibility of markets, were, as a group more completely barred off from escape or economic and social advance."[17] The simplicity of this life yielded a fundamentalist religious philosophy,[18] conservative politics, and intensely local loyalties. At the same time, the hill people were very much involved in populism—the politics of the "little man" opposed to big government; they fought the delta on everything from taxing and spending to prohibition.[19]

The Delta differs sharply from the hills. Located in the west-central part of the state, Key described the delta as "a flat shelf of fertile alluvial soil . . . , (that) produces a million bales of cotton a year."[20] According to Rainwater these soils are "among the most fertile on earth." Even its "dark tough sticky clay . . . when drained . . . is very productive."[21]

This region was home to the planter class. The practice of politics here was a high art, albeit to protect cotton, property (including slaves), and power. Though bourgeois, these planters had aristocratic pretensions. Many of them cultivated a style of sophisticated openness, obligation, and honor.[22] But all this was done to protect the leisure life and privilege guaranteed by property, another fact that distinguished them from hill people.

This geographical cleavage, however, has been the driving force behind local politics in Mississippi for many years. Even before slavery became an inter-sectional issue, the different types of economies characterizing the delta and the hills were of political consequence. Each area entered political alliances designed to protect its economic base. "[In] the western half of the state, where the property was concentrated, the people were unequivocally attached to the whig party. [In the hills,] containing comparatively little property but . . . the great majority of the white population, adherence to the Democracy Party was the rule."[23] These variations explain much about subsequent political preferences and regional mores.

Yet there is still another pattern that marks the historic South, including Mississippi. For all the elements of fragmentation that characterized many states, there was a remarkable similarity attributable to a common resource base and demands for labor. The entire region sustained itself on the basis of agriculture. The yeoman farmers had their truck patches and the planters had their plantations. The climate everywhere was conducive to the agricultural economy, although the delta farmer far outproduced anything a single planter family could service. Since the enslaved Africans were already deemed appropriate for performing agricultural services, a ready labor supply was available. Herein lies the base for one of the greatest contradictions in the otherwise highly fragmented southern region. The presence of Africans as a free labor class, while economically acceptable to planters, posed a distinct disadvantage to small farmers who had no use for such labor. But because of racism's complicated dynamics, the hill people opposed improved status for blacks, despite the white planter class's hegemony.

How does one explain this white solidarity, seemingly opposed to material self-interest? Clearly racial considerations that contrived Africans inferior were more important than material interests to whites. In Mississippi these attitudes were present among planters and hill people alike. Much of this was subjective ordering, whereby white superiority was sustainable only in the face of African inferiority.

> At the bottom was the slave, a chattel rather than a person; at the top, the plantation-owner and slave-holder. Ground between these two millstones were the proletarian 'poor whites,' 'hillbillies,' 'red-necks,' and 'clay-eaters,' and a middle class, mostly agricultural, of small farmers and town dwellers, who—as is usual with middle classes—to some degree looked up with veneration and emulative pride to the aristocrats, . . . [and] to some degree bitterly opposed them.
>
> It has often been said that slavery created a psychological bond among all whites by emphasizing the dignity of freedom; in this, at least, the dominant race was equal, and sharply contrasted with the black man. The white man's civilization was maintained, in a region nearly forty percent black, at bottom by force; not by violence, to be sure, but by the superior social strength which subjection always implies. Based on subjection, it was more or less precarious, and invited the cooperation of all free men to maintain it.[24]

It was only with the presence of slavery that the small farmer was not entirely squeezed out of the economic market. The almost exclusive rights the planters had to black labor left poor whites unfettered "to go to the devil in the absolute enjoyment of their liberty."[25] Thus the poor white, even in the absence of "legitimate virtue" in the white social hierarchy, received the appearance of such.

Separately, let us look at the interests of the planters and the poor whites. The planters and their chief spokesperson (like Calhoun) give all manner of evidence of their beliefs in African inferiority. The most prominent evidence is their willingness to use Africans to perpetuate the institution of slavery. Ironically, however, because the planters tended to live closer to the blacks, and because plantation livelihood absolutely depended on the institution of slavery, the farmer often exhibited a protective attitude toward the enslaved. This paternalistic attitude resulted because harsh and abject treatment could only be upheld with absolute violence that ultimately jeopardized the labor force.

Therefore in Mississippi (and other southern states), planters devised policies that often gave the appearance of protecting slaves, though most only provided the absolute minimum. Nowhere is the irony and myth of this proposition more prominent than in the debate over the Civil War. To the chagrin of the hills, the delta found itself largely in the apparently incongruous position of opposition to secession. The big farmers perceived this as an unnecessary disruption and sought negotiation. From their economic viewpoint, it was clear that there could be no victory. Many planters professed fear of the violence associated with war near the source of their livelihood.[26] The planters hoped that if they could maintain monopolistic control of the political economy of the South, then it would be possible to make satisfactory arrangements regarding the status of blacks.

This sectional competition continued just after the Civil War, with renewed strength found largely at the legislative level. The delta wanted to maintain the status quo in legislative dominance and plantation slavery. However, the decline in the cotton industry and the general state of uncertainty left the hills with a chance to break the delta hegemony. Notwithstanding a short period of coalition rule with blacks (reconstruction), this debate between white factions continued.

The delta fought virtually all proposals brought before the legislature that protected the "sectional interests" of the hills. Some examples follow: A proposal for redistricting was opposed because it would have increased the number of hill representatives in the legislature. Similarly, the wool tariff and increased education allocations earned disapproval because they were supported by the hills. At the same time, delta residents supported measures to improve the position of merchants on whom depressed farm operations were dependent for loans and transportation.[27]

The poor whites had a variety of other problems delimited by the presence of blacks in the economy. While the poor stood to gain power against the planters, they also had to suppress competition with the large enslaved population. To do so the delta economy and hegemony had to be destroyed. These "little men" and the politicians who emerged to represent them favored: "anticorporationism, the cause of the common man . . . and the advocacy of white supremacy."[28] These new men were categorically opposed to paid black labor (as required by policies established by the Union government after the war), as well as formal black participation in government. Kirwan speaks of this post-reconstruction period as "the revolt of the rednecks." In the jockeying for power among whites (especially given the economic misfortunes of the planters), the counties in the hills and in South Mississippi emerged victorious by gaining control of the legislature.

Perhaps the clearest symbol of their success was the emergence of a group of flamboyant, demagogic, populist political leaders. Their success was based on a constitutional provision that introduced primaries in state elections. "Under the [old] convention system, a candidate had only to win the support of convention delegates. Now, with primaries, he had to have popular appeal."[29] Their race-baiting claims were largely built on the contention of genetic inferiority. Yet they were populists who represented the interests of poorer whites. Ironically, their claims (like those of blacks) were in opposition to the policies that sustained plantation inequalities and planter hegemony.

Mississippi is especially noted for two of the most visible and outspoken of the populist race-baiters—John Vardaman and Theodore Bilbo. Vardaman was the first to take advantage of the primary law and quickly became governor in 1904. He eventually was also elected to the U.S. Senate in 1911, the same year that Theodore Bilbo won the post of lieutenant governor. The latter also later served as governor and U.S. Senator. Each was important in establishing the power of the poor whites in Mississippi politics at the turn of the century, and through the 1940s.

Few worked harder than these two in reorienting policies designed to displace the old hegemonic group. Vardaman helped secure the primary election law that gave greater power to the hills, and supported national policies to the same ends.[30] Bilbo was perhaps even more successful. He integrated his broad ideals with the populist orientation then prominent in Washington.

> He went down the line for the New Deal; all of its works were anathema to the delta. He was for farm-tenancy legislation; the plantation economy depended on tenancy. He was for old-age pensions which did not have to be matched by the states; to the delta this was an invasion of states' rights. He was for generous relief; to the delta this was destructive of moral fiber.[31]

This would seem to have created possibilities for black and white coalition. Instead, these demagogues saw the black presence as a "curse" that thwarted the material gain of poor whites.[32] To sustain this view leaders proposed that affiliation with blacks was polluting. Hence some of the most virulent arguments for white supremacy emerged in this period.[33]

These two leaders were more than up to the task of justifying continued racial division. Much of this centered on the most base and derogatory assertions of black inferiority. Vardaman, a journalist, initially used his newspaper at Greenwood as a vehicle for popularising the derogatory term "nigger." He asserted that the genetic inferiority of blacks negated their right to vote and called for repeal of the constitutional amendments that supported black citizenship and equality. As such, a wide range of schemes were devised to neutralize the race factor. Vardaman later attacked the education of blacks believing they could not learn effectively: "It is not only folly, but it comes pretty nearly being criminal folly. The negro [sic] isn't permitted to advance and their education only spoils a good field hand and makes a shyster lawyer or a fourth-rate teacher. It is money thrown away."[34]

Many of these fears emanated from a concern for white female virtue. Vardaman was obsessed with the possibility of black men raping white women. "His one exception to an abhorrence of capital punishment was his advocacy of a lynch law to deal with Negro men who raped white women. . . . [He said] there is nothing left to do with these human brutes but to kill them and at least get rid of them."[35] Theodore Bilbo, like Vardaman, feared interracial sexual contact. Since blacks were "mongrels" according to him, "[t]he purity of the blood of the

Anglo-Saxon, the Celt, and the Teuton in this America of ours . . . is now being threatened. . . . The offspring of intermarriage would be a motley melee of miscegenated mongrels."[36] His proposal was for a law that banned interracial marriage and sanctioned lynching to prevent interracial contact that occurred under other circumstances. He asserted that a black who dared to contrive a social situation with a white woman, however legitimate the circumstances, "would have decorated the tallest magnolia tree available nearby [so as to] avenge the honor and the good name of southern womanhood."[37] To rid the country of all these possibilities, Bilbo then proposed various legislation to transport blacks back to Liberia or Ethiopia.[38]

The views of both of these leaders represented the tone that characterized the political situation in Mississippi from the post-1890 period down to the civil rights movement. Vardaman and Bilbo cannot be thought of or adequately discussed without giving careful attention to their racial views and their obsessive assertion of same. It is difficult to identify their political platforms, for example, in isolation from their anti-black feelings. Consequently, views about white hegemony, based on racial criteria, were legitimately asserted for many years in Mississippi politics.

In large measure, the status and control of blacks was the object of the debate between the planters and the hill people. Each in their turn sought to devise a system that denigrated blacks and prevented their participation. The heyday of the planter was the enslavement era, and post-reconstruction that of the hill residents. The end product for both sides was the continued exclusion of blacks, even after the Civil War presumably settled the issue.

The nature of this system and the racial patterns that evolved from it nevertheless established the basis for mobilization politics for blacks. At every turn, even during the brief period of reconstruction, participation for blacks was to be realized on the basis of struggle as outsiders. Mass black activation was required to attack a system whose *de facto* operation circumvented their institutional incorporation. In the process, blacks have had to, largely independently, develop internal resources and activate them for struggle.

The next section looks at the fits and starts of the black community in Mississippi as it sought to break the racial pattern and achieve independent political benefits.

The Black Political Experience in Mississippi History

ENSLAVEMENT

The pattern for black "participation" in southern life was established by the system of slavery. The Mississippi system makes as good a case as any, though the state was a later entity to the agricultural development of the South. Mississippi was only admitted to the Union in 1817 and experienced but two peaks in its cotton production during enslavement: the 1830s and the late 1850s.[39] But as one student of slavery has said, the system that evolved was of special interest because of the prominence of cotton as a means of livelihood. While some of the earlier settled states had other crops or economic activity, Mississippi did not.[40]

So what differences did the special circumstances make in the lives of those enslaved? Daily life during the period was undoubtedly as harsh as anywhere. However, the greater preponderance of slaves directly engaged in the production of cotton suggests a more severe regimen in the state.[41] Notwithstanding allied slave policies, hoeing and picking cotton from "sunup to sundown" tells its own story. Wharton's argument to the contrary is even undermined by his own data that show the paucity of slave skills for work outside the fields at the end of the war.[42] But the system in Mississippi was sustained by the elaboration of equally harsh rules, regulations, and pseudojustifications. A recent summarization of these includes the following:

1. Reading and writing (and the teaching thereof) was proscribed.
2. Employment in printing industries was barred.
3. Financial exchanges allowed only with special permission.
4. Purchase of spirits completely barred.
5. Religious services conducted by blacks only with white presence.
6. Other public assembly of more than five persons, without white presence, barred.
7. Pass required for absence exceeding four hours. (The pass could not be used as a means of freeing slaves, as this too was barred.)
8. Possession of weapons barred.
9. Ownership of independent means of livelihood barred.
10. Flogging used as a routine punishment for offenses, including provocative behavior.
11. Independent legal standing in court barred, though trial in such courts was common.[43]

These "measures" were carried out by a patrol ("an adaptation of the militia to the control of slaves,") whereby "[e]very slave-owner and all other persons subject to militia duty and below the rank of captain were subject to patrol duty."[44]

In this context slave life in Mississippi was as inflexible as it was harsh.[45] Like South Carolina with its large black population, Mississippi's one crop had almost singular labor needs. Thus the enslaved were almost entirely consumed in the production of cotton, leaving a virtual absence of "free" blacks in the state. For example, "free" persons went from a high of 1,336 in 1840, to a meager 776 in 1860, according to Wharton. A partial explanation is that "[a]fter 1842, the freeing of slaves by will was absolutely forbidden,"[46] though a few blacks apparently avoided this by buying their own relatives as a "mere formality."[47] The intent of the slaveowners was to create a world of total isolation for the enslaved. Therefore, beyond the slave quarters there was little opportunity to participate in southern society on independent terms. At the same time there was little opportunity to develop social aspirations with so few examples of free blacks in the social order.

The most recent research on slavery, however, shows that notwithstanding their social isolation, blacks did independently determine some things about their existence. They began with a good deal of their "cultural baggage" from West Africa intact. Many of the habits and/or choices about coexistence with the natural world were preserved, such as "folk medicine." Many socialization techniques, direct customs and artifacts were recalled with enough regularity to form patterns among blacks.[48] Lawrence Levine is correct when he says that while the West African background was not directly transferred, it provided "a fundamental outlook toward the past, present and future and a common means of cultural expression which could well have constituted the basis of a sense of common identity and world view capable of withstanding the impact of slavery."[49]

Equally important is the way blacks used their "outlook" and "cultural expression" in order to survive in, and have an independent impact upon, the surrounding environment. There are a wide variety of such patterns that illustrate independent values held by them, notwithstanding the conditions of servitude. One such example is music and its complex adaptations. Owens has shown how the spirituals were a virtual blueprint of slave values in the messages they sent about the evils of slavery. But, in their typically West African structure, the songs were also cathartic—providing a release from the pain, and/or a sense of camaraderie—all within an acceptably religious context.[50] Many times the intended messages were coded, providing for antislavery expression.

But one of the most notable techniques for asserting independence was individual or organized revolt.[51] These varied efforts were constant and formed patterns. Little has been made of individual acts because the data have largely been ignored until recently.[52] For example, Genovese has shown that at least some of the inefficiencies and unprofitability of the slave economy was due to slave recalcitrance. He cites the breakage of tools and the low productivity in the absence of the overseer.[53] Aptheker points out still others: "sabotage, shamming illness, stealing, suicide, and self-mutilation, and strikes."[54] In addition, all of the legal codes of the period specified regulations against individual behavior such as impudence and disobedience, among others, suggesting that such acts recurred with some frequency. But the most feared act of resistance was the full revolt by an organized group, such as those raised by Denmark Vesey[55] or Nat Turner.[56] Herbert Aptheker has documented many of these revolts and conspiracies and argues that they represented the efforts of blacks to overthrow the system.[57]

During the enslavement period, Mississippi blacks exhibited most of the cultural patterns and adopted many of the survival techniques noted. The large enslaved population probably made this inevitable. Many African survivals could be found among the blacks living in the dense "slave quarters" of the delta region. Even though many of the blacks were imported from other southern states, settled patterns of existence in the system were already established. They merely reappeared in Mississippi. The same is true for the array of creative adaptations in traditional music, dance, religion and social structure that Gwaltney calls "core Black culture."[58]

While available historical analysis shows no overrepresentation of actualized revolts in Mississippi, there was plenty of known resistance and a plethora of regulations against potential resistance. It is no accident that policing was so important to officials; there were simply more blacks to police and a greater likelihood for revolt. Aptheker reports some of the numerous incidences of plots and acts of resistance in the state as blacks sought to independently mobilize to change their status. The perceived severity of some of these incidences led to punishments of floggings and hangings. Moreover, the general contentiousness and resultant fear caused the state authorities on occasion to seek external military support, or at least to refuse committal of internal police forces to external services.[59] But fear was equally important in the spread of rumors, or "hallucinations," and "phobias," as one writer has termed them. During these periods, insurrections or conspiracies notwithstanding, white "mob violence reigned supreme" against revolts imagined and real.[60]

Black Reconstruction—Mississippi Style

After the Civil War, blacks enjoyed greater political participation than in any period except that of post-1965. In record time they organized, sponsored independent black leaders, and committed themselves to active participation. This may be said to illustrate the first full mobilization of blacks in the state for the acquisition of political resources. Again, as in South Carolina, Mississippi blacks had much potential for participation because of their large population. In 1867 the black voting population of Mississippi was 60,167, compared to 46,636 for whites.[61] It was now possible for blacks to not only field candidates for election but to influence the outcome of elections by voting. They did both. In fact their rapid involvement and influence was evident in 1870 when the first reconstruction government was installed. Despite the presence of military rulers (many in collusion with the former confederates) just after the war, blacks began organizing and acquiring institutionalized political positions. Their successful mobilization lasted but five to seven years, but the achievements are instructive for the later mobilization of the 1950s and '60s. Also significant is the manner in which the mobilization was thwarted. This whole period of mobilization and demobilization has three stages: Cooperationism (1867–1870); Black Republicanism (1870–1875); and Fusion (1875–1890).

The Cooperationist period centered around reconstructing the state constitution in order to end military occupation. To accomplish this a state convention was called, an event that coincidentally provided the first formal opportunity for the newly-freed blacks to participate. They did so, but not without opposition from largely yeoman farmers and poor whites. However, blacks rapidly organized, both separately and in coalitions. The early purposes were political education and black candidate recruitment, both of which were successful. Huge numbers were registered to vote even before black candidates were fielded.

Wharton has suggested that much of this organization and racial identification for mobilization was done through existing associations called the Loyal Leagues. These were "an outgrowth of a Northern patriotic organization established during the war. . . . [Of local groups] there was at least one in almost every black-belt community."[62] Blacks called their own meetings for political purposes, and even at times thought of themselves as an independent party force.

However, the period gets its name from the cooperation that occurred between blacks and other whites in the constitutional convention of 1868. There were two basic groups of whites: "carpetbaggers," or whites who had migrated from the North; and "scalawags," local southerners who chose to seek political coalitions with blacks under the general rubric of the Republican Party. In this effort blacks are credited with making the coalition an effective body, despite their neophyte status.[63] In any case, these three groups pretty much controlled the debate about establishing the new state constitution, where these "radicals" lived up to their reputation. The initial document gave strong support to black civil and political rights, and disfranchised a large number of whites who promoted the confederacy. Not surprisingly, those outside the coalition largely withdrew from participation, while the local press labeled the convention participants "mongrels," "perjured scoundrels," and "wild and imported animals."[64]

Sixteen of the 100 convention delegates were black. They represented areas with a high concentration of blacks: the delta and loess bluff counties. (See Figure 2.1.) Rankin, Hinds, Washington, and Warren counties sent four delegates each; and one each came from other counties in this same area.[65] Some of these representatives continued in politics and became well-known government leaders of their time, especially Charles Caldwell and Thomas Stringer. This rapidly-assembled group included a wide range of talents, professions and qualifications: preachers, educators, former slaves, and immigrant freedmen. They performed their tasks rather well, producing a credible constitution consistent with the policy interests of their black constituents. However, opposition to the document remained among the white supremacists who voted against it in the referendum.

The second period, Republicanism, represents the watershed in black participation, albeit most noted by cooperation between black and white Republicans. In this period, blacks were in a position to (and often did) exert independent political strength. Prior to this they were assigned certain roles; after 1870,

Figure 2.1 Black Concentration in Mississippi

RELATION OF THE DISTRIBUTION OF SLAVES TO SOIL AREAS IN MISSISSIPPI IN 1860

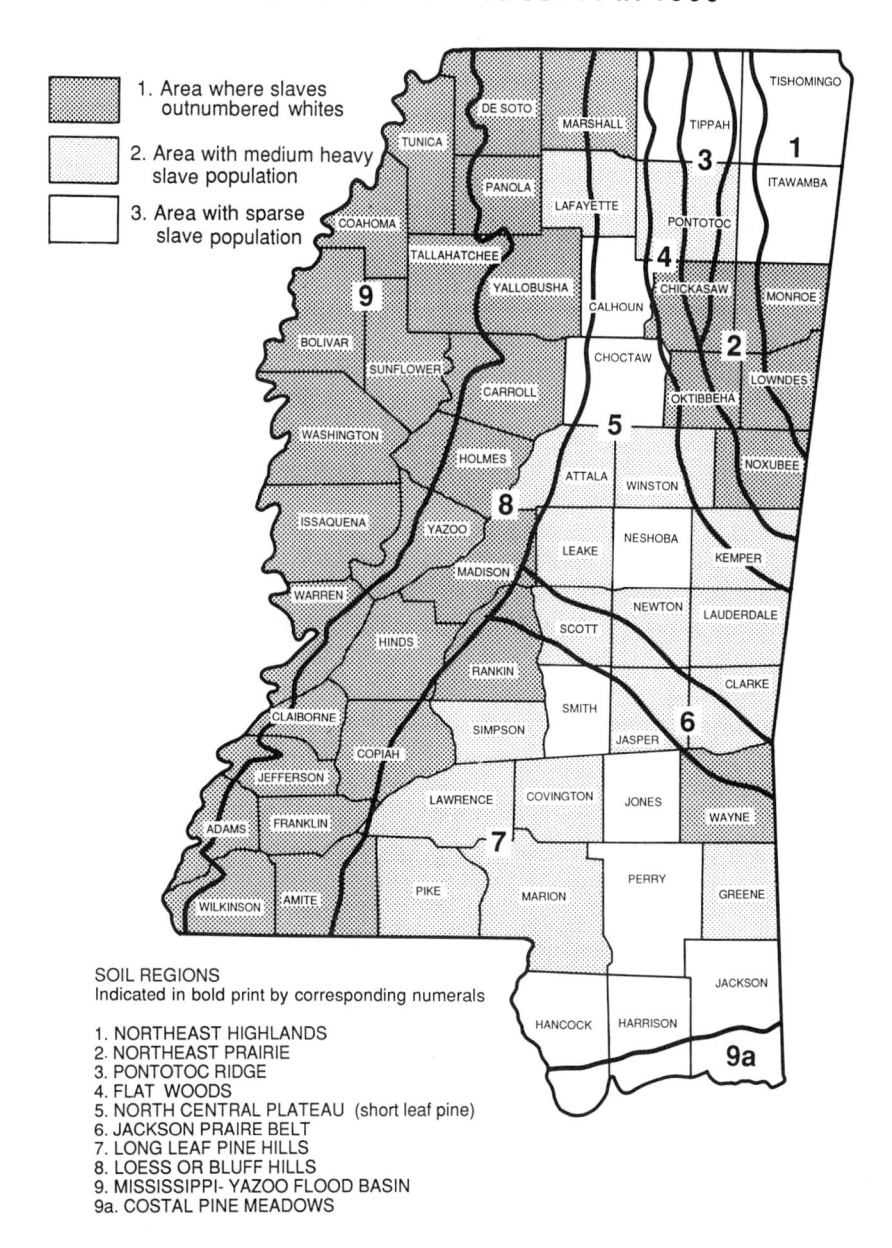

Legend:
1. Area where slaves outnumbered whites
2. Area with medium heavy slave population
3. Area with sparse slave population

SOIL REGIONS
Indicated in bold print by corresponding numerals

1. NORTHEAST HIGHLANDS
2. NORTHEAST PRAIRIE
3. PONTOTOC RIDGE
4. FLAT WOODS
5. NORTH CENTRAL PLATEAU (short leaf pine)
6. JACKSON PRAIRE BELT
7. LONG LEAF PINE HILLS
8. LOESS OR BLUFF HILLS
9. MISSISSIPPI- YAZOO FLOOD BASIN
9a. COSTAL PINE MEADOWS

Adapted from Rainwater, Percy. *Mississippi* (1938), p. 6.

however, these achievements were the product of leverage or traditional bargaining. Illustrative of this mobilization was that blacks won high state offices in the first legitimate election after the Civil War. James Lynch, a free-born from the North and a Methodist minister, was elected Secretary of State in 1869 on the Republican ticket. At the same time, 30 of the 107 legislators in the lower house were black; and so were five of 33 senators.[66]

The power of black representatives was bolstered by the caliber of elected leaders and their membership in the majority Republican Party. Four of the five senators—Hiram Revels, Charles Caldwell, Thomas Stringer and Robert Gleed—achieved great prominence and remained active throughout the period. In the House of Representatives, John R. Lynch was perhaps the most distinguished, though all but 14 of the rest were especially active in the legislative sphere and elsewhere. Such intensive political activity continued apace for a time. In the two succeeding legislative elections, black representation exceeded that for the first election. In 1872 black legislators numbered 38; in 1874 they numbered 55. Senators numbered nine in 1874.[67]

Meanwhile, blacks were attaining political offices and appointments in the state and national governments. In this period, one black served as Lieutenant Governor, five as Secretary of State; one each as Superintendent of Education, Librarian and Secretary of Agriculture and Immigration; two as Speakers of the State House of Representatives; two as United States Senators and one as Congressman. All of the preceding were elective posts, but many of these individuals went on to perform other political and civic functions after the end of Republicanism. Hiram Revels returned from the U.S. Senate to serve as Secretary of State, before dabbling in Democratic politics. He was also a clergyman and pursued this while he served as President of then-Alcorn University. B. K. Bruce, the other Senator, later received a federal appointment in Washington, as did John Lynch. Indeed Lynch had an exceedingly long and active career in Washington. He served as an auditor of the U.S. Treasury, an officer in the army, and later as a lawyer with practices in Mississippi and Illinois.[68]

There were also many local and municipal officeholders, though we know far less about them. There is definite notice of only one mayor in the period, Robert Wood of Natchez. And, "[w]ith the possible exception of Coffeeville and Greenville, no town had a Negro majority on its board of aldermen."[69] Both of these towns are located in black-belt counties—Yalobusha and Washington, respectively. But there were towns with aldermen and other city officials. Jackson in Hinds County and Natchez in Adams County were notable examples where blacks held a few councilmanic posts.[70]

The greatest concentrations of local officials, however, were in county posts with immense power. In Issaquena County, where Mayersville is located, there was a virtual hegemony of black officials. These new leaders controlled all but two elective offices. All of the county supervisors were black, as were the "members of the legislature, the sheriff, the clerks, the justices of the peace, and the constables." In addition, some 15 other counties usually had multiple supervisors in this period, positions that by law and tradition bore considerable power.[71]

The position of sheriff was also powerful and often occupied by blacks. Eleven other counties had black sheriffs—Adams, Boliver, Claiborne, Coahoma, De Soto, Hinds, Holmes, Issaquena, Jefferson, Washington and Warren—all in the black belt.[72] There were also lesser offices, such as treasurer, assessor, justice of the peace, superintendent of education, constable, and circuit and chancery clerk.

This heyday of mobilization was followed by a period of great conflict that led to the complete disfranchisement of blacks. This fusion period was marked by the efforts of the displaced whites to regain absolute control, even by making mock coalitions with blacks. The latter was seen as inevitable since these diehards saw that blacks were already participating to a considerable degree in concert with other whites. Thus the task was to disrupt the "Black-Carpetbagger-Scalawag coalition." The challengers were aided by mounting internal strains in the racial coalition. For example, many white parties to the coalition never reconciled their own beliefs about black inferiority and used every opportunity to exploit the racial angle. Their position was strengthened by the defection of many of their number who feared eventual black domination. Thus all of the old arguments began to hold sway as race became the standard by which sides were chosen.

Since black occupation of offices was extensive, the task was to either eliminate or co-opt them so that whites (now identified as Democrats) could gain an edge. This was done in a variety of ways, but the most prominent option was the formation of a "coalition" with black Republicans:

> Under this system, the white Democratic executive of a county would agree with the Negro leaders, who were generally Republican, on the number of offices in the county and in the county's legislative delegation that were to be held by Negroes. In theory these Negro candidates were chosen by those of their race; actually their choice was subject to review by the Democratic committee. The number and type of offices given to the Negroes varied according to local conditions. Generally they included a minority on the board of supervisors, a few other county offices of low pay and little responsibility, and one membership in the legislature.[73]

The result of this "fusion" was that Republicans (black and white) lost electoral posts so rapidly that by 1875 the Democrats were in near-absolute control of the public office arena. While blacks still held some offices, the terms of participation were very different. Bargaining was now required with those whose expressed aim was the elimination of black political influence. The black politicians, however, often accepted these arrangements. They would vote with Democrats, or with any other political group that offered concessions.[74] In point of fact, there were few other options. "[A]ll that was left of the once promising and flourishing Republican Party at the south was the true, faithful, loyal, and sincere colored men, . . . and a few white men."[75]

The dwindling numbers of black elected officials may be seen in legislative representation from 1870–1890. The data in Table 2.1 show that the peak years were the early ones: 1870, 1872 and 1874. At each of the first three elections, black representation increased. The rate almost doubled between 1870 and 1876, perhaps fueling the skepticism of whites in the coalition. However, representation dropped dramatically, by more than a factor of three, in the two-year period of 1874–1876. It leveled off at about seven. Subsequently, blacks as a legislative voting bloc were of no consequence.

Table 2.1. Black Legislative Representation (Lower House), 1870-1890.

Year	Number
1870	31
1872	38
1874	55
1876	16
1878	6
1880	8
1882	10
1884	9
1886	7
1888	7
1890	6

Total legislative membership: 107–115

Despite the apparent success of blacks in winning offices, their institutional integration into the political process was shortlived and hardly accepted as routine. It is in the irony of the success and the failure that we can account for the racial political history that so greatly affects black actions in Bolton, Mayersville and Tchula today. In the reconstruction period, blacks were seen to act in the interests of their constituents, though they often did so in concert with broader interest groups. Despite the contrary view that enslavement and inferiority handicapped them, blacks performed as well and/or as poorly as others. However, their success as well as their failure resulted from a system bent on their denigration and exclusion for racial reasons. The fears and assumptions of inferiority held by whites led to a consistent effort to destroy independent black influence, even after some whites coalesced with blacks to good benefit.

An assessment of the success and failure can be understood by evaluating some of the details of the periods. It has already been seen that many blacks had political influence between 1876 and 1879 in state and local positions. In the cases of some few individuals, such influence was exceedingly strong. The group in the constitutional convention was by all accounts vitally important to the radical coalition. Two state and legislative leaders, James and John Lynch, were typical of the small group of highly influential blacks. James Lynch served as Secretary of State with distinction and was regarded as a bonus to the Republicans because of his oratorical skills.[76] His early death cut short his career, however. The influence and power of John Lynch was even broader and longer. He began in Natchez at age 17, soon dominated Adams County, and effected what one author has called "black power," as defined in the terms of the civil rights era of the 1960s. Lynch mobilized and gained leadership control of the majority black constituency in the county and was a virtual "boss" in the period.[77] Not only did he control Natchez; his service as a state legislator and Speaker of the House has been evaluated as without equal. And so long as the Republican coalition held up, Lynch was as important as anyone in negotiating for the perceived good of black people and for social change. As a Congressman, from 1872 he and at least one of two senators did the same things in Washington. These men and several others like them bore much influence that overshadowed numerous others of talent. Their prodigious efforts provided Mississippi and the national government with examples that would have been outstanding in any era and to any constituency.

Notwithstanding influence, two other factors lessened independent Black success. The first was the lack of time to complete mobilization of the large constituency toward the goal of electoral participation. A striking fact about the period is its briefness. The "golden age" of reconstruction only lasted about four years. Confident black participation did not occur until about 1870, but by 1873 it was already declining. This means that independent black influence and control was never institutionalized. According to the population ratio, blacks fell far short of the majority influence that their numbers might have commanded. Their considerable population margin over whites was never reflected in state representation. Nor was it ever reflected on a broad scale in all of the populous black counties along the banks of the Mississippi River. Influence sufficient to get around coalitioning existed only in Issaquena and Adams Counties during the period.[78] The reality was that the white minority still possessed the most institutional power.

Perhaps because of (or in spite of) this incomplete mobilization, black leaders often did not perceive their tasks in terms of independent political action. Though bargaining was necessary, John Lynch was probably too optimistic when he argued that it was the blacks who determined who among the whites would have power in state politics; no one side could win otherwise.

The second factor was the philosophical belief held by most black leaders that cooperation with whites was desirable. There was no systematic effort by blacks to gain power commensurate with their numerical strength in the electorate. John Lynch articulated this measured and altruistic position in spite of an awareness of potential independent actions:

> While the colored men held the key to the situation, the white men knew that the colored man had no desire to rule or dominate even the Republican Party. All the colored men wanted and demanded was a voice in the government

under which they lived, and to the support of which they contributed, and to have a small, but fair, and reasonable proportion of the positions that were at the disposal of the voters of the State and of the administration.[79]

The choices made by blacks were of no greater consequences for failure than those made by whites, as an evaluation of the black-carpetbagger-scalawag coalition reveals. The whites in the coalition remained loyal for only a short time, thus affecting the Republican legislative majority. These defections made legislative success very uncertain from one day to the next. Indeed, the size of the Republican majority in the legislature declined from its high of 82, to 66 in the 1872 campaign, a mere two years after the coalition gained control. Moreover, "several of the white members . . . generally voted with the Democrats."[80] Therefore, even though black officials were increasing, their opportunity to coalesce was declining. This problem was exacerbated by the increasing activity and influence (legal and extralegal) of Democratic partisans at the local level. Their racist appeals were not easily resisted by local whites. And blacks who could not be forced to disavow the Republican Party were removed from offices by a variety of legal and illegal means. These tactics effectively ended Reconstruction.

Fusion politics replaced reconstruction and provided very few direct benefits for the black electorate. After 1875, the only blacks to gain were individual politicians who largely held symbolic positions and dispensed modest patronage. Real local power in this transformation was exerted only by the new Democratic Party, which used other whites and blacks to destroy the influence of the latter. Otherwise, some few gained by leaving the state for work. The most important of these had patrons in Washington who arranged federal appointments. These changes led to a precipitate drop in Afro-American electoral and other participation. Representation in the legislature, always easily maintained, now dwindled to a point of insignificance, and no other state-level officeholders exerted power of any consequence. Of course, local and municipal officials had come under attack much earlier and had already disappeared by this time.

Significant to this was the desertion of the Republican coalition by whites out of fear and social ostracism. Others merely found it opportune to opt out of an "unholy alliance."[81] This process was hastened when it was discovered that white Democrats, largely race-baiters, were actually recruiting blacks. White Republicans now found themselves squeezed from both sides. They quickly yielded to the Democrats, who after all had found a way to control black leaders.

There are other reasons for the re-emergence of white rule. A systematic campaign of extra-legal activities—intimidation, violence and media incitement—were also adopted by the Democrats. Stuffing of ballot boxes and defrauding voters became the routine in places where there was no white majority. Just as frequent was intimidation to prevent organized black and/or Republican activity. Beatings, burnings, economic reprisals and assassination were all used to prevent activities not affiliated with the new Democrats. Much of the violence and intimidation of blacks was carried out, especially in black-belt counties, by terror organizations like the Ku Klux Klan.[82] Moreover, this mob violence was also perpetrated against white Republican organizers.[83] This widescale use of violence was well reported and variously given sanction by the press.[84]

The Era of Disfranchisement

This end to Reconstruction left blacks in a status very similar to enslavement; it remained only to give it the force of law.[85] This was accomplished in the new state constitution adopted in 1890 that initiated the "Mississippi plan." The Democrat-controlled convention (130 of 134 delegates)[86] adopted two critical regulations designed to disfranchise blacks: the poll tax provision and the literacy clause.

The tax required payment two years preceding any electoral participation. It worked very effectively because it constituted an economic hardship, and provided one more legal regulation by which blacks could be trapped and disqualified at the polls.

But the "understanding clause" that required one to read and interpret a part of the constitution was the most effective; it "did provide a sure and regularized means of disfranchising Negroes as well as illiterate whites, if the group in power chose to do so."[87] The selective judgment of white circuit clerks routinely denied even literate blacks the vote. Thus ended the first great period of black political participation in Mississippi.

From 1890 down to the mid 1960s, there was virtually no consequential black American electoral participation. Data show that Mississippi, in consonance with a widespread perception, was the former confederate state most wed to the preservation of white supremacy. The white political leader of the day was most likely a populist, race-baiting demagogue, like Bilbo or Vardaman. Far fewer blacks were permitted to vote, let alone run for office or exert influence in the party. Table 2.2 illustrates that black registration declined from 67% in 1867 to under 5% in 1955, compared to white registration levels at well above 50% throughout the period.

The white primary bolstered this in 1907 when blacks were barred from Democratic Party membership.[88] Yet when one was not a member of the Democratic Party, there was no other meaningful option. The Republican Party no longer had a viable primary, or general election contest.

> The Republican Party, which had polled more than 52,000 votes for Hayes in 1876 and more than 43,000 for Blaine as late as 1884, cast less than 1,500 votes for Harrison in 1892. In no election thereafter until 1920 did the party poll as many as 6,000 votes.[89]

Table 2.2. Black registration, 1867-1955.

Year	Negro voting age population[a]	Negro registration	Percent of Negro voting age population registered	White voting age population[a]	White registration	Percent of White voting age population registered
1867	98,926	[b]60,167	66.9	84,784	[b]46,636	55.0
1892	150,409	[c]8,615	5.7	120,611	[c]68,127	56.5
1896	198,647	[d]16,234	8.2	150,530	[d]108,998	72.4
1899	198,647	[e]18,170	9.1	150,530	[e]122,724	81.5
1955	495,138	[f]21,502	4.3	710,639	[f]423,456	59.6

[a] Nearest decennial census is used for each voting age population figure, male only for the census years 1870–1900; thereafter male and female.
[b] *Jackson Weekly Clarion*, Sept. 19, 1867, p. 2, col. 1.
[c] Wharton, op. cit. supra note 14, at 215.
[d] *Biennial Report of Secretary of State to Legislature of Mississippi for the Years 1896 and 1897*, 68.
[e] *Biennial Report of Secretary of State to Legislature of Mississippi for the Years 1898 and 1899*, 171.
[f] U.S. Department of Justice figures, statement of Burke Marshall, T. 257.

Source: U.S. Civil Rights Commission, *Voting in Mississippi*. (1965), p. 8.

This remained the fact until the late 1960s when a Republican candidate was fielded against James Eastland for the U.S. Senate, and garnered over 100,000 votes. (Eastland got 250,000.) Intermittently over the years there were several Republican and Independent candidates, but these were never serious contenders and were largely ignored by Democratic opponents. A breakthrough in Republican fortunes only came with the new black mobilization which drove many whites from the Democratic Party.[90]

What remained of the Republican Party in Mississippi and much of the South was controlled for a time by blacks. This is both interesting and ironic. On the one hand, effective participation for blacks in the now "Solid South" was cut off. Yet the character of white southern isolation from the two-party competitive system actually allowed blacks to maintain a kind of alignment with the national Republican Party. The former confederates felt so absolutely confident of white solidarity that no concern was shown toward black Republicans. Though a few whites remained Republicans, organizationally they split with blacks.

After the turn of the century the blacks (Black and Tan Party) attained control of the small state faction and by the mid 1920s were actually dispensing patronage. The irony is that the patronage could only be delivered to whites since Mississippi blacks could not hold the available positions. Often the positions did not go to white Republicans either. The "federal jobs obtained by Howard (the black Republican leader) . . . were often sold to white Democrats. . . . There were never enough white Republicans to go around for all the available federal jobs in the South, so they went to the Democrats."[91] Over and above this the Black and Tans were active "every four years, when its leaders would campaign in the North, urging Northern Blacks to vote for a Republican president."[92]

This does not mean that blacks were dormant or did not seek other than formal office positions. The tradition of resistance continued during this long spell of disfranchisement. It is most noted in the efforts blacks made to either defend or protect themselves against white violence just after 1875. Wharton has cited the years 1874–76 as those of the most intense violence as whites sought to rout elected blacks from office, among other things.[93] There is repeated evidence, however, that blacks did not merely sit idly by in the face of violence. With their usually inferior weaponry, they put up a fight.[94] It appears that a great portion of the lives lost in the 40 or 50 years after the war occurred under such circumstances.

Contemporary Mobilization and Transformation

The momentum toward the transformative changes that were to characterize the 1960s in Mississippi began in the 1940s. Aldon Morris has shown that this effort was highly organized, insofar as it was dependent everywhere upon indigenous institutions. These "older relatives, black educational institutions, churches, and protest organizations,"[95] constituted a traditional "protest community" susceptible to mobilization. Mississippi fit this same mold despite the harsh nature of the segregation system. The following analysis reveals that the early local "protest community" included educators, the NAACP, and movement "halfway houses such as the Southern Regional Council."[96] Later the black colleges, independent organizations in local towns, and a "movement center"[97] such as the Council of Federated Organizations (COFO) emerged to sustain the mobilization.

The early protests were made by "black elites" and sought notably elitist goals. The concern was for independent use of the vote by the few blacks who had the franchise. Soon the issue was broadened to voter registration. By the early 1940s there were semblances of an organized campaign, not uncharacteristically, among those who were educated and of some means. Among them were school teachers, clergymen, and health care professionals. Their new spirit of aggressiveness led to the "Committee of One Hundred for the General Improvement of the Condition of the Colored People in Mississippi (which) urged Blacks to vote in the election for United States senator." Later they organized the Progressive Voters League that "encourage[d] voter registration and political participation" in the 1946 election, much of which was thwarted by white violence. Loewen and Sallis attribute such tactics to the overt campaign of racial bigotry from Theodore Bilbo. But the blacks were undaunted as they returned again several years later with the Mississippi Regional Council of Negro Leadership (1952), that had the same aims.[98]

Even at this early date, allied services were being provided by "halfway houses" and indigenous branches of national civil rights organizations. Mrs. C.C. Mosley looks upon the Southern Regional Council and its Mississippi branch as agents of change because they assembled information, put diverse people interested in change in contact, and took positions that isolated them from the mainstream. This "group of civil minded citizens, both white and Negro, which endeavors to solve the common problems of both groups" had recently "passed resolutions supporting the right of the Negro to vote; decrying lynching and the spirit which brings it about," *inter alia*.[99] These efforts served a bridging function whereby a group with broader goals made it possible for blacks to pursue independent goals with some quasi-support.

In the early phase, the civil rights organization of singular importance in Mississippi and the rest of the South was the NAACP, which survived on the strength of local black support. Though the headquarters for operation were in the North, it was southern branch organizations that provided the platform and leadership for the NAACP. It was not odd that the issues taken up by the organization were largely southern ones—this is where the membership and leadership strength was.[100] Local towns, such as Jackson, Vicksburg, Clarksdale, Belzoni and Natchez had branches. Eventually there was visible and very strong state NAACP leadership in the persons of Amzie Moore, Aaron Henry and Medgar Evers.

The importance of these homegrown local leaders in structuring the agenda for the NAACP can be seen in the issues the national office pursued. For the most part the big issues were those of interest to southerners: basic rights and desegregation. A major early victory was the 1944 *Smith v. Allwright* decision that outlawed the white primary, followed by the *Brown v. Board of Education*[101] decision that outlawed school desegregation. Both of these achievements became the catalysts for sustained mobilization activities. In Mississippi petitions were rapidly filed by local branches for school desegregation—especially Vicksburg, Jackson, Clarksdale, Natchez, and Yazoo City.[102]

Clearly these independent black actions were singularly significant in stimulating a national debate about such issues. The Democratic Party was forced to take up the question in 1948 when Hubert Humphrey offered a civil rights platform plank. Thereafter a coterie of congressional supporters put their weight behind change by passing new and far-reaching civil rights legislation. All this created more fluid conditions and opportunities than had existed in the South for 70 years; this provided great inspiration to black southern leaders and citizens alike.

Local organization continued and was tightened as branch units of the NAACP grew. The so-called voter registration clubs of the 1940s and early 1950s in Mississippi soon developed into NAACP branches and reinvigorated a cadre of leadership. Moore, Evers and Henry were soon joined by many others who began to work on many fronts in response to known needs and to take advantage of the spirit and opportunities of this new era. Local leaders began to follow up on the legal successes of the NAACP by instituting litigation of their own to challenge white recalcitrance on school segregation and voter registration. Sometimes these efforts were done entirely independently of the NAACP, but in the same spirit of rejection of racial exclusion. The black teachers, for example, were barred *de facto* from membership in the NAACP, but took their stand. When the then-Governor White presented what he called a "school equalization" plan, which would have perpetuated segregation,[103] the teachers publicly and categorically rejected it. That they did so put them squarely in the camp of the NAACP, membership notwithstanding. That such could happen with public school teachers illustrates that the base of mobilization was highly localized and broad.

These small efforts incited a great wave of reaction from whites. The backlash included legal maneuvering and violence not unlike that which accompanied and ended the reconstruction era of the 1870s. The Citizens Council was organized by some of Mississippi's best-known white leaders, to preserve white supremacy and to once again resist northern and federal encroachments. This was consistent with state actions, which in some states included legislative passage of interposition laws.[104] The violence, now widely and instantaneously reported by the media, ran the gamut of lynchings, assassinations, bombings, shootings, and riotous activity against blacks.

NAACP leaders were a particular target in the early days, as were community organizers later affiliated with the Student Non-Violent Coordinating Committee (SNCC). Leaders were killed or assaulted in all areas of the state, including Belzoni, Natchez, Tchula, Clarksdale, and Hattiesburg *inter alia*. Indeed, the head of the state NAACP and symbol of the movement, Medgar Evers, was assassinated in 1963 at Jackson.[105] Then in 1964, three civil rights workers (two white, one black) disappeared and were found murdered, but not before their case became an international *cause celebre*.[106]

This backlash in the late 1950s and early 1960s, however, did not stifle the movement. The pace of activities escalated so that after 1963, Mississippi, like the rest of the former confederacy, was in the throes of fundamental social change. Much of this intensification of effort occurred on the strength of organizational solidarity and amalgamation. It has already been noted that many local communities had independent organizations. By the early 1960s, however, all of the major civil rights groups were operating in the state. They created a coalition in 1962 in an effort to concentrate their energies in mobilizing against what they perceived as the most hostile environment in the South.[107] These forces referred to themselves as the Council of Federated Organizations, or COFO. They targeted voter registration, though a range of other activities were utilized: marches, demonstrations, sit-ins and boycotts. This represented the emergence of a statewide "movement center," an element believed essential by Aldon Morris. Indeed, the statewide effort made the movement center even broader and more highly organized than the cases discussed by Morris. His centers were all concentrated in a municipality. This in no way diminishes the utility of the construct. Rather, it highlights how the greater need and more intense mobilization in Mississippi yielded much greater solidarity for activation.[108]

Once state mobilization was underway, allied forces and other interests which the conflict incorporated were of major importance in sustaining the drive. Many of these allies were white students who participated in the "Mississippi Summers" of 1964 and 1965.[109] They left their college campuses and assisted with voter registration, demonstrations and the full range of other activities. Their work was buttressed by the Democratic coalition in Congress that was debating a strong civil rights bill and by the generally supportive work of Martin Luther King Jr. and the NAACP. Symbolically, President Kennedy had even put his personal prestige on the line in criticizing white defiance of law. Then in 1965 still another federal bill, the most far-reaching civil rights legislation since reconstruction, was passed to protect voting rights.

If developments so far can be characterized as indicative of social mobilization (activation for rights acquisition), then the next stage is indicative of political mobilization (goal of power acquisition). Though the local groups had combined into COFO, clearly the earlier NAACP dominance was being superceded by a group (SNCC) more interested in community organization for the assumption of power. In part this was an inevitable progression because of the earlier NAACP-led mobilization; "vulnerabilities" and "opportunities" were created in the environment that sustained broader group action. Thus despite white backlash, organized pressures from blacks opened up new spheres for exploitation. The federal government, for example, proved especially sensitive to these pressures by yielding ground to and protecting those demanding change. At this point the SNCC was a very prominent force in the "interactional network" (a collective of local organizations) that moved toward political mobilization. Their actions set the stage for individual town mobilizations like those in Bolton, Tchula, and Mayersville.[110]

The nature of the SNCC organization, and its tactics and goals, gave an indication of the shift in the mobilization to power. This largely student group was organized in 1960 and took advantage of the opportunities Martin Luther King, Jr. created for social action. Like King, they built on local black resources for support. They differed in that an initial concern was voter registration, which they sought to achieve via intense and highly localized programs of political education and community organization. This meant taking up residence in small towns and counties and confronting the most overt tactics of white violence and black fear. It was not accidental, therefore, that Mississippi was a special case for the political mobilization phase.

Once mass voter registration was made a goal, the entire organizational network was involved in its pursuit. The first areas where SNCC worked, however, were noteworthy for the white violence that accompanied any efforts to register blacks. Pike County whites in southern Mississippi were the most confrontational. The effort began in 1961 with a typical SNCC group of black and white college students who settled in the major town in the area, McComb. They were to encounter jailings, beatings, and murders as they organized adults for voter registration and conducted workshops for an independent direct action campaign led by high school students.[111] Eventually full-scale local mobilization was realized in Pike County, and gave momentum to similar activity being sponsored by COFO elsewhere in southern, central and delta Mississippi. The political mobilization was exceedingly important in light of the systematic state effort to disfranchise blacks. The data in Table 2.3 show the extent of this exclusion of blacks from voting in certain counties (where civil rights organizations were active and where the three towns in this study are located). Pike County (McComb) probably had no black registrants in 1962, and for certain had none by 1964. Issaquena (Mayersville) and Holmes (Tchula) Counties respectively had none and 9% in 1962. Little had changed by 1964, even where blacks did not constitute a majority. In populous Hinds County most of the registrants (10%) were in the urban Jackson area, while a relatively liberal tradition in the town of Greenville probably explains the 9% registration in Washington County.

Table 2.3. Black Voter Registration 1962-1967 in Selected Counties.

	1960 Voting Age Population	1960 Black Voting Age Population	Number (and percentage of Registered Blacks)		
			1962	1964	1967
Bolivar	25,970	15,939	NA	NA	10,269 (51%)
Coahoma	23,312	14,604	1,061 (8%)	NA	10,395 (67)
Forrest	29,926	7,495	22 (3)	236 (3%)	5,467 (68)
Hinds	103,974	36,138	4,756 (13)	5,616 (16)	26,383 (67)
Holmes	13,530	8,757	8 (1)	20 (0)	6,372 (73)
Issaquena	1,721	1,081	0	5 (1)	643 (73)
Leflore	23,841	13,567	281 (2)	268 (2)	10,547 (72)
Marshall	11,510	7,168	57 (1)	177 (3)	4,603 (64)
Pike	19,099	6,936	NA	NA	10,016 (75)
Sunflower	22,309	13,524	NA	185 (1)	5,548 (41)
Warren	24,256	10,726	NA	2,433 (23)	6,432 (60)
Washington	40,456	20,619	1,762 (9)	NA	10,448 (42)

Sources: U.S. Civil Rights Commission, *Voting in Mississippi* (1965) pp. 70–71; *Political Participation* (1968), pp. 244–46.

Moreover, there were all manner of difficulties in exercising the vote for the few who had it. The Democratic Party was virtually closed to them despite the Supreme Court ruling against the white primary in the 1940s.[112] And this explains the organization by COFO of the 1963 mock election as a protest against the exclusiveness of the Democratic Party and to demonstrate the level of mobilization of blacks. Subsequent to this the Mississippi Freedom Democratic Party (MFDP) was organized as an independent mechanism for pursuing political goals.[113]

The consequences of the shift to political mobilization were immediately evident in the symbolic sense, but only bore tangible fruits by 1967. On the symbolic side the MFDP made great strides by challenging the National Democratic Party to unseat the regular Mississippi delegation in 1964. This effort, while not successful, strengthened local organization and engendered mass participation. At this point mobilization was most evident in the willingness of local blacks to attempt registration and to make organized challenges to other aspects of segregation. Thus by 1967 registration levels were over 50% in all but two of the selected counties in Table 2.3. Even in Pike County this was evident where 52% black registration was coupled with a frontal attack on public accommodations and school segregation, via the courts and in the streets.

Also in 1967, the greatly improved registration levels translated into black elected officials. The first high-ranking post was won in that year by Robert Clark, who became a state legislator from Holmes County.[114] Then in 1969, the first black mayor from a bi-racial town was elected—Charles Evers of Fayette.[115] At the same time several other blacks were elected to lesser posts such as town alderman, county supervisor, election commissioner, coroner, justice of the peace and school board member.[116] As the data show in Table 2.4, the bulk of these were in local level posts by 1970. But the level of improvement in representation was dramatic. In five years, Mississippi blacks had emerged from almost total disfranchisement to the election of 81 officials. This was a greater increase than that of any other southern state with which Mississippi shared a similar racial experience.

Table 2.4. Black Elected Officials in Mississippi, 1967, 1970.

Year	State	County	Town	Judicial Enforcement	Other
1967	1	7	3	14	-
1970	1	22	35	18	5

Sources: U.S. Civil Rights Commission, *Political Participation* (1968), pp. 218–19; Metropolitan Applied Research Center and Voter Education Project, *National Roster of Black Elected Officials* (1970), pp. 57, 61.

By 1973, population concentrations were presenting an observable pattern. The most prominent areas of representation were those where the black population was large. These were the same areas where blacks had always been concentrated: the delta counties along the Mississippi River, and the central region where land was very fertile. Another pattern was that county and town positions (including school and law enforcement) were the easiest to win. For example, in bi-racial towns with a majority Afro-American population, mayoral posts and sometimes town councilorships could be won. At the end of 1973 there were seven mayors (up from the three in 1970), all in rural towns under 5,000 population, where the majority of residents were black.[117] There were also large increases in the numbers of blacks on town councils. The figures rose from 32 in 1970 to 54 by 1974, representing 22 towns. (Thirteen of these had multiple representatives.)[118] Most of these also were found in towns of less than 5,000 population.

To a degree, this mass mobilization represented the response to the national crisis in confidence about southern racism. The *Allwright* and *Brown* Supreme Court decisions were strong signals in this regard. But the much more important dynamic was the role blacks played in creating the crisis with an ideology of egalitarianism and exploiting the opportunities that devolved therefrom. The early and quite independent, if slow, work of the NAACP set in motion a collection of black voices bent on change. The process culminated in small towns all over the South like Bolton, Tchula and Mayersville, where mobilization sustained a complete transfer of power on the principle of egalitarianism.

In Mississippi, with its highly structured system of segregation and bulwarks for its maintenance, black organization and resistance was all the more intense. In the face of violence upon persons and properties, intimidation, economic reprisals, legal and extra-legal state government acts, the mobilization was rapid after 1960. Some of the earliest acts were the apparent individual choices to join a political organization, which later escalated and ran the gamut of legal challenges, public demonstrations and party affiliation. Perhaps the most significant symbolic and tangible act for the majority of blacks, however, was the trip to a voting registrar to be enrolled as a voter. Indeed, most people did not participate in a demonstration or become a named party to a suit (many would have gone to a mass meeting though); but there was a virtual certainty that everyone eligible would have been coaxed to register. Thus the presence of a voting campaign, while less obtrusive than other tactics, achieved almost total access to a town's black population. For example, in small places like Bolton and Mayersville it was difficult for potential voters not to feel personally engaged by this process; it affected everyone they knew.

Though the ideology of egalitarianism was omnipresent, there were practical considerations too. A major stimulus for voter registration mobilization was the realization that blacks could win offices in many places (and determine the outcome in others) if they used their strength as a bloc. In Fayette, the first biracial town to elect a black mayor, the result was inevitable with racial bloc voting; the population breakdown in 1969 was 1,318 blacks and 405 whites.[119] Hence a reason to vote was that there would be a direct consequence—election of one of their own. And the early electoral successes in most parts of the state were good symbols and proof that the process could work.

Hardly any of this large scale mobilization would have occurred, however, without the existence of a coterie of home-grown leaders, like the mayors of the three towns. It was they who dominated the mobilization campaigns by first articulating the ideas and later holding offices. As a product of their relative youth, few of these new leaders enjoyed prominence with local whites. The oldest of this lot (such as Aaron Henry and Medgar Evers) had started out in the

NAACP. The others were more likely to be students or recent graduates who signed on with the NAACP, SNCC and/or CORE. Many of them began as the footsoldiers of public demonstration, freedom schools and voter registration campaigns. Though they operated all over the state, in the post-1967 era they tended to concentrate on the political organization of a town or county region. Subsequently the new leaders usually won offices in places where they were long-time residents. In this regard they assumed the ongoing task of realizing equality in an environment where racism (or at least racial considerations) had stymied the participation of their constituents. That was not new. But what was new and interesting was the nature of the mobilization devised for resolution of some aspects of the problem, as the succeeding analysis is designed to show. Bolton, Tchula and Mayersville represent good cases for exploring this process and its consequence.

3

Neo-Populism in Bolton

Introduction

Mississippi is made up of many distinctive small towns and villages. Bolton is but one of these, with its several streets and small business establishments in the main part of town. A few church steeples rise, though not exceedingly high; and there is the train track and a cotton gin. Here and there an oil well is visible, for within the past 35 years oil was discovered in Bolton. Aside from the oil wells and some new, discordant edifices, what strikes the eye probably resembles appearances of 75 to 100 years ago. Walking its streets, one may get the impression of being in a black town, though a mere 15 years ago the powerlessness of blacks in the streets would have been all too obvious. And a mere 25 years ago equally obvious would have been their dependence upon a plantation cotton economy for work as sharecroppers. Labor engagement for the bulk of the employed would have been as field hands (hoeing, picking, tractor driving, etc.).

But much of this was swept away as the old agriculture system declined or was mechanized, and as the arrangement of power was completely changed from top to bottom. The changes that came to Bolton in the political sphere may be described simply. In 1969, three blacks ran for and won the position of alderman; one of these was Bennie Thompson. Four years later, a full slate ran for and won the mayoral position and all aldermanic posts. It was Bennie Thompson who won the mayoral office.

53

Figure 3.1   Town of Bolton, Mississippi, ca. 1980.

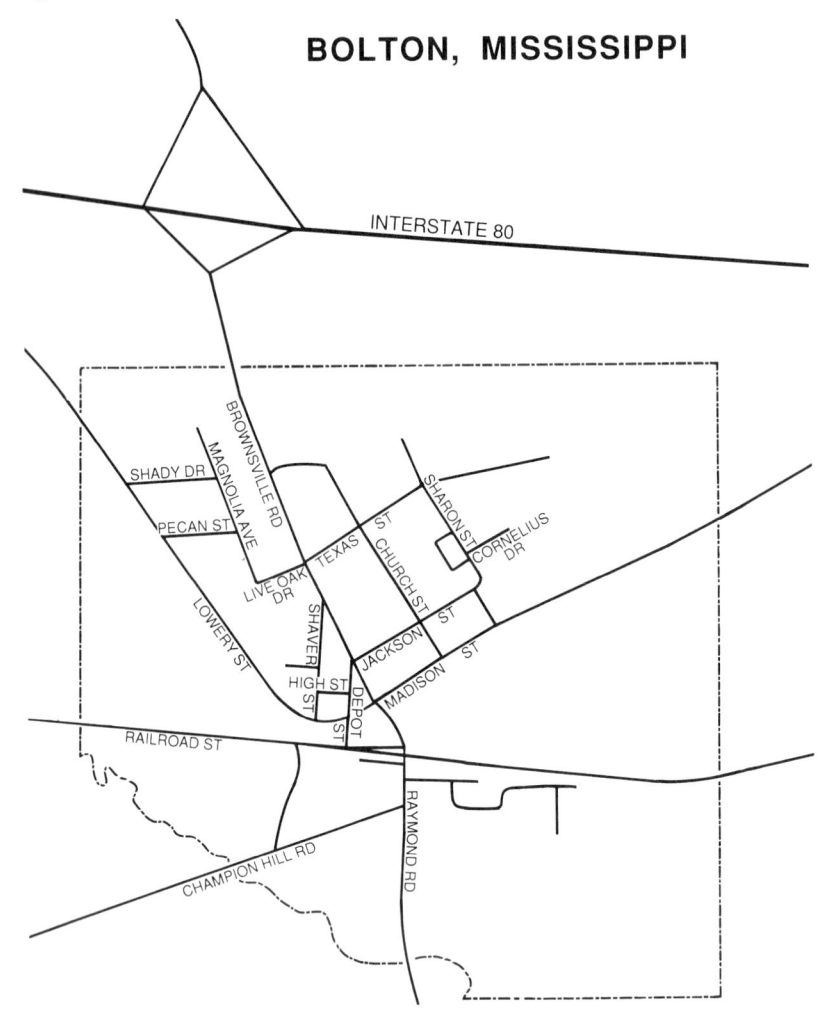

Adapted from Central Miss. Planning and Develop. Dist. (ND).

Bennie Thompson, the radical populist, came to preside over this landscape in 1969. No black had been elected or even tried, despite a mobilization campaign of considerable consequence since 1962. The combination of intensified organized civil rights confrontations in Jackson and Hinds County, and Thompson's arrival in 1969, served to bring the mobilization to a head. The result was a complete takeover of local political institutions by 1973.

It has already been seen that the radical populist Thompson is a grassroots-oriented intellectual, whose aggressive pursuit of progressive ideals and participatory democracy has been labeled militant. In his radicalism he is generally supportive of mass participation, with a strong ideological commitment. In this regard Thompson is like the cosmopolitan, often urban, and university-centered grassroots proponents, who are wed to the essential ideal "to make men equal in fact as in theory," or to "correct the balance between privilege and underprivilege."[1] In his populism he also fits the classical mold of those seeking to represent what often seems like the parochial interests of the excluded. But he is more like those who seek "devices of direct democracy like the referendum, to mobilization of mass passions, to idealizations of the man in the street, or to politicians' attempts to hold together shaky coalitions in the name of the people."[2] To some this would appear to be a combination of opposites, but for Thompson they serve as the base for successful leadership mobilization.

In this chapter the focus is on how Thompson's variety of populism and radicalism were shaped by educational experiences at Tougaloo College; the later, more radical national civil rights environment, and its accompanying activism, in which he was nurtured; and his independent analysis of local white racism in Bolton. However, this is undergirded (and preceded) by an analysis of local history and the conditions of disfranchisement that ultimately led to the present mobilization.

Bolton's population history is like that of so many other black-belt Mississippi counties. Before the end of enslavement, blacks outnumbered whites. At times in Hinds County the ratio was three to one. (See Table 3.1.) Even when major migrations occurred (viz. 1870s)[3] the huge black majority remained until 1950. However in the Bolton census tract, black majority status was never reversed. This population configuration was as important to the mobilization of blacks during reconstruction as it is to the present. It led to the development of a strong leadership class in the area, whose achievements and tactics are often invoked today as symbols of a glorious past.

Table 3.1. Hinds County Population, 1840-1860.

	White	Slave	Free Black
1840	6,778	19,098	261
1850	8,690	16,625	25
1860	8,940	22,363	36

Source: U.S. Census, 1840-1860.

Hinds County enjoyed a significant black mobilization during reconstruction. In fact, it may be argued that if white power was centered in the delta, black power was centered in the Central-Southern counties of Hinds, Warren and Adams. "Since Hinds County was highly industrialized and because of its strategic political position, it was under the control of the new class of Negro leaders as perhaps no other county during the Reconstruction period."[4] In this period, nine of the 33 counties with black legislative representation were within this central region surrounding Bolton. Moreover no other county had more blacks in the legislature than Hinds, with 13 between 1870 and 1884.[5] The concentration of these leaders and their active constituents in and around the capital (Jackson) made certain opportunities available that were conducive to mobilization. The area between Vicksburg and Jackson functioned as a metropolitan zone that facilitated communications between the blacks; they could take advantage of better information since there was a great concentration of newspapers in the area. And the independent organization among blacks was high and sophisticated. Many blacks were members of the Loyal Leagues, branches of patriotic groups that began in the North. Found throughout the South by 1867 with their memberships monopolized by blacks, it was they who fielded the first successful black candidates in Mississippi.[6] By any estimation, this rapid activation and application of black resources achieved a degree of constituent mobilization. (See Figure 3.2.)

There were many prominent leaders in the area who greatly facilitated local mobilization because of their organizational skills and impact on the public policy process. T.W. Stringer was one of these, "whose influence upon the constitution of 1868 was as great as that of any other man. [Then later,] wherever he went in the state, churches, lodges, benevolent societies, and political machines sprang up and flourished."[7] He was matched by two others, John and James Lynch. John was the young indefatigible scion of politics in Adams county, who became Speaker of the Lower House and U.S. Congressman. James Lynch of Jackson was a minister and Secretary of State, whose reputation and work in the Republican Party hierarchy greatly influenced the early local debate about black reconstruction, especially education.

Of these leaders, the homegrown Charles Caldwell perhaps had the most impact on the mobilization. From 1869 to his assassination in 1875, he was regarded not only as the most outspoken, confident black spokesman, but perhaps the one most effectively integrated into traditional power channels. He was born a slave, became a blacksmith and served on the Board of Police for a district that included Bolton.[8] Though his senatorial duties were important, his party work and activist feats were more important. As a part of the Republican Party cadre, he was engaged in all such functions and knew every governor of the party during his career. He saw this as the means to protect black interests among white Republicans whose ulterior motive was also deemed hegemony.[9] At the same time, Caldwell's lack of deference to whites and aggressive pursuit of personal and racial goals brought him notoriety. Whites found him an upstart because of his "daring,"[10] as when he shot a white who physically assaulted him in Jackson. That he successfully argued self-defense in court is a testament to the power he enjoyed; that he bore arms and owned up to their use against a white is an illustration of his presumption of absolute equality.[11] The same attitude was exhibited for the people when in 1875 he sought to stem the tide of disfranchisement by marching armed troops the length of the county (and back) through Bolton.[12]

This intensive mobilization and its leadership class were shortlived. Soon

Figure 3.2   Center of Early Black Political Participation.

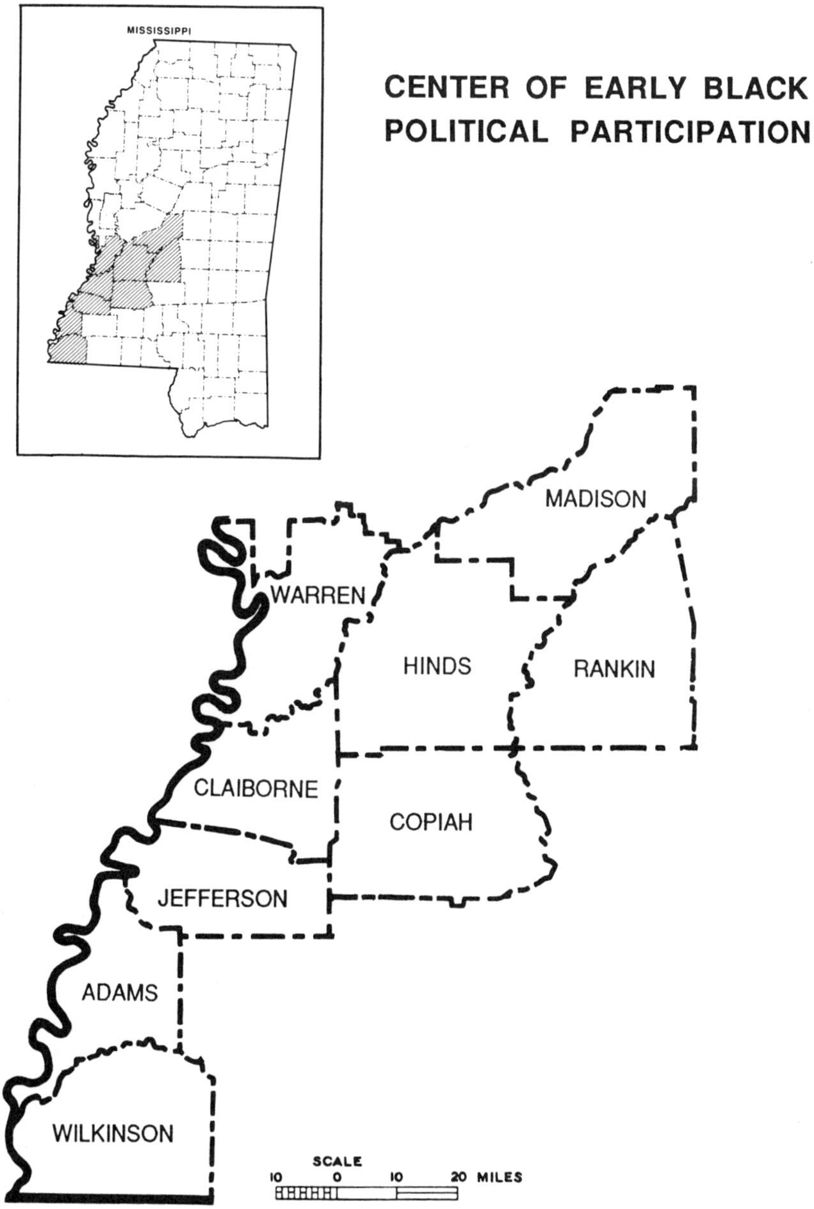

the interracial coalition was destroyed and remaining black leaders found it more politic to kow-tow to the new white Democratic majority. Violence was found in a good part of this. "Of the slain there was enough to furnish forth a battlefield, [including] the Negro, the scalawag, and the carpetbagger."[13] Between 1875–84, there was a single black legislative representative in Hinds County. Then after the four in 1884, there were no others until the mid-1970s. The formal scheme adopted for this displacement was fusion, a series of pre-election arrangements whereby Blacks agreed to accept certain positions designated by white Democrats.

> In some of the counties with large Negro majorities, the fusion tickets between Democrats and the Black wing of the Republican Party led by Hill and Lynch came to be openly recognized. Such tickets were formed by agreements between county Democratic executive committees and Negro leaders. Each party would name its candidates on a joint ticket previously agreed upon—Generally the Negroes were given a 'minority on the county board of supervisors, a few other county offices of low pay and responsibility and one membership in the legislature.' In Hinds County in the election of 1883 the fusion ticket gave the Democrats the sheriff, the chancery and circuit clerks, the treasurer, the state senator, three representatives, four supervisors, and an equal number of magistrates and constables with the Republicans. Negro Republicans were given the offices of county assessor, coroner, one representative, one supervisor, and their quota of magistrates and constables.[14]

Fusion ushered in a long period of black isolation from formal politics. For a time, the remnants of the Republican Party were dominated by three displaced blacks who had virtually no effect on state politics.[15] (Some like John Lynch received federal appointments outside the state with national party support.) Later this facade of power was maintained by members of the Black and Tan Party—blacks with links to national Republicans, but whose patronage could only be dispensed to local white Democrats. Not unexpectedly, the leaders of this party were concentrated in Hinds County. However, the pattern that most denoted black isolation was that their leaders became "out-group based" or chosen by whites.[16] These "Uncle Toms"[17] received instructions from whites and were thereby expected to maintain a favorable disposition by other blacks to status quo racial arrangements.

In Bolton and thereabouts, this isolation was maintained largely by these "out-group based" leaders. Caldwell had already been assassinated and the remaining Republicans either moved outside the state or were ineffective. These "new" leaders were variously workers in plantation houses, field foremen, and preachers; later they included teachers, business owners (especially funeral homes and stores), and farmers. Those in the employ of plantations were selected for their "smartness" given the "natural" handicaps of race; while the early preachers received tutelage from and replaced the white circuit preachers.[18] The crop of teachers susceptible to leadership only grew after the *Plessy v. Ferguson* (1896) decision sustained "separate but equal." Thus Bolton boasted schools (often one room) not only in town, but in outlying rural places too. Then as the town grew, so did small black businesses: stores, cafés, a funeral home, and insurance agencies. Since these catered almost exclusively to blacks, the owners were expected to also maintain the status quo or risk their bases of livelihood.

By any stretch of the imagination, these forces in Bolton and elsewhere cooperated in a system for a time that thwarted independent black progress. For many it was not deemed possible to develop independent bases of indigenous power in light of the violence and intimidation that whites could exact.[19] However, this forced outsider status did create conditions for a strong internal black community, dictated by a need to survive. The very institutional forces and arrangements that were used to maintain the status quo were the same ones used to sustain the mobilization that resulted in a transfer of power. Bennie Thompson was greatly aided by this kind of internal and complex survival organization that existed in Bolton since the 1880s.

Contemporary Mobilization in Hinds County

It is this class of leadership that was built upon and displaced by the emergence of Bennie Thompson in the late 1960s. The Thompson era ushered in a high level of mobilization and new office-holding reminiscent (but far broader) than that experienced in reconstruction in the Hinds County area. The shift in the political arena that accommodated his radical populism emerged from the southern civil rights movement (mobilization) dating from 1955 with Martin Luther King in Montgomery. When this movement was in full force in Mississippi, a large portion of it was near Bolton (around Jackson). In this sense Boltonians could observe and take part in the early movement that resulted in intense black mobilization.

The beginnings were slow and sometimes tentative in Hinds County, but afforded the opportunity in the principal city of Jackson for various organized groups to come together. In 1954 Jackson was one of several areas (such as Clarksdale, Natchez, or Yazoo City) where state NAACP officials met, issued statements and filed suits of one kind or another.[20] Though operating as indigenous black organizations, what these leaders sought was entirely within normally accepted parameters and principles in the institutionalized structure. The NAACP used litigation, while the Mississippi Human Relations Council arranged routine interracial gatherings on the assumption of equality.[21]

Much of the independent organization and activity by blacks was led by the NAACP. It made a broad assault on segregation, via litigation. Some of the cases, like that seeking the integration of the University of Mississippi, were so charged that mass activation accompanied them. The famous university case saw the governor openly defy a Supreme Court ruling that required the admission of James Meredith, a black student, in 1961. The governor's aggressive actions to preserve segregation included "standing in the school house door" amidst all the trappings of state power: police, ammunition, paddy wagons and dogs. Much of this took place in Jackson, and not Oxford where the university was located. Thus a litigation issue became a broad opportunity around which leaders and citizens in the county could coalesce. The international media assisted with its detailed daily coverage of events. Public demonstrations resulted, all of which were buttressed by federal intervention on the side of the NAACP. Few blacks were unopposed to the governor's actions and were more likely thereafter to find favor in NAACP programs. Bolton residents were very much affected by such a visible campaign being carried out 20 miles away. Aside from seeing it on television or hearing about it from neighbors, Bolton residents could experience this campaign personally. If they went to Jackson for any reason they were often caught in the traffic jams or spot searches that followed a defiant media event created by the governor, or a black-led demonstration. Since many county residents worked and/or shopped in Jackson, occasions like the above were not uncommon.[22]

Other forces emerging in Jackson and the surrounding areas involved the youth branches of the NAACP and college students. The latter became the standard bearers of much of the mobilization, and became a substantial portion of its leadership class. Their activities included several very visible projects that provoked vituperative responses from local white officials. In 1961 students from Tougaloo College attempted to use the city library that was designated for whites only, and were promptly arrested. The escalation continued when black supporters gathered at the courthouse for the trial and were dispersed by "Jackson police, using clubs and dogs."[23]

This overture was followed by the freedom rides, a series of bus trips made by integrated groups of students, designed to achieve "desegregation of southern transportation facilities." Several of these trips were made into Jackson over the summer, and formed a major part of the mobilization campaign in Hinds County. One author has suggested that the freedom rides were so significant to the ensuing mobilization because these leaders of "a self-consciously radical southern student movement . . . suddenly became aware of their collective ability to provoke a crisis that would attract international publicity and compel federal intervention."[24] This was precisely what happened in Jackson and the immediate area. The freedom riders were met by a massive police force and were arrested, even as the national media flashed pictures of the events all over the country and as the Kennedy Administration attempted to negotiate a settlement. Mississippi's hard-liners, however, were undaunted and continued the arrests.

> During the following months, more than three hundred protesters were arrested in Jackson. Choosing to stay in jail rather than pay the fines, the protesters were sent to serve their sentences in Parchman Prison and other Mississippi jails. White sympathizers in the North mobilized financial support for the campaign . . . [Meanwhile] the Jackson protests became a rallying point for activists from every section of the nation; [and] the Interstate Commerce Commission issue[d] a regulation prohibiting separate facilities for blacks and whites in bus and train terminals.[25]

The salience of the racial divide in Jackson gave much inspiration and credence to a locally directed movement of students and officials of the Jackson branch of the NAACP. These leaders became much more active and visible. The local branch at the time had the services and nearly ascetic dedication of Medgar Evers, then field secretary of the NAACP. He enjoyed great visibility all over the state, but residence in Jackson gave him high influence among area blacks. Evers' methods, though moderate, were perceived by many, especially the students, as being far beyond the litigation tactics of the NAACP.

Evers eventually sought activation and citizen application for social change in Jackson. He devised an independent plan that focused on the issue of economic discrimination, which he sought to exploit by orchestrating a mass protest of some kind, and forcing local officials to make some social changes in the city. He considered that the economic consequences of racial exclusion for blacks should be the subject of discussion, and action if necessary. In order to open up such a debate, however, Evers was required to orchestrate a mass protest of some kind. Public officials had not given any indication of a willingness to "negotiate" with the NAACP. But in order to achieve this end, Evers encouraged all manner of organizations and individuals with any activist sentiments to make public claims. A flood of demands were unleashed and unsatisfied. What emerged out of this was a black candidacy for Congress, as well as a full-scale boycott of Jackson businesses in 1962. The latter included public picketing, usually carried out by high school students in Jackson and college students from Tougaloo College.[26] This latter group was the most active and provided much of the public face of the movement as it manned picket lines and packed public protest rallies.

At the time, whatever happened in Jackson had direct effects on rural parts of Hinds County. In the first place any public protest (mass or otherwise) elicited a crisis response from city officials and police authorities. The mayor was prone to make statements about the public threat and its intolerability. Great police power was therefore mobilized in the form of cordons of officers, often in riot gear and accompanied by attack dogs. Usually these officers made an effort to contain the protest of whatever kind by encircling demonstrators and making mass arrests. Subsequently any such events yielded minor to massive traffic disruption for participants and nonparticipants alike, such as Boltonians. And those who were home could watch all the details on televised newscasts.[27]

In short, this environment of black organization and activity, and crisis conditions in Jackson, spilled over into Bolton. The spillover was sometimes direct between 1962 and 1966, as when all of the active civil rights organizations formed into COFO in 1962 and (among other things) began voter registration.[28] To this end a campaign was conducted in the nearly adjacent towns of Bolton, Edwards and Raymond, the latter being the county seat where actual registration was executed. While numbers of new voters placed on the books in this period cannot be specified, it was probably few. Justice Department data show a mere 1% increase in all of Hinds County between 1962 and 1964. It is known that the campaign was accompanied by violence and intimidation. The most common complaints were that volunteers were beaten or jailed while passing out leaflets.[29] Moreover, blacks who appeared for registration were still routinely rejected.

In addition, there were other local sectors within Bolton subject to independent mobilization. The most important of these were students, an active group with comparatively (for blacks) good educational institutions in well-to-do Hinds County and urban Jackson. Notwithstanding their inadequacy, there were two secondary schools available to black students in Bolton—at Sumner Hill in Clinton, and Hinds County Agricultural High in Utica. At the latter, students could get up to two years of college or terminal vocational training, an option many took. Then in the city of Jackson there was Jackson State College (now University) and Campbell College (then a two-year school); at the edge of the city was Tougaloo College. Bolton, therefore, had its own bloc of secondary and college students who were in tune with the ideas of social change emerging at the time. They constituted the force that completed the mobilization and produced Bennie Thompson.

The Emergence of Bennie Thompson and Radical Populism

It is in this milieu that Bennie Thompson got his entrée and situated himself for the role of leadership in the late 1960s. He is entirely a product of Bolton and its black institutional structure, having been born and entirely reared in the area, as were his mother and father. While his father died when Thompson was a youngster, his mother has continued to live and work in the town.[30] By tradition, therefore, the young mayor has always been a townsman. His early education was acquired in the elementary school at Bolton, where his mother taught. He had a reputation as something of a leader among his peers, though most of this was secured by his outspokenness. His intelligence was widely known, even when formal marks did not necessarily denote it. In high school, which he chose to take at Hinds County Agricultural, many of the same characteristics followed him. Indeed, he continued to do reasonably well, despite an increased reputation for fun. Even in this consolidated school where he competed with many new people, his influence generally grew as a spokesman. Thompson was well-known in the environment and began to appear at the forefront of discussions or actions that had to do with social change. Thus it might be concluded that he already possessed a number of those elusive leadership characteristics by the time he ended high school.

The significance of the past for interpreting the kind of leader that has emerged cannot be underestimated. While his elementary and high school experiences were entirely segregated, he lived his late teens in a radically changed and fluid Mississippi environment. He had been but a youngster when the Brown decision was handed down in 1954. But since change was slow, he had the opportunity to even take part in the public debate about school desegregation, which began after he left high school. As such he must be seen as a part of the transition period in Mississippi from an avowedly segregated way of life to at least a superficially more open one.

Largely, it was his generation that ushered in the swift changes over the South in the 1960s.[31] This began with the sit-ins by college students in North Carolina. But Mississippi had experienced its own version of this kind of protest, as we have seen. Hence Thompson was a part of that class of students who felt themselves specially called upon to inspire social change. Understanding him and his radical-populist vision is best done in the context of the student movement that swept the South in the 1960s. Prothro and Matthews talked to some of these students about why they were in the forefront of protest.

> 'If we leave it to the adults,' an 18 year old freshman in Atlanta said, referring to his longing for racial equality, 'nothing will become of it.' A junior in North Carolina went even further. 'You know,' he said, 'the adults still feel the white man can do no wrong.' In Mississippi a freshman girl concluded that 'most adults have given up hope or just don't care.' Only the young, many Negro students seem to have decided, could bring about a radical change in racial patterns. And they were 'tired of sitting back and waiting on the older folks.' 'Waiting is forever,' a sophomore in New Orleans said. 'You gotta do something.'[32]

Subsequently these same authors show that in the very early days of student protests fully 24% of the students had taken part in some public demonstration activity, like a sit-in. This is an extraordinarily high number, given that support for such acts does not always translate into actual participation. What is equally extraordinary is that in 1962 "(e)ighty-five percent of all Negro students enrolled in the predominantly Negro colleges and universities in the South approved of these activities, whereas only 5 percent were opposed to them."[33]

Thompson and his rural cohorts were emerging from high school at about this time and reaped all the benefits of the early student movement in and around Jackson. The effects of the earlier movement upon the commitment of people like Thompson were striking. The mobilization of the early period made it much more difficult for them to make an accommodation to old patterns. A few changes were already occurring in race relations and such opportunities made expectations much higher. For the increasingly more vocal students, activation was seen as a quite logical evolution to full equality. Indeed their challenge was much broader than that presented by an earlier focus on abstract and legal principles. Thompson and his lot quickly moved to much more fundamental questions about political and other material resources.

Thompson and the people around him exuded a degree of commitment that belied their youth. In some ways this was a natural attribute of youth; they also perceived that there was not anything to lose. In the first place, many of the young people around Bolton who may have otherwise gone into the job market, gave up the option in order to go to college. Some of those who were already in college now saw infinitely more reasons for remaining there, not least of which was the way their prospects for leadership and/or employment had changed. Still others in Bolton, like Thompson, were already destined to pursue college. Their backgrounds of relative privilege or academic achievement made this an attractive option.

Matthews and Prothro give us a clue as to who among those students in Bolton were susceptible to mobilization. They were both young men and women who rejected their parents' inaction, had enjoyed urban experiences at some point, and were from families with higher incomes and loftier social positions.[34]

To some extent circumstances in Bolton do match those described above. Clearly, students there rejected the inactive posture of their parents regarding social change. Many of them, like Thompson, had to buck their parents' authority in order to join protest activities. It is also true that women in this area were as active as men in inspiring change, though the top leadership group was and remained predominantly male in Bolton.

The other conditions were only partially met. It is noted that Bolton is in rural Hinds County, so that it cannot be argued that an urban experience existed there *a priori*. Yet it is true that Bolton's closeness to Jackson made it subject to certain urban influences that affected young people within the town limits. Thus it is not unrelated that virtually all of those who later achieved electoral power in the late 1960s and 1970s were from the town proper. In this sense they were townspeople, if not urbanites. Finally, social class surely was no standard by which they could be measured. Thompson was better off, but most of the others fit the general pattern of poor people found all over the town. They stood apart socially, insofar as they were students whose futures were likely to be enhanced by added training. It will be seen later that this advantage was indeed of some consequence in the new leadership class.

Having said all that, it is clear that this only partially explains the leadership class believed to be of vital importance to the mobilization that brought political power to a town like Bolton. It has been asserted that the leadership must be higher status, young and charismatic office holders with a commitment to civil rights and a welfare benefits public policy. In the following analysis this leadership group is explored through its central figure, Bennie Thompson, and his radical populist political style.

When Thompson won elective office several other blacks did also. In making a reputational survey of local leadership, town size and the scale of political activity made the tasks relatively easy. In the first place, the number of leaders was relatively small and those with affiliations were likely to have multiple ones that nearly exhausted the limited possibilities. However, four of the six very prominent leaders in the reputational survey held the elective positions of alderman. Two others, both women, held visible positions in local federal programs. This represented a critical shift from pre-1967 conditions, when most black leaders were without formal positions.[35]

The pattern above is decidedly new, but the next one is not—higher socioeconomic status. Thompson and virtually the entire slate of black office holders in 1973 were of higher socioeconomic status, defined in terms of higher education, status occupations, property ownership, and credit. This leadership class, like its counterparts almost everywhere, was much unlike the general constituency on these criteria.[36]

Thompson was easily a part of this newly emergent educated elite. At the same time certain aspects of his background set him apart. He, like few others, was from a comfortable socioeconomic position. Though his father was deceased, his mother was a long-time school teacher. This made her a part of a small class of local blacks who had a highly prized position, with relative security, and a comparatively good income. The family owned its home, a car, and had access to credit on the basis of considerable independent collateral. Then when Thompson completed college he had ready access to the short list of options for employment. He chose teaching and therefore had an immediately stable and secure income.[37]

The mayor's association with the civil rights movement and his purposive program for welfare benefits are also easily demonstrated. He was engaged by and sometimes participated in public demonstrations during the last stages of his high school education, and particularly while at college. Though Thompson and many of his aldermen and women were too young and too distant[38] to have participated in the sit-in phase of the movement, his development as an activist was solid. In time, he came to know all of the significant personalities and became involved on the cutting edge of the contemporary movement. As the mobilization in Bolton is detailed, his purposive welfare program, and Thompson's ideas that drove it, will be evident.

The scheme of radical populism has already been elaborated. It is significant to understand how and why Thompson appears to fit it by looking more carefully at both the roots of these concepts, and his own background and environment. In some ways the concepts of radicalism and populism may seem contradictory, particularly in the southern context. Many of the most demagogic race-baiters in southern political history were populists, who saw themselves as protectors of the poor little man who was unable to negotiate benefits from the powerful and wealthy. Nevertheless the latter did not prevent these anti-big government leaders from exhibiting great antipathy for the black poor, whose supposed genetic inferiority and labor power in the unskilled sector also threatened the poor whites.[39] Though much of the latter represented a great contradiction, many southern populists either expressed great pride in this position, or maintained a degree of ambivalence that leaves their view suspect. More generally, populism has often emerged in situations where a rural and non-cosmopolitan environment is present. The very origin of the concept, for example, goes back to the agrarians who felt left out of the mainstream policy process because they were farmers and isolated from the centers of power. Thus populists have been thought to have parochial biases, with an idealistic perspective on grassroots input. But as Carnovan's recent study shows, populists are far more concerned with the application of certain practical measures in the political environment. She calls this concern for measures like referenda and mobilization "political populism."[40]

For Bolton some aspects of both of these notions of populism are of importance. The town is surely sufficiently rural and has an almost simplistic cast to master the Jeffersonian requirements of "self-evident truths." This rural and racial isolation from the socioeconomic mainstream is all-important. But so is the emphasis, on the part of the leadership, on certain political actions for realizing political goals. In this case political mobilization is of strategic importance.

On the other hand, radicalism is a concept that is often thought to be opposed to populism because of the intellectual roots of the former. While radicalism may generally be associated with mass participation, it gets its inspiration for doing so from a strong commitment to certain ideals that almost borders on the ideological, as Sideny Lens has asserted in reference to equality and a balance between privilege and underprivilege.[41] These intellectual roots are generally supported by cosmopolitan, urban, and university-centered proponents. Many such proponents, however, see the "masses" as the base for which radical ends are to be achieved, since it is the former who benefit the least from the promise of the ideal community. Staughton Lynd articulates this as well as anyone.

> The proper foundation for government is a universal law of right and wrong self-evident to the common sense of every man; that freedom is a power of personal self-direction which no man can delegate to another; the purpose of society is not the protection of property but fulfillment of the needs of living human beings; that good citizens have the right and duty not only to overthrow incurably oppressive governments, but before that point . . . to break particular oppressive laws; and that we owe our ultimate allegiance, not to this or that nation, but to the whole family of man.[42]

Thus the radical movement or leadership often has an ideological component that guides its activities and structures its goals. In Bolton many of the attributes for radicalism are present. The mayor can be regarded as a highly trained intellectual who is comfortable with ideas. But he is ideologically wed to a body of ideas that have to do with the utter limits of equality for the black community. Present conditions of racial discrimination and exclusion are categorically rejected by the mayor. At the same time he exhibits all of the attributes of the urban cosmopolitan, though he is no urbanite, with his sophisticated mastery of the ways and means of social change in the world.

Therefore, the Thompson leadership in Bolton seems shaped by the combination of what seems on the surface to be opposites. How does he do it? On the populist side he is concerned about developing a social and political system in Bolton that is inspired by the popular wishes of the grassroots constituency. In this case "constituency" must be construed to mean, in large measure, the blacks that are such a substantial majority. More importantly, they are the "little" people who have been systematically denied the benefits of the system by a white elite previously. Thus the mayor believes that in most instances the informed people must make their own decisions because they know their own interests better than some far-removed government. But this is, after all, only based on material interest.

What is equally important under the special circumstances of the rural black South is a "vision." The "little man" certainly understands his situation, but the range of disadvantages present in his environment does not necessarily provide the skills for developing a vision to address the condition. Therefore, Thompson believes that leadership is of prime importance in developing a strategy for the community. He has attempted to do so by utilizing his own cosmopolitan skills acquired at college and in social activism. Yet he is in no way the classical cosmopolitan who developed an ideological perspective from living in and evaluating circumstances in a fluid urban community. The base for his ideological perspective is almost entirely homegrown. A rare combination of circumstances in the civil rights movement and his appearance on the scene serve to explain the pheonomenon.

He emerged in a southern area which was undergoing its most intense and transformative social change in history. The area had all the signs of a cosmopolitan landscape. There were a large number of proponents of radical social change working in Thompson's Hinds County. Moreover, the range of ideas being considered at the time was also greater and more radical than at any previous time in southern history. Though Thompson was entirely homegrown, he was privy to the full complement of these ideas and activities. His emergence was at an appropriate time whereby populist and radical ideas could be combined. Thus we have a grassroots leader who was inward-looking, insofar as he chose one small town as his base. But he sought to define that base by terms that were especially related to his radical vision of social and political transformation.

The Political Education of Bennie Thompson

Much of what occurred in Bolton between 1962 and 1966 was a radical attitude change, attended by new behaviors on the part of young blacks. The change was that the previous veiled racial antagonisms now began to appear openly. In the past, blacks who shopped at stores or received services from whites were likely to exhibit ritual deference, albeit with some begrudging. It was one of the ways to maintain racial peace and to receive benefits for survival. By the mid-1960s, however, it became a pattern of youth to violate all the old rules. After seeing all the demonstrations carried out by the likes of Martin Luther King, Jr. and CORE, often a mere 20 miles away, Bolton youths were intent upon making a local and independent contribution. Their ideas, while more avowedly political, were like those attributed to the largely middle-class white students who later developed their own protest movement: romantic, anti-authoritarian, egalitarian-populist, anti-dogma, highly moral, community oriented and anti-institutionalist.[43]

There was no single individual more prominent and outspoken in forging this new attitude than Thompson. Oftentimes the violations exhibited by the new behaviors were all too simple, but when analyzed in their context were revolutionary. Thompson was widely known to demand true equal treatment in local stores. Any indications, however small, of overt racist acts by whites drew an immediate and bold response. This was especially likely to occur in the provision of state services for schools, health and/or welfare. Of course, Bolton had very few of these, but enough for the new assertiveness to matter.

Yet, in the mid 1960s, Thompson, and many of those upon whom he had the greatest influence, were about to leave for college and to be temporarily removed from the community. As expected, Thompson went directly from high school to college, where he formed the ideas that became the cornerstone of a strong radical populist philosophy. Quite unexpectedly he chose the Mississippi Valley State College (now University) in the delta in 1965, and not one of the nearby colleges where many of his friends had gone. This seemed to be a part of his interest in "going away" to college. He only spent one summer there, however, before returning to spend one year at Utica Junior College, whose campus was shared with that of his old high school. The succeeding year, 1966, he joined many of his mates at Tougaloo College. He reportedly desired a more challenging academic and political environment. While at Tougaloo Thompson had access to remnants of the old line civil rights ideologues, as well as the new nationalists who had been in the forefront of social change in the state. These factors shaped his approach to the task of political change in his local town. By the end of the college experience, he had already determined to remain in Mississippi, as opposed to migrating to the industrial Midwest.

The Tougaloo College experience was significant for Thompson because it reinforced a range of commitments he had already made. Tougaloo had long been regarded as something of an oasis amidst the harsh realities of the racial divide in Mississippi. The college was established by the American Missionary Association (AMA) during reconstruction, and continued as a private school with church and United Negro College Fund (UNCF) support. Its curriculum evolved, like that of other such schools in the South, to provide a classical, liberal arts education. This was largely because their staffs were imported from East Coast schools with that tradition. These liberal white staffers usually had religious and/or political backgrounds that sustained commitments to racial equality. Tougaloo was a good example of this tradition with a majority white faculty, even when Thompson entered in 1966.

The college had already been dubbed "Cancer College" by local whites because of its "integrated" campus and progressive ideas. That is, a few northern white students had enrolled there and received public notice. What was more important in giving the college this reputation, however, was its rejection of the system of racial exclusion. The faculty was progressive in its teaching and opened its doors to the most progressive visitors on racial and other issues. Many state officials accused the college of fomenting revolution, with leftists and "communists" reputed to be among the faculty.[44] The administration was no better, as the president of the college headed the statewide Human Relations Council in the face of a vociferous opposition campaign by local whites.[45] This picture was completed by the students, who initiated the public demonstration portion of the local movement (sit-ins, public picketing and boycotting in the Jackson area). This student activism kept pace with the national movement that culminated in the community organization work of the Student Non-Violent Coordinating Committee. This academic and activist tradition was well established when Thompson matriculated there.

At the college, Thompson pursued a major in the social sciences. This made him more like the activist Tougaloo students of the past, many of whom also pursued the social sciences.[46] The training in social sciences was of high quality, with one of the most diverse and excellent faculties in the college. Moreover, the activist orientation of many of these instructors was well known. Thompson chose political science, not perhaps because it was the place where more activist students and faculty were found; sociology and history were more prominent in this respect. Rather, it seems that his choice had more to do with a concern about power relationships. Thompson saw the study of politics as a means of understanding the system and how to use power as a vehicle for change. That the political science faculty was not the most activist hardly mattered; he was confident that the highly skilled faculty was likely to expand his knowledge and not thwart his pursuit of progressive ideas.

The entire academic experience for this young radical was an encouragement to the pursuit of progressive ideals. While Thompson studied the social sciences for a degree, the classical approach to education then prevalent at Tougaloo also provided for a variety of courses outside his major department. Many of these other professors were equally activist and certainly no less progressive in what they taught. They could be found in virtually all of the other academic departments in the college. Hence, aside from the routine acquaintance with radical thinkers and literature in the social sciences, Thompson was also acquainted with their counterparts in everything from English literature and foreign languages to religion. This broad liberal arts curriculum merely provided the basis for Thompson to explore the full range of his possibilities as a community activist.

Thompson's ideology was significantly inspired by the experiences of growing up under segregation in Mississippi. He had never allowed his "social class" position to put distance between himself and those from "lower social class" positions. His aggregate of friends at high school and college always cut across the available spectrum. Thompson did not publicly or privately (so far as can be ascertained) harbor any thoughts of himself apart from the core black community. As such, he perceived the problems of all blacks to be similar in nature and subject to the same kinds of actions for social change.

The Tougaloo experience reinforced this perspective via the books he read and the social contacts he made. Moreover, this cemented his vision of what "ought" to be for blacks. In political science courses he was reading contemporary analyses of problems with effective democratization in the local and national political system. One of the notable books that he read at the time was *Black Power* (1967) by Stokely Carmichael and Charles Hamilton, which called for independent black political organization.[47] This was supplemented by materials from other courses that used the black context in academic work. He and his consorts built upon this with outside readings and discussions. They did not limit themselves to the American situation; one of the most prominent pieces was *The Wretched of the Earth* by Frantz Fanon, which analyzed the war of liberation in Algeria as being cathartic for the colonized mind. The Afro-American situation was equated with that of the Algerian peasants.[48]

Equally important in forming his vision was the sense of community that the college instilled. While not everyone at Tougaloo was a radical or an activist, relationships on the whole were close and personal. Thompson was able to know teachers and students in very much the same way, insofar as being able to share ideas with them. The college was small (about 700 students during his matriculation) and was residential for most students and faculty. Its appearance as an enclave was in many respects more real than imagined. Yet, inside its gates existed a remarkable amount of social leveling. For Thompson, who reports deep appreciation and respect for the experience, Tougaloo illustrated the extent to which his dreams for a democratic society for the masses could be realized.

Thompson gave as much to his consorts at the college as he took from them. He was well-known and influential. Radical faculty members knew him because he took their courses and took part in public protest activities. He was a campus leader, though not always in traditional campus organizations. His ideas were the ones likely to be put forth by student government leaders, especially in reference to campus democratization. Much of this was in the context of the student power movement, which sought broad participation in campus affairs. Thompson was in the vanguard for these changes, and by 1967-68 students were already found sitting on every college committee at Tougaloo—well before most other colleges.

At the same time, he was a part of what was left of the radical student activists who continued public demonstrations and external movement linkages. This is significant because by the time Thompson arrived at Tougaloo, most of the traditional direct action movement—i.e. mass demonstrations, picketing, and sit-ins—was over. The new focus was community organization and voter registration. But there still was an activist study group that organized campus rallies and maintained strong linkages with outside activists. Thompson was a strong member of this group.

These latter forces served to focus attention even more squarely on the issue of democratization for the broader black community in a system of racial exclusion. Thompson found his thinking more and more concentrated on the issue of liberation for students and all black people. Being an educated black person, as he perceived it, made little difference to his liberation. He was no less stifled by restrictions in the system than an illiterate black ditch digger. His circle of activist friends reinforced this because they too remained "in the streets" and loyal to the cause of community "liberation."

The ideas of SNCC regarding liberation were of strategic importance to Thompson's thinking about politics. The "SNCC [had] not used normal political channels to achieve its goals. It champion[ed] the use of Black Power," used variously to mean "political, economic, and social mobilization of an oppressed people . . . direct action . . . and electioneering"; or, later, "the unification of the Negro population to fight for their liberation."[49] Still later, the nationalist focus became paramount; "black mobilization, black leadership for black organizations, the promotion of self-pride, and the right to self-defense."[50] Perhaps Carmichael and Hamilton encapsulated the ideas best in asserting that black Americans exist in a classical colonial condition; institutionalized racism leads to political, economic and cultural domination.[51]

> There is no black man in this country who can live 'simply as a man.' His blackness is an everpresent facet of this racist society, whether he recognizes it or not. It is unlikely that this or the next generation will witness the time when race will no longer be relevant in the conduct of public affairs and in public policy decision-making. To realize this and to attempt to deal with it does not make one a racist or overly preoccupied with race; it puts one in the forefront of a significant *struggle*. [sic][52]

The task, they argue, is "to struggle for the right to create our own terms through which to define ourselves and our relationship to the society, and to have these terms recognized."[53] They speak of achieving this by having blacks "close ranks" or use "group solidarity" as a bargaining position of strength in a pluralistic society.[54]

It was not merely the ideas which made SNCC stand out. It was also the spirit that the members exuded as they went about their business. Many of them were college students with experience in direct action.[55] Even then (1960) their horizons included concern for the practical consequences of social change for the average black person. That they began activity with the daring and defiant direct action campaigns in the most violently racist portions of the South—Mississippi, Alabama and Georgia[56]—also indicated something of an emerging confrontational style. One author has likened them to the radical abolitionists because of the uncompromising attitude to racism and its vestiges. "They have a healthy disrespect for respectability; they are not ashamed of being agitators and trouble-makers."[57] They lived in the local, usually rural communities where they worked, sometimes with families. Oftentimes "living conditions [were] crude . . . an old frame dwelling with cots and blankets."[58] Moreover, they took the idea of local mobilization to the extreme. When a community was selected—e.g., McComb, Mississippi—the workers devoted an inordinate amount of time to that one town in achieving political education, direct action and voter registration. Though the goal was ultimately broad-scale mobilization, the focus for a local campaign was the intense concentration on a small geographical space.[59]

Thompson was highly influenced by this movement, which reached its peak in his middle college years. Looking at his own small town, it was relatively easy to accept the precepts of the SNCC. His town was one where a majority black population was as oppressed as any elsewhere in Mississippi. Moreover, his youth and experience gave him many of the attitudes that SNCC workers possessed—a "healthy disrespect for respectability" and an uncompromising attitude toward racial exclusion. That he only completed college in 1968, however, gave him enough distance from the mere expression of ideas to the practical application of some of them. He began this by making the decision to run for political office himself and by initiating an intense local mobilization campaign among blacks.

The Radical Populists and the Mobilization

Thompson's first move was toward holding office on the local Board of Aldermen. He did this as much as a test of his own appeal, as to test the effectiveness of a voter registration campaign that started in his area as early as 1964. He and two other blacks succeeded in their first outing to win offices, and thereby captured a majority on the board. He achieved this on the sheer strength of his popularity and the general perception that he was one of the average people. He had returned to the town regularly and took an interest in its affairs during his college years. Moreover, he did so with an uncommon sensitivity to the average person's problems, at least for someone whose economic position was clearly otherwise.

Thompson's small campaign in the first election was centered on educating the masses to the possible consequences of their new-found power as voters. He had to orchestrate a campaign that would appeal to those who had already taken the risk to vote, and to inspire those who had not borne the risk. Indeed much of the early work was designed to obviate people's fears and apathy about the political process. For we know that fear[60] and apathy[61] have each played a considerable role in the willingness of blacks to participate in the South. The campaign, conducted as a series of mass meetings and informal, routine, day-by-day conversations, was designed to reorient the thinking of the black community. The new challenge, it was argued, was for the black voting majority to use the vote to take control of their political lives. This point was of import for fear as well as apathy. On the one hand, there was nothing to fear because the new conditions actually gave blacks the upper hand in bargaining *vis-à-vis* the whites. In short, the whites would now be required to seek black votes if the former were to be a force in public affairs. On the other hand, apathy was now inappropriate because formally winning office was not only possible for blacks, but inevitable because of the substantial black electorate. There was virtually no possibility of "throwing away" a vote under the circumstances. Both of these were persuasive arguments on their face, and yielded considerable mobilization for this first electoral campaign for Thompson.

The preceding is also significant in understanding Thompson's populism. While he was a cosmopolitan and a sophisticate, these hardly affected his commitment to creating a political base in a town as small as Bolton. In this sense he defined his entire sphere of operation in grassroots terms. His early concentration on this area, but for the obvious cosmopolitanism, may have been viewed as parochial. He concentrated all of his early energies as a politician on realizing a transformation of the political environment entirely in the context of Bolton. And like any successful populist, he established his goals to correspond with what he deemed to be the aspirations of the average constituent. The tasks of his office would therefore be defined so as to fully represent these previously excluded citizens.

Thompson on the Hustings and at the Defense

Thompson's populism is evident in his policy proposals and in public speeches. In the policy proposals, the results of which are analyzed in Chapter Seven, it is evident that he perceived himself to have represented the masses. Even before election to office, he was on record in support of a wide range of welfare benefits for Bolton. After winning an office, he immediately sought to make such programs more available there. Special attention was given to Headstart, dependents' care, welfare assistance, and comprehensive health care. All of these programs were to have a direct and immediate impact on the lives of black constituents.

Headstart had several direct benefits. The program eased the problems of working women who now had a place to leave their children. The service was free and provided the children a nutritious meal. There was also an educational component designed to compensate for the lag in preparation that many such youngsters faced.

Other programs on which Thompson focused involved direct transfers from federal and state sources, such as family assistance packages for the unemployed and underemployed, and the provision of free health services. In any case these programs put him directly on the side of those most needy, the same group that constituted the new voting majority.

The concern for the little man as articulated in Thompson's populist rhetoric, was nevertheless not completely realized in the town. While historically populists seek to mobilize the entire "little man" sector of the community, this was not possible in Bolton. Racial segregation did not allow the mobilization of blacks and whites together. The poor whites hardly cast their lot with the black constituency, notwithstanding material position, for reasons already elaborated. Hence when Thompson focused his mobilization campaign on voter registration and electoral participation, such appeals to the poor white masses fell on deaf ears. They saw no advantage to casting their lot with Thompson, who then became *de facto* the exclusive leader of blacks. Thompson had no difficulty accepting this position. The blacks were the base of his support and easily most directly affected by his activist message. Subsequently, Thompson was never to make a separate appeal to whites. His concern for them was expressed in a way that assumed their regular membership in the community. In fact most whites voluntarily withdrew.

Thompson continued his populist claims even when racial segregation restricted his appeal to blacks. His own claim was that he represented the true grassroots, because blacks constituted such an overwhelming majority of the electorate by 1969. Even when he was only acceptable to blacks, that was appeal to over 70% of the active local electorate. The argument continued that this group did indeed constitute the "little people" of Bolton who were exploited and downtrodden by racial caste.

The populist spirit can be illustrated by an analysis of Thompson's speeches and public testimonies up to 1979 and a series of interviews conducted between 1977 and 1984. It is in these materials where his intense commitment to social change in the black community, and more generally in rural areas like Bolton, becomes much clearer.

In several wide-ranging interviews, he focused on black people in the context of the small town, and the complex of other factors that impinged upon progress. He argued that blacks in towns like Bolton suffered on two fronts: because of their race and because they lived in rural places. These factors combined to create an unusual degree of isolation from the policy process and material benefits. These places, Thompson argued, got less attention from both the state and national policymakers. In regard to race, the considerations were those traditional ones about black inferiority. But much of the isolation in this small, black-majority town resulted from a critical lack of local financial resources in an overwhelmingly poor and rural state.

The isolation from the federal government policy process was indicative of a much more fundamental problem. The government in Washington, according to Thompson, is so much farther away, and is so beholden to different kinds of interests (largely urban or big financial ones), that rural areas are shunted to the side. In short, since rural towns are not a major part of the national coalition, they do not greatly affect the policy process.

In interpreting this populist contention, Thompson adopted a view from elite theorists. He followed the line of argument that political influence is largely dependent on mobilized interests cleverly articulated by an organization; if one is not well organized according to the rules of the game, then not much can be gained.[62] Rural towns like Bolton are not highly organized for the political process (and most cannot afford to be), nor are they highly integrated into the ruling coalition. Thus it is not just race that creates these conditions, it is also socioeconomic dynamics. What complicates matters, by this view, is that race is a standard that doubly excludes blacks (most of whom are poor) from the policy process.

Thompson has been emphatic on this in reference to rural housing needs. In 1977 he testified at a conference on full employment in Atlanta and addressed the major points that he has repeated variously in speeches. In this his comments were addressed specifically to the federal government and its insensitivity to towns like Bolton. He addressed the problems of ignorance, outright discrimination, and isolation from the policy process:

> Since I have been mayor I have attempted to use many federal programs for housing community development (CD) purposes. To sum up my experiences, I have found that the various federal agencies do not address themselves to the problems. While there may be programs that exist in the *Federal Register* that would seem to address a particular problem, by the time you get down to the local office of a federal agency it is a different story. This is due to a number of factors. For example, a program may not have any funds appropriated, or it may have appropriations but for some reasons an agency elects not to expend the funds, or there just may be a complete lack of sensitivity or competence at the local agency office. In Mississippi 25 out of 82 counties have black majority populations. Yet there is not one black director of a Farmers Home Administration county office. The few blacks that are employed by Farmers Home Administration are in the lowest level positions. I feel that this tends to cause a lack of sensitivity to the problems such as housing, that affect blacks most acutely. Also, there is the problem of FmHA offices not knowing what their programs are. I once walked into our county office and asked about the Community Facilities loan section of the Rural Development Act. They did not know what I was talking about. However, there were several pamphlets on this very program in a wall rack in the room we were in at the time. This was an exhibition of maliciousness or incompetence or both. Further, unless a public official has the time to read the *Federal Register* or a variety of advocacy publications, one has no way of knowing what programs are available. Outreach is unheard of at either FmHA or HUD. You must go to them to inquire about what they can do, and then only maybe will you find out. Agency officials tend to forget that they are public servants and are supposed to be serving the people, and that means all the people.[63]

Thompson illustrated the isolation of Bolton by giving an example of his efforts to get a housing planning grant. He was told initially that "Bolton (was) too small" to receive a grant, since there was no "local comprehensive plan." The insensitivity of the government to such areas did not end there, according to the continuing testimony. Bolton was removed even further from the advantages of the program for housing when funds to Standard Metropolitan Statistical Areas (subject to allocation to surrounding "non-entitlement cities") were cut by 50%.

> This cut in CD funds was due to the priority given to suburban counties over small towns in a metropolitan area. This is a public policy that rewards the usually unplanned sprawling, higher-income, exclusionary zoned, unincorporated suburban areas at the expense of our older suburban cities and small rural towns within the metropolitan counties.

The populist perspective of the "little man" vs. the "big man" is in the mayor's testimony. Here he elaborates the starkly negative consequence of a system where some have undue influence and power in the policy process.

> I recently read that for the third consecutive year, portions of Mississippi were declared disaster areas, due to low crop yields and "untypical weather conditions." The Farmers Home Administration has been given the responsibility to help alleviate this problem. The method prescribed is long term low interest loans. This spring and summer, FmHA staff will be spending close to 100% of their time with these farming loans, with housing matters given a lower priority. Frankly, this disgusts me. Farms in these areas are characterized by huge plantations, often 1,000 acres or more. Many of these so-called farmers are already receiving thousands of tax dollars, paid by working men and women, not to produce crops on their land. One of these "struggling" farmers is a member of the U.S. Senate, another is the royal family of England. If any of you have been to rural Mississippi, it must immediately strike you that the "disaster" is not on the huge plantations but in the living conditions of the vast majority of the people of the area. The most visible disaster is the housing conditions. In fact, many of the animals living on the farms live in better housing conditions than many of the people of rural Mississippi. I never heard that a national goal of ". . . a super profitable plantation and an opulent living environment for every American planter . . ." had ever been declared. But, it sure seems that it is a high priority for Congress and the Administration. I propose that the appropriate steps be taken to declare within rural areas a housing disaster. To combat this disaster we create plentiful long-term loans with low interest rates for housing financing. Further, we need to make available sizable grants for the most desperate aspects of the housing disaster areas. Such a program would generate thousands of much needed jobs, put thousands of dollars into sagging small town economies and once again make our small towns viable and desirable places to live and raise families. Further, by solving today's rural problems, we are decreasing tomorrow's urban problems. If small towns and rural areas were able to retain their people I doubt that New York City would be quite the mess it's in. The same goes for virtually every one of America's large urban areas.[64]

Thompson's radicalism owes a great deal to the SNCC movement, but it is also very much in the tradition of American radicalism as defined by Staughton Lynd.[65] Even before he won an electoral office, Thompson had demonstrated a commitment to a conception of participatory democracy that made it difficult to restrict "public rights," even for the sake of efficiency or stability. At college he helped to bring to full reality student participation in virtually every sphere of college life at Tougaloo. Beyond the mere principle, Thompson also insisted that the human obligation was active engagement to fulfill the promise of participatory democracy; one should not appear to be on the wrong side by inaction. Equally important in his brand of radicalism was assertiveness, often called "militancy" by the media and public officials. Among other things, this assertiveness referred to the confident, sometimes abrasive pursuit of civil rights. Instead of fear, Thompson and others exhibited this bold new style with what seemed like abandon, and were actually winning considerable victories against the southern whites.

There were a wide range of actions and/or policies taken by Thompson that illustrate this uncompromising attitude about change. Two efforts will be explored in some detail. The first occurred at college, having to do with student rights and the obligation to act according to principle; and the second involved the white challenge to his assumption of the mayoral office.

The Confrontation at Tougaloo

The mid- to late-1960s offered one of the most intense eras of student challenge to authority, particularly that exercised by college and university administrators. After student involvement in external civil rights and antiwar issues, some argued that it was logical to question internal university policies. Indeed, many students came to see educational administrators as a part of the "establishment" that thrived on the undesirable and hypocritical social and political structures. This broad movement all over the country served as the training ground for the new student leaders as they protested, closed down buildings and campuses, and/or committed violent acts against properties.[66] Much of this was carried out by local students. Many white students were inspired by the Students for a Democratic Society,[67] or the May 2nd Movement and the National Committee for SANE Nuclear Policy.[68] Blacks were inspired by the SNCC.

We have already seen that Thompson entered college at a time when the involvement of black students in the "streets" was declining. The challenge had moved to other levels in community organization and also onto the college campuses. However, for black students the challenge to their college authorities began much earlier. Their heavy involvement in civil rights activity in the South occurred when most were enrolled in black colleges.[69] The magnitude of student involvement in making a radical critique of American society also made it inevitable that they would turn inward and that such would lead to conflict. In 1964, "more historically Black than white institutions experienced protests over academic priorities and campus governance."[70] This was likely a response to the largely conservative administrations of these colleges, such as that at Howard University, which looked upon campus activism as "lawlessness and anarchy."[71] Of course the responses of administrators at state-supported institutions were even more negative about the least civil rights activity.

To a degree what black students like Thompson were asking differed from many other students. As the victims of a lingering racial caste system, black students' radical critique of American racism gave them a more nationalistic perspective. Their black "community," as they analyzed it, was increasingly more oppressed. Indeed this community lacked basic self-determination, a condition illustrated even by the status and nature of black colleges.

Gurin and Epps have shown the development of this nationalism between 1964 and 1970. Students grew progressively more intolerant of college authority perceived to be inconsistent with the nationalist perspective.[72] "Demands [were put forth that] represent[ed] the students' desires to cast off traditionally accepted standards of what constitute[d] a 'good' and 'relevant' education."[73] In their eyes black colleges were merely carbon copies of white universities, a fact that hardly responded to the particular needs of the black community.[74] Therefore this critique led them to challenge the entire black educational framework, as the Howard manifesto shows:

> The Black University concept includes, among other things, a redirection of goals for the school as a whole and the instillment of a Black community concept within the Black students for generations to come. By this we mean a college that benefits and carries on a perpetual reciprocal relationship with the entire Black community. . . If the college cannot learn from and be designed to benefit from the Black community, then it does not need to exist; to hand America a carbon copy of itself is now archaic, insulting and irrelevant, in terms of outlook and practicality to the Black community. We Black people need and will have educational institutions that speak from a Black experience and address themselves to Black collective needs. Individual considerations are now secondary to a collective ethos—this is the order of the day. Survival of the Black population is of primary concern; therefore, individual pursuits as a primary concern can only be looked upon in this light: 'We all hang together, or we hang separately.'[75]

Notwithstanding the progressivism of Tougaloo College, it like all the rest experienced its share of conflict between the administration and traditionally active students. The students were even more concerned about whether their training was "relevant" to the tasks of improving the black community. Some of these questions had been settled rather peaceably with students being formally involved in numerous aspects of college organization. However, when Thompson arrived, students were beginning to articulate the notion of the college as a vehicle for direct service to the black community. They saw their fate and purposes tied directly to those of all other black people and looked upon the college as having special responsibilities to help fully realize the potential of such a national community. It meant curricular revisions that would virtually change the mission established for the institution of higher learning. Their vision was what Gurin and Epps have analyzed as a kind of collectivist nationalism.[76] This represented a linkage to external forces greater than any administration had considered before. And this was two years before the Howard manifesto.

Much of this looking inward began about 1964. The activist president, Adam Beittel, had resigned, some think because he was too active in the civil rights campaign.[77] Beittel was replaced by Tougaloo's first black president in history, George Owens. Though it was by no means certain where Owens stood on the involvement of the college in the movement, there was no reason to assume that his sentiments were any different than others on the need for social change. It was evident, however, that his style of leadership in this regard was different. He had not, for example, been known to publicly participate in demonstrations, while his attitude towards problem-solving generally was said to be cautious. Though some students were wary, as a black, Owens' appointment was consistent with the spirit of independent control.

These administrative changes hardly put a damper on the further elaboration of the nationalist perspective on the part of students. Nor did it decrease the tendency of these students to try and directly link the purposes of the college with the supposed collective national conscience of black people everywhere. In fact, it is probably true that their concern for this perspective was escalated because of the potential changes they perceived that the Owens administration would institute.[78]

During the early days of the Owens' administration there were several tests of the new president's approach to student participation and civil rights commitment. There were demonstrations about routine campus issues such as food and housing, and student governance. Most of these did not have the effect of creating a major schism between the administration and students, though some faculty (notably northern whites) evinced considerable dissatisfaction with the spirit and style of the new administration.

In matters of civil rights, on the other hand, while the president was no activist, he had not acted in ways inconsistent with general support for such. To be sure there had been few direct tests since there was hardly any question of campus civil rights demonstrations. Even the later adoption by students of an exclusionary rule (against whites) for certain organizations and general meetings, while not accepted, hardly led to great cleavage.

There was to be a hard test, however, in which Bennie Thompson centrally figured. It was a test which had all the elements for illustrating the mood of students in his day. It concerned student rejection of perceived irrelevant and irresponsible authority, and their assertion of a collective conscience in the interest of the core black community. The results of this test did not indicate any clear winners because of the complicated nature of the circumstances—yet it did create a cleavage in the college and left the administration with an "establishment" label.

The chief activities in this situation occurred not at Tougaloo, but nine miles away in Jackson. On the evening of May 10, 1967 the radio news reported a riot underway at Jackson State College. Policemen were on the scene to quell rock throwing on Lynch Street, a busy thoroughfare students wanted closed.

Apparently the events were triggered when two black policemen chased a speeding car through this campus street.[79] As they questioned the student suspect, others assembled to express opposition to the police presence and to the perennial traffic problem. As the numbers of students grew, the two police officers called for assistance. Scores of their number in riot gear appeared. Students also escalated their tactics.

The ensuing melée lasted two days. Jackson State students boycotted classes and had their numbers bolstered by community participants. Before it ended one was left dead and several injured. There had been localized burning and looting, even as the highway patrol and national guard were deputized with .30 caliber machine guns (with which they fired upon the crowd). Later the students negotiated a settlement with the city that closed Lynch Street.[80]

In one local newspaper account the following apparently innocuous notice appeared:

> And a group of Tougaloo College students who had joined the rioters called to police as they left the area early today: 'We'll be back.'
>
> Police said the violence Wednesday night accelerated with the arrival of the busload of students from Tougaloo College.[81]

There was indeed a busload, and at least one car, of Tougaloo College students in the area that evening. These students journeyed to Jackson State out of "solidarity" with the plight of the black students there. For the remnants of the movement cadre at Tougaloo, the campaign at Jackson State was merely one way to illustrate the new phase of activism that dictated direct defensive confrontation with authorities. The Tougaloo student cadre saw itself as being more deft at this because of longer experiences as activists. In any case the entire group moved into the crowd at Jackson State, though one would be hard put to assign them any leadership role in the activities.

At the hour of the activities in Jackson, there was no administrative official at Tougaloo on regular duty to authorize the use of the college's bus to transport students. With the full confidence that this was a justifiable act, the president of the student government, Constance Slaughter, authorized use of the bus to transport students to Jackson State. Miss Slaughter, a senior, knew that Bennie Thompson had access to the campus bus because of his part-time job as a driver. As the chief student spokesperson and herself an activist, it seemed quite logical to her (and her cohorts) that authorization was an act she could perform. Thompson's activism and ideological leanings all told him that this was a logical act, consistent with the obligations of one concerned with rooting out racial oppression. Therefore, he willingly brought out the college bus and took a load of willing students to the Jackson State campus and back.

The Owens administration did not respond lightly to the "unauthorized" use of the bus for this purpose. It became known to the administration almost immediately that Miss Slaughter authorized the trip and that Thompson executed it, since this was a matter of no secrecy. They were quickly charged with the unauthorized use of college property and brought to trial. After being found guilty, Miss Slaughter was denied participation in her upcoming graduation, and Thompson was placed on probation.

Even as the air at Jackson State cleared, the reverberations from this decision at Tougaloo remained. Though the academic year was at an end, the reaction of students was swift and not out of character for this college. They immediately instituted a boycott of classes and went to the college chapel, where rallies were traditionally held. Tactics were discussed for responding to what they perceived as a direct challenge to student power and an outrageous rejection of civil rights principles.

At this point almost everything was against the students. Since it was the end of the academic year, their boycott of classes meant boycotting exams. Moreover, they took the unprecedented step of challenging the judicial procedures and asked for a special body to negotiate with the college president, with whom the ultimate decision rested. In the interim there were various hit-and-run acts perpetrated against college properties that kept the campus in a state of mobilization and uncertainty.

The arguments made by Miss Slaughter and Thompson structured the debate that was to take place with the president. The two student leaders asserted that theirs was an absolutely rational and responsible act. They focused on the need for their solidarity with Jackson State because of the conditions that impinged black students everywhere. While their actions were understood to be political, they deemed them appropriate in light of consensus about abject racism in Mississippi. In other words, this was not just about student power; it was about the larger question of self-determination for black people. Quite obviously, they reasoned, a self-determining Jackson State community would not have left the wide and busy street thoroughfare open, nor authorized an external police force to fire upon students with live ammunition. By this view it seemed inevitable and mandatory that black people in the area present a united front in support of the "victims" at Jackson State. The clarity of the circumstances in Jackson and the required response was not at all doubted by these activist students. To Thompson and Slaughter it was inconceivable that a "relevant" black college administrator would see this matter any differently. For anyone who dared to place other considerations above the "legitimate" claims of the Jackson students was opposed to the total liberation of black people, or functioned as an Uncle Tom.

After the guilty verdicts the task of convincing the administration fell to other students (supported by liberal and activist faculty) on a special committee. These negotiators, with substantial continuing input from Slaughter and Thompson, also sought to turn the debate away from the narrow issue of illegal use of college property. Rather they too wanted to focus upon the circumstances in Jackson and the efficiency with which the Tougaloo students performed their task there. After all, they contended, the Jackson State affair did represent a very serious offense against black people, and in a not uncommon manner for "unredeemed" Mississippi. Not only had the city mobilized the full limit of the state's police power to quell student activities; but one member of the black community was left dead, some injured, and others in jail. This, they argued, left no doubt that the situation required black solidarity.

At the same time it was deemed of utmost importance that there had been no negative consequences from Tougaloo participation. The students did not get arrested while in Jackson, nor did they represent themselves in any way as leaders of the campaign, notwithstanding contrary news reports. Moreover, while it was in their possession no damage was done to the bus, nor were any extraneous uses made of it, they claimed. Indeed all reports indicated that Thompson drove directly back that night. Therefore the students believed these seriously outweighed any culpability for the unauthorized use of the bus.

The president was supremely aware of the case building against him as he pondered the final decision. In the circumstances he was not entirely inflexible about various propositions from sectors of the community. He did not refuse conversations on the matter and ultimately agreed to meet with a specially appointed group of faculty, students and administrators to sort out the dilemma. Yet a general student perception was that he was not listening to their point of view, and was largely out of touch with their sentiments.

In part, this was true. The president apparently never accepted that the extenuating circumstances somehow outweighed the first illegal act of taking the bus. Such an act, for example, directly challenged his formal authority and responsibility for college property. Indeed the president adopted this legal-formal approach, which made it exceedingly difficult for him to consider the purpose for which the bus was used. In short, those who perpetrated crimes had to take the consequences for their actions. To do otherwise, in this view, was to sanction behavior like that of the literary "trickster" who succeeds in "doing bad things and getting away." Therefore, on the question of punishment for the students, he was implacable.

The president's final decision affirming the judicial ruling was made on the eve of commencement, largely thwarting student response. The rumor that student terror would ensue under the cover of darkness to disrupt commencement was countered by another from the administration that hidden cameras would record any such acts. In the end "disruptions" that did occur came from the faculty. After leading the invocation, the college chaplain stated his objections to the president's decision and left the podium. He joined other faculty who had also refused to participate in the required ceremony.

How did Bennie Thompson find himself the leader of this effort to activate the student body and then define the terms of their actions? It has already been argued that in some ways the Tougaloo environment contributed directly to this. Though Thompson was vocal and visible before he got to Tougaloo, clearly this experience contributed to his vision of populism and radicalism. His associates and studies all led him to directly challenge anyone or anything seen to be opposed to the best interests of repressed black people. The very act of driving the bus must be seen in this light. Not any student with the keys would have exercised the option to drive the bus, other drivers did have keys. Thompson's activities made him a likely choice for such a task. Even as the discussions about how to respond to the radio announcement were going on, Thompson was present. Neither he nor any of the rest of this activist group was oblivious to the fact that use of the bus should be authorized. But their very consideration of taking it required a broad range of prior commitments. For Thompson this was based on ideas internalized from the civil rights movement. All of his experiences said that this act was a necessary and appropriate response to oppression. The actions of Jackson police firing on students in a "legitimate" protest campaign was clear evidence for him of unacceptable racist practices that had to be opposed. Moreover, any blacks on the other side of this issue were no less dangerous, and also had to be opposed.

Meanwhile, the cautious administration at Tougaloo engendered skepticism in students like Thompson. The social change movement was well in force on black college campuses by the time of Owens' accession. Therefore Thompson and the students around him were perhaps more concerned with their symbols of power than previous groups. Though students already had considerable power at the college, there were still routine symbols of administrative authority that students desired to contest. This does not mean that the new administration represented any remarkable retreat; the college remained a fairly open and vibrant place. It was rather the caution and the lack of encouragement of change that bred skepticism. Thus it was almost inevitable that students would test the strength of their commitments against those of the president and administration. Thompson was always involved in this, though the conflicts did not often boil over. The students continued to work at what they perceived as cross-purposes *vis-à-vis* the administration. Much of what they did actually had no everyday consequence for the operation of the college; as such they were left unfettered. The students read, held workshops, carried on external projects, and sometimes held rallies on civil rights issues. However, when conflicts did boil over, the lines were so drawn as to inspire a challenge on all the anti-establishment issues being commonly raised at the time. The posture of the Owens administration made it a relatively easy target.

In interviews Thompson has argued that this experience had another, more significant, effect on him. As a young radical and populist, his ideals necessarily opposed those of an administrative structure based on a system of the "oppressors." He has said that the way the lines were drawn at Tougaloo gave him a clearer idea of the real world of politics and the need for political education. Clearly the debate about the bus was no game. It was a direct conflict about how blacks were to proceed in a racist society. Owens believed that there had already been some progress, while Thompson felt that blacks remained an almost singularly oppressed class. By this view racism was no respecter of distinctions between the poor black and the educated one; each was subject to the same exclusion. Thus Owens was seen as trying to draw a distinction between the students' concerns and community issues. Thompson sought to sustain the view that the Jackson State affair was such a larger black community problem. He interpreted the kind of political education needed by the college administration as a "baptism" for the battle he was to fight in electoral politics for control of Bolton. The whites he assumed to be racist and to reject virtually all of his ideals. But he now also saw that there would be a need to guide and nurture the mobilization of an unevenly committed black community.

Litigation and the Assumption of Office

Much of the preceding reveals the personality, ideas, and political training behind the behavior of Bennie Thompson. These fully evolved into the radical populism that characterized his early political career. His application of these principles began with the very act of seeking office. In the small town of Bolton he was required to display a full panoply of militance *vis-à-vis* whites, and to violate all the taboos that sustained racial segregation. His assault upon the white power structure was done assertively and in a relatively short period. His easy support within the black constituency owed much to this attitude and to his considerable charisma. With the latter, Thompson inspired the community to accept and act on his contentions. They in turn strengthened his independence and ability to take risks.[82] Moreover, this young leader brought a wealth of contacts and sheer knowledge of political matters with which he buttressed the intense mobilization that emerged in the town. All these considerable resources were required in his assumption of office.

The electoral successes of Thompson were rejected by local whites with extraordinary vigor. On May 13, 1969 in a Democratic primary election for aldermen, Thompson and two other blacks were nominated. After the general election the three blacks (constituting a majority of the five-member board) were certified along with the others. Then four years later Thompson led an entire slate of blacks for all electoral posts in Bolton. The results seemed straightforward—the blacks had won. However, in neither of these cases was the result to be as simple as it seemed. A long battle ensued with whites who contested the results. In the process Thompson reached the pinnacle of his leadership influence and oversaw the most massive activation of blacks for political participation ever realized in the county.

The reputation of Mississippi whites as being the least "redeemed" among the southerners was probably sustained, at least in Bolton in 1969 and 1973. The reaction among whites was swift, though not as violent as had been the case during reconstruction or the early registration campaigns. In this case their physical reactions were legalistic, although the principle on which they reacted was the same: white supremacy—few hid their contempt for black participation. In their view the majority of blacks were merely being incited by "smart niggers" like Thompson and "outside agitators" (northern civil rights workers). It was submitted that most blacks remained satisfied with their traditional roles, and were in any case incapable of taking up other ones.

The efforts to prevent blacks from assuming office were relentless. In 1969 whites challenged the primary election result in court, and the federal court ruled against them. A similar challenge was made in 1973 that generated a total of eight separate court actions between May and July of that year. These challenges the whites also lost. Then to show their ultimate disapproval, virtually all whites withdrew from voluntary participation of any kind in the new black government.

In the 1969 challenge the whites charged irregularities in the May 13 primary. Specifically, they alleged that the verifying Democratic Executive Committee was not in compliance with the Mississippi Code as amended in 1968;[83] and that the individual behavior of Bennie Thompson caused undue influence upon the election outcome.

> They said Benny [sic] G. Thompson frequented the polling place for the better part of the day and observed the regulation books and argued with the poll workers if certain names were not found on said book, all this in view of the fact that he already was represented at the polls by a poll worker.[84]

On the strength of these charges the defeated whites asked the Democratic Executive Committee to void the election. When the Committee did not hold a hearing, a legal petition was filed for court review of the election. Meanwhile, Thompson sued for removal of the case to Federal District Court and was denied; the case was remanded to county court. Then Thompson instituted another suit seeking removal to the Federal Circuit Court, an effort at which he succeeded.

The energetic manner in which Thompson pursued this case is indicative of many aspects of his radical populist leadership. In the first place, he exhibited no fear of the threats and other efforts at intimidation from whites—he was clearly their chief target. Instead of yielding, Thompson began to call upon the vast array of internal and external contacts. Locally, any number of supporters were prepared to actively assist the first duly elected black officials to occupy their seats. Thompson utilized them to maintain a state of agitation and mobilization about the issue. This was a tactic for activation and education: voters were encouraged to focus their independent electoral achievement, and told that they stood to lose it if they did not fight. Thompson was the chief symbol of this resistance by his avowed public rejection of the whites' contentions and his announced intention to fight the challenge legally.

It was at this point that Thompson sought the counsel of Frank Parker and those at the Lawyers' Committee for Civil Rights Under Law[85] in Jackson. The two had worked on many projects from which other civil rights litigation had resulted, and thus worked confidently together in devising a strategy for the case at hand. The first tasks were to ascertain the base of the white challenge, and then to determine the applicable law on which to argue. To them the issues in the case were deemed beyond the jurisdiction of the state courts and removal to the Federal District was sought. Their reasoning centered on three problems: changes made in the election procedures in 1968; the requirement that election commissioners be freeholders; and the question of Bennie Thompson's actions on election day. Specifically, the claims were:

> The Mississippi primary election contest procedures were void because of failure to comply with Section Five of the Voting Rights Act of 1965, . . . that the freeholder qualification for county election commissioners, who were required to play a substantial role in determining primary election contests,

denied them rights secured by the Equal Protection Clause of the Fourteenth Amendment . . . and that the contest was brought to oust petitioners . . . for conduct by petitioner Thompson which is protected by . . . the Voting Rights Act of 1965.[86]

In this instance the District Judge, without giving a hearing on the issues, sent the case back to the state court. (This decision was upheld by the full District Court.)

Thompson immediately appealed to the Fifth Circuit Court on the grounds that the District Court should have taken up the issues and removed the case to the federal level. They established the grounds for removal on precedents from 1880 [*Strauder vs. West Virginia* (1880) and *Virginia vs. Rives* (1880)]. These seemed to indicate that when a state law was in violation of a Constitutional provision or statute the grounds for relief were outside the state courts; in such instances the controversy was required to be removed to the federal courts for settlement. In the Bolton case several such violations were noted.[87]

The burden of Thompson's legal claim rested on the 1968 legislative changes in election procedures that appeared to violate the Voting Rights Act. This act provided that any post-1964 changes in voting regulations in certain states required approval of either the Federal District Court or the U.S. Attorney General. (Mississippi was one of the states to which the statute was applicable.) The suit charged that no such approvals were sought and that the changes spawned even other violations of law. It was reasoned that the electoral changes had the direct effect of lessening the potential participation of black electors. They cited section 11(b) of the Voting Rights Act which prohibited threats and intimidation, and section 1981 that guaranteed rights to all persons equal to "those enjoyed by white people." There was already a precedent for this, Parker argued, in the recent *Allen vs. State Board of Elections* (1969) that voided similar changes.

Moreover, they argued that the new requirement that election commissioners be freeholders violated the Fourteenth Amendment and the Voting Rights Act of 1965. They showed that the requirement was only instituted by the state legislature after blacks challenged the existing statute that resulted in an allwhite county commission.[88] Just prior to the resolution of the legal challenge, the state legislature changed the law to permit commissioners to be elected, with the qualification that they must be freeholders. The petitioners in Bolton said that represented a blatant tactic to thwart black participation on these commissions.[89]

On the points of law it was reasoned that the violations were both economic and racial. In regard to economic discrimination, the petitioners cited a recent combined decision (*Bryant vs. Blunt* and *Williams vs. Reed*, both from Mississippi) in the Federal District Court, where it was decided that indeed the requirement of freeholder status was economically discriminatory and thus in violation of the Fourteenth Amendment.[90] In light of this Thompson and his lawyers presented a detailed analysis of land ownership in Hinds County from the 1960 Census. This showed great disparity between black and white land ownership, allowing the conclusion that blacks were far less likely to be freeholders. They buttressed this conclusion with historical evidence that showed how such economic discrimination was used to disfranchise blacks.[91]

The matter of racial discrimination that violated the equal protection clause and the voting statute was put more simply. The petitions asserted that the new laws were expressly designed to exclude blacks because of their race. They focused on how the changes had been instituted in the face of a legal challenge from blacks. The 1968 legislative actions were specifically designed to circumvent the election of blacks, it was reasoned. The petitioners then cited the chronology of events that led to the changes and said:

> The clear inference from this chronology is that the state legislature changed the manner of selecting county election commissioners from appointment to election in *anticipation* (emphasis added) that this Court might grant the relief requested in *Allen* and require that the state election commissioners cease their systematic exclusion of Negroes from appointments to the county election commissions. The only reason for retaining the freeholder requirement was to prevent blacks from being elected to office.[92]

Finally, the petitioners took up the question of actions by Bennie Thompson on election day. The commissioners alleged that Thompson had unduly influenced the electoral outcome by exhorting people to vote. Again Thompson and his lawyers argued that this claim was made solely for the purpose of harassment and intimidation because Thompson had every right to do the things he had done. Indeed every citizen had the same rights. It was demonstrated that the Voting Rights Act provided that one "has a right to be free from intimidation, threats, or coercion, or attempts to intimidate, threaten, or coerce him for voting or attempting to vote, or for urging or aiding any person to vote or attempt to vote."

The Fifth Circuit Court upheld the claims of Thompson some six months later in December. It was only at this point that the three aldermen, including Thompson, were able to take their seats with full confidence.

The importance of this dispute to the constituency should not be underestimated. This was the first clear test of the strength of social and political change that Thompson had sought. It was the first election since the Voting Rights Act where he was the most visible leader of the new ideas and mobilization. For both him and the electorate much of the future hinged on success in this battle. The Court's agreement with Thompson's side was both a relief and a boon to further political mobilization. The constituents were now fully prepared to invest in the special qualities of this young college graduate. They had seen him refuse to back down to the challenge from whites and to issue challenges of his own. His confidence and aggressive pursuit of all venues to sustain the election results inspired constituents to continue their mobilization.

This was merely the first phase of the battle. It has already been noted that blacks won a majority of the five aldermanic posts. Two of the five seats, however, were won by whites. And the mayoral position was also won by a white. From an administrative and policy standpoint the apparent black advantage was illusive. Efforts to form a bloc to exact concessions from the whites did not work. "The mayor (white) had a veto, and because the state attorney general has required that four votes is necessary to override that veto, the white minority on the board continued to block progressive action . . . designed to serve the interests of the majority population."[93] For this period of time, then, the new leadership under Thompson was largely frustrated in attempts to deliver goods to their black constituents.

Discussions about remedies soon turned to attaining even greater control of local political institutions. Thompson led the move to seek additional offices on the grounds that a working relationship with whites on "good faith" was proving unsuccessful. He contended that if whites could not be persuaded to accept the principle of black participation (a reality in the newly elected, integrated board), then blacks were required to work independently to guarantee the exercise of their rights. The decision was to run a full slate in the next campaign dedicated to an open political community, and to brook no alternative effort based on the old ways. Thompson and his emerging cadre left the opportunity for everyone to join, but only blacks accepted the offer; whites who were active sought to maintain segregation.

The Thompson slate carried the day by sweeping all the offices in the 1973 election, as can be seen in Table 3.2. The negative reaction of the whites was swift and broader than that in the 1969 contest. They immediately moved to block the Democratic primary election result and to have a special election called. A list of 9 "irregularities" were detailed as cause for voiding the election. According to the petition filed against Thompson[94] the following charges were made:

1. Eleven municipal voters who were unqualified in the county illegally voted.

2. Nine county voters who were unqualified in the municipality illegally voted.

3. Four to eight residents outside the town's corporate limits voted illegally.

4. Twenty voters with delinquent municipal taxes illegally voted.

5. The ballot box was not properly sealed or delivered to the Town Clerk as required.

6 Duplicate receipts for blank ballots were not provided.

7. An excess of the total ballots issued was returned after the election.

8. Challenged ballots bore distinguishing marks and were thereby invalid. Moreover one such ballot was counted even though the elector tendering it did not meet residency requirements, and another was not properly registered. Still six others had other inappropriate distinguishing marks.

9. Twenty-six voters marked with a check (✓), instead of the legally required (X) or (V).

Table 3.2. 1973 Election Returns, Bolton.

Office	Black Candidate	Vote	White Candidate	Vote
Mayor	B. Thompson	217	D. Beard	119
Clerk	H. Harris	225	J. Condia	188
Aldermen	L. Leach	211	J. Milano	187
	L. Butler	208	A. Payne	185
	D. Davis	208	J. Giambrone	179
	J. Hill	199	R. Mashburn	176
	M. Green	198	J. Brewer	170
Democratic Executive Committee	E. Jones	203	J. Mashburn	186
	E. Dixon	201	D. Mashburn	184
	E. Heard	195	C. Lancaster	180
	H. Hulitt	194	T. Cox	178
	D. Robinson	193	W. Culipher	177
	A. Campbell	193	R. Heard	176
	M. Rollins	188	R. Boyd	174

Source: Frank Parker, Memorandum on "Bolton Election Contest Litigation," (Sept. 17, 1973), pp. 1-2.

Then matters became exceedingly complicated because the challenges were made to the Election Commission (that which had overseen the May 8th election).[95] This commission, with a white majority, accepted the challenges and set aside the election result. Meanwhile, in preparation for the general election (scheduled for June 5) an election commission had also to be appointed by the Board of Aldermen. The mayor made these appointments (including one black) in anticipation of the June general election, though no independents had qualified to oppose primary winners. (There was no Republican primary.)

Quite by accident, Frank Parker, Thompson's lawyer, overheard a conversation about two whites who had secretly qualified to run in the general election as independents. They were planning to run for the two most important offices—mayor and town clerk. Thus if the primary challenge did not succeed, the whites could stand for office in the next round. Secrecy was important so as to "lull [blacks] into a sense of complacency regarding their primary victory . . . [Moreover] it was unlikely that black candidates could muster as many votes for a general election contest as they had for their primary election. Many college students . . . would [now] be out of state working in summer jobs by June 5."[96]

By now Thompson, used to the tactics of his opponents, prepared for the litigation. The white mayor's appointment of the Election Commission appeared to be illegal since the Board of Aldermen were assigned that responsibility. Acting on this information, Thompson and the other black aldermen had a meeting on May 19 to exercise their prerogative in appointing a new commission. This they did, though the white aldermen and mayor refused to appear at the meeting. Now the town had two election commissions, "and there was a substantial question as to how the May 19 Commission would vindicate its authority."[97] Clearly Thompson had set the stage for some kind of confrontation, one of which Frank Parker speculated may have been to exercise arrest powers against the commission earlier appointed by the mayor.

Questions about the secret candidates led to the overt confrontation. When Thompson was tipped off about their existence, he directly approached the town clerk about how such information could be concealed. No full response was given. Meanwhile the Thompson Election Commission instituted hearings to ascertain how this happened. It was revealed that these candidates filed only with the town clerk (white), and not the Election Commission as required by statute. With this information the Thompson Election Commission denied these candidates a place on the ballot.

There were now at least three outstanding legal issues: legality of the primary; which electoral commission had power; and who was to appear on the general election ballot. Neither side saw possibilities for compromise, and between them instituted eight legal challenges between May 29 and July 13 to reach closure on the issues.

The first of these cases came when the Commission appointed on May 1 by the white mayor brought an action to enjoin the Thompson Commission from conducting the upcoming June election. The May 1 group prevailed when "an *ex parte* injunction [was] issued without notice or hearing" by a Chancery Judge. Thompson's attorneys quickly challenged that order and were also granted relief after a hearing, to the effect that the May 19 commission had legal standing and should conduct the June election. However, attorneys for the May 1 commission refused to honor or participate in the hearing, as they deemed it illegal.[98]

In the interim much maneuvering occurred. The May 19 commission did proceed to conduct the June 5 election in spite of one judge's ruling that enjoined such action, and despite the fact that the primary results had been voided. The ballot listed only the black candidates who had run in the Democratic primary. This left virtually all the outstanding issues unresolved, though Thompson and his supporters felt they had gained advantage.

One outstanding dispute that had to be taken up, even though the general election had proceeded, was how to undo the decision that voided the primary results. After all, the general election had been conducted directly on the basis of the primary returns. Once again, Thompson's lawyers decided that the best route was to seek removal of the case to the federal courts. Indeed their rationale was based on the ruling that settled the previous election dispute. This action was filed June 8 and bore the title *Thompson vs. Bolton Municipal Democratic Executive Committee*.

Just days later (June 13) the Democratic Executive Committee filed a claim in the Hinds County Chancery Court against the Primary Election Commission. They claimed that since their committee "had voided the May 8 Democratic primary, . . . that therefore there were no Democratic nominees for municipal office in the June 5 general election, and that therefore the June 5 general election was void." These petitioners sought denial of the petitions of office to those so elected.[99]

For the Thompson forces this required still another legal petition. Their strategy was the same—to seek removal to the federal level to avoid what Frank Parker called "an ambush in state court," since "it was apparent that [the] chancellor . . . was prepared to grant the [Mashburn] injunction." Time was of the utmost importance, as revealed by the swift action of Thompson's lawyers in filing a reply less than 24 hours after notice of the June 13 action.[100]

The frenetic activity resulted in almost daily petitions. The whites wanted to maintain the offensive by keeping Thompson's forces off-balance. In this situation the protection of information was valuable. Frank Parker, for example, lamented that when the challenge to the general election was filed on June 13, he was not informed until "five p.m. on the 14th," and that the hearing had been scheduled for "nine a.m. . . . the next morning." On the other hand, Parker and Thompson wanted very much to create as much publicity as possible with each of their legal challenges. They played to a highly mobilized local constituency and a broad "external audience." Therefore, their court actions were never downplayed. In fact Thompson cleverly used the media to his own ends as he readily made himself available to reporters and always provided a "story angle."

Evidence of the tactics of the proponents of the old regime can be seen in their next two legal challenges. Again on June 13, this group submitted a money claim to the county Circuit Court against those who organized and oversaw the general election. They asked for $37,500 from the Thompson Municipal Election Commission, to be paid to the losing white primary candidates.[101] Then, just one day after filing in Chancery Court (June 13) to have the general election voided, the Democratic Executive Committee also filed another action.[102] They did this even before any notice was received by Thompson of the action of the 13th. Their claims were virtually identical to those previously filed. This time they contested the general election because since "the primary had been voided there were no Democratic nominees to be placed on the ballot for the general election, and therefore the election was void." Now their best hope was that one of these challenges would be successful.

The strategy of the Thompson team was the same again—to seek removal of the last two actions to the federal court. Their reasoning was that if the challenges were accepted, such would constitute violations of guaranteed rights under the Voting Rights Act. They contended that the decision to void the election result was both "without lawful authority and racially discriminatory"; and that there was otherwise no violation of the legal standards for contesting elections. The decision to go ahead with the general election, they said, was an obligation required by law. It was pointed out that no one, including the courts, had otherwise made arrangements to carry out an alternative primary. By this view the state-designated election date stood and in the absence of other qualified candidates, those who prevailed in the primary were listed on the general election ballot.

Frank Parker's detailed memorandum sets out the full weight of the complete victory that the Thompson challenges achieved in the federal court. This victory was particularly significant because although blacks expected to win eventually, they did not necessarily expect the victory to come at this level in the courts. After all, "a civil rights removal case had never before been won before any of the federal judges in the Southern District."

> With unusual speed, Judge (Dan) Russell handed down his decision on August 17 ruling for us on every point, including points that were not directly involved in these cases, but which were directly applicable to the *Thompson* case (Suit 2). On the basis of our 1970 Fifth Circuit decision in *Thompson vs. Brown*, Judge Russell held that these two cases were properly removed to Federal Court and denied the motions to remand. He held that the Democratic Executive Committee lacked the authority to set aside the May 8 primary, and that the contests should have been heard by the new Committee which had been "elected" in the primary. He held that the winning Black candidates were properly in Federal Court because the state statutes permitting an appeal from the Committee decision, amended and reenacted in 1968, were unenforceable for failure to submit under Section 5 of the Voting Rights Act of 1965. He also held that the Governor and Secretary of State should be ordered to issue to the winning black candidates their commissions of office. He found that there had been "no significant irregularities" in the conduct of the primary election, and that there was no evidence of fraud which justified the Committee's decision. The principal justification for the decision, that the ballots had been initialed on the front rather than on the back, was not sufficient to void the election. Judge Russell further held that the Municipal Election Commission was justified in holding the general election and including on the ballots the names of the Democratic nominees declared on May 9.[103]

There were minor skirmishes in court thereafter by the whites, but for all intents and purposes the transfer of power was to be effected on the basis of the Federal District Court decision. But what did it all mean for Thompson and his black constituents? In the first place it must be seen that Thompson was the central moving force in all these actions. He insisted that the legal challenges be made and he operated in a manner to sustain the momentum that went into the election at the outset. Moreover, his sheer visibility at every crucial juncture was of utmost importance in establishing his centrality in the campaign. Thompson was named in virtually all of the suits filed by the whites and was more likely to have his behavior denoted offensive or violative of the law. Clearly he was a major target for the opposing side, a factor heightened by his press notices and testimonies when required at court.

Conclusion

The prominence of Thompson in this critical debate illustrates both the general patterns of the new mobilization leadership and his political style. It is evident that his youth and civil rights commitments gave him the energy and the perspective to take a radical and populist approach to the challenges raised by his electoral victory. When one observes the tactics, notwithstanding litigation, clearly the politics of accommodation was not his object. Thompson's direct influence was important in forging the ideological commitments for social change that citizen activism (in voting) had wrought. Moreover, he won the important right to establish the local agenda as he deemed consistent with constituent demands and ideals. His initiatives were bold, as with the opportunity to appoint a "favorable," though legal, Election Commission—this despite the availability of other options, such as going directly to court. However, this required more time. And in the end the risk he took preserved the initial electoral victory and was sustained in court. The decision thereafter to go forward with the general election was just as revealing of the radical break with traditional routes to power.

Thompson's political perspective was firmly grounded in the principles of participatory democracy and his commitment to black people. For him, to leave the white contentions unchallenged was tantamount to perverting constitutional principles that allowed the people to decide. It hardly mattered that all the representatives were black; they had been democratically chosen and there was no way around it. His special leadership position allowed him to serve as the bridge to effect their wishes. He perceived an obligation to be their spokesman and benefactor as he sought to fulfill the promise of a purposive, welfare-oriented program.

4

Heroine in Mayersville

Introduction

Mayersville is, for all the glamor of its contemporary experience, a dusty spot at the edge of a great river. It is typical of so many exceedingly small places in rural Mississippi, where scale and isolation combine to give an idyllic picture of calm parochialism. With its many weather-worn houses and trails of dust across so many miles of cotton or soybean acres, Mayersville very much looks its part. It even has a kind of *piazza* at its center, except that residents do not routinely congregate there to "cool their heels" at the end of a sultry day.

Contradictions abound in Mayersville. The mid-town square is actually the seat of county government, with a courthouse and offices. This signals that Mayersville is the largest town in the county (albeit an unincorporated one until 1976), with barely 500 inhabitants and a mere two stores. A further contradiction occurred when this idyllic setting was transformed in 1977. A black woman, Unita Blackwell, succeeded in getting the town incorporated, became its mayor, and subsequently became an international figure.

What is evident when one focuses on Mayersville are the heroic and inventive acts of Unita Blackwell in moving the town successfully through the early civil rights period to her subsequent election in the late 1970s. The mobilization in this town, unlike the others in this study, began earlier and moved systematically through phases related to the strategies of Martin Luther King, Jr. and the early student movement. It is in this context that the

96 BLACK POLITICAL MOBILIZATION

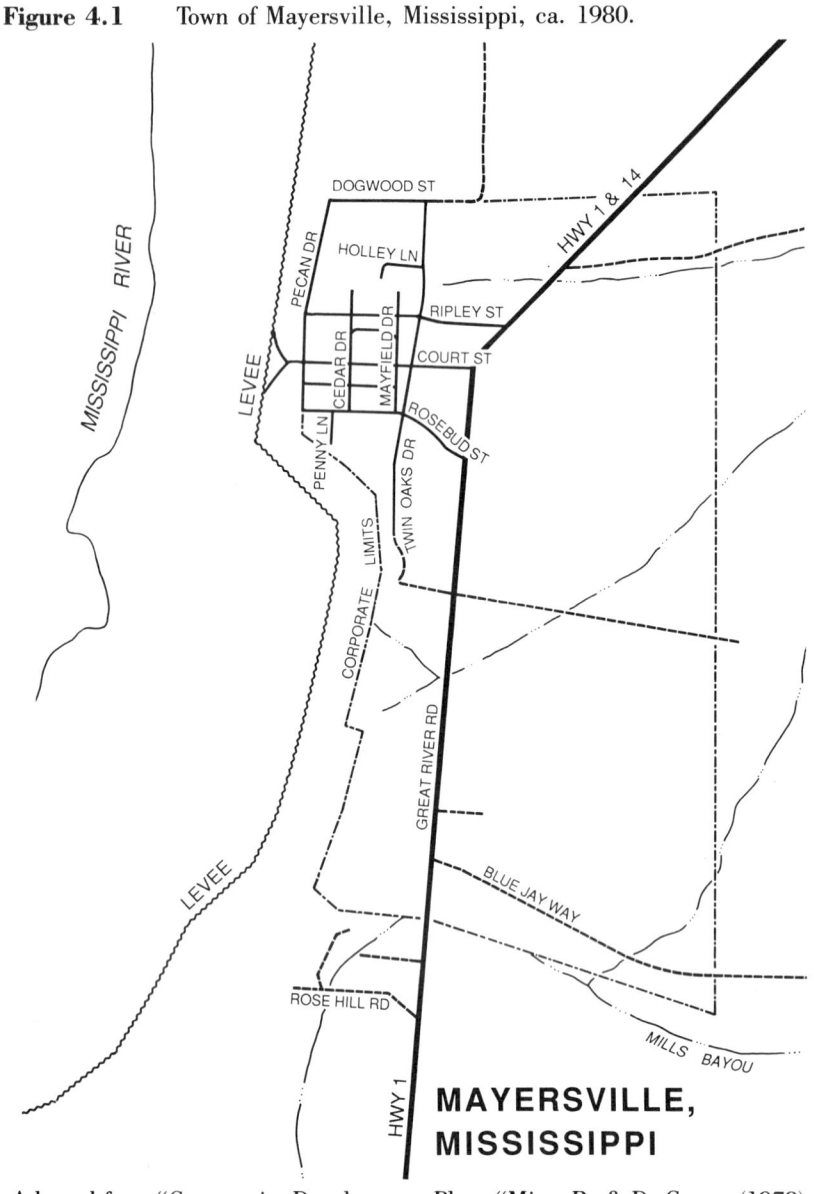

Figure 4.1 Town of Mayersville, Mississippi, ca. 1980.

Adapted from "Community Development Plan, "Miss. R. & D. Center (1978).

theory of heroic invention obtains significance. The isolation of the Mayersville black community (marked by fear, apathy, and complete black disfranchisement) created a static situation that was most easily activated by a catalyzing symbol. Unita Blackwell used a creative, individual approach in cultivating and building on local organizations and unpublicized but generalized sentiments for change. She melded this with traditional American values as espoused by King and others. In seeking to mobilize her racially isolated community, she could be creative, even daring because this community was in another sense inchoate—ripe, open, and malleable. In part this explains why Mrs. Blackwell is older; she spent a much longer activist period in the social mobilization campaign that culminated in the assumption of power.

The analysis begins by evaluating the special background of Mayersville and Issaquena County, and how it may relate to the present. It is reasoned that the broadness of the agricultural economy and the high proportion of enslaved in this heart of the delta region led to hardship for the blacks and opportunities for the present mobilization. It was here that plantations had hundreds of slaves, instead of a score; that these same blacks nearly dominated the political structure during reconstruction; and where disfranchisement resulted in their near-complete isolation thereafter. Unita Blackwell spearheaded the campaign that yielded an extraordinary reversal of the disfranchisement. The assessment of how she did it focuses on the delta environment and her heroic and inventive visions. All these are elaborated by an exploration of her charisma and ideology, and her active work on the issues of education and town incorporation.

Mayersville History and the Slaveocracy

The poverty, even the apparent extreme absence of a resource base,[1] masked a "glorious past." Mayersville enjoyed tremendous wealth betweeen 1840 and 1870. Its prime location on rich, alluvial soil was complemented by proximity to waterways that bathed and drained the soils and provided ports for marketing.[2] This fertile land required much labor and led to a population over 90% black, virtually all enslaved. (Table 4.1 shows that only seven were "free.") Even until 1890 (40 years after emancipation), the labor requirements led to an increased black population.

These conditions sustained a slaveocracy somewhat different from other places. In the first place Issaquena was organized as a unit relatively later than

Table 4.1. Population in Issaquena County.

	Blacks	Whites
1850	4,112[a]	366
1860	7,244	587
1870	6,146	714
1880	9,174	761
1890	11,579	695
1900	9,771	586
1910	9,946	577

[a]seven were free.
Source: *U.S. Census of Population*, years indicated.

other counties (1844).[3] Its large tracts of land[4] were owned by usually wealthy, northern or border state absentees[5] and managed by stewards.[6] Soon Issaquena had the highest median enslaved population in the country (188),[7] and nearly 40% of the plantations had over 50 slaves.[8] Thus the investment motive was unusually high among these absentee owners, a fact that had dire consequences for the welfare of blacks. In order to enhance their own positions, the stewards used excessive rigor in enforcing rules. Sydnor claims that in concentrations over 30, blacks "fared worse when supervised by overseers . . . [for] nonresident owners," a condition for "the plantations [such as Mayersville] of over fifty slaves . . . bordering the Mississippi River."[9]

Black Reconstruction in the Delta

With such a large enslaved population, black control was possible after the war, but its success in Issaquena County and the surrounding area was only partial. "In 1874, every member of the board was alleged to be an illiterate negro. . . . The members of the legislature, the sheriff, clerks, justices of the peace, and constables were all colored. In fact there were only two white officers in the county."[10] Perhaps the highest-ranking of these blacks was Richard Griggs, who served as state Commissioner of Agriculture and Immigration in 1873.[11]

Despite these favorable conditions, those occupying offices in this county hardly measured up to the influence black leaders enjoyed in Hinds County (or even in neighboring Washington County).[12] Even when the board of Supervisors and most officers were black, there is little evidence that they succeeded in dominating affairs. Evidence is sketchy, but it appears that the most significant of these officials were more sensitive to the concerns of whites and the political party hierarchy than to the black community. H.P. Scott held the potentially powerful position of sheriff for four terms in the county.[13] In refusing to protect black officials from white violence and intimidation, he asserted that he lacked authority.[14] Much of his difficulty stemmed from personal fear and promotion of a certain political perspective. On the one hand, he had seen whites eliminate other blacks.[15] But Scott also sought to protect his healthy relations with whites. He was active in the Republican Party and later with the Democrats; in positions he hoped reminded whites of their immorality and illegality in local government. When this proved ineffective, Scott became little more than a collaborator.[16] This is revealed in his appointment of deputies. He reported that his permanent assistants were more likely to be whites, whose qualifications were not questionable. Blacks received *ad hoc* appointments, especially if they were "qualified."[17]

Intimidation often led the overwhelming black majority to adjust their alignments after the Democrats overturned Republican government in the county between 1875–76. This meant fusion politics, a practice most glaring in its inequity in this delta county. The most serious decline in black participation was local. One fusion ticket is an illustration. "In Issaquena County, where the Negroes outnumbered the whites almost ten to one, the Democrats reserved for themselves in 1877 the office of sheriff, treasurer, surveyor, coroner, three supervisors, and one justice of the peace and one constable in each district."[18] What blacks maintained was representation in the state legislature, a body now completely dominated by whites. However these Black legislators remained until as late as 1890.[19]

In Mayersville and the surrounding area, nothing of the fusion plan survived the new constitution of 1890. The county was rural and exclusively dependent on agriculture, leaving blacks in the most extreme isolation for the next 50 years. The absentee owners had built no large towns since they lived elsewhere. Even the Mayersville port declined when surface transportation gained in importance.

The economic dependence of blacks deepened as they owned little land and remained attached to large planters, in a capacity reminiscent of enslavement. As sharecroppers and tenants, their labor was still deployed in plowing, planting, hoeing and picking cotton. They remained outside of the direct wage economy, and completely divorced from the power structure.

The Emergence of Unita Blackwell

For a long period Mayersville appeared to languish. A black child could only look forward to a future on the farm that paralleled that of the parents. Mayor Unita Blackwell explained that her own life had been made up of a cycle of hoeing and picking cotton. One either lived as a tenant, or hired oneself out on a daily basis to white plantation owners.

This cycle served as the prototype for the future, since one was directly tied into it virtually from birth. The total immersion of adults in the plantation economy meant that children were equally engaged. About the time they reached school age, children began to learn the trade, which exceeded education in importance. During the hoeing or picking season children were routinely let off from school to assist in the preparation or harvest of the crop. This was a factor that affected Mrs. Blackwell's early life. As a child in another delta county, she tells of having been spirited away (with her sister) to Arkansas so that the school year would not be interrupted by working the fields. As an adult she observed the same pattern repeating itself in Mayersville; time seemed frozen.

But for Unita Blackwell time was not frozen, as she always visualized a different life for black people. It was not readily evident how or what was to be done. For her, certain factors were more important than others for change. Higher education was extremely important to her; it would provide advantages neither she nor her mother had. Also important to her was public recognition of the values and independence of black people. Both of these put her at odds with whites in the environment, for she chose to emphasize two elements out of bounds for blacks in the system of racial exclusion. In espousing these values she won praise from the core black community as one who "did not bite her tongue."[20] Thus even as she lived within the racial confines, she had limits. For example, though she conceded that living on the plantation was inequitable, such a life was tolerable when a minimum of human dignity was allowed. Mrs. Blackwell was known to take considerable risks to preserve this standard, even prior to systematic change. It was this individualistic daring within the context of her environment upon which Mrs. Blackwell's heroism was built. The bonding between her and the community resulted from her strength of personality, which provided a base for identification and organization. She came to fit the mold of the individual who "personifies [an] important period of history. [For] consolidating the deeds of whole classes of men in a single person seems initially to result from popular incapacity to follow clearly the great stream of history in all its complexity."[21] The "great stream of history" that Mrs. Blackwell found impossible to follow was the racial division whose institutional base she challenged.

The local environment was also conducive. The isolation of blacks from 1876-on has been noted. Thus, the Mayersville community was ripe for the talents of someone like Mrs. Blackwell to exploit the opportunities for social change. Extreme poverty for blacks was coupled with overall economic decline in the region. Mechanization put most blacks out of work (many migrated). Also, cotton lost its economic value when improved seed led to a saturated market and synthetic fibers became more available. Meanwhile, blacks who remained were affected by the "revolution of rising expectation." They could regularly see via the media what other Americans enjoyed and how other blacks were challenging the system of racial exclusion. Not surprisingly, sentiments in Mayersville were affected, increasing the chances for local mobilization, with Unita Blackwell as the centerpiece.

Sidney Hook has described the melding process between a heroic figure and followers under conditions such as these. "The great men (in history) were thrown up by 'chance' in the processes of natural variation while the social environment served as a selective agency in providing them with the opportunities to get their work done."[22]

Unita Blackwell was the center of all this activity. Unlike either of the other two mayors, she was not born in the county to which she offered her leadership skills. Mrs. Blackwell was born to poor, farming parents in Coahoma County, Mississippi. This delta county north of Issaquena is also on the Mississippi River, and has a similar history. Mrs. Blackwell and her sister (the only sibling) grew up in a home of integrity. Her mother, anxious for them to continue their school year uninterrupted by plantation chores, regularly sent them across the river to an aunt in Arkansas. Her father demonstrated equally strong if not uncommon convictions. In a manner that Mrs. Blackwell equates with her own behavior, her father was said to reject the efforts of white men to tell him what to do with his family and stuff," though this got him into trouble. The whites sought to destroy his independent spirit in ways she notes are common.[23] Absent much detail, she relates that her father's activities created great anger in some white men. The outcome is quite familiar—her father was required to leave by night because "they wanted to kill him." He settled in Memphis, providing what she calls her extended family context—a triangle between Memphis, Arkansas, and Coahoma County.

After marriage to Jeremiah Blackwell, the mayor settled down to raise a family (that included one son), and to make a living in the cotton plantations of Coahoma County. Already, however, the industry was beginning to decline with smaller acreage in cotton and with the entry of mechanical cotton pickers. Yet for her family, migration North was not a ready option. They had already committed themselves to staying in Mississippi by starting a family. For Jeremiah Blackwell, however, with a piece of property in Mayersville and roots that included a great-grandfather in the legislature during Reconstruction, there was every reason to stay home with his family.[24]

The Mobilization Campaign

Mrs. Blackwell made her permanent home in Mayersville in the early 1960s. At the time she was struck by the familiar range of inequities blacks had to endure there. The southern civil rights movement, however, placed all of this in a new light. That Martin Luther King and the students were mobilized against the segregated and racist character of southern life was exceedingly important for Mrs. Blackwell. Since the routines of race relations were now being openly challenged, these mores became much less acceptable even in the remotest places. And so it was that Mrs. Blackwell felt swept up by the ferment all around her. It provided a way of thinking about the "unease" she always had about the way things were.

In some ways Mrs. Blackwell was unlike a good many of her cohorts, most of whom were young college students. She was neither young nor a student. At 30, she was older than most of them. Moreover, she was a married women (with a child) who had never been to college. Yet she was captivated by their sentiments and her own real-life racial experiences.

If Mrs. Blackwell was unlike the typical early mobilization leaders, some of this was due to the characteristics of her community. The population of the town had continued to decline, with many black youths migrating. Therefore, when the civil rights ferment began in the early 1960s, Mayersville had no group of local college students to disseminate the new ideas. This task of agitation and ideological delineation was largely home-grown. Mrs. Blackwell was at the center of this youthful leadership that was almost a half generation away from that of college students elsewhere. The group in Mayersville raised the same issues and used similar tactics employed elsewhere for stimulating mobilization.

Unlike Thompson in Bolton, Mrs. Blackwell was an early mobilizer insofar as she began to develop in the earliest phases of the civil rights movement. She was much more involved in creating opportunities and establishing conditions for constituency activation. The activities that ushered her into the limelight were those that challenged the system of social segregation on moral and philosophical grounds. Hers was tinged with aspects of the moral crusade reminiscent of Martin Luther King, Jr., then the most prominent leader in the southern movement. His campaign of protest demonstrations, designed to prick the Christian consciousness of America, were the first activities that Mrs. Blackwell considered and in which she would participate. Her immediate goal was to prevail upon local blacks to reject old ways. This required activating them to challenge or to systematically violate the racial taboos in a manner consistent with Christian principles. It was deemed easier to exact actions once the appropriate interpretations about the past were made.

Mrs. Blackwell's personal commitment to move in the direction of the students, who were also inspired by King at this juncture, occurred when two black civil rights workers came to the town of Mayersville. "These two strangers came walking into this little town, while I was sitting on the porch with a friend. . . . And, they were walking right fast. . . . And we know when you walked fast in 1964 in this part of the country, you weren't from here. . . . There weren't a lot of cars; there weren't a lot of things; and people walked two or three times slower in the South." Virtually every behavior set these young men apart from the average Mayersvillians. "They said 'hello,' and then we knew they weren't from here, because we say 'how y'all feeling.'" Yet, this was to "break open my life, and I didn't know it. It was the beginning of a whole new era."[25]

The men, later identified as early SNCC workers, remained for some days and attempted to get acquainted with people and the environment. They talked with blacks, and when possible focused the conversations on social and political change, consistent with the grassroots techniques of SNCC.[26] Proof of their sensitivity to local sentiments was their early appearance at local churches. This made an especially strong impression upon Mrs. Blackwell, for the church was personally important to her, and represented so much about cultural life and organization in the community. Since these strangers had an interest in starting at this nerve center of the community, Mrs. Blackwell was impressed that they were also honest and clever. In her own experiences she knew that this was where one had to begin to capture the local masses. She was to adopt this as a base.

Mrs. Blackwell was one of the earliest local people to become an associate of these "strangers." She was readily engaged by their conversations and the commonsense manner of their reasoning; and that they sought to be guided by indigenous sentiments. At a Sunday School class, for example, one of these men established a connection between the lesson for the day and the necessity of political mobilization. The point of the lesson had been summarized by Mrs. Blackwell, the class teacher, to be that God helped those who helped themselves. Then in the discussion that followed, she relates, one of the SNCC field workers adapted her point to the racial problems at hand by illustrating how the church could be a partner in the movement. He emphatically asserted that one was obligated to use the moral injunction of self-help for the purpose of changing the immoral racial caste system. This could be done, he reasoned, by small measures—the first of which was registering to vote: "If you all go and register to vote, this is the way you help yourself." According to Mrs. Blackwell, the young man proceeded to outline some benefits of voting: decent housing, education, etc. This struck a responsive chord with her, a devout Christian. Philosophically, she had already concluded that the principles of Christianity were inconsistent with racial division. In part this explained her devout faith. But in deeply personal ways it all made sense. In her own words:

> I know I need (all that he was saying) because I was in a house that was falling down; falling down on the ground at the time. And I was terribly concerned about my son. Was he going to get a good education? You see, here in this area at the time, if it was cotton chopping (or picking season), the children had to come out of school.[27]

Civil rights activity and mobilization moved rapidly from that point for Mrs. Blackwell. That Sunday she agreed to take a bold new step. She, her husband at the time, and four others attempted voter registration. That she was not the first in line, as she relates it, was due only to deference to her husband, who was an equal partner and supporter. The others who joined them were school teachers and several older persons.[28] Mrs. Blackwell noted that the entire group was more than sufficiently educated to meet literacy requirements.

The reaction of the small white community was swift. When the six blacks turned up to register, they were summarily refused. Rapidly, masses of local whites surrounded the courthouse. Mrs. Blackwell reports that many of them had never been seen before, indicating a well-planned response. Their presence was punctuated by the shouting of provocative racial epithets. There were also comments that reminded the six that their "aberrant behavior" was due only to "outside agitators" (a euphemism for any non-local civil rights workers). Mrs. Blackwell also reports that many whites boldly displayed guns in their pickup trucks, a sight that became routine as the activation intensified.

Mrs. Blackwell went three times before she succeeded in passing the literacy test. She explained this in the minutest detail to the Civil Rights Commission (which held hearings on Mississippi voting in Jackson in 1965).

MR. TAYLOR   Is there currently an effort to get Issaquena County to vote?

MRS. BLACKWELL   It is now. It has been since June of 1964.

MR. TAYLOR   Could you tell us a little bit about it and your part in it?

MRS. BLACKWELL   Well, I am now a COFO worker, and we are getting people to go down to the courthouse to register to vote. They are afraid, but they

[go] now, because . . . since COFO came in there and explained to the people that they had a right to register, . . . [they] are going out now. . . . They [are] afraid to go and get cut off their welfare and get thrown off the farms and everything else, but they're standing up because we are talking to them and explaining everything.

MR. TAYLOR Do you know of any Negroes who were registered to vote in the county prior to the summer of 1964?

MRS. BLACKWELL No, because they didn't even want to talk about it. They used to talk about it and they just said "You know the white folks, they don't want us over to the courthouse, and you just can't do that."

MR. TAYLOR Can you give us an estimate of just how many Negroes attempted to register since the drive began?

MRS. BLACKWELL About 150 attempts.

MR. TAYLOR Do you know of any Negroes who have passed?

MRS. BLACKWELL Yes. I do.

MR. TAYLOR About how many?

MRS. BLACKWELL Well, about nine or ten.

MR. TAYLOR Have any of the applicants for registration had better than a sixth grade education?

MRS. BLACKWELL Yes.

MR. TAYLOR Have there been any high school or college students?

MRS. BLACKWELL There [have] been . . . teachers.

MR. TAYLOR Have they passed?

MRS. BLACKWELL Well, I know of a teacher; she went twice, and then she passed the last time. And I know a college student; . . . he didn't pass; and I know another college student [who] didn't pass. And that's the way it has been.

MR. TAYLOR How far did you go in school?

MRS. BLACKWELL I went through the eighth grade.

MR. TAYLOR Have you attempted to register?

MRS. BLACKWELL I have. Three times.

MR. TAYLOR Well, tell us about your first attempt.

MRS. BLACKWELL Well, the first time I went over with my husband. [Everything had] started the day before then. The COFO workers came in, and we had a mass meeting, and they [asked] "Well, who would volunteer to go over to the courthouse and try to register to vote." And we had people—to start off, we had three or four go that day and three or four go the next day. We were in the group that went the [second] day. And my husband and I went in, and [the registrar said] "What do you want?" and we said, "We came in to try to register." And she [said] "Well, all of you can't—one at a time." And so we just went out.

And she told me to sit down, and I [sat] down at a little table, and she gave me this slip of paper—[which] I had never [seen] before—and I looked at it and took my time, and I filled it out, and she stood there hanging over the bannister. And then she gave me a book, pointed out a section for me to copy, and I copied it and tried to interpret it like it said. And then the next [part was] about the citizenship—obligations of a citizen—and I put that down.

And then I asked her [which] oath [I should take]—general oath [or] minister's oath. She said "I can't help you. You have to do it yourself."

MR. TAYLOR She gave you a copy—she gave you a section of the Mississippi constitution to interpret?

MRS. BLACKWELL That's right. The first time I went in [it] was 182.

MR. TAYLOR Do you have a copy of your application form?

MRS. BLACKWELL That's right, I do.

MR. TAYLOR Could you read that section that she gave you to interpret?

MRS. BLACKWELL (reading):
The power to tax corporations and their property shall never be surrendered or abridged by any contract or grant to which the State or any political subdivision thereof may be a party, except that the legislature may grant exemption from taxation in the encouragement of manufactures and other new enterprises of public utility extending for a period of not exceeding 5 years, the time of such exemptions to commence from date of charter, if to a corporation; and if to an individual enterprise, then from the commencement of work; but when the legislature grant such exemptions for a period of 5 years or less, it shall be done by general laws, which shall distinctly enumerate the classes of manufactures and other new enterprises of public utility entitled to such exemptions, and shall prescribe the mode and manner in which the right to such exemptions shall be determined.

MR. TAYLOR Thank you. Did you go back to find out whether you had passed the test?

MRS. BLACKWELL She said come back in 30 days.

MR. TAYLOR Did you pass?

MRS. BLACKWELL No, I didn't. And I asked when could I take the test again and she said about 2 weeks.

MR. TAYLOR Did you go back again a second time?

MRS. BLACKWELL I did go back.

MR. TAYLOR Do you know what section of the constitution you were given to interpret the second time?

MRS. BLACKWELL Yes, I do. 111.

MR. TAYLOR That is the section dealing with the judicial sale of land. Did you attempt to interpret—

MRS. BLACKWELL   No. I had wrote out affidavits showing that I had had over a 6th grade [education] and I gave it to her and explain[ed] that—and she says "Well, that's all right; you'll have to do it anyway." And so I just didn't fill it out. I just wrote it and signed my name and came out.

MR. TAYLOR   Did you go back a third time?

MRS. BLACKWELL   I did.

MR. TAYLOR   And what section did you get on the third time?

MRS. BLACKWELL   Ninety-seven.

MR. TAYLOR   Did you pass?

MRS. BLACKWELL   I did. And this time she helped, because . . . so much had been going on; all the civil rights and Justice Department, everybody running in. And she was all upset,—and I filled out [the registration test] and I had section 97 and I wrote it down and looked it over and I picked some of the words [for explanation and] put [them] there and turned it over. And I misspelled "length" and I said, "Oh, my Lord." And so then I filled out the rest of it and when I got through I handed it to her, and I said "Well, I misspelled this, and well, I didn't date the top," and she said "Oh, that's all right, it's all right, it's all right." And then she ran and got the book and, you know, she was just tired of looking at me.[29]

Local registration was achieved, but not without frustration and not before Mrs. Blackwell was radicalized to invest all of her time in the effort for local mobilization. The experience surrounding her efforts to vote catapulted her into a formal position as a SNCC worker and as a perpetual thorn in the side of Mississippi officials at all levels. As was a common practice for those who became too involved in challenging the system, Mrs. Blackwell became unemployable at the only local outlet for making a living—the cotton farms. Quite suddenly she had undertaken a level of commitment not unlike that for her student counterparts. Yet her commitment was much harder to maintain and was fraught with greater risks. She had none of the advantages of students, who only bore partial responsibility for themselves; their parents bore the rest. For Mrs. Blackwell, however, there was an existing family, a household, and the full panoply of additional adult responsibilities.[30]

In the early mobilization campaign one could already see some heroic feats in Mrs. Blackwell's accomplishments. By associating herself with the only forces of change available, she dared to engage in activities unacceptable to the white power structure, (Most of those around her feared intimidation and violence from whites, though they agreed that social conditions were inadequate.) She accepted these challenges at a very early time in the movement when personal risks were greatest. When COFO inaugurated its concentrated 1964 summer campaign, Mrs. Blackwell was thoroughly involved, locally and elsewhere. (Her local strengths had already earned her notice among other movement leaders.) In Mayersville she continued to move from house to house as a SNCC worker (elsewhere described as a Council of Federated Organizations worker)[31] to convince blacks to register.

In the beginning there were many negative and frustrating occurrences. In testimony before the Civil Rights Commission she related two of these incidents. "The other day (Wednesday) we [were] coming out—we had been to Mr. Jackson('s) house, and was talking to him about coming to parent's meeting, and some white guys came up in a truck and blocked us and got out and told us all kinds of nasty things, 'Get out of here and don't come back.'" Then, the previous Sunday "the same truck . . . [ran] a lot of school kids out because they were down talking to people." The men in this truck also "had a shot-gun out and [were] flashing it . . . and saying 'I could have killed you [a] way back yonder in the woods.'" Yet she explains why these events had little effect in changing her ways: "you just get to the place [where] you know it's [these incidents] going to happen but you've got to stand up and got to do something."[32]

Still other frustrating experiences occurred when those with whom she worked appeared at the courthouse to register. Their encounters often exceeded her initial ones in level of difficulty. Mrs. Luetishie English, a housewife with a ninth-grade education, related her unsuccessful attempts to register, and carefully described how she thought the literacy test requiring interpretation was biased against blacks.

COMMISSIONER GRISWOLD   Mrs. English, do you know how you happened to get these particular sections of the constitution to interpret? Were they handed to you by the registrar or did you draw them from a box, or how did you get these particular sections?

MRS. ENGLISH   They were given to me by the registrar. They pick it out in the book and . . . put a circle around it with a pencil . . .

COMMISSIONER GRISWOLD   And you copied a section—

MRS. ENGLISH   Out of a book.

COMMISSIONER GRISWOLD   Which she told you to copy.

MRS. ENGLISH   That's right.

COMMISSIONER GRISWOLD   But you don't know on what basis the particular section assigned to you was chosen?

MRS. ENGLISH   No; I do not.

COMMISSIONER GRISWOLD   Did she seem to open the book and put a number around a number, or what?

MRS. ENGLISH   She opened the book and laid it on the table and circled around it, the section she wanted me to copy.

COMMISSIONER GRISWOLD   Then you think the section was picked by her—

MRS. ENGLISH   Yes.

COMMISSIONER GRISWOLD   —not by chance?

MRS. ENGLISH   I believe it was picked by her.[33]

Immediately after this testimony a lawyer for the Commission confirmed that there were gross irregularities in the administration of the tests between blacks and whites. The latter were routinely assisted in preparation of their applications and were certified to register even when they erred on the forms. Attorney Charles Humpstone showed that blacks were given more difficult sections of the constitution for interpretation, and received no assistance at all. Moreover, blacks were for a time summarily failed, notwithstanding how well the tests were executed.[34]

There was much occurring in the state at the time for the purpose of political mobilization. This very fluid period included the development of civil rights and political organization on all fronts. Mrs. Blackwell's opportune timing allowed her to tap these resources for her own local campaign. In a manner consistent with the preconditions for leadership, she made aggressive efforts to develop linkages with the important organizations and operatives in state politics and civil rights activities. She already had links to SNCC. But because of the confederation of all the major organizations into COFO, she also knew the workers of CORE, NAACP, and many local campaign organizers.[35] She was involved in the Mississippi Freedom Democratic Party (MFDP) and served as one of its delegates during the 1968 challenge to the local Democrats.[36] The NAACP was particularly important at this time because of the huge amounts of litigation it sponsored on everything from voting to school desegregation. Mrs. Blackwell's contacts with the organization gave her access to such vital resources as lawyers and bail money.

It is noteworthy that while her attention had always been focused on Mayersville Mrs. Blackwell earned a reputation in politics and public affairs far beyond the town. She was involved in state and national Democratic Party politics, and was appointed state co-chairperson in 1980.[37] Her expertise is widely sought for consultations on "the needs and aspirations of the poor."[38] In 1977 she became co-chairperson of the U.S./China People's Friendship Association, in which capacity she has traveled to China many times.[39] Moreover, she has extended her contacts vastly with the upwardly mobile and public affairs-oriented American members of this group. Overall she has found through these associates considerable access to resources for her small town.

The Personal Role of Unita Blackwell in Mayersville's Transformation

It is easy to describe Mrs. Blackwell's civil rights activities as heroic, for she was the spark of a major transformation in the thinking and behavior of blacks in Mayersville and the surrounding area. Yet there are several policies and other actions that signal both heroism and acts of invention. Four aspects will be explored: charisma and ideology, the introduction of freedom schools in the mid-1960s, litigation to desegregate the schools in the Issaquena and Sharkey County district, and the incorporation of the town of Mayersville.

Charisma and Ideology

Both charisma and ideology have already been discussed as separate variables in their relationship to preconditions for leadership. At this juncture the two are combined to illustrate the complicated way in which Mrs. Blackwell used them. It has been seen that there are two aspects of charisma. The first is where great power is achieved on the basis of personality. The other is where mastery of certain cultural parameters enhance power acquisition (for example, the florid and romantic style of idioms for successful oral presentation in black culture). Ideology, on the other hand, is that perspective that specifically disdains racial exclusion justified on the basis of inherent black inequality. This abiding conviction is converted into a "functional, organizing, unifying, and purposive role."[40] Mrs. Blackwell has used these together so that her charisma stretches the horizons of her people along lines consistent with her ideological vision.

Much of this has to do with language, for in the black community the way one uses it is important. Within this culture there is a premium on embellishment, much of it related to similar usages in language of West Africa.[41] In any case the importance and desirable nature of this "self-expression is evident." "The black culture is a culture in which, relatively speaking, oratorical-debating competence is far more praiseworthy than technical bureaucratic skill. . . . A black preacher . . . had better be a good talker! The same thing is more often than not true for the black politician."[42] All the same, mastery of such techniques has been known to sway an audience. Indeed, evoking a direct response is a very important measure of the level of success, a fact ever present in field observations.

Mrs. Blackwell is particularly skilled at the use of language required for success in her community. In personal interviews one is struck at the fullness of her explanation of matters. She uses considerable time to elaborate upon her various points. Sometimes this is true of relatively simple things—a barn is not merely a barn, but it has a kind of personality that must be shown. And so, in describing the barn, it is invested with a good variety of characteristics. But this is equally true for other phenomena. In her fast, staccato speaking voice, Mrs. Blackwell tells one a lot, using many words, gestures, and so on. In an early interview she warned me that I might need to stop her once she got "cranked up." She remembers incidents and situations in the minutest detail, and they are relayed in a convincing manner. On subjects in her areas of expertise she quite literally is never without words. When she was describing the process of incorporation for the town, she was able to talk close to an hour without interruption; she did equally well in detailing her personal ordeal in registering to vote, as noted.

Another aspect of the successful use of language is the repertoire of words, phrases and inflections used in structuring a conversation. It is evident that neither Mrs. Blackwell's educational level nor her language is that of a university graduate. Her daily language is like that of those around her, simple and earthy, using the slangs, code words, and idioms of blacks in the rural delta.

Every speech and interview are sprinkled with these everyday usages. For example, occurrences/phenomena (of a negative kind) were usually referred to as "this kind of *stuff*," with a deprecatory smirk. To a query about what existed in Mayersville prior to incorporation, a flood of responses were uttered in an almost symmetrical cadence: "There wasn't no city hall; there wasn't no telephone; . . . there wasn't no nothing!" This kind of tautological statement, whose repetitious phrases highlight the meaning, indicates seriousness. Her ability to maintain this facility marks her station as being one among the people. Power, as they might say, "has not gone to her head," it has not caused her to relate differently to the people. She turns as good a phrase today in classical rural delta style as she did before the transformation.

The other significant part of the use of language is the tendency to use aphorisms or proverbial statements. These statements are often commentaries upon the unacceptable aspects of life, but just as often they are statements about how life ought to be lived. In contemporary times such statements are likely to be evaluations that are made according to dicta of long standing. Unita Blackwell uses language in this manner to assert an ideological position. When she was describing how the civil rights worker reinterpreted the Sunday School lesson "God helps those . . . ," here was one of those proverbial statements pinpointing local conditions. This represents one of her abiding ideological postures—that God is available (Holden's Moralism), and that one is under some obligation to right the situation (Holden's Defiance).[43] She feels that blacks in Mayersville must use the strength of their faith to sustain a meaningful life. She looks upon this as an injunction from God to defy the "immoral system of segregation." Consequently much of the proverbial language is inspired by the Bible, a much-favored local guide. Mrs. Blackwell often cites God as the inspiration and protector for her endeavors. To wit, "[What I do here] is not patting myself on the back, but it's just choosing what *God* has chosen for me." That God has chosen her is a certainty in her own mind. Leadership "is not with the people who have the money, it is not always with the people who have the know-how, and so forth. He has chosen me—a person with no money and no status. It shows you that leadership can come out of the strangest places."[44]

Other aspects of her ideological perspective are mostly secular-based. A good sample of these include the commitment to integration, the centrality of blacks to social change, and a grand vision for the political community. Also important are sacrifice, the rural community ethos, and a "third world" perspective.

Integration was the guiding force for her work in the civil rights movement. Her vision of integration in America is one where blacks will have full and equal access to all benefits of society. It was a given that she rejected the southern racial exclusion that remained in the 1960s. Her ideas, at least on this, were very much like those of Martin Luther King, Jr., whose "ultimate goal [was] genuine intergroup and interpersonal living—*integration*." Moreover, "we are tied together in the single garment of destiny, caught in an inescapable network of mutuality."[45]

The depth of Mrs. Blackwell's commitment to this perspective is best illustrated in her response to the issue of white participation in local affairs in Mayersville. Obviously the substantially larger black voting bloc could effectively eliminate all white participation. This circumstance arose immediately after the incorporation process when Mrs. Blackwell was nominated as interim mayor. It was also necessary to appoint a board of aldermen and women. The overwhelmingly black audience desired a complete takeover. Mrs. Blackwell argued, however, that everybody had to live in the town in some peace and that some compromise was in order. "Let us find out [whether] we want to start our town off this way, or do we want to find out if we can work together?" After polling the people "some said [it should be] all black, and some said we'll give them one seat. . . . I said, how about two seats? After some discussion this was agreed."[46] She has said that this illustrates how to achieve the good in society, without flaunting power.

Notwithstanding devotion to the notion of integration, she also believes that blacks are at the forefront of social change. She asserts that as an oppressed group, blacks have historically been more apt to understand and to support fundamental change. Definitionally, this is akin to some contemporary thinkers who argue that the most serious movements for social change always emerge in this or similarly oppressed communities. Usually these materialist scholars believe that a change always goes from the bottom up because of the inherent oppressed conditions there; revolt is inevitable, at least in the classical statement of this view.

Mrs. Blackwell is in agreement with this. She elaborates when asked if her being black gives her greater potential for achievement. "There is something in us—being in a suppressed situation—some drive." Since blacks have always had to struggle against "suppression," they maintain a special expertise on the problem and are obligated to keep such issues before the larger community. "I don't think whites have the 'get up' and drive; they have had access up to a point."[47] She describes how local whites thwarted their own progress because of efforts to restrict blacks. Many times, she says, whites withdrew from or denied themselves things in order to deny blacks.

That this specialness exists can be sustained by a reading of history. She sees blacks being in the vanguard of social change as an enduring phenomenon. It is a part of a long historical process (Harding's river)[48] whereby blacks have resisted and proposed alternatives to the racial divide. "In history the aggressiveness and push for a change has always come from us . . . , from slavery on up. . . . Any change that you now see . . . it is the blacks that have laid their lives on the line and have died." She uses the emancipation as an example: "These kinds of things even put Abraham Lincoln in the position that he could sign the paper" freeing blacks.[49] Or it can be observed in the history of Issaquena County. The roles of her ancestor by marriage, Saul Blackwell, and the other reconstruction leaders, are cited as examples of the continuity of blacks in the efforts for social change. Aside from forming her ideological base, this continuity allows her to explain the necessity of continued involvement for local blacks.

Sacrifice is important to Mrs. Blackwell's ideology as she seeks to be at one with the sentimentalities and realities of the local people. As such her personal life is simple and quite consistent with that of a wide variety of local black citizens. Her sacrifice, like theirs, is that she endures the harsh terms of existence in a poor, rural town. In Mayersville there are hardly any options. But for those who stay, life is a constant struggle of managing extreme scarcity. Inhabitants either work on farms or work in surrounding towns where there are small industries or service sectors (Mayersville has neither of the latter). The choice to remain, or to be forced to remain, virtually relegates one to a life in impoverished conditions.

The mayor's personal existence is a testament to the nature of the sacrifice. She alludes to having not been gainfully employed since she was barred from the cotton fields in the mid-1960s. Yet, in point of fact, few are engaged in this activity as technology has displaced this labor. The mayor's point is telling, however, as it illustrates that for those who stay, there is very little to do. She ekes out an existence, as does everybody else. While what she gets in the way of perquisites resulting from her official positions does distance her considerably from others, she gets but $100 per month as mayor, and $50 per month as judge. Other monies come from consultancies and the like. She explains her ability to get along as a product of her upbringing. "We learned to make it with nothing, more or less. And it has been helpful; that skill has really been helpful in terms of getting this town off the ground."

Meanwhile, the strong ideological posture is strengthened by a special sense of "rural place" in American society. Much of the reason why she remains in Mayersville is because its flatlands along the banks of the Mississippi River represent a place and a style of life which she has always known. She sees special virtue in the opportunities that rural living provides, with the accompanying values of family and small-scale participation. There are examples that she regularly uses to illustrate these points, especially given the breakdown in such values elsewhere. The migration of youth to urban centers is lamented because they lack understanding of the rural virtues of "closeness . . . [that] really makes man work and survive." Moreover, "I have found [by] traveling in other countries and other parts of the world, that people don't really know what they have here." A good part of the understanding they lack, she continues, is how much potential they (especially blacks) have for reorienting the political system. All this emerges from voter registration, which then allows one to build a power base in such small-scale communities that can last from one generation to the next.

Her vision about the importance of the rural area is broader still. She describes rural areas as the backbone of the American civilization and economy, believing if places like Mayersville are abandoned, then a decline in the entire economic system will follow. In this sense she makes the classical argument that the traditional rural areas are the breadbasket of the country. Though technology has affected rural areas, "machines cannot run unless somebody runs them. I don't even think the rural people [themselves] really understand their importance to the rest of the world. Without the farmers, our prices in Chicago or New York City . . . for groceries will skyrocket." She used the drought of 1981 to illustrate. "Regarding soybeans . . . we were all crying for rain. So we got some today. [But] if we don't get a certain amount of rain, to produce a certain amount of beans . . . it hurts everybody [who has] got to go out and buy anything. . . . You see, Wall Street cannot be there unless some of us out here are doing the things we are doing."[50] Therefore, her vision is that people ought to remain in and be proud of these areas because of their centrality to the entire American social and political system, Being located in such an area gives one a special position in the hierarchy of national values.

This vision is completed by the innovative and bold manner by which she attempts to convince local Mayersvillians of their connection to the rest of the world. Mrs. Blackwell argues that the strong interest she has in social and political change is consistent with the perspective of Third World people who have taken courageous steps to alter their existence. She believes, as did the SNCC with its Pan-African and Third World ideology, that local conditions of racial oppression could be equated with the conditions of people of color everywhere, especially those colonized.[51] Black people were "caught up with a sense of destiny with the vast majority of colored people all over the world who are becoming conscious of their power and the role they must play in the world."[52] She believes that blacks have much to gain from the knowledge of others' campaigns for change.

One practical example shows the extent to which Mrs. Blackwell has assimilated these arguments—her interpretation of her Chinese experience. She intimates that seeing the revolutionary changes on the first trip to China taught her a lesson about conditions in America. She describes how communal efforts among the rural Chinese have led to so many national achievements, in the face of circumstances similar to those in rural America. Theirs was a struggle, too, since the old forces had to be swept away. They had achieved:

> . . . the almost universal availability of health services . . . [and] the young were taught from early childhood to cooperate rather than compete. . . . One of the things I learned in China was who I was and what I could do and to assess what has been done in the struggle of black people in America. So I came home with a greater sense of purpose that the struggle I was in was more important than personalities. The struggle is against oppression and three-fourths of this world is with you. . . . Now I don't mind sitting here being black and [a] minority in this country because I'm black and [a] majority in the world.[53]

The upshot of these ideas is that they constituted a fresh, new perspective of possibilities in a desperately poor rural area. Mrs. Blackwell assimilated these ideas and used them in a manner that was challenging and sympathetic to her environment. She dared in the heyday of the movement to think and utter these thoughts in a town where the risks were great for her personal safety and that of the black community. Her courageousness in standing firm indicates a part of the independence and tenacity necessary for accomplishment of heroic feats. In her stated ideological commitment she was seen to achieve changes vital to black American betterment.

EDUCATION

Still another example of Mrs. Blackwell's heroism and innovation is illustrated in her activities towards education, when little was noteworthy about local schools. She had a strong interest in education that was sustained by memories of her own experiences of oppression. For her, like so many others, "education is valued . . . highly . . . as an instrument of partial or total escape from whatever the oppression happens to be—sex, race, age, religion."[54]

At the time Mayersville schools remained segregated with blacks, as she puts it, only "receiving the hand-me-downs" from the white schools. There was apparently little independent expenditure on basic school materials, for even textbooks were sent to blacks only after being discarded at white schools. In Mrs. Blackwell's mind this was only one of a variety of practices that relegated blacks to low educational achievement. Like Len Holt, she wondered: "Is there guilt in having a reality made of fictions when the manipulators [power structure] deny access to other than make-believe?" The whites could "seek their philosophical escape from their hells in a caricature, which mawkishly causes their whiteishness to shout . . . 'All is well.'" For blacks, though, "the public schools are the arch tools of the fictions and the conformity to 'Alice in Mississippi-land,' which answer the Negroes' question of 'Who am I'? with the word 'Nigger.'"[55] Thus Mrs. Blackwell wondered what future her own son could expect if the system continued. She, her husband and other parents determined to mobilize the black community for change.

The initial activity that challenged the education structure was the freedom school. The ideas for these "freedom schools" were propagated by Mrs. Blackwell in the early 1960s when she had responsibility for a six-county area as a SNCC field worker. They provided an alternative to the existing school system by extending the regular school curriculum materials on the one hand, and by fundamentally challenging it on the other. The argument of Mrs. Blackwell and SNCC workers was that the schools performed little of their desired function in preparing black children for the opportunities available. They felt that this was by design, and that alternative learning facilities could serve as a supplement. Moreover, the freedom schools could be used as a vehicle for educating people about change and the requirements for mobilization. Thus the schools were to be an arm of the movement. Subsequently, the first few of these schools were a direct part of the consolidated 1964 statewide campaign dubbed "freedom summer" or "Mississippi summer."[56] They would "fill an intellectual and creative vacuum and [get] young Black Mississippians . . . to articulate their own desires, demands and questions,"[57] or to "provide an educational experience for students which will make it possible for them to challenge the myths of our society, to perceive more clearly its realities, and to find alternatives, and, ultimately, new direction for action."[58]

These schools were not just limited to children. Eventually there was as much involvement on the part of older persons who received political education. The emphasis for them, who attended rallies at the centers or who met with the children's teachers, was "to help them to understand themselves, and thereby to understand their society and the need to change it . . . . to take themselves seriously, to articulate their ambitions and their discontents."[59]

Mrs. Blackwell became heavily involved in this effort in her six-county area, but it is in the statewide organization that the full flavor of the challenge is revealed. In combination with existing volunteers, this massive challenge to the Mississippi authorities called for 1,000 new volunteers to staff these schools.[60] Between 650 and 700 "young people, mostly Northerners and mostly white and mostly students"[61] arrived. They plunged immediately into a full-scale style of integrated living never experienced before. They were rapidly given assignments and ferreted out to well over 40 centers in every area of the state.[62] New volunteers worked and planned with local black leaders or SNCC field workers. Mrs. Blackwell was one of these local leaders overseeing and planning the work of these students.

The formal curriculum of the schools varied but there were certain basic ingredients. "The courses included normal academic subjects, contemporary issues, cultural expression, and leadership development, the last course covering the history of the black liberation movement and the study of political skills."[63] A "Curriculum Guide for Freedom Schools" provided a list of penetrating questions that helped the volunteers focus their teaching on the racial reality and how to challenge and change it.[64] Formal academic subjects might include literature, political science, or French as dictated by student demands or volunteer skills.[65] Curriculum was also dictated by issues in a local community, such as fire-bombings or economic reprisals. Limitations sometimes resulted because resource materials, such as books, were scarce or unavailable. Most such resource materials were donated in any case, and making do with what was available led to frequent improvisation.[66]

In addition to involvement in the broader campaign, Mrs. Blackwell assisted in founding several schools in her local area, an act that flew in the face of physical dangers to herself and clients because of widespread terror against such schools. At least four of these schools were organized, all in churches in and around Mayersville. The Rose Hill Baptist Church Center was located right in town and also accommodated mass meetings for COFO and the MFDP. The other centers were in the outlying communities of Valewood, Tallula and Hopedale.

It is not known how many students were served. The numbers were undoubtedly sizable since the Issaquena County freedom schools developed in direct response to the massive expulsion of blacks from the public schools. As will be detailed in the succeeding section, they had been expelled for wearing "freedom buttons." The freedom schools accommodated these students, whose parents sued the public schools (a suit initiated by the Blackwells) and instituted a boycott for the remainder of the academic year. Meanwhile the high school students in this lot, some of the most highly mobilized and enterprising, were sufficient to establish a local newspaper. Their rhetoric challenging the educational structure easily matched that of their parents.[67]

The challenge of the alternative school went far beyond re-education and supplementary education. These factors were important enough because they presented a fundamentally different view of racial history for blacks. Yet it was more mundane matters that created heroes and innovators out of rural workers like Mrs. Blackwell in Mississippi. The greatest challenge to white supremacists was how these schools symbolized an integrated life. In little isolated towns like Mayersville, black children and civil rights workers of all colors could be seen consorting together. The perception of the white Mississippian was that interracial intimacies were occurring that threatened "white supremacy" and violated "white virtue." Equally forceful in this symbolic sense was the "loss of control" that authorities experienced because events were occurring so fast and with such force that routine measures rarely worked. After all, there was no white solidarity to be appealed to regarding the white "outside agitators;" their avowed purpose was to destroy the white authority structure.

The local whites responded violently in a way that created crisis, but also provided continuous opportunities for intensified mobilization. They did so in traditional ways designed to put "blacks back into their places." A favored tactic was the exercise of economic reprisals against local leaders. Mrs. Blackwell is a prime example. Her meager income from chopping and picking cotton quickly evaporated after she was identified as the "ringleader" in the Mayersville area. Plantation owners simply refused to hire her. Not only was she a personal target, but so were her associates and the black institutional facilities utilized for the schools. Many black parents who sought to enroll their children in integrated schools lost their plantation jobs and were evicted from homes there. The Ku Klux Klan was also very active, at least at cross burnings. On a single night twelve crosses were burned in Issaquena and adjoining Sharkey counties.[68] The plantation owner adjacent to a black church threatened to burn it down if civil rights activities there did not cease. Another church, St. John's at Valewood, served a similar function and was destroyed by fire.

Despite a highly mobilized effort on the part of state authorities, Freedom Summer continued. It attracted something over 2,000 students, but it also led local leaders to become much more of an organized force for post-summer work. Many of the schools continued after northern volunteers left.[69] It was in this context that Mrs. Blackwell and her associates spread the freedom school model throughout the county. The summer activation provided a cadre of farmers, church deacons, students and retired persons to continue teaching youngsters in the four local schools. In the context of mobilization, this indicated broad organizational commitment to the ideology of change, and active work in obtaining new benefits. Mrs. Blackwell's success in this campaign finally settled the question of who would lead the continuing mobilization drive in Mayersville. In her, most agreed they had found the appropriate home-grown leader.

Mrs. Blackwell's next challenge was to the orthodox school system on its own territory, since the alternative schools were never designed to fully meet all educational requirements. In 1965 she and her husband began a major assault upon the inequities between local black and white schools and continued segregation in violation of the Brown decision. Their action followed not only a growing concern by parents, but also the mobilization of their children in other aspects of the local campaign. Again Mrs. Blackwell was at the center of an activist effort that escalated to provide favorable opportunities for broader realization of practical goals.

In January 1965, a number of students at the all-black Henry Weathers High School wore buttons to school that bore the acronym SNCC and a black and white hand clasped together. Many were openly discussing the civil rights movement and the implications of the buttons. Consistent with the harsh sanctions usually associated with any such activity, the principal ordered the buttons removed and threatened further action if buttons reappeared or disturbances ensued. The students were hardly deterred. Well over a hundred of them returned the next school day wearing the buttons and still more in succeeding days. The principal proceeded to expel those involved, which amounted to well over 300 students in Issaquena County. Moreover, since the students also instituted a boycott of classes, the principal ruled that those who remained absent for 20 days would be expelled for the rest of the year.

Since the town of Mayersville was already in a state of mobilization, the Blackwells set about organizing a campaign to have the students reinstated. They first made an appeal to the black principal, which was not satisfactory. Later the all-white school board was approached, also without relief. Subsequently the Blackwells and other parents conducted a broad educational program to convince others that the children's campaign was legitimate and that litigation was necessary. Many parents rapidly agreed to support a court challenge. They turned to the NAACP, where Mrs. Blackwell's influence was instrumental in securing immediate involvement from lawyers in Jackson. Moreover, this was seen as a fitting case for the NAACP, whose highly organized challenges to segregation were much a part of the mobilization.

The grounds on which the Issaquena case was brought were violation of the First Amendment right of free speech and the Fourteenth Amendment equal protection clause. The parents argued that their children were denied their constitutional right to free expression when barred from wearing the "freedom buttons." At the same time their expulsion was deemed to be an unequal application of school "discretion." Their claims were bolstered by a partially favorable ruling in a similar case in Philadelphia, Mississippi. There, high school students had also been expelled for wearing buttons that read "One Man One Vote" and "SNCC." Their parents sued on the grounds that rights protected by the First and Fourteenth Amendments had been violated. The Federal District Court agreed:

> [The] high school regulation prohibiting students from wearing 'freedom buttons,' which had the words 'One Man One Vote' and 'SNCC' and which did not appear to hamper school in carrying out its regular schedule of activities, was arbitrary and unreasonable and an unnecessary infringement on students' protected right of free expression, and refusal to grant application for preliminary relief (in the lower Court) was an abuse of discretion.[70]

In Issaquena County, however, the case turned on the activities that accompanied the wearing of buttons. In the court proceedings it was noted that

Issaquena students not only used the buttons as a symbol, but used them to engender discussion about local issues. None of this was denied. (The students reported concern with issues of school operation, curriculum and resources.) The school administration went further with its charges. The Trustees' affidavit said: "Many of these children were accosting other students in the corridors whether they wanted them or not, and generally tried to persuade all of the students to wear and exhibit these buttons."[71] The principal gave a more detailed explanation.

> On February 1, 1965, more than one hundred students came to school wearing these buttons. Hazel Lamb, a teacher, reported to me that students were going up and down the corridor passing out buttons to those who did not have them and pinning buttons on other students who did not do so voluntarily. I investigated the matter and found this to be true. This activity on their part had created a state of confusion and had disrupted the orderly procedure at school. I assembled all the students wearing buttons at the cafeteria and requested that they remove the buttons so that some order of discipline could be restored. Two students were particularly hostile to my request and displayed a nasty attitude.
>
> At this time some of the students had on as many as three buttons varying in size. At this meeting several of the students present took over from their leader and one boy, Dan White, went so far as to call me 'Uncle Tom.'[72]

It is not inconsistent that these issues were raised, for they were integrally linked to others already under discussion. Mrs. Blackwell and the local cadre were constantly talking about education as the key to full realization of most other goals. Indeed, voter registration was regarded as but a necessary first step that would make it possible to confront other aspects of the segregated system. Since educational change was so critical to Mrs. Blackwell's vision, the students were a strategic part of the general mobilization campaign. She reasons even today that the buttons were merely a means for opening up the question of how blacks were to be educated equitably.

Despite the energy that went into the case, with many parents offering depositions, this was one of the few instances in which the Federal Circuit Court was to rule against the interests of the black mobilization. The same judge who had ruled favorably in the Philadelphia case, did not find the pleadings in Mayersville and Issaquena County acceptable. He ruled that the activities of the students in this case had exceeded those rights protected by the First and Fourteenth Amendments. It was first established that freedom of speech was not absolute: "Constitutional guarantee of freedom of speech does not confer an absolute right to speak and law recognizes that there can be an abuse of such freedom." The activities of the students, beyond merely "expressing" themselves, the judge argued, were abusive of the rights of others.

> Where the record showed unusual degree of commotion, boisterous conduct, collision with rights of others and undermining of authority as result of school students wearing and distributing "freedom buttons" which depicted a black and white hand joined and word "SNCC" regulation of school authorities

prohibiting students from wearing such buttons was reasonable, so that refusal to grant preliminary injunction to restrain enforcement of such regulation was not abuse of discretion.[73]

However, there was another vital question on which the parents had sought a ruling. They asked the court to "enjoin the defendant school authorities from operating compulsory racially segregated schools." That is, they took this opportunity to make the major assault that local leaders thought was the broader problem. And on this point they won the assent of the court. The judge ruled that the previous negotiated agreement that only allowed voluntary integration of schools was unacceptable because it in no way guaranteed the process. This set the stage for the appointment of a court master who oversaw the development of elaborate desegregation plans for transferring black and white students. The early favorable ruling in Issaquena County put the area in the forefront of what became a consolidated court challenge to remaining segregation all over Mississippi.[74] But for Mrs. Blackwell the mere mobilization of her constituents around this single issue is regarded as a masterful achievement. Though almost all of the white students eventually withdrew from the school system, blacks perceive that they are ahead because of the improved resources and access they obtained in all public schools.

Incorporation

Little symbolizes or illustrates the heroic and inventive acts of Unita Blackwell in the Mayersville mobilization as the achievement of town incorporation. She achieved this status for the town in late 1976, and was thereupon appointed its first mayor. Before, Mrs. Blackwell says, Mayersville was merely a "village." Whatever independent affairs were carried out by Mayersvillians were done in the context of the county, of which the town was the seat. Though the county offices were always located there, this did not provide for the local "personality," or any independent development or vision for the future. Nurturance of the town was not the concern of those who lived within its boundaries; indeed it had no boundaries.

In her mind, lack of incorporation created certain critical problems. In an abstract way a town without this formal status was unlikely to make any progress in the contemporary political arena. Unofficially designated towns did not even show up in the record books. In addition, she already knew that many of the federal programs awarded to Mississippi towns were unavailable to Mayersville as long as it remained an unincorporated town. If any of the benefits she had held out before her "constituents"—both black and white—were to be realized, Mayersville had to become a fully recognized town. This was especially important for blacks. Mrs. Blackwell had seen the continuous decline in the town's population, its agricultural base, and the socioeconomic status of virtually everyone. The blacks who remained were hardest hit by these circumstances. Their traditional jobs in the cotton fields were disappearing, and few other options appeared. The blacks who remained therefore were largely in a state of subsistence. Mrs. Blackwell believed that incorporation would improve their lot considerably by either providing jobs or supplements for the basic necessities that most Americans enjoyed.

Others were long aware of the problems the lack of status created for the town. However, it seems that prior to the civil rights movement, county politicians saw little or no need to change the status. Their livelihood was based on farm ownership. Their decreased agricultural production was in fact encouraged and their economic shortfalls sustained by federal subsidies. Many of these farmers also did not live in the "village" proper; they lived in plantation houses in the outlying farms or in adjoining counties. Incorporation was of no immediate concern to them, but would be of prime benefit to their former black laborers who did live in the village. Mrs. Blackwell suggests that the latter reasoning, combined with ignorance, explains why no one ever pursued the arrangement of townhood. "[Townspeople] had been asking the men around to do it. And none of the men would take it. . . . They had been asking the Board of Supervisors. One of them was black [and] he didn't bother to mess with it either, [he] had no interest. . . . [But] another thing I found out [was] that they really didn't know how to do it. And they just didn't want to venture out."[75]

Once the soon-to-be mayor took on this project, the task seemed daunting, requiring skills that she did not have. Perhaps this was what had deterred others in the past. But she was undaunted, and applied her personal instincts and style to management of the issue. She held the firm commitment that in a true democracy it was inconceivable that the system could not be negotiated, even by the average citizen. To be sure, she was operating with deficits that neither of the other two mayors in this study possessed: the absence of college and higher educational experiences. The leadership cadre around the state with which she had consorted had been a full education in itself, however, that gave her more of the skills and still more access to expertise than was readily obvious. She brought all of these to bear. In the end she acquired the required lawyers, engineers, airplanes (for surveying) and a full complement of paraphernalia with which to present her case.

The initial phases of the work required Mrs. Blackwell to talk with state officials and lawyers about the requirements for incorporation. She did this and in short order discovered that the process could only be set in motion on the basis of a formal referendum, in which the concerned community expressed its desire for the status.[76]

This was to require a major organizational campaign that would be more challenging than most local organizational work Mrs. Blackwell had done for voter registration or school desegregation. The latter two could be achieved in stages, over time. The referendum, however, required everyone to exercise judgment at an agreed-upon time, as in an election. The trick was to politically educate the constituents so that the importance of the measure would be understood, and then to get them to a central meeting place for the vote. To do this, "first I used the style I know best—this is to organize people [by] call[ing] a meeting. I called a meeting in the church . . . [to which] everybody that showed up was black."[77] At this meeting the virtues of achieving new status were explained and a consensus to go forward was reached. From this group she selected a team of eight people to do a house-to-house survey to verify the broader commitment of all citizens in Mayersville.

The house-to-house campaign was organized around a "survey instrument" that Mrs. Blackwell and the group had prepared. It asked simply whether one wanted the town to be incorporated. This detailed work was required in order to guarantee the participation of at least two-thirds of those registered in the upcoming vote. This process, according to Mrs. Blackwell, was completed in two days, to the amazement of the lawyers who advised her. But this was not the end because a series of meetings were still required for explanation of additional details prior to the formal vote. It appears that all of this went rather smoothly, including the final vote. Indeed, it was a lone white, Mrs. Blackwell reports, who refused to sign. His reasoning was that "he didn't know what he was signing and . . . wasn't going to fool with it."[78]

It is of note that once this campaign was afoot, there was no obvious racial divide within the community. In part this was due to the political education that accompanied the effort. The literature in circulation did not make any obvious appeal on the basis of race. Instead it singled out the improvements that were bound to occur for the town—there would be a water system, sewers, and all of the usual service items, which in the short run were likely to be more beneficial to whites than to blacks. (The blacks, for example, would have to bear considerable independent costs in using a sewer system because most did not even have the common indoor plumbing which utilized a cesspool; pit latrine toilets were still widely used.) Therefore, most citizens did not see that they would be especially disadvantaged by such a change. The whites who were skeptical recognized this as a part of the general degree of black mobilization, but did not see this to be as threatening as some of the other measures that had occurred in their recent past, such as voter registration.

Much more than mere organization of a referendum was required. Mrs. Blackwell also had to spend considerable time demarcating boundaries and thinking about resource capabilities. It was in this phase that the considerable outside resources available to her were useful. To this end she enjoyed the services of black attorneys in nearby Greenville. They helped her research the problem and to execute appropriate documents. There were local meetings with farmers whose land within the new corporate limit would be taxed. This was a delicate phase because "some white farmers were shook up [at the thought] of having to pay [such] taxes." Discussions showing them how "they would have to give a little if they wanted the best for people in the community"[79] eased this somewhat. Afterward the engineers and airplane surveyors completed their task of setting boundaries. This was followed up with complicated discussions regarding a municipal tax. (As an unincorporated area, Mayersville had no provision for raising taxes or for being a center of government business.)

In short order, the last meeting to vote on the final decree was scheduled. It was here that all present, except for one, signed the document after appointing an interim government. The crowning achievement for Mrs. Blackwell's leadership was her unanimous selection by the body to hold the office of mayor. Thus she became Mississippi's first black woman mayor that we can identify in history, and the first black mayor ever in Issaquena County. The latter is especially significant because this delta county had such a large number of officials during reconstruction, none of whom, as far as is known, was a woman. An ironic twist is that in a delta town where the racial divide was maintained with such fervor in the past, it was a white farmer who put Mrs. Blackwell's name in nomination for mayor. She says, "the place was packed that night, and a white fella stood up in the back of the room and said, "I nominate Unita Blackwell for mayor. She knows what this stuff is all about, and I think she should be the mayor.'" With a second to the nomination, they proceeded to discuss and negotiate for the other offices.[80] Her heroism and inventor capability thus noted, Mrs. Blackwell continued in her role as premier leader in Mayersville. She was now in a position to execute the feasibility studies and applications for a wide range of projects she had promised earlier on. Then in 1977, when regular elections were scheduled, as expected, she easily won this first electoral campaign.

Conclusion

This episode is one of the briefest in Mrs. Blackwell's career, but it may be the most important in illustrating her heroic and visionary role in contemporary Mayersville. Her actions in achieving incorporation of the town are the quintessence of what the local constituents see as her special ability to adapt to the needs of the community. While hardly any other single individual may have had the confidence to seek incorporation, such an action which gave Mayersville "status" certainly was desired. But most Mayersvillians had no idea how to bring such a dream to reality, or even how to articulate it. They also needed her forceful personality in combining the broad range of educational issues and mastery of local idioms for mobilization. Mrs. Blackwell was successful because of the way she captured constituent sentiments on these issues and gave them definition. The rallying around her by the locals gives every indication that they understood and accepted the connections she was making regarding problems and opportunities. In short, we observe a good degree of merger between the Blackwell personality and the fluid environment in Mayersville. That the town was open to her suggestions and to some degree malleable made it quite safe for Unita Blackwell to put her mark on local history.

The perception of Mrs. Blackwell's inventive and heroic contributions are widely felt and articulated. In the first place, it is not uncommon even today to find people in and outside Mayersville who credit Mrs. Blackwell with "founding" the town. They mean that she had given it its first significant definition in history. Before, many citizens imply, Mayersville was merely a place whose definition was little more than that of myriad communities named after churches that dotted the rural landscape here and there. There was no power that went along with the small settlement along the banks of the Mississippi. The campaigns led by Mrs. Blackwell had changed all that.

5

Agrarian Townsman in Tchula

The delta, of which Tchula is thought by sentiment and livelihood to be a part, is very flat. In the geographic sense Tchula is a part of this flatland, but it is just at the edge of the bluff hills. Arriving by road from the East, the descent from the modest hills is perceptible. That this is the largest of the three communities examined shows the instant the town's center is seen. There is a business district with its main street and several others running perpendicular thereto. A portion of a through road (U.S. 49) also constitutes a major part of this district. Included in local businesses are grocery, department and hardware stores, a bank, an auto dealer, etc. It looks every bit the small town center for a delta community. Its population of just under 2,000 is a tremendous increase over its 800 plus in 1960, when there was an expansion of the city limit. One does not see cotton fields amidst this city center as might be the case in many smaller delta towns. Rather one sees the small clump of houses that surrounds the business district and effectively blocks the not-far-distant cotton and soybean fields. For it is these crops that give a sense of place to Tchula, as is the case in Mayersville. Though there is a factory here and there in the county, the base for financial resources is still agriculture. Riding into Tchula one is struck by its tranquil and old-fashioned appearance, with men about on "lazy benches." All this belies a five-to seven-year period of extreme change and great political conflict. Such a

Figure 5.1 Town of Tchula, Mississippi, ca. 1980.

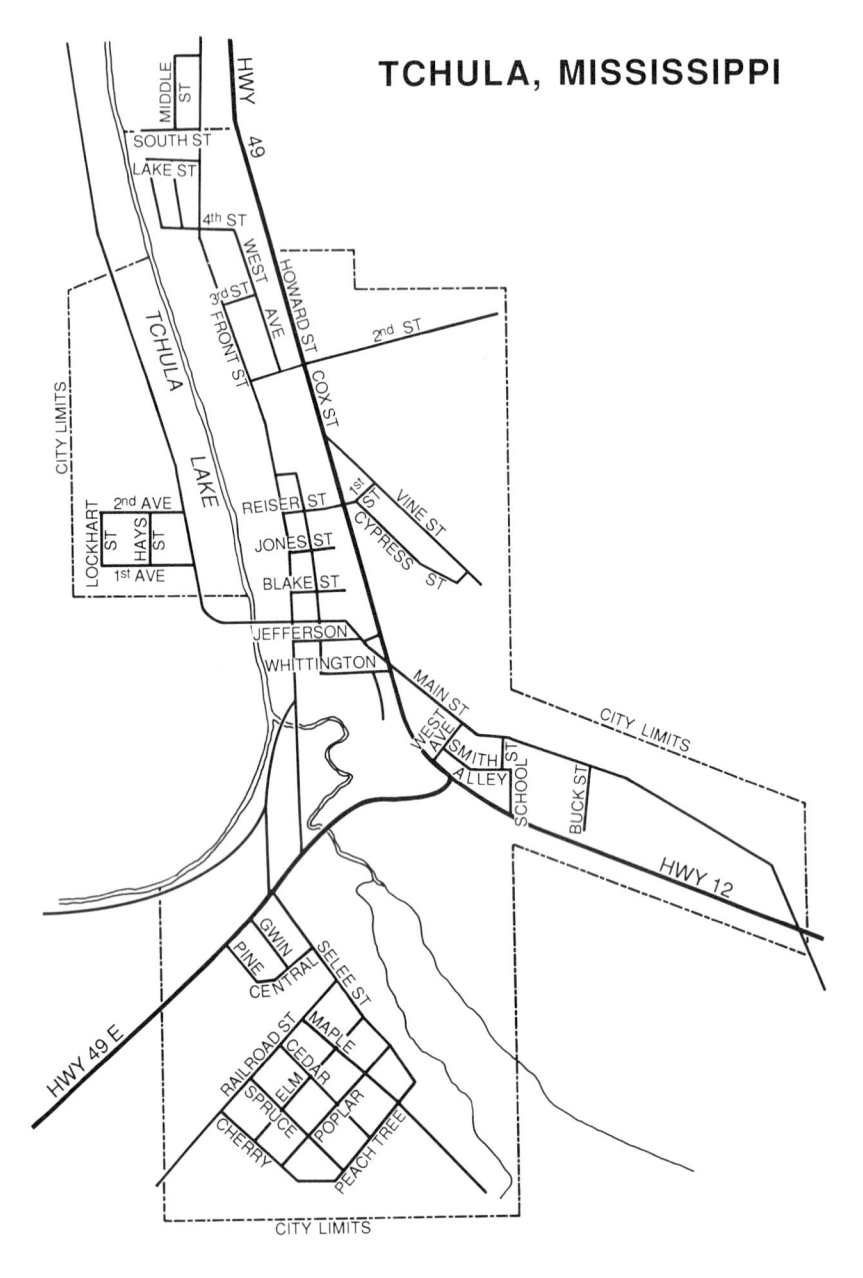

Adapted from a map by Southern Engineering (1979).

small place has been described, not entirely incorrectly, as seething with dissent.

The contemporary era of intense political mobilization of the black community in Tchula and surrounding Holmes County may easily be dated back to 1968. It was then that Robert Clark became the first black since reconstruction to win a post in the state legislature. This was widely seen as the beginning of the phase when blacks moved from the streets to the elected political sector. Yet it was to be nearly 10 years, 1977, before the substantial black majority in Tchula was to achieve municipal success. In that year Eddie Carthan, who was running for the office for the first time, was elected mayor. In that particular campaign he had been opposed by two whites (one the incumbent), and another black (who had run for the office before). At the same time four other blacks won aldermanic posts; the fifth position was won by a white farmer. Though the black candidates originally planned to run as a slate, in the end they split into two blocs. Thus, unlike in Bolton and Mayersville, the political mobilization did not yield a victory sustained by solidarity. In the town of Tchula a large number of blacks were swept into office, perhaps on the mayor's coattails, but with considerable differences in outlook on the task of black betterment. This ignited the intense conflict that affected the rule and partial failure of the agrarian townsman.

This analysis also begins with a brief historical overview that shows both the paucity of black political activity in the area and white extremism. Much of this can be related to the harsh economic conditions of Tchula and Holmes County. Relatively recent history showed that the old patterns remained much the same. The early mobilization movement was greatly affected, for example, by efforts of the White Citizen's Council to maintain white supremacy. These efforts, often violent, were exercised as much against progressive local whites as blacks. Yet because of and in spite of such reaction, an intense mobilization, part of the civil rights movement, occurred in Tchula and the surrounding county.

However, when political power was achieved at the pinnacle of the mobilization, the analysis shows a rapid deterioration due to conflict. In accounting for the rise and fall of Mayor Eddie Carthan, the focus is on both interracial and intraracial conflict within the leadership class. The administration of the agrarian townsman was almost immediately marred by disagreements with some black aldermen about who should rule, and by a white alderman who exploited the dissension. In the end, the combination of forces led to a host of legal charges against the mayor that culminated with his removal from office. He was to endure a long cycle of trials—many of which had political motivations—and was imprisoned. Ultimately, most of the new black leaders (including the opposition) were decimated and the former white leadership returned to power.

The Political and Economic Development of Tchula and Holmes County

Tchula became a town in 1833[1] and was integrated into Holmes County, an area topographically astraddle the hills and the delta. Cotton agriculture characterized the economic activity, which led to a larger black population. Relative to the other towns in this study, however, this area of mixed topography was always poorer. Plantations here were smaller than in Hinds or Issaquena, and had fewer laborers. Scores of farms in the latter counties had over 100 enslaved laborers, compared to a mere six farms in Holmes in 1860. Moreover, the county ratio of blacks to whites, prior to the Civil War, was just over 60 per cent.[2] True to the intensive labor demands of cotton, productivity was always low. In 1850 a mere 12,635 bales were ginned. This improved to 40,000 in 1860, but ten years later declined to 19,027.[3] The war exacerbated these dire economic conditions when dislocations virtually cut off this interior county from waterways for marketing.[4]

The isolation of blacks was so nearly complete, and maintained with such severity, that there is little known successful local political activity among them after the war. There is notice of one who served as sheriff,[5] but no others. Moreover, their activity at the state level was also less salient. No black participated in the constitutional convention of 1868, but six served in the lower house between 1870 and 1880 (without distinction, according to one scholar).[6] Some of this was a product of the size of the black population in the 1860s, but much of it was sustained by white violence. The success of terror groups like the Heggies Scouts in harassing, injuring or killing blacks involved in politics was widely recognized. Their tactics were so feared that no blacks (unlike in other counties) appeared before the U.S. Senate committee investigating illegal disfranchisement efforts after the war. Two whites who did appear indicated great fear of retaliation.[7] Consequently, there was never any great need for fusion politics to take hold in the area. The dominant white politicians remained in control, even though the war devastated their economy.

The county and the town rebounded somewhat in the mid-1880s with the introduction of the railroads. The agricultural sector thrived, especially in that part of the county near Tchula, and created a pattern of near-servitude for blacks that continued until contemporary mobilization began in the 1950s. Eventually two railroad lines traversed Tchula[8], connecting the town with Memphis and New Orleans. While the black population grew to accommodate the new labor needs, their political participation was naught. There was no black legislator here after 1880.

The Last Stand of White Resisters: The Citizens' Council and White Supremacy

There was to be little independent Afro-American participation in the mainstream of county affairs until the late 1960s. Yet significant markers in the recent political history of the county show the developing activation of blacks favoring social change, and the extremism of whites supporting segregation. Elements on both sides adopted quite radical measures as they pressed forward.

It is against this backdrop that Eddie Carthan, the agrarian townsman, emerged in the 1970s.

The spotlight began to focus on Tchula and Holmes County in the early 1950s, not just because of local black resistance (which remained of little consequence), but because of the reaction of white segregationists to racial changes occurring elsewhere. The "diehard" perspective of the whites made them feel threatened by the increased national acceptance of integration. As such, the Brown decision on public schools excited more immediate interest in Holmes County than in many other delta counties. Tchula and the large towns in the surrounding counties of Indianola, Sunflower and Leflore became a center of organized white resistance to potential school integration. The area was significant not merely because of a congeries of disgruntled residents. It also boasted support and encouragement from one James Eastland of Sunflower County, then senior U.S. Senator from Mississippi, whose sentiments for the preservation of segregation and white supremacy were well known. For example, he had used both his powerful office as chairman of the Senate Judiciary Committee and his party seniority to block virtually any legislation that had an avowed aim of furthering the civil rights of black people.[9] These forces soon formally organized and called their movement the White Citizens' Council.

The catalyst for the development of this new organization was first and foremost the desire to keep the schools segregated, but overall maintenance of white supremacy was also important. In anticipation of a favorable ruling for school integration by the Warren Court (cases pending from the NAACP),[10] white Mississippians in authoritative and powerful positions in their communities determined to resist this encroachment on states' rights. "Included among their members were bankers, industrialists, lawyers, doctors, judges, congressmen and governors."[11] The speaker of the lower house of the legislature "took up its cause,"[12] and when Ross Barnett became Governor in 1960, he boasted of his membership, appointed Council members to state offices and distributed state money to them. They (the councils):

> . . . enjoyed apparently limitless access to the corridors of state power during the administration of Governor Ross Barnett (1960-64). Indeed, by forging political alliances and adroitly manipulating public opinion, it managed so thoroughly to obscure all distinctions between public and private authority that by the early sixties the organization was the almost unchallenged arbiter of Mississippi politics.[13]

The first Council meeting at Indianola (40 or so miles from Tchula), was soon followed by an organized group in Holmes County, again including some of the most prominent white citizens. Their ideals were summed up in a primer written by Leflore County Circuit Judge Tom Brady. His arguments were the traditional ones about black inferiority and the possibilities for tainting the white race by "racial amalgamation." On pain of destruction from "the cup of black hemlock," whites had to resist if even to the point of declaring "an economic boycott" on relations of any kind with blacks.[14]

Meanwhile, in Holmes County (in the towns of Lexington and Tchula) there were already symbols of racial moderation that could provide targets for the Citizens' Council: a newspaper whose independent white owner was attacking a wide range of county privileges and illegalities, and a farm cooperative where "communal" social organization was being tried. Massive resistance was exercised in the efforts to destroy these institutions that appeared to challenge the status quo. This foretold the pattern that characterized white reaction to independent black activation for change.

Hazel Brannon Smith was the newspaper editor, an Alabamian who came to Holmes County in 1936 and in time purchased and printed four newspapers. From the early days this self-styled segregationist indicated an aversion to the usurpation of public power and the callous disrespect for common human dignities, even for blacks. At first this was to be observed in her editorial rejection of apparent widespread corruption in the county. "With the purchase of the Lexington *Advertiser* in 1943, Hazel stepped up her fight against the slot-machine operators, liquor racketeers, gamblers, and conniving officials who were finding easy pickings and little opposition in the clique-ridden rural county." In a series of exposés she subsequently succeeded in getting some public officials indicted.[15]

Later, this odd perspective (for rural Mississippi) was applied to matters regarding race relations. For the first time in memory, a local journalist began to presume standards of dignity for white behavior toward blacks. In 1954 Hazel Brannon Smith castigated the sheriff for willfully shooting a black man at a cafe, who had committed no apparent crime. She asserted that "the laws in America are for everyone . . . black and white," and continued that the sheriff "has violated every concept of justice, decency and right. He is not fit to occupy office."[16] For this the sheriff sued and won an initial judgment (later set aside) of $10,000 for libel. Undaunted, in 1954 Smith went further into the fray by reporting the shooting of a black school teacher who expressed umbrage at an act of white trespassing. The trespasser was never arrested, while both the school teacher and her husband were fired from local jobs.[17]

Fairly soon, a small rural publisher was catapulted into the role of "crusader." Increasingly the challenges of the time inspired the editor to print more and more editorial material demanding transition in race relations. These "included refusals to attack President Eisenhower for his conduct in the Little Rock imbroglio, to condemn [then state] Governor Coleman for his moderation, and to go along generally with the powerful local Citizens' Council."[18] Mrs. Smith eventually became involved with some of the more progressive forces in the state, sometimes by direct actions and other times because of her editorial comments. She received many prestigious awards for journalistic accounts,[19] was singled out by *Ebony* Magazine as an admired southern integrationist;[20] and later found herself printer for a local civil rights paper—the *Mississippi Free Press*.[21] She later sat on the local advisory committee to the Civil Rights

Commission, which produced a two-volume exposé on white violence and other violations of federal laws.[22] All of these factors earned her the infamous epithet of "nigger lover," and made her a prime target of white resisters.

The Providence Cooperative was a 2,700-acre farm run by two whites near Tchula, but which catered mostly to blacks. "For twelve years Eugene Cox and Dr. David Minter, both southerners, had worked closely as manager and physician for the white and black families" there.[23] However, the communal lifestyle adopted on the farm was perceived to threaten the very fabric of private enterprise. It was seen as communism by average white Holmes Countians. The effort to have farmers pool their resources against a presumably unfair market was anathema to them. It was especially abhorrent to the plantation farmers whose livelihood depended on the availability of cheap and unorganized black laborers. At the same time there were continuous suspicions that the presence of whites and blacks in the cooperative led to unusual interracial interaction. This perception was strengthened by the seemingly misplaced sympathies of the white leaders. They were widely perceived to be "pro-Negro" and to be using their considerable influence to instill ideas averse to the southern way of life. For example, Cox had "admitted his belief that segregation [was] unchristian."[24] And earlier Dr. Minter had testified in defense of Hazel Brannon Smith in the libel suit brought by the county sheriff. Thus the cooperative and its leadership also became targets.

The campaign against the newspaper began when the county sheriff publicly identified Hazel Brannon Smith as a threat. Initially it was thought that she could be silenced by legal entanglements or embarrassments before people whose sentiments she was supposed to know and perhaps share. Therefore, in the first phase she was merely sued, or borne upon in individual conversations to right her ways. After litigation and strategic visits from authorities and friends did not work, an advertiser boycott and public harassment ensued. Hodding Carter reports that her advertisements dropped by 50 percent and her husband was fired from his local position because "his wife has become a controversial person."[25] But none of this was to stop her; indeed the editorials seemed to harden.

The last effort was categorically designed to break her as a force in local opinion-making—the creation of an alternative newspaper. In 1958, local white citizens organized and underwrote the *Holmes County Herald*. Many of those contributing to the coffers for this new venture were founders of the local Citizens' Councils.[26] They asserted that it was necessary to have their own organ to express their sentiments which was not communist-inspired.[27] Soon the state legislature took up the cause and passed a statute purely designed to allow the town government to "produce its proceedings outside the municipality" so as to prevent transaction of business with this local editor.[28]

The preceding was but an overture as to what was to come with the cooperative, and with blacks who confronted the old ways. The targets in the coop, once again, were whites. They had already brought attention to themselves by supporting Hazel Brannon Smith, and questioning the system of segregation.

Moreover it was rumored that blacks and whites routinely interacted on the farm, a claim that caused the Citizens' Council to intervene. Amidst charges of "interracial swimming . . . and conducting mixed classes . . . advocat[ing] integration" a meeting of the Council was called in September 1955 at which the two cooperative managers were formally accused. The evidence sustaining the claims came from several young blacks who had been interrogated for allegedly "making obscene remarks at a white girl."[29] This meeting at Tchula reportedly drew 700 whites who "adopted a resolution" to the effect that "Dr. D. R. Minter and A. E. Cox . . . should move from this heavily Negro-populated area."[30]

All this was done without the cover of law, but had the force of legitimate action because of the people involved. As has been seen, the Citizens' Council in Holmes County included a good many public officials and wealthy private citizens. Therefore, as far as the average white citizens of Tchula and Holmes County were concerned, these two men were guilty and the resolution had the force of law. It was perfectly reasonable to them that refusal to obey the resolution order should be followed by other measures. Subsequently, "threats of violence were made against both men and their families and, his patients having been intimidated, Minter's medical practice fell off about 50 per cent." These actions were sometimes accompanied by equally threatening local governmental actions. "With threats of arson increasing, and a dubious roadblock arranged by the sheriff, Cox sat up, a rifle across his knees, from midnight to dawn for ten straight nights." He left the next month, while the doctor left seven or so months hence.[31]

This represented the beginning of a long and violent mobilization campaign in the struggle for civil rights in Holmes County and Tchula. In destroying these symbols, the local power structure created new opportunities for challenges to the "local way of life." Though neither Smith nor the cooperative managers saw themselves presaging transformation or giving credence to continuous black discontent, such was inevitable. Clearly, Hazel Brannon Smith's editorials were reinforced by the civil rights movement, itself buttressed by modest federal collaboration. Previously, her editorials would have been systematically ignored. However, now that information on civil rights was more widely available, segregationists were more threatened and took increasingly more direct methods to preserve the status quo. This ushered in the considerable turmoil in the county that affected the pattern of black mobilization adopted by Eddie Carthan.

The Mobilization in Tchula

As in Mayersville, Tchula was a center of concentrated action at the height of the Mississippi civil rights mobilization. Indeed, Tchula was a prime staging area for community organizers from SNCC and a center for the "Freedom Summer" campaign of 1964. The designation of Tchula as a center had to do with the perceived gravity of problems affecting black participation. Because of the almost total isolation of blacks, the level of violence against them, and the highly organized white resistance, Tchula and the surrounding area was a glaring symbol of the need for mobilization.[32]

The civil rights campaign in Tchula began relatively early and was intense. Even prior to Freedom Summer, there was some civil rights presence in support of Hazel Brannon Smith, but most work began in 1964. A number of northern workers were assigned to Holmes County, and most of them worked within a 10-mile radius between Tchula, Mileston and Lexington. Though voter registration was the initial thrust, many other issues were taken up in a comprehensive approach. There were freedom schools at Mileston and Tchula[33] that sought to develop a cadre of high school students to continue the work beyond Freedom Summer. One result of their activity was a boycott of the public school system where at least one principal sought to deny admission to students who had participated in the freedom schools.[34] But the pinnacle of achievement, which also illustrated the high level of involvement with Holmes County mobilization, was the construction of a community center near Tchula. The center was constructed at a cost of $20,000 by "white friends of our Mississippi Freedom Movement," and housed the myriad mobilization activities underway. It was of particular advantage to Holmes Countians who were turning out in such large numbers at mass meetings, but who had virtually no access to large public spaces elsewhere in the county.[35]

A report by one of the workers in August 1964 detailed some of the active projects underway and those in the planning stages. First the report indicated that five of the summer workers intended to remain instead of returning North. Programming at the center included adult literacy, clothing and food distribution, political education classes, a library, clinic, and a recreational area for dances and movies. The facility, therefore, sought to respond holistically to the needs of the community.

There were other projects on the drawing board. Discussions continued regarding a large medical clinic for the county, and for the maintenance of political education and freedom schools beyond the summer. To this end a novel program was suggested. The concept sought to have individuals or groups from the North "sponsor" local workers who would carry on movement work beyond the summer. These sponsors would provide the resources to make it possible for local people to commit their time fully. In this way the workers would not be subject to the economic reprisals so often exacted by local white employers. Another "intended consequence," according to the report, "will be the inhibition of threatened violence after the summer project is over."[36]

The reaction of the white community was immediate and intense. The most usual response was frontal or threatened assault upon civil rights workers in integrated situations. Many altercations or instances of verbal abuse occurred in the early days in public places where blacks and whites were seen together in collegial interactions. Other more frequent physical or verbal abuses occurred when such integrated groups sought to transact routine business. For example, in some situations the integrated group may have been seeking information at the town hall or the county courthouse about services. Most of the time they were denied such services in an abusive manner, ejected from the premises, or arrested. In these situations it did not matter whether these requests were usually granted to black people. It was the integrated character of the group that seemed to elicit most negative reactions. This was only exacerbated when such "integration" occurred in places previously reserved for whites. Violations of racially reserved waiting spaces in conveyance centers or doctors' offices are examples of acts that often set off violent confrontations. Yet the workers' intense involvement created an integrated experience. White volunteers revealed in their letters that they ate, slept, and interacted fully in these rural black homes.[37] Hence these amply integrated situations provided many opportunities for arrests or citations, some even to integrated groups merely riding in cars.[38]

More systematic and violent reactions occurred as the fundamentals of southern life were more intensively challenged and local overt mobilization and engagement became obvious. As blacks began to appear in droves for voter registration, intimidation increased by methods such as job removal and the denial of credit. Later these tactics escalated to include cross-burnings, bombings and arson.

An early example of the violence designed to silence one of the most salient local black leaders was the bombing of the home of Hartman Turnbow. He had been very active in voter registration work. "They . . . firebombed the living room, the back bedroom, and shot all in it. Made 'bout five shots right in the living room here."[39] Even after exchanging gunfire with what he identified as white assailants, Mr. Turnbow was charged with setting the fire to "increase racial tension."[40]

Then there was much activity associated with the attempt of blacks to integrate Holmes County schools, or at least to raise new issues in these schools. These black students were dismissed from school for singing "freedom songs at lunch."[41] Moreover, those whose children made appearances at white schools had their names posted throughout white neighborhoods in Durant, East of Tchula.[42] They were then susceptible to loss of jobs, threats, etc.

Since Tchula was a center for civil rights forces in the county, a large number of blacks, notwithstanding fear, were mobilized. Many of these were older persons whose commitment was based on a lifetime of denial. Thus a branch of the Mississippi Freedom Democratic Party (MFDP) was organized very early in the county, with the avowedly political aim of fielding black candidates for office. This organization, therefore, became the vehicle through which blacks defined their ideological goals and activated the masses. The SNCC Papers reveal that, in hindsight, the Holmes County effort was well-organized and more successful than members believed at the time. There are long lists of local individuals who took up positions in the organization. The most notable of these early leaders was Ralthus Hayes, who as MFDP county chairman succeeded in getting over 250 residents to a central meeting in August 1964 to formalize the Holmes County unit.[43] Later he was to run for the U.S.

House of Representatives and to serve on the state executive committee of the MFDP.

The rapid success of the MFDP signified much about the level of mobilization in Tchula and Holmes County. It has already been noted that MFDP represented an intensification of the mobilization and a shift in political focus to community organization or "building grassroots political strength."[44] The shift began in 1964 with the MFDP challenge of State Democratic Party representatives at the 1964 presidential convention. Tchula leaders rapidly sided with this effort, and by 1966 fielded their own candidates for office. Ralthus Hayes ran for Congress, two others from Tchula ran for county supervisor, and one each for justice of the peace and the board of education.[45] None of these were successful, but taking advantage of the opportunity to run was seen as an important step in personal activation and community stimulation. Just a year later the work all paid off when Robert Clark was elected as a representative to the state legislature, the first black since reconstruction. And though only Clark won, at least 12 other blacks were candidates for one office or another that year.

Gaining this access was not easy. Once again white reaction was extremely negative. The county clerk still refused to certify many black registrants, a condition only corrected with federal registrars (as sanctioned in the 1965 Voting Act). There were also other obstacles. In 1966, when black candidates first contested posts, the white election commissioners refused to permit them to assist in managing the election, despite presentation of a list of 52 suitable blacks.[46]

Needless to say, those blacks designated to watch the polls fared hardly better. Mrs. Elra Johnson told the Civil Rights Commission that while she and another were permitted to enter the polling place at Durant for the 1966 election, they were able to do little else.

> A Durant policeman directed them to remain at least 20 feet from the two tables where the election officials were seated, preventing them from closely observing the activities of the officials. Although the polling place was in the city hall where many chairs were available, the election officials, all of whom were white, told the two Negro poll watchers, according to Mrs. Johnson, "You'll have to stand all day."
>
> During the morning, Mrs. Johnson related, she used the lavatory facilities . . . , but found them locked when she returned to use them again. Election officials told her, she said, that if she left the polling place for any reason, no one could undertake her duties for her. . . . According to this account, poll watchers who arrived at the polling place around noon to relieve the two women were not allowed to do so.

Later the poll watchers were allowed to sit after Mrs. Johnson formally complained to the federal examiners and local officials. Then:

> ... during the counting of the ballots, Mrs. Johnson reported, she was not able to get a tally of votes because the counters did not call out the votes as had been the custom, but exchanged notes to tabulate them. She reported also that she was not permitted to see disqualified ballots adjudged by the election officials to be spoiled. The Chairman of the election commission, in an interview, indicated that upon request poll watchers customarily are permitted to see spoiled ballots in Holmes County.[47]

In 1967, when Robert Clark and others sought offices, the now-accepted black election managers had other problems. They were often superceded by whites who insisted on helping black voters who required assistance. In one instance a black official "helped one voter all day long. . . . Scores of others who asked for his help specifically were aided by his white counterpart who, while not forbidding him to take any action, merely prompted it by being more aggressive."[48] Indeed, Holmes County officials appeared to have gone to greater lengths than other counties in 1967 to prevent any black impact on the election. "In Tchula, Lexington, and Thornton no one was allowed to use sample ballots," a common means of facilitating participation by illiterate people. "In Ebenezer [the home of candidate Robert Clark] . . . illiterate voters were not allowed to use sample ballots, although other voters were."[49]

The Emergence of Eddie Carthan

Thus was the stage set for the emergence of a new generation of leaders in Tchula that was to be exemplified by Eddie James Carthan. The new generation, like that in Bolton, was much younger than any that had preceded it. Most of its members had attained college degrees and were in strategic, if traditional, positions in the local black community. Most of them would have had an opportunity to be affected by and to have possibly been a part of the local civil rights movement. Most were barely out of high school, at their first jobs, or were college students. They were often personally inspired by the ideology of the movement and could actually see themselves occupying public positions. These were persuasive images for young people whose horizons were already broader than those of any blacks before them.

Eddie Carthan and the four others that accompanied him to office in 1977 were remarkable examples of the new guard in several respects. In the first place, as in Bolton, the mayoral campaign was run with a slate of blacks for aldermanic posts. Unlike the situation in Bolton, the slate did not hold up through the election, but for a time it was seen as such. Most of the candidates were young. Carthan and two others were in their late twenties; another was in his mid-thirties; and the eldest was in her mid-fifties. All had college education, and at least three had received or were working toward advanced degrees. Professionally, all were or had been involved in education, and three remained public school teachers. Not all, however, were affected by the civil rights movement in the same manner, a fact that led to divergent ideologies. Three of the new group were townspeople who were fairly close to movement activities and participated in one organization or another. Two others were of rural backgrounds and evidently far on the fringes of the movement and exhibited hostility to its vestiges.

As the agrarian townsman, Eddie Carthan attempted to respond to both the rural and town masses. In doing so he sought to combine opposites. He was born on a farm; his father was always a farmer and the family livelihood was basically acquired from farming. He still describes himself as a rural person—one who resides in town, but whose experiences and sentiments provide an understanding and appreciation for the rural life. And indeed his personal involvement in farming was noted; he owned a farm and engaged in farm work with his father (recently deceased) and siblings. He argues that this kept him abreast of agrarian aspects of Tchula life, still so vital to many black citizens.

Yet he now lives in the town and exudes comfort and satisfaction in this more cosmopolitan environment with its concentrated population, quicker pace, and opportunities for broader communications. This seems to be explained by several factors. As independent farmers with land, the Carthan family was in a better economic position. The profits from the land routinely gave the children access to the town and they were conversant with its ways. Moreover, the independent business occupation that Eddie Carthan himself eventually took up in Tchula was concentrated mostly in the town and required the development of acumen for the task.

In Eddie Carthan's view, standing astride these two worlds provided him particularly good benefit for displaying effective leadership. For him this was seen as a strategic benefit in representing all sides of the black community without prejudice. He cited his special talent for relating as easily with those in the rural area as with those in the town. Indeed, he, like Thompson and Blackwell, saw these black constituents as monolithic, all equally susceptible to racial exclusion. They together constituted the grassroots community, whose contemporary identity was based on oppression. When Carthan thought of the average constituent, he saw one massive bloc long denied political participation he explains. His task as a leader was to mobilize them around this central identifying characteristic, not as farmers or as townspeople.

His methodology and style of mobilization also had another component akin to urban cosmopolitanism. In this he had a tendency, like James Q. Wilson's "amateur" politician, to structure arguments around "principles" and "ideas."[50] Carthan, as did Mayor Thompson of Bolton, framed his arguments for action around a conception of the "public interest" identified as the requirement of democratic theory that everyone participate fully in the political system. When they did not, as was the case with his black constituents, a violation of a basic principle had occurred. Correctives should not be based on bargaining or compromise, but on the most direct means to full realization. Thus while he was solidly grounded in the local environment, he was outward-looking. Merton says that such an individual is "oriented to the world outside" and envisions personal integration with that larger world.[51] For Carthan it is clear that he was greatly influenced by the issues and methods of the larger world; he showed conversance with these. Yet he seemed much more wed, as was Thompson, to the local scene; to grafting aspects of the former onto the Tchula environment. He never lost sight of the grassroots dimension because it was all too important to the larger principles espoused in the interest of the black constituency.

During the tumultuous years of civil rights activity in Tchula and Holmes County, Eddie Carthan was fairly young. He was merely fourteen in 1964 during Freedom Summer. Thus he was not a leader of the movement in any sense. It may be more important, however, that at his age he was one of those thrust forward to test the limits of racial exclusion. Young high school students like him were the first to challenge their local black schools by singing freedom songs and discussing local daily movement events. Some of these youngsters were arrested for exhibiting behavior inconsistent with the racial taboos. Then they were the first to endure the pain and humiliation of entering newly integrated white schools.

In many ways they developed a harder edge in their approach to change because they bore the brunt of the offenses that followed efforts at change. At the same time they were challenged to measure all of their possibilities for the future, whatever transformation took place. According to Carthan, this was especially important for his later ideas, though at the impressionable age of fourteen it was difficult to separate youthful enthusiasm and energy from a more somber, critical understanding of activities. He asserted that this reckoning made him and his generation perhaps the freest and most aggressive of their lot in the history of blacks in America. Not even during reconstruction was there such intense integration and mobilization of youth into a movement for political change.

Like most blacks of his station, there was little question that Carthan would go on to college after finishing high school at Tchula Attendance Center. Thus in the late 1960s through the early 1970s, he was completing college studies at a state school near Tchula—Mississippi Valley State University (MVSU). He studied social science there and reportedly settled on law as an area for further study. He did enter law school at the University of Mississippi, but remained only one year, before pursuing graduate studies in educational administration at Jackson State University. There he earned a masters degree.

Carthan was not an activist of the Blackwell type that emerged in the heyday of the 1960s movement. In the first place, there was far less opportunity for activism when he reached his late teens and went to college. Much of the intensity of the concentrated movement in Tchula had gone. What he was a part of in MVSU, or at least privy to, was a high level of student mobilization (albeit intermittent), opposed to what was seen as an "Uncle Tom" administration. The long-time college president rejected the tenets of and changes wrought by the civil rights movement. Many of the students, however, had (like Carthan), come from activist delta and other communities that routinely challenged the status quo. Carthan once again found himself amidst a campaign for social change.

Though Eddie Carthan was not a ringleader in what was occurring at MVSU, one source has described him as having always demonstrated strong commitment.[52] Thus it is of interest to explore this environment and its possible effect upon Carthan's development. Trouble at MVSU surfaced with some force in early 1969 just after Carthan matriculated, when student government leaders demanded reorientation of aspects of the curriculum to accommodate black needs. They sought courses on Afro-American history and increased library acquisitions on blacks, and remediation courses. Lack of response to the demands eventually resulted in a sit-in at the administration building.[53]

The administration found it very difficult to accommodate the students in light of a conservative temperament and fear of the consequences from the state college board if students were not effectively controlled. The initial response, therefore, was to call the police to execute student arrests while some others were arrested via administrative procedures. Some 15 were arrested for disorderly conduct and nearly 200 were expelled.[54] The impasse ended only after the president agreed to about half of the student requests, including reinstatement of those expelled and the withdrawal of charges against those arrested.[55]

The confrontations at MVSU did not end with this first round. Many of those expelled sued for reinstatement without prejudice and eventually won. At the same time, since MVSU did not exist in isolation from the statewide mobilization campaign, Charles Evers from the state branch NAACP appeared on the scene to assist with the negotiation process because "sending the students home was unwarranted." He continued that "if it means marching on campus in support of these kids because they haven't done [anything] wrong then we'll march [even] if everyone of us is arrested."[56]

The greater challenge, however, was still to come the following academic year. The new student government leader continued the spirit of protests[57] by issuing a longer list of demands in early 1970. These 30 new demands were more banal, but also were more challenging to the administration. Students asked that refund policies on certain fees be revised; that student insurance be clarified; that room and board fees be separated; that "harassment" clauses be deleted from the student handbook; that "calling hours" at female dormitories be revised, etc.

Some points, however, were not so mundane. There were four or five demands that had to do with faculty hiring, where the students made revolutionary requests and raised charges about faculty competence. For example, they asked for a say in the selection of faculty, and that "mentally" incompetent teachers be released. The demands appeared to be widely supported as over half of the student body, according to some news reports, took part in an associated protest march and rally.[58]

These demands were more challenging because they exposed not just administrative conservatism, but the absence of local independent decision-making power. While many of the issues for example, regarded simple in-house regulations, changing them internally was another matter. Such a decision would have meant a fundamental reorientation of administrative temperament and power. The president temperamentally could not concede that students had a legitimate right to make claims; but neither could he concede that social change (already rejected by the board) should be fully integrated into the regular policy process. Yet few of the students who experienced the ordeal could accept the old ways. Eddie Carthan was one of a number who report that much about their commitment to the ideology of change and activism was nurtured in this restricted environment.

After leaving the law school and completing a master's degree, Carthan began teaching. His first and only job in this area was at a junior college located in nearby Lexington—Saints College. He reports finding this a sobering experience, though his intense interest in education did not decline. Other things began to attract him, especially electoral politics and business. He believed himself to have certain acumen for both of these fields and began gradually to take actions to further those goals.

On the business side he used the ideals espoused by his father and the family financial advantages to get ahead. The most salient ideal was that of financial independence, which the father had always enjoyed. Carthan reports that until he finished college he had never had to work for anyone else. All of his energies were dedicated to the profitable farm interests of his father and grandfather. This experience, it is believed, also provided the base for some of his personal interest in private business. Moreover, his father and siblings could provide vital assistance and expertise.

He pursued it with determination, speed, and success. By 1980 young Carthan had acquired considerable wealth from an array of businesses. He owned a stretch of property at the edge of downtown Tchula about the size of a city block. There were several edifices on the property for personal, public, and business use. His temporary home was a huge trailer at the center of the plot and beside it was a small house of three or four rooms that had been converted to office use. In this same row of buildings was a large grocery store. Though the square footage would not compare with larger chain supermarkets, it was well stocked for its scale and represented a considerable business venture. It compared easily with others of its kind in the town. The block of businesses was completed by a café (a small eatery and amusement tavern) and a service station. For its place it amounted to the all-purpose shopping center/mall. Elsewhere in town Carthan owned or controlled some rental properties.

Meanwhile, he was achieving more visibility in public affairs. He now started to take part in matters on which he had previously been little more than an interested and committed spectator. In typical fashion for the contemporary American politician, Carthan began by being ubiquitous. It became another part of his business to know what was going on in town, the personalities involved, and to align himself with appropriate organizations. He continued regular participation in the Baptist church and took the office of deacon in the church hierarchy. Carthan was also a member of many of the other available civic, social, and fraternal organizations, some of which had direct links to politics or business.

Some of this local activity was directly political. Carthan knew and campaigned for the significant number of movement leaders who sought local offices. This group included ministers, MFDP leaders like Ralthus Hayes, and the few blacks who already occupied electoral positions. Combined with this old guard leadership was a cadre of younger people who had been influenced by the civil rights mobilization campaign, some of whom had finished college and returned to Tchula. They were readily available to a young, aggressive leader like Carthan, who proposed to take control of the political system.

Carthan was first elected to the local school board. Though the experience of acquiring this local office was satisfactory, he quickly became aware of the need to expand his contacts. He has said that in order to realize any of his dreams for transformation of a poor place like Tchula, he had to also have access to and influence upon external resources. Therefore he rapidly began to court state and national leaders and to align himself with other black politicians. He did this exceedingly well—ingratiating himself with black leaders and (though a self-styled independent) aligning with the Democratic governor (Finch) and President Carter. This was of particular benefit for advancing his own political stature, which by the middle 1970s gave him sufficient local standing to command his own following.

Incipient Class Dynamics and Leadership Ideology

It is useful to think of the decision by Carthan to run for mayor as having been influenced by a desire to give black people the kind of political independence that he sought in his personal affairs. It may also be useful to visualize his business model as instructive for understanding the political style he was to adopt. All of these, of course, would also seem to be heavily influenced by the time of his emergence and his age. Only one of his age and in this particular stage in Mississippi history could sustain a belief that all the taboos of racial caste could be violated to benefit social change for blacks.

Coming into his own as a local leader may well have been difficult for Carthan, whose status was different from that of most of his constituents. However, he succeeded in rapidly gaining broad popularity with his agressiveness, independence and cosmopolitanism. Many saw this as merely an extension of popularity he enjoyed when he was a school boy. Even then he was known as a "hard knot"—one usually able and more than willing to protect self and property.[59] This same perception informed contemporary comments. Much of his attractiveness came from a willingness to speak his mind and "stand up to white people" in Tchula. This behavior inspired pride and awe among many blacks, who themselves desired but lacked such courage. In this regard he was like Bennie Thompson of Bolton.

His campaign approach had a kind of pristine quality, but was one which sought to extend mobilization immediately to all sectors of this oppressed community. This approach was not novel for he concentrated on activating an existing base—that from the civil rights movement of a few years past. He said that this movement and its leaders gave him his inspiration and entirely matched his sentiments. His own dedication, he said, began when he used to drive with his father to NAACP and other community activities bearing on civil rights. This extended to voter registration and canvassing at a later time, so much so that he considers himself "a product of the civil rights movement." Now he sought electoral leadership to be of assistance to the people of Tchula, especially the black people who were very poor and in many cases illiterate, unemployed and badly housed.[60]

Though there was an aspect of paternalism in Carthan's expressed approach to the average poor black of Tchula, there was also an ideology of nationalism or solidarity. He clearly was aware that his educational and economic position put him some distance from the average person, but his ideas were built on a notion of solidarity born of the ubiquitousness of racial division in the local community. He argued that the system made no separation between himself and them; they were all seen as the same by white racists.[61] Thus he could claim with some validity that all blacks were the same in Tchula and that his wealth and other accoutrements were unimportant. In taking this position he went against the grain of an evident divide between the townspeople and the rural plantation people. These younger people in the towns, for example, in recent years had had a rather different direct relationship with whites than those on the plantations. Many of those on the plantations, for example, continued to live in a directly dependent relationship on whites. As tenant farmers or sharecroppers, they were not accustomed to bargaining with their labor in ways that some semi-skilled townspeople were. And yet Carthan succeeded in putting forth the argument that townspeople enjoyed no greater degree of independence, with their access to salaries and cosmopolitan ideas that naturally emerged in the town or were brought by transients.

This very idea of linkage or solidarity in Tchula was itself an aspect of cosmopolitanism in Carthan. The purpose of the argument was to create a base for political mobilization in the town. The later civil rights movement leaders more concerned with ideology had long since concluded that the way to achieve this was via mobilization of the community as a bloc. One could easily do this around certain issues that critically affected all blacks, or one could focus on the generalized theme of racism as it affected the total existence of blacks. Carthan chose, as did Thompson, to pursue what may have been a mere abstraction by focusing on creating solidarity around the generalized condition of blacks. What made this more than an abstraction in this case is that Carthan could develop any list of public policy areas and illustrate their differential effect upon *all* blacks. In discussing schools, housing, taxes, jobs, etc. he could prove that there were disadvantages to blacks of any economic or educational station. This complex and academic argument was sufficiently grounded in local experience that Carthan could effectively merge apparent opposites between the town and the farm communities.

Black Leadership Conflict and the Development of Power Axes

If Carthan was successful in creating a monolithic constituency, he was not able to do the same within the black leadership class. Even on the eve of his mayoral election, the ideas of the agrarian townsman came into direct conflict with the diametrically opposed ideas of an opposition group. The group was made up of two axes, that ironically fed into each other. The first part of the axis was evident even before the end of the 1977 mayoral campaign, when two black candidates withdrew from the slate to wage a quite separate campaign. They did so, it was alleged, under the auspices of the other axis—the whites—one of whose number also ran for office. It was widely believed by many blacks in the early 1980s that an arrangement was made by the latter two axes to cooperate in furthering each others' political interests. Some residents report having been solicited, for example, to vote for candidates from these two axes as a kind of slate.

After winning aldermanic posts, the two blacks (Roosevelt Granderson and Jacyne Gibson) became somewhat of a formal opposition to Mayor Carthan. Together with the one white who won an aldermanic post, they remained locked in conflict with the mayor and effectively created stalemate in government.

These two opposition blacks, like Carthan, were prominent community leaders who enjoyed some popularity. They were young college graduates who returned home with an apparent interest in public affairs. They were of the same age range as the mayor, had also gone to the nearby MVSU, and were school teachers. However, their economic position was not commensurate with that of the mayor, though their incomes were respectable. More importantly, their backgrounds diverged significantly from that of the mayor. Though these men were now residing in the town, they were not townsmen by attitude or experience. Most of their lives had been spent on traditional rural plantations as dependent tenants or sharecroppers. In short, they were of a different class than the mayor.

The ideology of these two men was most easily observed from their activities, as we shall see later on. However it was possible to extrapolate some philosophical understandings from the general attitudes and behaviors they exhibited in local affairs.[62] It is all-important that some attention be devoted to their plantation background. Their early willingness to cooperate with whites, some of whom had held political offices before in Tchula, suggests that status quo arrangements appealed to them. Indeed the mayor was believed to be going too fast by the opposition. Carthan was thought to be too pejorative toward whites and too prone to exacerbate conflict in order to institute new policies. These two aldermen are said to have been especially annoyed because the mayor's tactics alienated whites in the local community who were potential friends of blacks, or who controlled significant economic resources to be reckoned with. Without the support of such whites, this bloc felt, it was impossible to enjoy any political success. The whites could simply refuse to utilize their economic resources to the benefit of the community, or worse, could withdraw from the patron-client relationship still widely practiced in the area.

Their philosophy assumed the necessity of cooperation between whites and blacks in the political arena. This led them to place a premium on a working relationship with the white alderman. Like the "house Negroes" of Malcolm X, they did not exercise the full limit of their opportunity to undo dependence on whites.[63] Indeed they recognized that such an arrangement provided them personal benefits and privileges. Hence, like the preferred slaves before, they were unlikely to attack the system as readily. Contemporaneously, their sentiments and approach earned them the label of Uncle Toms. But when the mayor referred to them he invariably used the disparaging terminology of "house niggers." His opinion was that they were merely managed by their previous plantation bosses.

Unlike Carthan, these men had no wish to achieve solidarity within the community. To do so meant acceptance of a philosophy that would undermine their basis for maintenance of power. Their conception of the political community and its involvement in decision-making was as restricted as their vision of their independent potential for exercising power. For them, if solidarity (or nationalism) were exercised, this would also require a theory of democratization sustained by the will of the constituency. For them this was unacceptable. Instead, they preferred a system of bargaining based on certain givens. One of these givens was that the past racial exclusion gave certain advantages to whites in the bargaining process. The rest of the power structure, therefore, was based on a delicate balance of forces activated in the political community and the ability of their representatives to bargain as "trustees."[64] Democratization would defeat their purpose, as it would cut off the intra-leadership bargaining process. Given this vision, Carthan's philosophy was easily more threatening than that of even white political contenders. Thus it was in their political interest to try and defeat the efforts of the agrarian townsman.

This is but one axis that was in opposition to the mayor. The other was made up of representatives of the white community, many of whom sought reelection as incumbents. Only one of their number, however, was successful—John Edgar Hays. He came to symbolize the presence of the now politically "dispossessed" white community, that would seek to "divide and conquer"[65] the majority black administration.

That Hays was able to win a position in a highly mobilized, majority black town was a testament to the success of his method. Many of those blacks interviewed refer to the fact that of all the white candidates, Hays had been convincing enough in his rhetoric about a willingness to cooperate with some inevitable degree of black leadership. His friendliness and eagerness to seek out black sentiments were cited as evidence. Once in office, however, the perception of many was that he inserted himself into political debates in a way that exacerbated conflict between the opposing blocs of black leaders.

The general perception of Hays' tactics and policy perspective results from the relationship between him and the mayor. The mutual distaste between them became evident fairly soon after the election. The mayor made it widely known that he distrusted Hays, whom he called a "scalawag." Hays' personal sentiments were just as strong, but he also rejected Carthan's philosophy of democratization and cosmopolitanism. The alderman simply could not accept a system whose population configuration spelled the exclusion of whites from a position of power for the foreseeable future. Under these circumstances, Hays stood a much better chance of preserving white influence by bargaining with the other side. In striking an alliance of sorts with the black opposition Hays could even create the appearance of being a part of an integrated, black-majority coalition.

The efforts of divide and conquer also had a practical policy import. For example, if it was indeed true that Hays merely represented white interests as part of a coalition that included blacks, one would expect that there would be little policy initiative on his part aimed at the black community. Instead he might have been expected to defer to black leaders for such initiatives, after which bargaining would ensue. It would appear that the opposite occurred, with Hays not only dominating the coalition, but taking a range of independent positions clearly detrimental to the socioeconomic welfare of large sectors of the black community. Many of the mayor's supporters, for example, assumed that Hays was the driving force behind almost categorical rejection of any proposition put forth by the mayor after about one year of the regime. This reactionary posture included rejection of services, federal programs, and refusal to honor legal prerogatives designated for the mayor.

The mayor was especially convinced of the white alderman's dominance of the opposition axis. It was alleged that Hays led a campaign to isolate Carthan from the black constituency by denigrating the higher social class position of the mayor. In this so-called whispering campaign, other blacks in salient community positions (such as black aldermen Granderson and Gibson) were touted as being better-suited representatives because they were more like average people.[66] Still other actions cast suspicion on Hays' partnership in any coalition said to be favorable to blacks. Some of these were regarding the location of federal projects in town, which were rejected by Hays as being too costly and out of line with the needs of the black community. On other occasions he was said to discourage private industry for similar reasons. The mayor noted one instance in which Alderman Hays is said to have rejected location of a new factory in Tchula "because black people were already satisfied with what they had."[67]

In all this, however, an actual and very public working relationship existed between the two black opposition aldermen and the lone white. This sometimes made it exceedingly difficult to track leadership within the coalition. Otherwise there were instances when the political sentiments and ideologies of these three aldermen matched in such a way that divide and conquer was hardly operable. Each was merely seen to be representing his own best interest.

Governance and Conflict: Phase One

Therefore a base for high-level conflict existed in Tchula almost from the beginning. The two groups of power contenders in the black community and the refusal of the whites to withdraw (or accept black control) yielded a situation quite unlike that in either of the other two towns. The intense mobilization in Tchula was deflected at an early stage into an effort at maintenance of political power by two classes of black leadership—the mayoral bloc and the aldermanic bloc. After the first year of the regime, it was no longer possible to speak of local governance in the traditional sense of the word. The leadership forces were battling each other with such ferocity that public business was either in stalemate or in such a highly confused state as to be ineffective. Before the process was over, the mayor had been barred from city hall property, there had been physical altercations between the forces, the mayor had been alleged to commit such serious illegal acts that he was forced from office, and an alderman had been murdered and the mayor charged with the crime. Amidst such fierce competition it is not unreasonable that the vision of Carthan was further from realization than that of the other towns, where class conflict or a prominent contending leadership group was absent.

The succeeding analysis will focus on the conflict-ridden early phase of the Carthan regime. In this context I shall detail some of the early issues that caused extensive conflict and led to the second phase of mass litigation and criminal charges. The early battles focused on abstractions about how the political community was defined, though it did not take long for whites and the black opposition to find Carthan's philosophy and actions of democratization unacceptable. As Carthan saw it, entities in the political community were not only able to bargain on the basis of the size of their membership in the community, but also on the basis of need. The smaller white community obviously had less bargaining power in this scheme. At the same time the whites were at a deficit in making political claims because their needs were far less. They had always enjoyed the benefits and resources of the community, while blacks had not. Though this was not a theory of reparation or white exclusion, it was one which refused to award whites any "honorary" position in the hierarchy of claimants. The mayor's ideology put him to great limits not to award special privileges to whites because of the past.

This latter dimension was particularly important because it epitomized another aspect of his style that aggravated tensions with whites. He was aggressive in their presence and sought to make full use of the prerogatives that accrued to him as mayor. As a young man highly influenced by the so-called militant phase of the civil rights movement, it was very important to Carthan to disdain the appearance of deference or dependence upon white gratuitousness. The young mayor wanted to be seen to have a reputation for independence from whites. This independence was to be exerted with great fervor in the interests of blacks, whom he sought to bring into the mainstream of American society—hence his cosmopolitan outlook. However, the behavior that emanated from such abstract ideals made whites exceedingly uncomfortable. For them Carthan was a "smart nigger" or a "bad nigger." In white mythology such a black did not know his place and could unfavorably influence others. And for the black opposition it was a combination of political and class factors that led them to reject Carthan.

The first series of policy actions by the mayor consistent with his philosophy of fully integrating blacks into town life was his aggressive use of the prerogatives of appointment. He sought to replace the local city hall staff with blacks in which he had confidence. This included the appointment of a new police chief, town clerk and garbage collectors.

This met with strong opposition from the white community and from the opposition aldermen (who had formed a majority voting bloc). The local whites initially accused the mayor of not seeking their input in decision-making, since he had neglected to seek meetings with them or to apprise them of policy changes, and the like. Within the aldermanic opposition group, a variety of measures were being used against the mayor. For a period of two months the voting majority refused to pay the salaries of town employees. The rationale was that they were illegally appointed, though the mayor looked upon this as harassment. Eventually Carthan's black city clerk was reportedly forced to resign because of personal and family intimidation. She alleged that because of her clerk position, the employment of one of her children elsewhere in the delta was jeopardized.[68]

Still other incidents of this nature occurred as the conflict escalated. In a chronology of events since 1977 issued by proponents of the mayor, and from accounts reported variously in newspapers, some of the following incidents occurred in Tchula: The mayor was denied certain reimbursements for what he claimed was business travel. He argued that some of these trips were in connection with solicitation of federal funds or meetings with other officials in the associations. The now three-man working aldermanic majority (Gibson, Granderson, and Hays) disagreed and argued that these trips represented the mayor's personal travel. The same was true for telephone calls. In 1979 "the telephone company cut off service to the town hall because of the board of aldermen's refusal to pay a $1,289 bill. Hayes (sic), Granderson and Gibson voted against paying the bill because many of the calls had been made from Carthan's home and office phones."[69] The mayor insisted that these were business calls, most of which were made after he had been locked out of his town hall office for a two-month period.

The lock-out began a more intense phase of conflict. The mayor was ostensibly barred from the premises because he was denying the voting majority on the board any input. Granderson said "We have been preaching and praying, and begging and saluting to the mayor . . . asking him to let us have some input into what is going on in the town." The mayor was accused of hiding town records. "Every time we asked for the minute book, it was gone some other place. Every time . . . [we ask for] the bank statement, the city clerk doesn't feel like giving it to us." All this was said to be symptomatic of a broad range of illegal actions whereby the mayor "refuses to hear the majority of the board. . . . He doesn't have to agree, but just abide by the rules. We don't make the rules, the Mississippi Code states the rules. . . . The only thing we [aldermen] are doing is trying to abide by them."[70] The consequence of this dispute was that the mayor was barred from the building by the majority of aldermen. According to many sources the town hall was locked for eight weeks with the police chief stationed at the door and a sign that read "all trespassers will be prosecuted."

Meanwhile, these events caused reverberations elsewhere. By 1979 the mayor's program for "modernization" of the town had come virtually to a halt. Prior to his becoming mayor and in the first phase of his regime, Carthan had been instrumental in initiating a number of federal-and state-supported programs. Some of these programs began to be affected by the political circumstances within the leadership class. Ultimately the mayor and his proponents charged that the opposition aldermanic bloc caused "all federal programs to be halted."

Notwithstanding the theories of conspiracy, a variety of programs were cut off. Some of these difficulties began as early as 1978 when a $476,592 Community Development Block Grant was terminated after federal auditors found "discrepancies" in fund allocations and expenditures. Ninety-nine thousand, six hundred and seventy dollars ($99,670) of this housing rehabilitation grant could not be accounted for.[71] In this case the mayor was not accused, though as mayor he bore authorizing responsibility. Then the next year a day-care center, named for two outstanding figures in the civil rights campaign of the 1960s (Hayes and Turnbow), was also closed because of charges and countercharges about propriety of operation. During this period there were many other similar disagreements between the contending forces that crippled everyday governance.

Governance and Conflict: Phase Two

Eventually the opposition challenged the legal authority of the mayor to act without the consent of a majority of the board. This represented a continuation of the conflict over appointment powers. The issue of the mayor's authority was eventually litigated (1980) after he forced the resignation of one black police chief (Sharkey Ford) and replaced him. The aldermanic bloc contended that the mayor had no such authority and sought to have Ford reinstated with back pay. The Circuit Court of Holmes County agreed with them, but on appeal the state Supreme Court overturned the decision.[72]

This was not to be the end of the matter. In April 1980 the board appointed an acting police chief, at what they dubbed a special "call" meeting of the board, Their reasoning was best stated by the Justice Court judge, who in adjudicating the case, said this meeting was for the purpose of hiring "Jim Andrews . . . until we can get this town straightened out."[73] According to supporters of the mayor, this meeting was illegal and took place not at the town hall but in a "Jitney Jr." food store. When the mayor was informed of this meeting and the subsequent efforts of the new police officer to exercise his duties, considerable consternation was expressed. The mayor gathered up the remaining five police officers and a supportive alderman, and proceeded to town hall to prevent this "illegal exercise of authority." The new police chief refused the mayor's orders to put down his arms and to leave the premises. When the mayor insisted that the new "officer" be disarmed, a scuffle ensued between the contending forces. In the altercation the acting police chief was injured, some say by gunfire.

Legal charges brought in the interest of the aldermanic bloc eventually went to trial. Acting chief Andrews and James Harris, (an off-duty officer who claimed injury) made charges for aggravated assault against a police officer. The mayor and his six cohorts were formally arrested. The most serious charge was leveled at Carthan, who was "accused of firing a pistol at Jim Andrews." All of the defendants were convicted by jury. The mayor was sentenced to a three-year prison term; the five police officers received three-year suspended sentences with three years of probation and $500 fines; and the alderman received a similar sentence but a fine of $1,000.[74]

The process of the trial and the tactics adopted caused many Carthan supporters to charge that a conspiracy was afoot to end the mayor's rule. Indeed in this first major trial there were discrepancies in procedures and evidence that led to conflict escalation. Initially there was some discrepancy about whether shots were ever fired during the altercation and by whom. The plaintiffs apparently charged that shots were fired directly by the mayor; others contended that there were no shots or that they were fired accidentally. The court and jury appeared to accept the contention that the mayor fired the shot(s) or bore the responsibility for firing them. Later, the charges of the chief complainant (the acting police chief) were dismissed against the mayor[75] and the actual case was made on the claims of the off-duty police officer. This is especially curious because it was the acting police chief who had allegedly been shot in the altercation.

The mayor's proponents asserted that Harris, the off-duty officer, was pressured by whites to maintain his charges of assault. Various incidents were cited. For example, it was alleged in the *Tchula Times* that even prior to the altercation, Harris was under pressure from the aldermanic bloc to disobey directives from the mayor. This was significant because ordinarily policemen appeared before the mayor (who sat as town judge) to defend summonses or other charges for ordinance violations. But this was all complicated because the aldermanic bloc had preempted and delegated these judgeship responsibilities to a Mrs. Deane Taylor, a sitting Justice of the Peace, in order to reduce mayoral power. According to the *Times'* report, James Harris was "told by the Board of Aldermen to take all tickets and cases to Justice Court Judge Taylor . . . and failure to follow their instruction would result in him being fired and not paid."[76]

The pressure upon Harris to participate in the alleged conspiracy also included a supposed payoff of a new car and a job from the family of the acting chief, Andrews.[77] The mayor and his proponents contended that the proof of the conspiracy was that James Harris later saw the error of his ways and sought (but was not permitted) to recant the charges implicating assault during the altercation. He even denied the charges in open court. "James Harris was asked if he was assaulted. He said no one hit him and he wasn't hurt, but Mayor Carthan supposedly pointed a gun at him." After the trial, "James Harris admitted that he lied on WLBT-TV3 (a Jackson television station) before the eyes of Mississippi and subsequently went to the sheriff to give a sworn statement to that effect, but the sheriff refused it".[78]

It was later contended that the conspiracy extended to the county court system. The mayor and the other defendants asserted that the court never took up their counterclaim against Andrews for interfering with a police officer in the performance of his duties. The ruling on this was apparently that Andrews was not subject to prosecution because of "immunity" given for his testimony in the trial against Carthan, *et al.* But the "conspiracy" in the court system, the defendants argued, continued with instructions to the jury during deliberations. The mostly black jury gave early notice to the judge of difficulties in reaching a decision. Thereupon the judge gave additional instructions. It has been alleged that some of the jurors in hindsight believed the further instructions were designed to trick them into convicting Carthan and the others. The judge is said to have alluded to the simple nature of the crime and the likelihood of merely a fine if the conviction were handed down. According to this view, when some of the jurors returned to deliberations with what they perceived to be encouragement, a guilty verdict was soon reached. Surprise and consternation marked jurors' responses and those of the Carthan forces when the judge delivered a sentence of three years in prison and a fine for the mayor. "Shortly after the sentencing several jurors came forward with sworn statements admitting that they were given false information and instructions. One juror said that his conscience was bothering him(;) he had no peace within himself, so he had to come forward and tell the truth."[79]

After the mayor's various appeals to higher courts were all denied, charges of racial conspiracy became more prominent. In arguments before the state supreme court, attorneys asserted that the original charges were illegal because Carthan had the authority to appoint a police chief in the face of a resignation that had already occurred. It was charged that only racial motivations led to a political climate where such claims against the mayor could be made in the first place. Later the attorneys attempted to introduce a range of new arguments before the courts that included information about jurors' post-trial comments and the alleged recantation from the chief accuser. These were all denied by the state courts, and so was a final appeal to the U. S. Supreme Court.

The prominence of the arguments about unfairness in the judicial proceedings was highlighted when a group calling itself the "National Campaign to Free Mayor Eddie J. Carthan and the Tchula 7 and to preserve Black Political Rights" marched on the state supreme court. The group, estimated by local papers to number about 35, appeared at the court building and proceeded to the appropriate offices where a statement was delivered demanding bail for Carthan. "We, the people of Mississippi, demand that the Mississippi Supreme Court Justices set bond for Mayor Eddie James Carthan immediately, so that his release may be effected."[80] The group also sought a meeting with the judges on this general problem.

Though all of their demands were rejected since they were not "representing Carthan as his attorney," this represented a critical stage and an expansion of the conflict. Since they took the unusual step of appearing directly at the court it signified a belief that the judicial system was the chief sustainer of a conspiracy against the mayor. At the same time, the demonstration in Jackson attracted far broader attention and support. Soon the campaign for the "Tchula Seven" was nationalized with support groups appearing all over the country, as will be seen.

This local case was followed by several charges from the federal government that the mayor fraudulently used federal funds. The first of two cases to be discussed charged that Carthan submitted claims for foodstuffs that were never delivered to a federally supported program. During the summer of 1979 Carthan was a vendor for a program that provided free meals for poor children. The grantee for the program was a black corporation designed for the "development and expansion of minority business." Its chief officer, Koai Meuchy, was indicted and eventually pleaded guilty to charges of issuing false receipts. He then testified about alleged transactions that led to government charges against Carthan. The latter was accused of making three false transactions with Meuchy that totalled $8,546. Then in August of the same year, two additional claims were said to be submitted: one for $6,294 for food and another for $703 for supplies. The contention of Meuchy was that the two men colluded to illegally convert federal monies to private, personal use.[81]

The mayor pleaded innocent to these 1980 charges and argued that they were once again a part of a conspiratorial effort to remove him from power and influence in Tchula. Indeed there was never any resolution of these charges, since the government chose to drop them after many trial delays and critical changes in the evidence available for court presentation. Perhaps the most important of these events was the death of the chief witness, Koai Meuchy. The latter was killed in a shoot-out with Madison County police.[82]

Following close (1981) on the preceding indictment of Carthan was another for federal fraud. This case was a complicated web of charges and insinuation about the mayor's relationships with several Mississippi politicians and businessmen. Harold "Hap" Foreman was a former Jackson businessman, and R. L. Bolden was former Director of the Office of Minority Affairs for Governor Cliff

Finch (1976-1980). The allegations were that Mayor Carthan had received a $2,000 kickback using a Tchula day-care center as collateral in seeking federally insured loans. The loans, a total of $32,547, were secured by Hap Foreman after he produced documents showing that $40,000 worth of equipment had been delivered to the Tchula Day Care Center. The government charged that no such delivery of equipment had ever been made and that the documents were false.

The involvement of Mayor Carthan resulted because he allegedly signed the receipts indicating that the equipment had been received in Tchula. Foreman, who had other indictments pending, pleaded guilty and agreed to testify to the nature of the scheme. As a government witness, Foreman alleged that he, Carthan and Bolden had earlier entered an agreement whereby each would receive a kickback of $2,000 for expediting the false paperwork. According to Foreman, Bolden's part was to sign Carthan's name to the appropriate documents by previous agreement. In detailing how the alleged scheme worked, Foreman provided the FBI with a tangled web of charges indicating kickbacks involving virtually every federal program with which he did business and other prominent state personalities. These included bank officers, to whom Foreman said he routinely paid a five percent kickback.[83] At the trial R. L. Boldon also became a government witness and made similar allegations against Mayor Carthan.

The mayor's testimony diverged considerably from that of his accusers. Carthan and a host of officials and former officials from Tchula testified that while some knowledge of Foreman's equipment deal existed, there was no collusion to commit fraud. The mayor detailed how Bolden, from the governor's office, recommended Foreman as a reputable businessman who could provide assistance in getting the day-care center rapidly equipped. Apparently the mayor assigned the town planner the task of equipment procurement, which she did by deriving a list together with Foreman. At this point what occurred was not clear, though the mayor and town clerk seemed to indicate possible impropriety by the town planner. The mayor then testified that what he knew of the possibility of wrongdoing came from a state official inquiry about the cost of certain items.[84] Thereafter he sought to take appropriate action against the official he deemed implicated by firing the town planner.[85]

In October 1981, the mayor was convicted in this trial, sentenced to three years and given a fine of $5,000. By now he was subject to six years in jail and $6,000 in fines on state and federal charges.

These charges and convictions were followed by what some have called a "bizarre," continuing set of violent circumstances and general mayhem in the town of Tchula. As a result of the fraud conviction, the mayor was forced from office, to be replaced by one of the black opposition aldermen (Granderson). The costs of the uncertainty in government were borne by the larger society in many displays of exaggerated violent confrontations and what appeared on the surface to be psychological dislocations. There were numerous reports of police-citizen altercations, sometimes with shots being fired and other times with individuals being beaten. Some of these violent confrontations were between citizens and the police, where the former often enjoyed notable success in "fighting it out." There was also evidence in this period that many more persons armed themselves, especially public officials. One alderman noted that he always carried his pistol. The mayor was even disarmed in the courtroom on an occasion.[86] Then there were mysterious deaths and observably perhaps more public drunkenness and subsequent intergroup quarreling than may have been expected in a town this size. Some respondents reported feeling personally threatened due to their closeness to both sides of the divide in the black conflict. For them the ready resort to violence meant that they could easily be accused by one side or the other, with dire consequences.

As if to prove the point of an "outlaw" town, the chief black opponent of Carthan, who now occupied the mayoralty, was gunned down gangland style. The murder occurred at the "Jitney Jr." convenience store where Granderson was employed part-time, and where routine board meetings allegedly took place. The murder occurred late on a Sunday evening at the end of June 1981, in what was initially billed as a common robbery. According to two female employees at the convenience store, Granderson and two unknown men approached the store from outside about closing time. When one of the men brandished a gun, the women opened the store and allowed them in. After dispatching the women variously about the store, Granderson was shot and $5,000 taken by the unknown men.

In the succeeding days a tale that matches one made for television unfolded: police officers combed the area for the two men. On the Friday Granderson was buried, gross bedlam broke out in and around the town as men thought to be the perpetrators were pursued. The pursuit started several miles away in Lexington when these men allegedly stole a truck from the local hospital. Said to be heavily armed with guns and dynamite, they eventually drove to Tchula where still another truck was stolen. After being spotted once more, police charge that the men stole still a third vehicle. Thereafter, they unleashed a flurry of gunfire and blasts with machine guns and dynamite.[87]

Later two men were caught and subsequently charged with the murder of Granderson. Vincent Bolden and David Hester, of East St. Louis, Illinois, were convicted after turning state's evidence, which led to the subsequent charge of capital murder against the mayor and his brother. In short, the two out-of-state men argued, after plea bargaining, that they had been hired by the Carthans to murder Granderson and to create a scene consistent with a robbery. This was but the culmination of what those who argued for a conspiracy against black rule said was inevitable—that the mayor would be charged with the murder. Carthan was indicted, arrested, and tried for capital murder, as well as armed robbery and conspiracy to commit bank robbery.

This trial was as complicated and confusing in parts as were the others against the mayor. The case was based on the apparent testimony of the two suspects that they had been hired by Carthan and his older brother to execute Granderson. According to the suspects Carthan had known at least one of them for five years and had made arrangements at various sites (including a down payment) to expedite the deal. The total payment said to be agreed upon was $10,000. Despite inconsistencies between some of the testimony of the suspects, the state pressed the line of reasoning about the mayor's involvement with some vigor. In order to exact supporting testimony, the state allowed the suspects to plead to charges less than capital murder. Both men were sentenced for the lesser crime of murder—Bolden for life and Hester for 30 years.[88]

The trial itself did not clear up the question of how the mayor supposedly expedited the plans with the out-of-state suspects. Carthan's defense team offered an entirely different set of circumstances and motives behind the murder and the subsequent charges. In the first place, they proffered alibis for the mayor at the time when he was alledgedly executing arrangements with the suspects. This made the state's scenarios about what occurred seem implausible. Moreover, the credibility of the suspects was questioned. Carthan's attorneys argued that because of the past criminal records of the suspects, reliability could not be expected; each reportedly had previous arrests and jail sentences. The suspects themselves, already accused of being drug dealers, created deeper suspicions when one of them claimed to be a Baptist minister who supported churches with proceeds he acquired from heroin sales.[89]

In the eyes of the public, much doubt was cast on the state's case because of the conflicting stories about who was actually involved in the act of killing. Some of the questions centered on the fact that four men were thought to be on the scene when the mayhem occurred on the day of Granderson's funeral. Some who claimed to be witnesses to one part or another of the shootout indicated that four men were indeed involved in the shooting. One press report recounted the statements of four people who said that at least one of the four suspects was white. Only two persons of this alleged group were ever apprehended. The only other arrests were those of Eddie Carthan and his brother, who were never alleged to be a part of the shootout.

The other tangled allegation centered on illegal drugs. It was suggested that the real motive for the killing was not robbery, but an execution of a partner in a bad drug deal. It was alleged, for example, that Granderson had long had such dealings and was involved with other powerful figures in the delta in supplying the region. In one such report the *Tchula Times*, which was unabashedly biased in favor of the mayor, sought to link the accused men with supposed local drug interests. The paper asserted that Granderson was in cahoots with some unnamed white lawyer from nearby Greenwood. The report rather confusingly related that illicit activities stemmed from a drug bust involving higher-ups, who covered up their involvement. The paper did not elaborate on how such a scheme led to involvement by Granderson or his murder.[90] The jailed suspects, however, furthered their claims when they gave evidence that money for South American cocaine purchases was the object of an attempted bank robbery several days after the murder.[91]

Many of those who were supporters of Carthan (and others who were not) found the escalating series of charges against him suspicious. To these individuals it seemed unlikely that coincidence would result in such a watershed of criminal charges against a single individual, in a small town in Mississippi. There was an emerging belief that some element of design was involved in the challenges. Gradually a broad consensus emerged among activists, both locally and nationally, to sustain the mayor's claim that he was being framed and was in fact a political prisoner.

The energies that Carthan had been unable to utilize in mobilizing for local political change, he now turned to his defense. He became his own best spokesman in claiming political imprisonment. He was temperamentally suited to making these claims given his observation and understanding of local racial history during the 1950s and 1960s. Even so, he made no systematic argument that whites were organized to defeat him until the trial regarding the police altercation. With this case Carthan began to articulate the position that a conspiracy existed with the intent of destroying his political influence. He said that the nature of the trial and the sentencing were all indicative of his contentions. The trial proceedings were thought to be flawed because of the anomalous dispositon of his countercharges against the accusers, and the fact that he was never tried on the stated but withdrawn charge of shooting Andrews. And he recounted all the other issues of payoffs, denial of witness recantation, and misinstructions to the jury.

From the mayor's standpoint this all came down to his imprisonment for his legitimate political beliefs. He equated his case with that of the "Wilmington 10," where the courts were utilized to silence those with progressive views and an activist orientation.[92] He and his chief supporters argued that this represented the same kind of campaign that had been traditionally mounted against black success in Mississippi. Allusions were made to the elimination of black influence during the reconstruction period. Here they attempted to show that at a time when blacks were on the verge of controlling Mississippi politics, a campaign of violence and intimidation was used to put down such efforts. The mayor saw his personal difficulties as symbolic of such a new campaign in response to the increased voting power of blacks. Since he saw himself as a direct product of this voting power, the conspiratorial campaign was designed as much to stem voting as to remove their aggressive new leaders. In the nature of the circumstances in Holmes County, this was especially critical because the overwhelming black population was likely to entirely dominate the political process. If he could be removed, he asserted, it would be possible to undo all the changes for which the civil rights movement had been responsible.

The mayor made similar arguments in all the succeeding cases. For example, he said that the charges of submitting phony receipts for foodstuffs were directed at his successful efforts in bringing federal programs to the town. This plethora of programs, he argued, were so altering the fabric of racial relations in Tchula that the whites wanted to cut off old programs and prevent new ones. According to this theory, if a cloud of suspicions and doubt could be created among federal officials about the propriety of operations in Tchula, then the financial support would possibly be withdrawn. (Indeed virtually every federal program of any magnitude was withdrawn during this period.) On the charges about the day care equipment, Carthan suggested that the federal government was using circumstantial evidence to link him with known criminal forces. It was contended that the charges could only result from a stretch of the imagination, the motives for which could only have been a pre-existing will to so associate him.

At the murder trial the mayor elaborated this thesis fully in a scathing indictment of the justice system. News reports indicate that the eloquence of this charismatic presentation left a largely supportive courtroom cheering. He began by discussing the system of racial segregation in American society where he alluded to the indelibility of blackness that thwarts achievement of the "American Dream." This dream was part of his desire to be a local politician. Much of his dream was short-circuited, however, because of this system. "He reminded the black jury that not too long ago, they could not sit in the jury box, because of segregation, or 'drink at a certain water fountain, ride on a bus . . . but it was justice at the time.' "[93] He provided examples of the continuity of racism by asking rhetorically what the consequences would be of attempting to integrate one of the schools to which whites had fled after public school desegregation.

He then discussed the role of the courts in furthering the conspiracy to get rid of strong aggressive black politicians like himself. This collusion on the part of the judges and lawyers to jail blacks was a contemporary kind of "lynching." "I'm here because I'm an illustration to the poor whites and blacks that when you step out of your boundaries and refuse to be a little boy to the power structure, you'll be punished." Then, Carthan likened himself to certain Biblical figures and to Martin Luther King, who were struck down despite their righteousness, and before their work was completed. None of this, he argued, should be a deterrent to seeking the benefits of the political kingdom (which he likened to the "Promised Land"):

> 'Moses died like Martin Luther King: without reaching the Promised Land. . . . but God brought Joshua. I submit to you today, we're in the time of Joshua . . . we didn't make the Promised Land. But we shouldn't stop here.
>
> [Then], his voice taking a[n] edge as he finished his 30-minute speech, he said the Liberty Bell has a crack in it, to symbolize freedom. And he told the jury, a 'not guilty' verdict 'is striking the Liberty Bell . . . and let it be heard in all 50 states. Let it be heard in the great delta plains of the South. Strike it! Let it be heard in the hinterlands of Mississippi.'[94]

Eddie Carthan and the Tchula Seven: The Making of a Cause Celébre

There were many people of different political persuasions who also were convinced that Eddie Carthan's experiences were akin to those associated with political imprisonment. And fairly rapidly after the first trial result was in, the "Tchula Seven" were taken on as a *cause celébre*. The reasoning of these several support groups and individuals was somewhat more simple than that of Carthan, but the conclusion was nearly the same. They accepted the contention that his troubles were far more related to his political ideology and behavior than to any criminal activity. There was a common belief among these supporters that it would have been impossible to sustain the charges against the mayor, even circumstantially, if he had not been a public personality in a highly visible position. This was all the more important in his case because he was known to oppose the status quo and to have instituted policies designed to undermine the singularly powerful position of whites in the community. It was these political actions, these supporters believed, that led whites in Tchula and Holmes County to use what remained of their traditional power to silence Carthan.

A large part of the argument of supporters was based on charges of racism. In that Carthan was located in Mississippi, perceived as the least redeemed of the old confederate states, it was relatively easy to make a connection between his fate and racism. It was said that his political imprisonment, and other outstanding political charges, were related to the fact that Carthan, a black man, was violating all of the taboos of the racial divide with his aggressive behavior and supposedly anti-white views. The traditions of Mississippi and especially Holmes County had never supported an individual of this sort; such people had always been destroyed. Examples were usually given from contemporary experiences to illustrate the immediacy of the problem. Such illustrations could include bombings and other violence against blacks in the county, or the murder of Medgar Evers and other state civil rights leaders. For some supporters who knew intricate details of Mississippi history, it was possible to relate the range of similar circumstances encountered by black leaders just after 1875 when reconstruction was overturned. Therefore contemporary supporters could use a plethora of past and present situations to formulate the argument that Carthan's problems were related first and foremost to political factors, largely determined by race. These ideas could not be separated in their minds and formed the base for a wide range of activities designed to free Carthan from prison.

The most striking fact about this effort is how rapidly it became national in scope. In short order there were branches in many urban American areas, and among traditional progressive and liberal organizations. Though there were several local groups and lawyers who surrounded the mayor and gave legal assistance, it was perhaps the national campaign that gave the movement the true flavor of a *cause celèbre*.

The first organized group to make a public issue of the political nature of charges against Carthan was the Mississippi Conference of Black Mayors.[95] Since Carthan was one of their number, they all were well-informed of the nature of political affairs in Tchula and personally knew the mayor. When the verdict of the 1981 trial for assault was announced, this group was incensed. Its chairman called the charges "a disgrace to the judicial system of not only the state of

Mississippi but also to the United States; . . . political assassination." The chief contentions were that the trial process had not been fair, what with the possibility of jury tampering and the length of the sentence *vis-à-vis* the magnitude of the alleged crime. These mayors thought it uncharacteristically harsh that a sentence of three years should be meted out for simple assault. It was argued that if those within the judicial system were not intent on merely silencing a man whose political views were unacceptable, then a far lesser sentence would have been warranted. The upshot of their complaints was that they established a defense fund to assist the mayor in appealing the conviction.[96]

With the addition of federal charges, still others organized to either create defense committees or to mobilize public support for the mayor. At this stage the proponents extended their claims to suggest that Carthan was but a symbol of a much broader campaign to rid the country of successful black politicians. By this view black politicians were under attack everywhere and Carthan was merely a glaring symbol of this strategy of white backlash. At a news conference in July 1981, it was evident that local and national groups were organizing around this theme with the effect of greatly expanding the conflict, in Schattschneider's terms.[97] Two local groups were organized for the purpose: the Holmes County United League, and the Committee to Defend the Tchula 7. The former was an existing organization that sought to maintain some of the mobilization achieved early in the 1960s and to channel it toward electoral politics and continuous social change. The group now chose to use its resources for a campaign regarded as its routine business in a hostile racial environment. The Committee to Defend the Tchula 7, on the other hand, was established specifically to assist the mayor in defending himself against the assault charges.

These local groups were joined by the first out-of-state group, the Equal Rights Congress of New Orleans, whose apparent concern was largely the extension of the voting rights legislation that was about to expire.[98] One of its leaders met Carthan in 1979 and saw the problems in Tchula as integrally linked with the national efforts of the Congress. Indeed Tchula and the local organization there, the United League of Holmes County, were seen as a means by which the Congress could expand its efforts into Mississippi. Even though the issue of political imprisonment was not a major objective of the Congress at the time, organizers did find a way to link their broader concerns of voting rights with the problems in Tchula.

Eddie Carthan's fate was thought to be indicative of a broad effort by southern whites to circumvent or completely destroy the usefulness of the Voting Rights Acts of 1965. This act had been specifically designed to improve black voting conditions in the southern states, but was now about to expire and the Reagan Administration appeared at the time to favor its expiration. The Tchula case, however, was good evidence, according to this group, that the legislation was still needed. For if blacks could again be successfully disfranchised by fear or intimidation, as in Tchula, then without any federal legislation whites could easily regain their power.[99] This meant that the Equal Rights Congress also accepted the view that Carthan's was a political trial,[100] and made their resources available to Tchula in the hopes of also advancing their larger cause of mobilization for voting rights.

By the time of the murder trial a national organization had emerged. It had the aim of freeing Carthan from the array of state and federal charges, all of which were seen as acts of political repression. The group bore the name of the National Campaign to Free Mayor Eddie Carthan and the Tchula 7 and to Preserve Black Political Rights. It represented a collective body of national leaders and groups, especially among social activists, churches, and civic-minded groups. Its truly national character was evident in the numerous offices and contact people maintained around the country. In one of its newsletters a "partial list" of coordinating points indicated the following places: Alabama, California, District of Columbia, Florida, Georgia, Illinois, Kentucky, Massachusetts, Missouri, Michigan, Louisiana, Minnesota, New York, Ohio, Oregon, Tennessee, Texas, Utah and Wisconsin.[101]

The headquarters for much of the national effort was located at Dayton, Ohio. It was run by a college professor, Jim Dunn, whose task was greatly advanced by big-name figures who lent their names and efforts to the cause. The national organization was eventually headed by Ossie Davis, the well-known actor and political activist. Dick Gregory, the comedian and political activist, also joined the campaign, and joined the fast that Carthan began while jailed in Holmes County. At the same time many officials of civil rights organizations also joined the ranks, including Joseph Lowery of the Southern Christian Leadership Conference, various state NAACP officials, and the Delta Ministry of the National Council of Churches. Indeed, the coordination committee of the organization looked like a Who's Who of human and political rights leaders.

The chief work of the national committee was to mobilize public and media support for Eddie Carthan by political education and sponsorship of public protest activities. Their initial project was a national speaking tour featuring Carthan prior to his final arrest. It was estimated that the mayor appeared before over 60 support groups to tell his story. Thereafter the group organized an information campaign directed at known human rights activists and the mass media. During the highwater mark of their operation, several newsletters and open letters from the mayor were published. These one-to four-page documents routinely updated the trial, announced upcoming events, and solicited funds. Oftentimes there was a direct statement or appeal from the mayor.

The campaign was relatively successful on both counts. The Carthan case became widely known and attracted sufficient support to maintain the media blitz, to publish a well-presented newsletter, and to develop national coverage for later activities, including the murder trial. One of the newsletters noted that:

> National representatives from CBS are at the trial and *Time/Life* magazine [sic] has been in Holmes County for several weeks collecting information for a major story. A representative from Amnesty International, sent from Canada by the

London, England office has been present at the trial since it began on the 19th. In addition, the *New York Times* ran a front page story on the case—See *N.Y. Times*, Wednesday, October 20.[102]

The major part of the mobilization included nearly a week of activities leading up to the murder trial scheduled for October 19, 1982. The national committee planned four major events to focus attention on its contention that the trial was political. First, because much of the support for the national effort had come from churches or church people, October 10 was designated National Church Day. Special prayers were to be said and a collection for the defense fund raised. October 11 was the date of the "long march" from Tchula to Lexington, where Carthan was incarcerated. The intent was to dramatize the conditions in Mississippi before the national media and to take advantage of local sentiment favorable to the mayor. On October 15 a rally was planned in Tchula. All of this was to culminate the following day, October 16, in the urban capital of Jackson. Here it was expected that the full weight of the national campaign would be exerted as thousands jammed the streets in the name of a small town mayor. This event was expected to attract speakers of national reputation to discuss political repression and the ordeal of the Carthan family.

Though these were not the first protest activities outside of Tchula for Carthan, they probably garnered more attention and support for his cause. The large rally and auxiliary activities occurred on schedule and with some degree of organization and success. The newsletter, for example, reported that more than two to three thousand people took part in the march on October 16 in Jackson, Mississippi. "The marchers walked 5 miles, mostly through the Black community, singing freedom songs and chanting slogans like 'Free Mayor Carthan' and 'We're fired up, ain't taking no more.' As they reached downtown and entered a city park next to the governor's mansion, they were greeted by a couple hundred cheering supporters."[103]

Otherwise the national campaign stimulated many sympathetic national officials to take note of the effort and or to make statements in support of Carthan. This was especially true among Afro-American leaders. On the roster of partial endorsers the national committee indicated the support of Jesse Jackson, Julian Bond, Congressmen Ronald Dellums and Mervyn Dymally (both from California), Mayor Richard Hatcher (Gary, Indiana), and Vernon Jordan (formerly of the Urban League). Many groups also endorsed the weeklong campaign. Some of these included the American Indian Environmental Council, Catholic Committee of the South, Center for Constitutional Rights, Coalition of Black Trade Unionists; the National Council of Churches, United Methodist Voluntary Services, National Urban League, Operation Push and the National Conference of Black Mayors. Moreover, the officials of many of these organizations mobilized their members to write letters or to make financial contributions.

The direct impact of all of these groups on the resolution of the issues surrounding Eddie Carthan is not clear. It is obvious, however, that the national leadership succeeded in creating a *cause celèbre* in the name of human rights. They felt that the notion of "southern justice" as a special category of American jurisprudence had some practical meaning.[104]

It is also said that the combination of forces had an impact on the eventual conduct and resolution of the remaining litigation surrounding Carthan. It is widely held that the national mobilization for the mayor provided an array of resources—personnel and finances—such as separate contributions of over $10,000 from both the Methodists and Presbyterians.[105] The mayor could afford competent counsel and a host of legal and political advisers that assisted in developing strategies. At the same time the rapid development of such a substantial following was thought to have affected judicial officers and even the hostile community in unusual ways. One of the newsletters reported that the courtroom was always filled to overflowing with supporters. "Some longtime Mississippi residents have stated that they have never witnessed Circuit Judge Tom Clark be so courteous and cooperative as in this trial. They are convinced it is due to the presence of out-of-towners and the national news media, including Amnesty International."[106] Their presence was seen as a deterrent to the prolongation of the trial and overt violation of legalities that some thought had marked previous litigation.

The murder trial represented the culmination of the charges against the mayor. He had already left office by the time of much of the litigation, and was serving the three-year jail term at the county prison on the assault charge. The end of the murder trial and its resolution also seemed to represent a turning point in the public's mind about the inappropriateness of much of what had preceded. Carthan became a symbol and martyr to so many of those mobilized and those merely on the sidelines. As such there was the appearance of pressure on public officials to somehow dispose of the whole affair. After the jury in the murder trial promptly returned a verdict of not guilty in early November of 1982, the state decided not to go to trial with the charges against his brother or to pursue any of the several additional charges said to be associated with the murder. The general agreement seemed to be summed up by one juror who said: "The state didn't prove nothing to us."

Meanwhile another of the assault charges regarding the altercation at town hall was dropped. According to the county district attorney (in press reports) "there was some question whether Andrews was legally a police officer since he had not been sworn in and had not posted bond" at the time of the altercation.[107] The following March the governor suspended the balance of the assault conviction, after which the mayor immediately proceeded to federal prison on the fraud conviction regarding the day-care sentence. He served eight months at Maxwell Air Force Base prison, before the sentence was reduced leading to his release in October 1983. The other outstanding fraud charge, regarding false receipts for foodstuffs, had already been dropped in June 1982 as indicated, when the government's chief witness died. Thus ended the saga of political mobilization and turmoil surrounding Eddie Carthan. He returned to private life in Tchula, where political administration was now in the hands of the old regime. Lester Lyon, the incumbent unseated by Carthan, had been returned as mayor.

Conclusion

The mobilization in Tchula was in many ways broader in its organization than in the other towns. However the realization of the benefits from the transformation was incomplete and shortlived. This analysis illustrates two interrelated components that contributed to the failure. First there was the concentrated efforts of the whites to maintain white supremacy and a willingness to use divide and conquer tactics to do so. And on the other side, there was a critical divsion within the black leadership class that prevented solidarity.

The role of whites in attempting to thwart the black mobilization was deeply imbedded in history. The relative poverty of the area had always left these whites feeling especially vulnerable. This had been so even during plantation slavery and reconstruction when their smaller, less productive farms made them poorer. The blacks they enslaved or maintained as tenants were thus more of a threat, kept in check by harsh measures. By the time of contemporary civil rights mobilization in Tchula, little had changed in the economic status of whites or in their willingness to use violence to protect their political supremacy. The growth of extremist organizations in the area was ultimately to fuel the violence that preceded Carthan's election and that stimulated an ongoing effort to undermine the emergent solidarity in the black community. The lone white alderman was often seen as but the point man for these interests that rejected the claims for social change by the blacks.

Despite the intensity of the mobilization among blacks—the development and activation of organizations and leaders—the local class of leaders was not in agreement about the task. Much of this seemed to be based on differing backgrounds. The traditional townspeople, represented by Carthan, had some degree of independence because of their properties and educational resources. They also had acquired a degree of cosmopolitanism because of contacts and travel. On the other hand, the newcomers had only their education and the potential for enjoying some independence for the first time. Their backgrounds were rural. Immediately, the newcomers' motivations for political power clashed with the ideologically more progressive motivations of the townspeople. The differences in the two experiences made this almost inevitable, since they came to see themselves in competition with each other. And given the racial past and the known continuing sentiments of the whites, this black intragroup conflict created a vacuum for exploitation. Clearly it was exploited for all it was worth.

Therefore leadership mobilization in Tchula was ultimately directed more at external matters than to the "committed" constituency. This was a critical difference from the other towns where the efforts never ceased to be trained on needs defined by blacks and the development of appropriate projects. Though

Carthan himself was sufficiently committed and developed an appropriate vehicle as agrarian townsman for mobilization, the ideal could not be fully realized. Largely this was because after election the mayor was required to exert his energies, even as the aggressive agrarian townsman, to fending off opposition in the white community and among some black leaders. Hence the aggressiveness, cosmopolitanism and nationalism of Carthan, when fully elaborated, did not have a sufficient local base for positive utilization. As an example, instead of creating jobs for development by expanding federal grants, he had to fight with his opponents for the very right to solicit such funds. In these debates Carthan's ideals and commitments were always sumptuously elaborated, but reviled with equal force by the opponents. His failure therefore must be understood in the full context of local history where whites have continued the resolve to maintain supremacy. At the same time the incomplete absorbtion of the black leadership for the ends of the mobilization left the process truncated.

6

The Electorates: Politics, Economics and Ideology

In the drive for political mobilization in these Mississippi towns, constituents have proved to be all-important. Without their broad dissatisfaction with the old ways and their impetus, the new leaders already described would have found little place to register the ideals of political change. Indeed the people, these new black constituents, were the foundation upon which the general ideals of populism and participatory democracy were built for the transfer of power symbolized by the mayors. The people's commitment to this process was distinguished by their readiness to act in new ways in public affairs, and by their utilization of all organized resources to such ends. This chapter details what the mobilization of these constituents was like, and how it was critical to the realization of political change and power transfer.

As in the analysis of the leadership of these towns, the focus on the constituents is political mobilization in progress. The major question is how did the local constituents sustain a process that included their collective activation of local resources for the acquisition of political goods? In the first place their activism and commitment are known by the dramatic changes they wrought in the past twenty-odd years. However, this analysis defines the commitment and measures the activism as they occurred. This is done by singling out four key variables for sustained exploration that are important in circumstances of democratization like that occurring in these rural, small-scale societies. The variables are participation, political information, efficacy and ideology. Elections and registration are indicators of participation; knowledge of leaders and a wide variety of issues are indicators of information; perceptions of citizen impact on government are indicators of efficacy; while principles used in sorting out issues and policies are indicators of ideology.

In the analysis, contrary to conventional wisdom, (which is elaborated) the intense mobilization of these constituents focused upon domestic affairs. (They faltered in depth only in their facility with the international sphere, a factor introduced to establish the boundaries of citizen sophistication.) The depth of their mobilization broke all the best known rules about the impact of demographic and socioeconomic factors upon citizen participation. Though expected to be non-participant and uninformed, these poor and uneducated rural folk had undergone a transformation that gave them remarkable political sophistication. It is this which made them of such critical importance to the local mobilization.

Blacks in the American Democratic Process

There are many things we as political scientists think we know about American political culture or the value system which undergirds American democracy. At the same time, there are also many things we think we know about the political culture of various regional and ethnic groups participating in the American political process. Many of these truisms in academic parlance result from the behavioral revolution in social science that made it possible to take large samples of opinion on issues and policies, with great regularity and speed. These massive compilations of data on political attitudes and behaviors then allowed us to make certain conclusions, and even predictions. Richard Niemi and Herbert Weisberg have recently pointed out two of the influential models that have allowed us to amass such data. The earlier model they refer to as the sociological, which allowed political scientists to focus on "a person's socio-economic status (SES)—education, income, class, religion, and place of residence (rural or urban)" as the strongest determinants of voter choice. Later a psychological model was developed that focused on "the person's attachment to a party, the person's orientation toward the issues, and the person's orientation toward the candidates." The upshot is that such socio-psychological factors were thought to be extremely important in allowing us to predict who would vote, for whom, and how often.[1] And the critical finding using either of these models was that higher-status individuals were more likely to be participants and more likely to be mobilized for political action.

By these measures blacks were usually described as non-participant, but also with less interest in and inclination toward activation for political purposes. The importance of this axiom was heightened when it was said that such conditions were especially exaggerated among blacks in the South.

Earlier studies pointed out that blacks, like other Americans, were more likely to participate if they were of higher SES. Since most blacks were not of such status, they voted less. But there was also the additional factor of less motivation on the part of blacks that further depressed their participation levels. Angus Campbell et al. reported "persistent non-voting among Negroes" in the South, notwithstanding "restrictive electoral laws" whose "greater impact . . . [was] a function of the relatively low motivational levels among Negroes."[2] While blacks in the North voted more often, they "participat[ed] in politics substantially less than their white neighbors."[3] Another source strengthened the claim of habitual non-voting among blacks. "Deprived social conditions or inhibiting cultural values lead to low interest in, little concern with, and little information on politics and that in turn, leads to non-voting."[4] Even the quality of participation by those with lower SES was flawed, since their level of competence was so low.[5]

This general view of black activism was sustained by all manner of empirical surveys. In Table 6.1 (illustrating voting between 1952 and 1976) lower black participation levels can be observed. The lowest levels were in the 1950s when disfranchisement was still a major factor in the South; the increase in the 1960s may be attributed to the mobilization of the civil rights movement. Even when region and restrictions were controlled the same pattern was confirmed. (See Table 6.2.) Even in presidential elections, which usually engendered more participation, blacks were less active. It was found in the 1960s that 52 percent of whites reported voting in all presidential elections, compared to 38 percent of

Table 6.1.   Percent of Eligible Voter Participation, 1952-1976.

Year	National	White	Black
1952	61.6%	79.0%	33.0%
1956	59.3	76.0	36.0
1960	63.1		
1964	61.8	70.7	57.5
1968	67.8	69.1	57.6
1972	63.0	64.5	52.1
1976	59.2	60.9	48.7

Sources: National, 1952-1968: U.S. Bureau of the Census, *Statistical Abstract of the United States: 1972*, 93rd ed., Washington, D.C.: GPO, 1972, p. 373. National, 1972: U.S. Bureau of the Census, *Current Population Reports— Population Characteristics*, "Voter Participation in November, 1972," Series p-20, No. 244, December, 1972, p. 1. National, 1976: *Statistical Abstract of the United States*, 1978, p. 520.

Abstracted from Barker and McCorry, *Black Americans and the Political System* (Cambridge, Mass.: Winthrop, 1976). p. 84.

northern blacks; Southern blacks at this time had the lowest level of participation, with but 11 percent reporting voting in all such elections. It was also demonstrated that southern black participation decreased precipitously for "less elevated and visible" offices. Of the white participants, 71 percent reported voting in all or most presidential elections, and 48 percent said the same for posts as low as local school board elections. Blacks, on the other hand, voted at a 55 percent rate for presidents and at a mere 28 percent for local school board posts.

Table 6.2. Relations of State Restrictions on Voting to Past Frequency of Voting.

	\multicolumn{4}{c}{Negro}	\multicolumn{4}{c}{White}
	\multicolumn{2}{c}{Suffrage Laws Restrictive}	\multicolumn{2}{c}{Suffrage Laws Moderate}	\multicolumn{2}{c}{Suffrage Laws Restrictive}	\multicolumn{2}{c}{Suffrage Laws Moderate}
	North	South	North	South	North	South	North	South
Voted in all elections	20%	3%	23%	10%	55%	26%	49%	34%
Voted in most elections	10	0	31	10	20	22	23	19
Voted in some elections	35	12	24	20	9	24	16	19
Have never voted	35	85	22	60	16	28	12	28
	100%	100%	100%	100%	100%	100%	100%	100%
Number of cases	49	95	62	89	753	315	1,515	439

Source: A. Campbell, et al., *The American Voter* (New York: Wiley, 1960), p. 182, 279.

The Political Socialization of Blacks

If it were true that blacks participated less and did so as a result of less motivation, was there a way of accounting for these conditions? Once again the behavioral method allowed scholars to measure what seemed to be some components of the problem. There was a mass of evidence that pointed to political socialization and ideological commitment to the political process as being significant. Blacks seemed to be socialized differently, and their lack of engagement rarely sustained ideological attachment to the system.

Even though political socialization is deemed of first order importance, blacks seem to have followed a different route in this training process and evince skepticism toward the system. Political socialization is deemed to occur very early in the family, school, and primary group contexts of childhood. "[These] shape ideals and give insight into political aspects of life."[6] But the black child has been largely cut off from this process, and has learned a whole set of different rules and has a different relationship to the political system. Even though blacks are some of the strongest supporters of the abstract principles and symbols associated with American democracy,[7] they learn as children to distrust political leaders and have little confidence later that the government will operate in their interest.[8] In the early studies it was argued that SES, especially education, was seen as a chief determinant. "The educated stand out with great clarity on the motivational dimensions of what we call 'sense of efficacy' and 'sense of citizen duty' . . . with more formal schooling an individual is more likely to feel that he has influence on political events."[9] Data collected between 1952 and 1974 sustained this conclusion as the perceived ineffectiveness on the part of blacks remained almost two times that of whites in many of these years.[10] Indeed Dwaine Marvick's findings using 1960 data showing 49 percent black distrust of political leaders (versus 90 percent for whites)[11] have not been reversed. For example, blacks believing that government was run for the benefit of all declined from 69 percent in 1964, to 19 percent in 1974.[12] What emerges, according to these scholars, is a situation among blacks of deep-seated estrangement from the political system.[13]

It followed from this that principled commitment for blacks would likely also be low. They would be unable to develop "a highly differentiated attitude structure [whose] . . . parts are organized in a coherent fashion"[14] or to develop "a configuration of ideas and attitudes in which the elements are bound together by some form of constraint or functional interdependence."[15] This was true for two reasons: (1) Very few people could be classed ideologues in American democracy; the system was largely based on consensus since "the fundamental political problems of the industrial revolution have been solved: the workers have achieved industrial and political citizenship; the conservatives have accepted the welfare state; and the democratic left has recognized that an increase in over-all state power carries with it more dangers to freedom than solutions for economic problems."[16] It was the end of ideology.[17] But (2) with particular reference to blacks, there was less likelihood of ideology because only the most active and participant citizens were ever likely to exhibit sufficient principled commitment.[18] And even these were only the most highly educated.[19] Insofar as blacks were the least participant in orientation, then the absence of ideology was easily accounted for. To the extent that blacks deviated from the norm it was rather a product of their primordialism (ethnic or racial chauvinism), and not principled commitment of the sort denoting an active ideology.

These conclusions would seem to suggest an absence of potential among blacks for the type of mobilization that characterized the Mississippi towns. For in these three places very intense general activation occurred in the 1960s on the strength of existing community bases. Is it possible that the data could be wrong, or how is it that activation in Mississippi is aberrant? It has already been seen that the three new leaders were independently strong, but only insofar as they were buttressed by their small town constituents and local organizations. This does not appear in any way aberrant, as it was occurring all over the South. The critical difference, according to scholarly evaluation, resulted from the virtual isolation of the core black community from the American mainstream. The independent facilities were always what made for survival (but also invisibility) in a system of racial exclusion. Yet when the match-up occurred between revitalized leadership and a simmering constituency it was relatively easy to forge ahead with mobilization. All of the sentiments of distrust and principled commitment for black betterment were organized and directed toward the goal of social change and acquisition of political benefits. The results of this process are detailed below by relating the content of mobilization within the three local black communities—the extent of their knowledge, participation and principles.

The Demography of Rural Black Electorates

The isolation of blacks after reconstruction, especially in politics, was broad, and the first breaks came in the North. There was little opportunity for mobilization within the framework of the routine American political process. It will be remembered that though blacks were largely linked to the Republican Party, this was of little practical consequence for receipt of political goods. A more concentrated focus began to emerge, however, with certain demographic changes in the community and in the ruling American political coalition. Much of this was occurring in the North,[20] where large numbers of Blacks had migrated. They were inspired to participate in electoral politics because of recruitment by the urban political machines and because the new national coalition dominated by Democrats appeared amenable. The latter was much impelled by Franklin Roosevelt, the party's standard-bearer whose "unprecedented gestures toward the race . . . managed to convey to them that they counted and belonged."[21] Soon blacks independently elected some of their own to office.[22]

The circumstances leading to electoral participation in the South were very different. Because of the ubiquitousness of racial exclusion, and in spite of the concentration of potential black electorates, there were few avenues for the exercise of the franchise. At the same time many of these potential citizens had adopted an attitude of non-participation as one of the means of survival in a system where violence often accompanied efforts or ideas for political change. Therefore what was required in the South was a mobilization campaign that focused directly on destruction of the racial caste system, and eventually its political attributes. This was largely achieved in the civil rights movement that was inspired by the work of Martin Luther King, Jr. and the legal work of the NAACP. The legal campaign had started before the entry of King, with successful challenges to white primaries and school segregation. Nevertheless it was only in the mid-1950s when the sundry civil rights activities and actors began to converge on the issues and tactics. Simultaneously there was a distinct and critical effort to captivate and motivate the masses to action. It was a conscious decision to expand the campaign to the people whose corporate existence was defined by the confines of Southern white racism. In this sense the social change movement in the South was dependent upon mass mobilization from the start. It is doubtful whether the slow and arduous process of bargaining and negotiation in often isolated circumstances could ever have achieved the status of a generalized campaign, without ultimately being buttressed by the mass constituency of black people. The local campaigns however did radically expand the opportunities and base for actions, as Morris has shown.[23]

Meanwhile, even broader opportunities were created due to general support from the New Deal coalition for change in Southern racial relations. The importance of blacks to the coalition made it practically impossible for the party to ignore the glaring nature of southern discrimination. This began with the Roosevelt Administration, which while not of substantive programmatic importance in the early days, had all of the appropriate symbols. He was aware of the practical importance of blacks to the party's growth and sought their support. (See Table 6.3.) Blacks seized the opportunity for all its symbolic worth. "Far

Table 6.3. Population in Standard Metropolitan Areas (SMAs) by Regions: 1900, 1930, and 1950 (in thousands)

Area	1900 Total	1900 Nonwhite	1930 Total	1930 Nonwhite	1950 Total	1950 Nonwhite
United States	75,900	9,200	122,700	12,500	150,700	15,700
	30,800	2,200	64,700	4,900	85,600	8,300
Northeast	15,200	350	27,700	1,100	31,900	1,900
Northcentral	8,800	250	19,300	1,100	24,100	2,000
South	5,000	1,500	10,900	2,500	17,500	3,500
West	1,700	83	6,600	260	11,900	690

Percent Increase Over Previous Period

Area						
United States	...	...	61.6	36.0	22.7	26.2
	...	...	110.2	122.4	32.1	67.9
Northeast	...	...	82.0	213.5	15.3	79.2
Northcentral	...	...	111.8	307.5	24.5	92.3
South	...	...	119.7	65.2	59.6	42.8
West	...	...	291.5	215.1	79.3	164.5

Source: Taeuber and Taeuber, in Marcus Jones, *Black Migration in U.S., With An Emphasis On Selected Cities*, p. 50.

from being surprised at the failure of the New Deal to embrace a racial agenda, most blacks in the 1930s remarked on how much attention the Roosevelt administration seemed to be paying to them."[24] Subsequently, over the next 20 or so years, blacks and others in the Democratic coalition moved the agenda further along to the point where the executive became an advocate for at least the minimum of social change: establishing legal guarantees for blacks consistent with provision of the Constitution. In sustaining these opportunities the Supreme Court, under NAACP pressure, was of critical importance; its interpretations would make or break this approach. After 1945 its rulings were more often than not consistent with the views espoused by blacks and by the executive. This created a preponderant succession of activities that culminated in the black mobilization. After a point, it even became difficult for Republican executives to deviate radically from this perspective, as Eisenhower proved in the matter of school desegregation at Little Rock, Arkansas.

Black Constituency Mobilization

What was there to activate and mobilize in the South and what was its political importance? It has been seen that massive numbers of blacks migrated from the South to the North, beginning in 1890. Yet data reveal that in 1940 about 77 percent of blacks lived in the South, compared to 68 percent, 60 percent, and 53-plus percent in 1950, 1960 and 1970, respectively (see Table 6.4). The 1970 figure shows this population at over 12 million in the South alone, when a modest reverse flow of black migrants became important.[25] Hence even at this peak, the out-migration did not see more than half of the population leave the South. On this one count there was a tremendous mass of people to be mobilized by the civil rights campaign. We know that this population was both urban and rural in its distribution, and constituted a major proportion of the entire population of many of these states. However, because of the generally more rural character of the southern states, a considerable part of this population remained rural. This is especially indicative of a state like Mississippi, with but two major urban concentrations: Jackson and Gulfport/Biloxi. Yet a substantial proportion of the 35-40 percent of the state's black population lived in other than rural areas.

The formal electoral participation of these blacks was miniscule, even after the white primary, which barred blacks from party membership, was outlawed. Most blacks still did not vote. In Alabama in 1947 a mere 6,000 (1.2 percent) of blacks were registered. By 1956 this figure had only improved to 53,366 (11 percent). In Mississippi the circumstances were worse. In 1947, 5,000 (0.9 percent) were registered, and 10 years later the figure had only improved to 20,000 (5 percent). These conditions were only slightly better in the other southern states in 1947, where not a single state showed registration levels exceeding 30 percent for blacks.[26] Moreover, V. O. Key's conclusions from 1949

Table 6.4. Racial Population Distribution, 1940-1980.

	Total Population	Afro-American	%	Caucasian	%	Other	%
Mississippi							
1940	2,183,796	1,074,578		1,106,327		2,891	
1950	2,178,914	986,494	45.3	1,188,632	54.6	3,788	0.1
1960	2,178,141	915,743		1,257,546		4,852	
1970	2,216,912	815,770	36.8	1,393,283	62.8	7,859	0.4
1980	2,520,638	887,111		1,615,632		17,895	
S. Carolina							
1940	1,899,804	814,164		1,084,308		1,332	
1950	2,117,027	822,077	38.8	1,293,406	61.1	1,332	0.1
1960	2,382,594	829,291		1,551,022		2,281	
1970	2,590,516	789,041	30.5	1,794,430	69.3	7,045	0.3
1980	3,121,820	947,969		2,147,825		26,026	
Louisiana							
1940	2,363,880	849,303		1,511,739		2,838	
1950	2,683,516	882,428	32.9	1,796,683	67.0	4,405	0.1
1960	3,257,022	1,039,207		2,211,715		6,100	
1970	3,641,306	1,086,832	29.8	2,541,498	69.8	12,976	0.4
1980	4,205,900	1,238,472		2,915,310		52,118	
Alabama							
1940	2,832,961	983,290		1,849,097		574	
1950	3,061,743	979,617	32.0	2,079,591	67.9	2,535	0.1
1960	3,266,740	980,271		2,283,609		2,860	
1970	3,444,165	903,467	26.2	2,533,831	73.6	6,867	0.2
1980	3,893,888	886,283		2,873,289		24,316	
Georgia							
1940	3,123,723	1,084,927		2,038,278		518	
1950	3,444,578	1,062,762	30.9	2,380,577	69.1	1,239	
1960	3,943,116	1,122,596		2,817,223		3,297	
1970	4,589,575	1,187,149	25.9	3,391,242	73.9	11,184	0.2
1980	5,463,105	1,464,435		3,949,583		49,087	

Source: *U.S. Census*, by year as indicated.

remained appropriate that restrictions on registration were greatest in areas where the proportion of black population was highest. Figure 6.1 illustrates that "increases in the proportion Negro up to about 30 percent are *not* accompanied by substantial declines in Negro registration. As the proportion Negro increases beyond 30 percent, however, Negro registration rates begin to decline very sharply until they approach 0 at about 60 percent Negro and above."[27] In this context, therefore, it is obvious what there was to mobilize—virtually the entire black population.

Figure 6.1 Median Percentage of Voting-Age Negroes Registered to Vote, by Percentage of County Population Negro in 1950, in 11 Southern States.

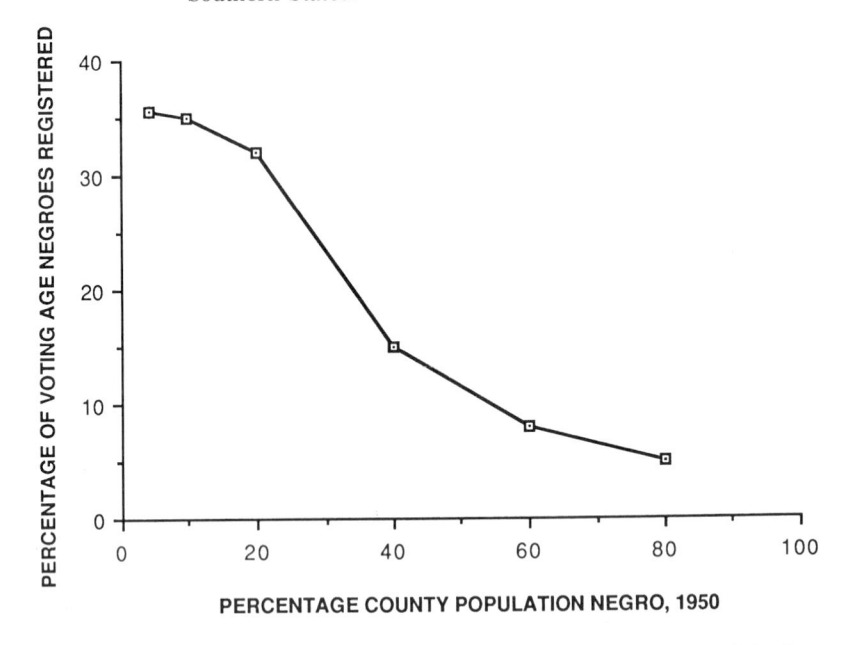

Adapted from D. Matthews and J. Prothro, *Negroes and the New* . . . (1966), p. 116.

It was not principally the question of voter registration that stimulated the mobilization campaign. It was the totality of the southern racial experience, of which voter registration was a part. In the early days the focus was on a variety of other phenomena, many of which were merely symbolic and abstract. The overt aspects of segregated society were some of the easiest upon which to direct attention. A great deal of energy was expended to focus on the obvious mistreatment of blacks in the routine actions of whites. These included white refusal to use courtesy titles such as "Mr." or "Mrs.," preferring "boy," "auntie," or "nigger-nigrah." Then there were the host of trivial symbols of segregated life, as in separate water fountains, waiting rooms, movie theaters, and outdoor recreation facilities. In some places a black man was not even to gaze at a white woman with whom there was no employee status. Though these were simple matters, they constituted powerful symbols that excited anger and almost universal rejection within the confines of the black community.[28]

Moreover, at least from the standpoint of black leaders, the racist symbols represented a continuing fundamental rejection by whites of the basic human quality of blacks; that blacks were not covered by the basic principles of democracy and human rights as elaborated in the Constitution. In this sense the civil rights forces saw a need to mobilize blacks around the familiar theme of basic rights. That is, the mobilization task was partly defined by the necessity to convince whites about the applicability of abstract principles and ideals.

But the consequence of the small symbols was also seen to be far beyond the mere abstract idea of rights. It was generally believed that the poor socioeconomic conditions of the black community were largely a product of the ideas and symbols of racial caste, and required equally forceful action. One was not only denied access to swimming pools and restaurants, but one was denied the basic resources required to develop an independent, if equal, institutional base. Education and employment were all affected in such a way that blacks were guaranteed to make less of a living than their average white counterparts. Such conditions provided the base for leaders and the masses to make claims against the southern power structure.

These were the circumstances that created an especially fluid atmosphere for political and social mobilization. Many sources have documented how the early phases that culminated in the electoral effort of the late 1960s were executed. Darlene Hine has traced the battle to overturn the white primary,[29] while Steven Lawson and Pat Watters have focused on the early registration and voting efforts between 1944 and 1969.[30] But nothing is more indicative of the campaign than the words of its own footsoldiers, such as Martin Luther King, Jr.

In the early period there was no more substantial regional leader than King. His crusade initially issued forth via the Southern Christian Leadership Conference (SCLC), as a result of the Montgomery bus boycott of 1955. His leadership was supplemented by that of national officials in the NAACP, CORE, the Urban League and the technical skills of Defense Fund lawyers. King and the others argued for politically educating the masses (and for the benefit of a larger public) that it was time for "America to live up to the true meaning of its promise" by ending segregation. In short, the early aims of the emerging movement were to revitalize the masses with the fact that certain rights were entitlements and that it was entirely appropriate to demand them.

King added another dimension—the assertion of moral imperative. He associated the rights he sought with moral rights as dictated by the Christian faith. While he did not reject the political dimensions of these issues, he sought to infuse them with a moral component. King sought to instill the idea that good Christian faith required one to overturn the immoral system prevalent over the South. By this view, the masses were required to achieve their general rights in order to attain political ends, but also in order to "save their souls" in the sight of God. As a Christian man, with an intensely moral message, King was guaranteed a certain amount of success among these rural blacks who were devout

Christians. The message was in a form and a tone that were eminently understandable.[31]

King's leadership was supplemented by that of many others in the local communities. These local populations gave their independent leaders the same degree of support that Montgomery citizens provided to King. They matched their talents with volunteer support from students and other organizations with similar aims, and thus developed the strongest mobilization campaign yet seen among blacks. From their local strengths they created new opportunities and took advantage of others, as they were activated for the assumption of previously denied political goods. The myriad ways this happened were seen in the analysis of leadership development in the three towns. The success of the process, however, remains to be accounted for in the everyday political experiences of blacks since mobilization ensued. For this, the succeeding analysis will be devoted to the role of the constituents' behavior in the assumption and maintenance of political power.

"Conventional Wisdom" and Contemporary Black Political Behavior

The first factor to understanding contemporary black behavior is the realization that its orientation is not non-participant or unmotivated by principle. Some objective facts about contemporary black life appear to deviate radically from "conventional wisdom." Since the time of the civil rights movement and the ensuing passage of civil rights legislation in the mid-1960s, there has been remarkably improved black participation. This participation has occurred at virtually all levels and among all classes, leading us to challenge the thesis that SES is the best predictor of political behavior among blacks. In the particular circumstances of the small Mississippi towns, it is observed that the phenomenon of radically increased participation levels is perhaps more prominent than similar increases in urban settings elsewhere.

What is it that explains this turnaround in electoral participation? While the three Mississippi cases may not be adequate to specify with absolute certainty how this process is driven all over the South, it is possible to illustrate its larger meaning under certain general regional circumstances. For example, there is no doubt about the improved electoral success of blacks all over the rural South. Moreover, there is little doubt that many of the same factors that impinge upon black politics in Mississippi also affect other regional states. Consequently it is not unreasonable to evaluate what seem to be very important variables to political scientists as being illustrative of the nature and consequences of rapid mobilization for political life. The variables selected in this instance are political participation, knowledge, efficacy, and ideology. It is expected that high mobilization will be indicated in places where ideology is strong. Contrary to popular belief, it is expected that this relationship will persist even when SES is controlled. In this sense it may be concluded that political factors in the environment far outweigh other explanations in accounting for black behavior and attitudes.

The four variables are defined as follows. *Participation* is operationally defined as voter registration and voting. In measuring voting in the towns, turnout in three elections is used—the 1972 and 1976 presidential elections, and the 1976 governor's race. *Knowledge* is also operationally defined in terms of politics, by asking respondents to provide information on a wide variety of local, national, and international political issues and personalities. *Efficacy* is the perception of the respondents about their abilities to influence the government before and after the election of a black administration. And *ideology* is operationally defined by citizen principles and preferences on issues and ideas relevant to their political environment.

These variables were selected with a view to understanding circumstances where blacks have come to exert considerable power. It is of interest to know what differences may have emerged in black perceptions and behaviors as a result of the intense mobilization experienced in the civil rights movement. It is reasoned that the rural South is the best scene from which to base analysis because it is the region from which most of our conventional empirical assertions (that black participation especially in the South was exceedingly low) were sustained. Moreover, that our three cases seem to be diametrically opposed to conventional assertions makes this study even more significant. Indeed, it is the contention here that it was the great susceptibility of the South to the civil rights mobilization campaign that subsequently yielded the intense political mobilization, and greater political participation and sophistication, among blacks.

These three southern towns illustrate that contrary to popular belief, SES does not overwhelmingly determine the nature of black participation and sophistication. Political factors such as leadership mobilization, and size of the black electorate seem to be far more significant under contemporary circumstances. Hence, it seems not accidental that in towns like these (with a black majority population, black leadership and the benefit of a civil rights mobilization effort), there is uncharacteristically high participation and sophistication. This is a radically changed black electorate, whose behavior has implications for the broader role of this group in American politics. Even in larger urban communities and at the national level, there is remarkable similarity to the linkages these rural towns exhibit between mobilization, leadership and political success. When the numbers are favorable, and there is a black candidate to spearhead a mobilization campaign, other variables are of considerably less significance.

The Mississippi towns have already been described in such a way that one gets a picture of the population of these small communities. Though there are clearly differences in the three towns and the people who live there, much is very similar. In short, these are poor people, who live in poor towns, in the poorest state in the union. Some have attained about as much as is available to anyone elsewhere in the state, but most are off the average by a considerable amount. The data below (also see Table 6.5) give a general comparative picture of the people who were surveyed between 1977 and 1980. In Mayersville, the smallest town, we acquired 59 usable surveys; 64 from the town of Bolton; and 150 from Tchula (the latter over twice the size of the other two towns); for a total sample of 273. Forty percent of the sample was male, while 60 percent was female. Most had long been residents in the communities, having lived there for life (39 percent) or over 10 years (another 38 percent). It is interesting that the population in Bolton and Mayersville consisted of a much larger number of lifelong residents—55 percent and 63 percent, respectively. In Tchula, only 23 percent of those residents had lived there all their lives. This is not to say that many people in Tchula had not been long-time residents, because 51 percent of them did report residence for more than 10 years.

Table 6.5. Socioeconomic Characteristics

	Bolton		Mayersville		Tchula		Total	
Age:	N	%	N	%	N	%	N	%
18-29	24	(38)	15	(25)	53	(35)	92	(34)
30-45	9	(14)	21	(36)	23	(15)	53	(19)
46-60	6	(9)	4	(7)	24	(16)	34	(13)
over 60	23	(36)	18	(31)	49	(33)	90	(33)
Education:								
None	0		3	(5)	3	(2)	6	(2)
Primary	13	(20)	11	(19)	18	(12)	42	(15)
Junior High	18	(28)	9	(15)	45	(30)	72	(26)
Secondary	14	(22)	30	(51)	68	(45)	112	(41)
Some College	8	(13)	6	(10)	11	(7)	25	(9)
College Degree	6	(9)	0		0		6	(2)
Advanced Degree	3	(5)	0		3	(2)	6	(2)
Occupation:								
Unemployed	13	(20)	15	(25)	70	(47)	98	(36)
Laborer	24	(38)	32	(54)	39	(36)	95	(35)
Semi-Professional	12	(19)	5	(9)	2	(1)	19	(7)
Housewife	2	(3)	4	(7)	13	(9)	19	(7)
Retired	5	(13)	3	(5)	16	(11)	32	(12)

There are some interesting variations in the other characteristics of the towns worth highlighting. While there is little that is startling about the ages of the respondents, it is noteworthy that a sizable proportion of them were younger.

Thirty-four percent of those in the general sample were 18-29 years old. It is only in Mayersville that under 30 percent of those sampled were 18-29 years of age. In that town an unusually large percentage (36 percent) of the respondents were in the mature adult group (30-45 years of age). In the other towns, however, mature adults and the middle-aged group (46-60) averaged 12-14 percent. This could be accounted for by the higher rate of out-migration in Mayersville, which affects younger adults more than other groups. All of the towns do demonstrate a common pattern in reference to the elderly—over 30 percent of each sample is over 60 years of age.

Education and occupation characteristics highlight the distance between Bolton and the other towns somewhat. In the former, there are no respondents without some schooling, while there are a few in both Tchula and Mayersville. For only high school completion, 51 percent and 45 percent are reported for Mayersville and Tchula respectively. Bolton is much lower, with 22 percent, but only because a much larger number in that town have continued beyond high school. Twenty-six percent have training beyond high school, 14 percent are college graduates or hold advanced degrees. Their educational levels are far and away beyond those for the other towns. None of the Mayersvillians had a degree, and only three Tchulans (in this case, advanced degrees). Bolton and Tchula, in fact, split the lot of respondents with advanced degrees (three in each town).

Occupational status showed some similar differences, but was also interesting in other ways. It is evident that Bolton had a higher educational level because of the number of professionals or semi-professionals in the sample. Nineteen percent of them reported such a status, compared to 9 percent in Mayersville and barely any (2 percent) in Tchula. The other striking dimension is the rate of unemployment. It is high in every town; Bolton is low with 20 percent, followed by Mayersville with 25 percent, and the figure in Tchula is astoundingly high at 47 percent—nearly half of the able-bodied, working age population is without independent means of livelihood.

It has already been observed that past patterns of participation among southern blacks have been very low. We also know many of the reasons why, given the racial caste system. However, the central thesis of this work is that mobilization and leadership have radically altered these patterns. In the three Mississippi towns an initial evaluation is made of participation levels as an indication of the shift that has been facilitated by leadership and mobilization. The concept of participation has been operationally defined in terms of voter registration and voting, though it is clear that there are a range of other kinds of participation that are of importance. In the theoretical sense, the focus is on formal participation such as elections, because it is this form that was most difficult to achieve by blacks. In the past, informal mechanisms such as using a hand picked notable in the black community were used more often to achieve participation, but without any rights to fair bargaining or sanction. It was the formal avenues to power that remained blocked as a sign of blacks' outsider status. At the same time the formal mechanism of voting is the symbol, the quintessence of the democratic promise. It is the ultimate means by which one may express bonafide membership in the political community and affect the course of events. The attempts of blacks to achieve this kind of participation over the years, and particularly during the 1960s mobilization, have been all-consuming. In the times when leaders were most antithetical to aspects of the American system, voting rarely ceased to be a highly sought prize.

Voter Registration and Three Electoral Campaigns in Mississippi

The first task is to evaluate the status of voter registration in the three towns. If the evidence in these towns is consistent with the pattern generally observed in the South, it can be expected that registration levels will be high. Moreover, it can be expected that due to the special cases of mobilization used to win the mayoral office in the towns, registration levels will even exceed those for the general black population. But because of the additional special circumstances of racial exclusion in the South, particularly in towns like these with a majority black population, it is also expected that the length of registration (or potential for participation) will be only so long as the height of the mobilization campaign between 1963 and 1969. That is, most are likely to be fairly new participants in the formalized structure. The succeeding data appear to confirm these expectations from one town to another.

A series of three questions was asked respondents regarding voter registration. The first was whether one was registered; if not, whether one had ever been registered; and for how long had one been registered. Overall, the pattern was that an overwhelming majority reported current registration (88 percent-plus), and nearly 50 percent of the remainder indicated that they had previously been registered. The variations between the towns in this regard were too small to be of any significance; registration levels were remarkably high in all towns (see Table 6.6). The success of the 1960s mobilization is probably best illustrated by the small number of persons who had never been registered. A mere 6 percent of the sample of 273 had never registered and presumably never voted in the interest of the new regime.

As was expected, most of these respondents had only been registered since the beginning of the civil rights confrontations and voter registration drives in the early 1960s. Though there were isolated and individual efforts to register all along, 1962-1963 stand out as the years of concentrated activity in the counties of our concern. It was in 1963 that the campaign pressure in Holmes County led to bombings there, and in 1964 that Mrs. Blackwell sought to break the bar to registration in Mayersville. Indeed, the 1964 report of the state Advisory Committee of the Civil Rights Commission noted this growth. "Prior to the spring of 1963, efforts to bring about change were primarily confined to a small number of persons. During the spring and summer of 1963, civil rights organizations accelerated efforts to achieve registration of Negroes at the polls and to eliminate other discriminatory practices." And despite "mass arrests, private violence, and violence on the part of law enforcement officials," it was only during these years that black registration began to improve.[32] Then in 1965, with the passage of the Voting Rights Act, this was to escalate into a virtual flood of first-time registrations. Therefore most of the registrants encountered between 1977 and 1980 had been on the books for little over 11 years.

Table 6.6. Voter Registration and Length of Registration in Three Mississippi Towns, Post-1977

	Number	Percent
Registrants	241	(88.3)
Length of Registration		
Under 1 year	24	(9)
1-10 years	125	(46)
11 or more years	87	(32)

Total N = 273

Data show that there were two distinct waves of registration, believed to signal two distinct periods in the mobilization campaign. There was a sizable group in the first wave (32 percent) who constituted the initial registrants. This group was believed to be inspired by the early civil rights mobilization that culminated in the 1965 voting statute. They were registered at least 11 years, and tended to be older.

The second group was somewhat younger, but larger, and was made up of those inspired by the new leaders of the civil rights movement. These new leaders were more avowedly political and largely locally based, and thus more successful in inspiring registration. This wave is among the 46 percent of the sample that was registered between one and 10 years. Still another 10 percent were registered for under a year.

Respondents were then asked about their electoral participation at local versus national levels, to test Matthews and Prothro's thesis that national elections engendered far more voter attention among blacks and others. Three elections were selected. Two were national: the 1972 and 1976 presidential elections. The other was the 1975 gubernatorial election.

The 1972 election was of interest because of George McGovern's (the Democratic presidential candidate) perceived radicalism, which isolated him from the party cadre and many party identifiers, even blacks.[33] The 1976 election was also of interest because the now-salient indigenous leaders were active in the Jimmy Carter Democratic campaign because of sentiment and recruitment. Carter's rhetoric and overtures led many leaders to drum up local support for his candidacy. The 1975 local election, on the other hand, saw both strong Democratic and Republican candidates courting the black vote—one with a lunch pail to symbolize the working man and the other with rational appeals to state modernization. In their way, each of these contests allows us to tap the depth of a behavioral attitude toward participation by highly mobilized blacks.[34]

The data in Table 6.7 indicate that there was considerable Afro-American turnout for each of the three elections. The least was in the 1972 election featuring George McGovern (50 percent). Improvement occurred for each succeeding election, however. In the gubernatorial campaign of 1975, 56 percent of respondents indicated they voted; as did an exceedingly high 71 percent in the 1976 presidential campaign.

Table 6.7. Voting for State and National Executives, 1972-1976*

	Number	Percent
Governor 1975	153	(56)
President 1972	136	(50)
President 1976	194	(71)
	N = 273	

*Marginals omitted.

Just how high these turnout levels are is indicated by a comparison with general turnout levels, both in Mississippi and nationally, in the recent past. In the past, Mississippi gubernatorial campaigns, unlike in many other states, have generated more excitement than presidential ones. However, overall turnout has been comparatively low. In gubernatorial campaigns between 1951 and 1963, for example, the average turnout was 36 percent. During this time it is of some importance that competition and black involvement were virtually non-existent in the state. But when some blacks offered competition beginning in 1967, gubernatorial turnout improved dramatically. In 1967 it was 56 percent, and in 1971 it was 52 percent.

For presidential elections (in which Mississippians exhibited less interest by far), the average between 1948 and 1964 was a mere 24 percent—more than ten points lower than turnout for gubernatorial campaigns. Then in 1968, when the new black vote was of importance in its first national election, turnout rose to 53 percent, and only dropped slightly in the 1972.[35] In short, Mississippians generally have not exhibited great interest in formal democratic participation in contemporary times, except when racial competition threatened the routine intraracial base in the "Solid South."

National turnout, while much higher than that for Mississippians, barely measures up to the strong sentiments for voting expressed among the blacks in these small towns. In the 1960s, before these southern blacks had the franchise, overall presidential turnout approximated 60 percent. This dropped in the 1970s when the voting age was lowered, but only by about 5 points.[36] In the state of Mississippi, while respondents voted less often in 1972, there had been a precipitous rise to 71 percent. Hence, at least for the time being, it would seem that blacks were exhibiting a rate of interest in elections at all levels that far exceeded the usual political science expectations for communities with similar backgrounds.

To some degree these data are explained by the increased confidence that blacks must have acquired as a result of finding that the act of participation could be achieved without undue violence. On the other hand, there are factors about the elections and the personalities involved that help to fully situate the changes. In the first place, by the gubernatorial campaign of 1975 most of the new black leadership had easily earned its place in the three towns, and was beginning renewed and politically focused mobilization with the aim of achieving a transfer of power from the whites. Bennie Thompson was already mayor and Blackwell and Carthan were easily recognizable as the heirs to the center of power in their respective places. Moreover, these leaders and others were now wielding a degree of partisan power (as Democrats) that was not known in Mississippi since reconstruction. This gave them a broader interest than the politics of the local town; there was an interest in who was to be governor and president. It was reasoned, at least by the leadership cadres, that there was some linkage between all levels of party activity because the success of local programs depended on broader working relationships with others. It was politic to mobilize for national as well as local elections.

The prize of politics was no longer "hollow," and all the old rules about who participated and where were broken. Presidential elections were generally known to inspire greatest turnout elsewhere,[37] and in these small towns such participation was also high. The 1976 election would seem to suggest that this resulted from the blacks' competition for political goods.[38] It is suggested that by 1976, the stakes were so different and expectations so high, that black participation skyrocketed. These expectations were built not only around routine political promises, but also the particular character of leadership involvement in the competitive arena. In influencing events, the local leaders were seen to have clout beyond their borders. This was even evident in the gubernatorial campaign just preceding the Carter election, when the competitive advantage of blacks led most of the Democratic contenders to develop strategies for garnering the black vote. It must be remembered that this was an off-year election, which ordinarily elicited even less of a turnout.

These findings would seem to confirm a long-standing thesis in political science: that it is the intensity of competition in the electoral sphere that determines active formal participation.[39] But the weight of this evidence is even strengthened when this competition is measured in local elections, also not known to inspire intense participation. Our own case of Bolton may be taken as an example of how some such circumstances worked when Thompson first became mayor. The intense and competitive campaign, inflamed by racial polarization and a majority black constituency,[40] led to a near-100 percent turnout. The total vote was 405, indicating that over half of the total population participated. This corresponds with census data (1970) that show slightly more than 50 percent of the citizens above the voting age of eighteen. The vote for Thompson was 211 (52 percent); his white opponent (Beard) garnered 194 (47 percent). This gives credence to the rural respondents' report that 80 percent of them have participated in local elections since being registered. Forty-one percent of these indicate participation in up to four such exercises, while 39 percent say that they have done so on greater than four occasions (see Table 6.8). Perhaps the model citizen, as these rural voters illustrate, is one who "is highly interested, informed and concerned . . . and turns out to cast his ballot on election day" even for small town mayoral offices.[41]

Table 6.8.   Voting in Local Elections, Post-1967

	Number	Percent
Up to 4 times	111	(40.7)
5 to 10 times	107	(39.2)
	N = 273	(79.9)

Political Knowledge and Electoral Sophistication

It is widely assumed in political science, and probably correctly, that knowledge of political events and political leaders indicates the depth of one's involvement with the system. Those who are more knowledgeable are likely to be participants, or at least engaged enough by the process to follow its outcome. At the same time, it may be argued that information and knowledge provide the fundamental base upon which intelligent judgments or any decisions can be made.

> Some information about politics and government would seem to be a precondition for political participation. . . . The act of voting presupposes that the elector *knows* when it is election day, that he *knows* how to get registered, that he *knows* where his polling place is, that he *knows* how to mark a ballot, and so on.[42]

The best-known evidence about the general population of blacks and/or those in the lower SES category is that they tend not to have much political information. Matthews and Prothro found striking differences between southern whites and blacks regarding political information prior to the intense mobilization campaign in the region. While information in the South generally was only modest, that for blacks was piteously low. Out of seven questions on knowledge about politics and leaders,[43] blacks could answer only 3.1 of them compared to 4.6 for whites; 9 percent of the blacks could not provide any answers. In this regard there appeared to be a correlation between information and voting. "Almost all whites participate . . . to the point of voting . . . ignorant or well informed." But this was true for only a very small segment of the black population. While "90 percent of the highly informed Negroes have voted, (only) 35 percent of those with low scores on the [information] quiz" have done so. Hence the "politically ignorant tend to be the politically uninterested, and vice versa. Thus both the motivation to participate and the cognitive equipment to do so tend to be found in the same person."[44]

We also know much about what information is possessed. Consonant with more interest in the higher electoral offices is possession of more information about such office holders. Of course such officials are much more salient and thereby affect voting behavior. "The visibility of the office [or candidates for the office] will affect the information the voter is likely to have in hand . . . and the way he makes his decision." Therefore while information has been low for both gubernatorial and senatorial campaigns, it has been relatively high in presidential campaigns. This would at least partially seem to explain the higher participation in presidential elections.[45]

In ascertaining the knowledge level of the rural Mississippi respondents, a wide range of questions were asked about individuals and issues of political importance. Some of these questions were designed to tap purely local information, while others were broader in scope. Some of the standard questions were asked about the identity of local, national and international leaders; about issues in a similar context; and about political organizations relevant to the black community. It was reasoned that because of the highly politicized and mobilized nature of these small town environments, political information levels would be high across the board, but especially so for local affairs. These data will allow us to see how far such a reverse ordering of information may be sustained. Then, because overall information levels are expected to be so high, socioeconomic phenomena (while somewhat relevant) are not expected to have overwhelming explanatory power. On the other hand, it is expected that there will be correlations between formal participation and the highly informed.

At a higher level of abstraction it is expected that domestic "information sophistication" among these voters may also translate into some higher level of information sophistication about issues and personalities, with some bearing on social change at the international level. That is, our suspicion is that those who possess a wide range of domestic information may also possess greater information about the wider world. We already know that information among Americans about the wider world is very low generally, and notoriously inconsistent with views on other matters.[46] In the case of the rural towns there is expected to be some measure of agreement with the general population. Yet there is one international area for which many scholars have led us to believe that blacks may exhibit greater interest. This is on the subject of Africa, due to African ancestry of black Americans.[47] The latter are expected to have a desire for a continuing linkage to the motherland,[48] as demonstrated in many circumstances of history, especially in the era of cultural nationalism of the 1960s.[49] From this it is assumed that sentimental interest translates into more information, etc. This proposition is tested by an evaluation of information by blacks on personalities and issues in African affairs.

On the domestic side, the respondents were asked to correctly identify the local mayor, aldermen and women and the county supervisor. In state government they were asked to identify the governor and the district legislator. And of national officials they were asked to identify their Congressman, a Senator, and the President. The results show that information levels were extremely high at one end and extremely low at the other, though overall exceeding that for the broader American population. Ninety-seven percent identified the black mayor and 90 percent the President (Carter). Moreover, information on most other state offices was above 70 percent. Least well known were state legislators (20 percent). Nationally, information was very sparse on Senators and Congressmen, with information on the former unexpectedly exceeding the latter. Even so, when compared with results like those obtained by Matthews and Prothro, substantial improvement has occurred in what blacks know about politics, especially at the local level (see Table 6.9). In addition, these high information levels compare more than favorably with that for the general population, where information is rather low.[50]

These results would seem to be due to the salience of the particular office holders to these respondents and their perceived needs. In the nature of political mobilization, it was not difficult to see why the mayor had almost complete recognition among the citizens. It was a combination of the size of the political community and the singular involvement of this individual in contemporary politics. The mayor (as well as aldermen and women, who also had high recognition indexes) was the direct representative and embodiment of all that these constituents perceived as their political gains. Knowledge of the President was thought to be unusually high for similar reasons. This President had been presented to the people as a symbol whose fate was intertwined with theirs. Carter's reliance upon them and their local leaders provided a sense of camaraderie and common sentiment on issues of race. Moreover, he was an incumbent President during the survey and very much visible.

Knowledge of the state governor and county officers was also remarkably high. Again, this was believed to be a product of the salience of these offices in the contemporary experiences of the towns, as opposed to that of a U.S. Senator, Congressman, or state legislator. For example, two of the counties had a black supervisor, and a well-known black contemplated competing in the other county. (The interest in these positions was so great because supervisors maintain considerable power in Mississippi's decentralized system.) The situation with the Democratic governor has already been described with reference to the particular style of campaign (the lunch pail) and the cultivation of his independent contacts with black leaders. The relative mobilization of blacks within the party structure gave considerable advantage to the governor in acquiring local recognition. But in the state legislature and in the Congress, little success or visibility for these offices was achieved. Not a single black had won one of these districts at the time. And since the incumbents were routinely unavailable to blacks, these representatives were least identified.

Table 6.9.   Political Information: Local, State and National (1972-1980).

Political Office	Percentage Correct Answers
Mayor	97%
U.S. President	90
Alderman or Woman (11)	78
County Supervisor	78
Governor	72
U.S. Senator	26
State Legislator	20
U.S. House	12

The next task is to see whether these unusually high information levels and behavior at the polls were affected by socioeconomic factors. It has been hypothesized that there is little effect, based on the belief that the new leadership and the size of the mobilized black electorate were the overwhelming influences on behavior in these cases. Yet this goes against the grain of what social scientists have generally found in regard to SES for blacks and others: that high SES is a better predictor of participation than lower SES. Consonant with our expectation, the data indicate that generally high levels of information and participation in the towns occur at virtually all SES levels; education, occupation, sex and age do not markedly alter the conclusion. The clearest pattern, in fact, shows that participation has consistently risen since the Presidential race of 1972—from 61 percent to 82 percent.

In evaluating comparative participation and information, sex, age and education were the more interesting factors. In these towns women participated slightly more often than, but had information levels about equal to, men. Women outvoted men in all three elections, and by 10 percentage points or more in two of the three campaigns. This would appear to reverse what is the more common impact of sex on voter participation, particularly for southerners.[51]

Table 6.10. Electoral Participation: Gubernatorial and Presidential.

	1972 (Pres.)	1975 (Gov.)	1976 (Pres.)
Male	59%	61%	72%
Female	62	71	88
Total N	(135)	(151)	(192)
18-29	41%	53%	67%
30-45	71	72	88
46-60	83	87	100
60-plus	63	70	85
Total N	(134)	(153)	(192)
Primary	63%	56%	87%
Junior high school	65	80	84
High school	56	61	80
Some college	50	64	68
College	60	60	83
Advanced degree	83	80	83
Total N	(133)	(150)	(191)
Unemployed	60%	68%	83%
Laborer	59	67	81
Professional Semi-professional	58	65	74
Housewife	71	82	100
Retired	65	58	79
Total N	(131)	(148)	(188)

Education also deviated from the usual patterns. Consistently lower levels of education were on par (and sometimes better) with the other variables as predictors of participation. Only age follows the more routine pattern whereby younger individuals were less apt to participate, though their information was no worse.

These results were maintained when respondents were asked to identify political leaders. Virtually everyone in the sample knew the local mayor and the President; sex, age, education, and occupational status affected this very little. This further substantiated the view that local officials matched the national executive in importance. In identifying less visible state legislators, however, this general pattern floundered. First, far fewer respondents could make identifications (12 percent). Moreover, SES analysis showed an eclectic pattern, particularly for education and occupation, but only within the low-knowledge range. It did occur that the percentage of knowledgeable respondents between those having primary education and some college training ranged from 67 percent to 100 percent. On the other hand, the number of respondents was too low to claim any reliability in the result. The most reliable conclusion therefore would appear to sustain the hypothesis that high levels of participation and information exist independently of social status (see Tables 6.10 and 6.11).

Table 6.11. Correct Knowledge of Elected Officials: Local, National, and State.

	\multicolumn{6}{c}{Officials Identified}					
	Mayor		U.S. President		State Legislature	
	%	n	%	n	%	n
Male	98	104	98	99	78	25
Female	99	159	100	149	71	29
Total N		263		246		55
18-29	100	93	99	89	77	20
30-45	98	52	100	48	74	14
46-60	94	31	100	33	73	8
60-plus	99	86	99	74	87	13
Total N		262		244		55
None	100	6	83	5	—	—
Primary	100	40	100	31	67	4
Junior high school	99	68	100	61	100	8
High school	99	112	99	110	85	33
Some college	96	24	100	25	75	9
College	100	6	100	6	0	0
Advanced degree	83	5	100	6	20	1
Total N		261		244		55
Unemployed	98	94	100	90	86	18
Laborer	100	95	99	88	79	23
Professional/						
Semi-professional	100	19	100	18	22	2
Housewife	95	19	100	17	80	4
Retired	100	31	96	26	100	3
Total N		257		239		50

An evaluation was made on some additional information of a more abstract nature. This line of questioning was pursued because of an interest in testing the depth of respondents' domestic cognition, and to establish its linkage with broader pheonomena not having a direct bearing on their exercise of rights or their political activism. Yet the phenomena were deemed to be of potential, indirect or symbolic force in local affairs. If the respondents did well on these questions, then it could be concluded that some principles might be operative with which to sustain a broader range of behaviors. In this context the names of two organizations and two leaders were supplied that were of some presence in the area. The organizations offered were polar opposites: the NAACP and the KKK. It was assumed that each of these was commonly enough known for their interest in or opposition to blacks in each of our towns, while the symbol of the robed klansman or cross burnings was also known in at least each of the counties. The leaders offered were a recent black candidate for governor and a gadfly (Henry Kirksey), plus an up-and-coming black contender in the regional area (Fred Banks and/or Aaron Henry, both of whom later won posts at the state legislature). As can be seen from the data below, the information levels were high for the organizations and low for the individuals. This provides a mixed picture for association with a broader range of behaviors, or presumed, consistently high, cognition levels.

In two of the three towns, there was more information about the NAACP than about the KKK. The levels were very high with 69 percent of the respondents professing to know the NAACP and 66 percent the KKK. Far fewer of them knew who the regional leader was or who the previous candidate for governor was (30 percent and 22 percent, respectively) (see Figure 6.2). Since the regional experiences with the various organizations and leaders had been somewhat different, these data were separated by town to ascertain whether this made for any difference in who possessed information. As Figure 6.3 illustrates, a town does account for some variation. At the higher end on the information index, Tchula and Bolton exceeded Mayersville by a considerable degree on knowledge of the NAACP, while in the latter more respondents knew the KKK than the NAACP. At the lower end the differences were of somewhat greater magnitude, with Bolton doing modestly well, while the others did not.

On the surface it does appear that the experiences of the towns may be somewhat accountable. Though Mayersville experienced much of the movement, the organized base for this was not always evident. Mrs. Blackwell was evident and had a personality large enough to overshadow that of other organizations and leaders. She was much more of a singular force than the independent organizations and leaders in her area. Moreover, Mayersville was much more isolated than either of the other towns, and as such had less exposure to the full range of forces acting upon the black community.

Tchula, on the other hand, seemed much more affected by its intense association with the traditional organizations and symbols, the NAACP and the KKK. In the recent political history of Tchula, each of these outfits has played a prominent role. The intense mobilization in the town only followed a longstanding association with the NAACP and its older leadership. At the same time, the white reaction in the area had been more salient, with bombings, cross burnings and a host of activities that blacks associated with the Klan. It was not surprising that Tchulans exhibited more sophistication about the traditional organizations.

Figure 6.2 Information on Organizations and Indirect Local Leaders in the Three Towns

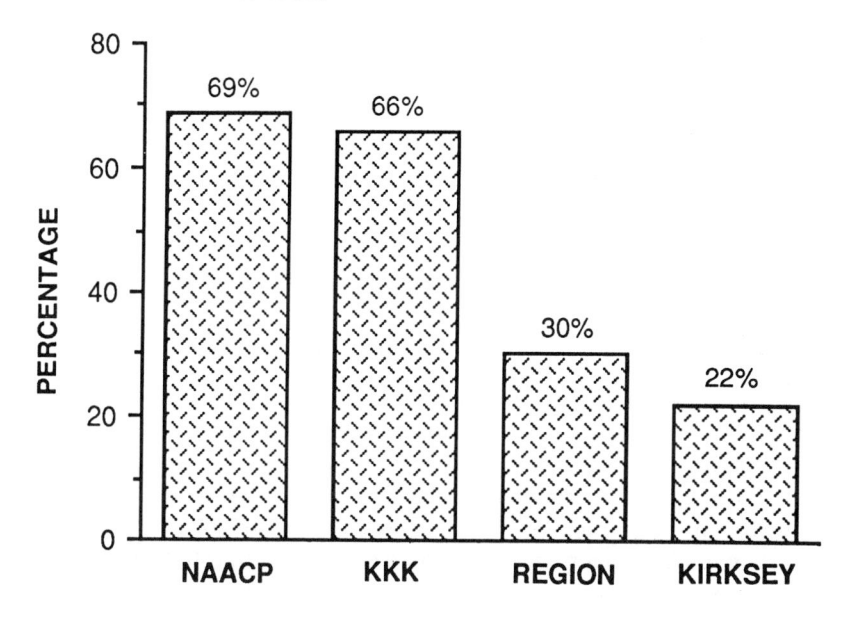

NAACP 69%
KKK 66%
REGION 30%
KIRKSEY 22%

Figure 6.3 Information on Organizations and Indirect Local Leaders, by Town.

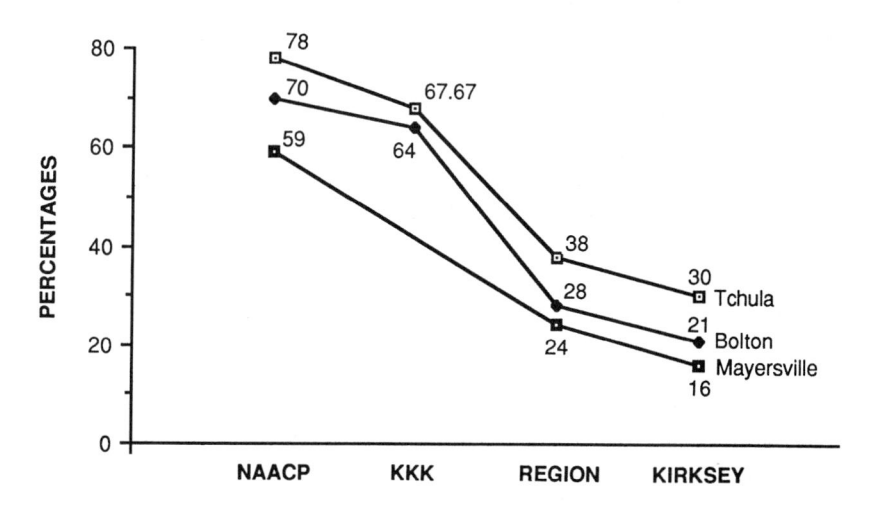

	NAACP	KKK	REGION	KIRKSEY
Tchula	78	67.67	38	30
Bolton	70	64	28	21
Mayersville	59	64	24	16

Bolton differed from both Tchula and Mayersville insofar as its information levels were higher across the board. This is of particular note regarding more recent political information. More Boltonians knew the regional contender and the gubernatorial candidate, but by a greater margin than for organizational leadership. Fully 38 percent of Bolton respondents identified a county contender who did not live in their town and may not even have ventured there for public business. Yet he was a prominent person sufficiently involved in negotiating political resources so that people knew him. Not even thirty percent in the other towns could identify a similar regional figure. It was believed that the expressly contemporary character of the Thompson leadership accounted for this situation. Unlike Tchula, Bolton did not have much of a base from which to structure the mobilization campaign. It was built more on the strength of Thompson's personality and contacts.

The Transferability of Domestic Sophistication to the International Sphere

With this mixed picture there is some question about the depth of domestic political sophistication. In sorting this out an evaluation was made of the transferability of the sophisticated domestic behaviors and attitudes to the international sphere. First cognition was explored. Several questions were asked of respondents regarding Africa, about which it was hypothesized that there would be special interest. First we asked for the identification of leaders—Andrew Young, Henry Kissinger and Idi Amin—and then for the definition of an issue: apartheid in South Africa.

For the purposes here, information was sought on the two American leaders because they had something to do with Africa policy specifically, or foreign policy in general. Kissinger had served as Secretary of State under presidents Nixon and Ford, and was a major international foreign policy spokesman. He was widely known in Africa because of several well-publicized policy positions he had taken on southern Africa.[52] Andrew Young was a good source because during much of the research he was U.S. ambassador to the United Nations, a visible and vocal foreign policy official, who took African affairs as a special interest area. That he was the only such Afro-American official at the time was also significant, given the ideological perspective of respondents on domestic issues.

Knowledge of American leaders was compared to that for an African leader and issue. The task was more difficult because of the large number of possible leaders and issues in Africa.[53] However, the range of choices for an American audience would have to be restricted if previous research was accurate about the lack of knowledge on Africa. The dilemma was how to find representative leaders or topical issues that would tap the meager information of even a progressive American audience. Idi Amin emerged as the leader most apt to elicit some response because he had received more than scant attention in the American media and boasted a kind of nationalism in the early days that had some appeal among blacks.[54] Then *apartheid*, easily one of the most prominent issues in African affairs, and widely reported in the American media, was utilized under the *Afrikaans* nomenclature.[55]

On the whole there is little comparison between information on Africa and that for the domestic arena. These respondents were far less informed about individuals and topical questions regarding Africa. Even though some lessening of information was expected, broad lack of information among these domestic activities was striking indeed. This was especially evident on internal matters in continental Africa. The data in Table 6.12 illustrates this and can be divided into two distinct parts. The first part, where the results were fairly predictable, involved information on the American leaders Andrew Young and Henry Kissinger. While comparatively low, a sizable number of the 273 respondents correctly identified each: 36 percent and 33 percent respectively. They associated Young with his United Nations post and Kissinger with the office of Secretary of State. Knowledge on Young probably exceeded that for Kissinger because respondents were more likely to personally identify with the former, a black southerner. Young was also widely remembered as a civil rights leader because of his association with Martin Luther King, Jr. in the 1960s.

Table 6.12. Knowledge of Issues/Leaders in African and Foreign Affairs (N = 273).

Issue/Leader	%	N
Andrew Young	36%	92
Henry Kissinger	33	90
Idi Amin	17	47
Apartheid	2	5

In the second part of Table 6.12, however, a precipitous drop is observed in the correct identification of Idi Amin and defining apartheid. These internal, country-specific matters collectively elicited less than a ten percent response rate. Seventeen percent (less than 50 persons) correctly identified Idi Amin, who had frequently been covered in the American media, and often in a mirthful or derisive manner. Nevertheless, only a small number of respondents recalled the man who was object of much caricature—perhaps it was this factor that yielded much more information on Amin than on apartheid. A mere five individuals, in all of the three separate towns, could identify apartheid as racial segregation as practiced in South Africa. In short, almost none of these respondents could transfer the benefits of their sophisticated, domestic activism to knowledge about African affairs. To the extent that they could it appeared that a direct, internal United States affiliation was required. Young and Kissinger were distinguished in this context by their executive positions in the United States government. These findings, therefore, lead to the suspicion that perhaps a connection between black domestic activism and concern for African affairs cannot be confirmed. Comparatively, blacks are far more occupied with domestic concerns.

The analysis was then carried further to see if an assumed linkage between domestic activism and international progressivism could be sustained by higher SES. It was believed that there was a greater propensity for the higher-educated, better-employed, and younger respondents to possess information on African affairs and to have progressive views on continental issues. The assumption that this would be true was based on some of the highly generalized findings of empirical social science that show SES to correlate with interest, activity and formal participation. Of course, the far removed geographical location of Africa suggests that higher-status people would find appropriate information far more accessible than others.

Cross-tabulations of these data with SES variables confirmed this hypothesis only modestly, and thus weakens the interpretation. There was very little evidence of a strong relationship between SES and information about African leaders and issues. Undoubtedly much of this was due to the relatively low amount of information overall. What can be demonstrated from the cross-tabulations is that men and women were very similar in the information they possessed about Africa, though it is noted that four of the five persons who define apartheid were men. Age, however, tended to correlate fairly strongly. Younger respondents (18-40) were far more knowledgeable in identifying African leaders and defining apartheid in the small number of cases where information existed. Education was of significance for only the most highly trained. Those who had advanced degrees were far more knowledgeable. Occupation had a similar effect insofar as professionals possessed more knowledge. Other employment categories presented no clear pattern. In sum, it may be concluded that SES did seem to affect our respondents' attitudes and behavior in the expected ways. Even the modest patterns found were irregular, making it difficult to isolate how the SES variables interacted with each other regarding international progressivism. For this we turned to other statistical measures.

Pearson's correlation analysis was used to determine the association between opinion-knowledge variables and SES. The principal aim was to ascertain whether the tendency of higher SES to correlate with international progressivism could be strengthened or was spurious. In addition it was critical to ascertain the degree of significance of the individual variables. That is, could it be confirmed that education, occupation, age, and sex (in that order) best depicted the process by which progressivism was achieved? The data in Table 6.13 immediately showed that at least the pattern by which progressivism was thought to be sustained did not hold. This was the case for both information and knowledge questions. There was not a single instance in which education, hypothesized to be most important, was found to be significant at the .05 level. For the information variables (Andrew Young, Kissinger, Amin and apartheid), only two of the relationships seen in cross-tabulations were associated: age with identification of Andrew Young (.001), and occupation with Idi Amin (.01).

Table 6.13. Pearson's Correlations (SES) with Africa Knowledge.

Africa Variables	Socioeconomic Status			
	Sex	Age	Education	Occupation
Andrew Young	−.010	.185[a]	−.293	.301
Henry Kissinger	.073	.212	−.273	.079
Idi Amin	.110	.212	−.295	.095[b]
Apartheid	−.017	−.008	−.078	−.116

a = .001
b = .01
c = .05

In zero-order partial correlations this pattern, opposed to the hypothesis, continued (see Table 6.14). In this case each of the SES variables was controlled to determine the independent association of the other variables upon knowledge and opinion about Africa. The stronger relationships were prevalent for knowledge about Andrew Young. Henry Kissinger also emerged. Still, the expected relationships were not strong. Education, for example, had an independent impact only when age was controlled for identification of Henry Kissinger. Otherwise, it was age that was consistently of some importance. Its significance was noted at least once against all the Africa variables except apartheid.

On the basis of these data, therefore, it would appear that the hypothesis that domestic participation and knowledge lead to greater knowledge of African affairs among blacks cannot be sustained. While it was true that these rural respondents exhibited broad domestic participation and knowledge, this did not seem to transfer. There was very little general information exhibited about Africa. Yet for those few who did possess information, there were some modest correlation with socioeconomic phenomena. Age appeared to be the strongest determinant in this regard, with education, sex, and occupation (respectively) being of less importance.

Table 6.14. Zero–Order Correlations/Knowledge and Opinion Variables.

SES Variables	Africa Control Variables (SES)															
	Andrew Young				Henry Kissinger				Idi Amin				Apartheid			
	Sex	Age	Educ.	Occu.	Sex	Age	Educ.	Occu.	Sex	Age	Educ.	Occu.	Sex	Age	Educ.	Occu.
Sex	—	-.026	-.030	-.011	—	.062	.060	.076	—	.094	.095[c]	.107	—	-.016	-.022	-.013
Age	.187[a]	—	-.061	.185[a]	.140[b]	—	.044	.183	.205	—	.092	.192[a]	-.007	—	-.049	-.032
Education	.294	-.238	—	-.291	.232	-.192[a]	—	.242	-.290	-.228	—	.291	-.079	-.079	—	-.086
Occupation	.321	-.032	-.015	—	.081	-.137	.095	—	.092	—	.082	—	-.116	-.120	-.121	—

a = .001
b = .01
c = .05

Efficacy and Political Participation

It has been noted that a considerable number of those who actively participate do so because they believe that they can influence what the government does. These are the same people who tend to be most knowledgeable. From what we know about traditional empirical social science findings, blacks supposedly lack such efficacy. They do not participate in great numbers and lack political knowledge, the argument goes. In the present research, however, no such assumption was made. It was hypothesized that dramatic increases in previously low efficacy levels would be found among these constituents who had experienced the transformation from white to black power. Our contention was that one's faith in the government, and knowledge about it, radically improved when one had a perception of closeness to and responsibility for that entity. It was expected that the transfer of power, therefore, made a remarkable difference to the sense of efficacy in these respondents.

The survey was designed to test the relationship of the constituents to the old and new regimes. Those in Bolton and Tchula were asked to explain whether they had frequented city hall before, and for what reasons, under the white mayor.[56] The first question was, "When there was a white mayor here, did you ever go to city hall with your problems?" The data in Table 6.15 show that in neither town was there any overwhelming direct interaction with city hall as exhibited by visits there. A mere 11 percent in each town reported ever going for problem resolution. When asked if they had ever gone to city council meetings when there was a white mayor, the number responding affirmatively was also very small, in this case 6 percent in Bolton and 12 percent in Tchula. If it is assumed that presence at such meetings or in the environs of the center of power indicated a degree of efficacy, then there certainly was very little at the time of the white administrations. Yet it must also be realized that perhaps many had not frequented these places because they were generally barred from doing so. In the segregated lifestyle marking these two towns it would have been unusual for blacks to even know about such meetings, unless one was to appear for an express purpose. In Bolton, for example, the new black administration charged

Table 6.15. Interactions with Local Government, Old Regime.

Interaction	Bolton		Tchula	
	N	%	N	%
Visits to City Hall During Previous Regime	7	(11)	17	(11)
Participation in Council Meetings During Previous Regime	4	(6)	18	(12)
Total N	64		150	

that such formal council meetings often did not even occur because of informal arrangements among whites.

As expected, when respondents were asked the same questions in reference to the black administrations, dramatic increases were reported. There was improvement by a factor of more than two in all cases. Interestingly, the greatest overall improvement occurred in interactions at city council meetings, which proved least accessible under the white regimes. That this is the case may give some indication about the influence of racial taboos upon past behavior, as opposed to assumed apathy or lack of efficacy.

Moreover, there was a clear distinction in the two towns, with Bolton showing the most dramatic improvements in interactions. Those who went to city hall and/or attended council meetings in town were above 40 percent of the respondents in each case. Tchula showed marked improvement, however; its average of 25 percent is a considerable distance from Bolton's. Here too one should be reminded of the considerable difference in the exercise of power by Thompson in Bolton and that by Carthan in Tchula. In Bolton there was always broad solidarity in the leadership group, while at Tchula there was virtual stalemate after a time due to leadership conflict. Consequently some citizens we interviewed in Tchula expressed fear about interactions too close to the center of power. Yet the improvement did represent considerable new interaction by blacks under these circumstances. (See Table 6.16.)

Table 6.16. Interactions with Local Government, New Regime.

Interaction	Bolton		Tchula	
	N	%	N	%
Visits to City Hall During New Regime	27	(42)	35	(23)
Participation in Council Meetings During New Regime	29	(45)	43	(29)
Total N	64		150	

It was assumed, however, that past dislocation of blacks from the center of power would complicate their present feelings of efficacy in both places. We already know from Abramson and many others that under ordinary circumstances, blacks demonstrate some of the lowest levels of efficacy and exhibit great distrust in the government. These findings, we also know, were even more indicative of blacks in the South than in other places, prior to the mobilization campaign. Therefore it was not expected that efficacy would grow so quickly among these constituents, for under the best circumstances scholars have attributed the growth of such feelings to socialization. Given this, it was expected that black efficacy, even under conditions of intense mobilization, would be uneven; it takes time for the constituents to fully accommodate themselves to the participatory process. It would seem that our assumptions in this regard were correct, for somewhat less than an overwhelming number of respondents felt they could influence government actions.

When the Boltonians and Tchulans were asked this directly, under 50 percent of each sample believed that they could influence what the government does—in spite of the fact that these same respondents turned out in great numbers to elect their black mayors and to help in the election of U.S. presidents. The data are interesting, however, for they reveal (at least in Bolton) feelings of influence not grossly out of line with willingness to visit the offices of the government. In Bolton the same number of respondents who reported visits to city hall (42 percent) also believed they could influence what the government does. In Tchula, on the other hand, fewer believe they have influence than those who go to city hall or to council meetings. In short, it was easier for these citizens to go to government offices than to believe that such actually achieves results. (See Table 6.17.)

Table 6.17. Percentage in Bolton and Tchula Who Believed They Could Influence What the Government Did.

	N	%
Bolton	27	(42)
Tchula	27	(18)

Total N = 214

What else is there to possibly explain the distinction between Bolton and Tchula, since more sophisticated statistics tell very little? It has already been observed that the considerable conflict in Tchula led many citizens to adopt an aloof attitude. But because there was so much conflict between the leaders, little clarity was left about who was in charge and to whom one should direct efforts in order to receive political benefits. In fact, after a time it was not evident that anyone was in charge. This state of affairs affected the perceptions of the young electorate.

In Bolton, on the other hand, aside from leadership consensus, the process had been at work almost twice as long as in Tchula. It will be remembered that Bennie Thompson was the first of these mayors to be elected and was beginning his second term when Carthan and Blackwell were beginning their first. As such, the people in Bolton had much more of a basis for their feelings about the efficacy of black rule. The absence of conflict, the easy reelection of the mayor, and his perceived success in producing welfare benefits all combined to give Thompson an edge that Carthan could not claim.

It may be concluded from this that there was some evidence that efficacy in these rural towns was connected with the political changes that occurred in recent years. It has been seen that participation and information levels were very high, but were not matched by levels of efficacy. This, however, was no necessary contradiction since we would expect efficacy to grow at a slower pace. After all, the independent art of going to city hall for meetings is a difficult one that requires a high level of absorbtion of the ideals of the system. In light of this difficulty it was significant to observe that behavioral changes have occurred since the beginning of the black regimes. This would seem to indicate that there was indeed a conscious awareness of the changes and their implications for citizen influence.

Ideological Commitments and Political Attitudes

Next, ideology was considered as a means of further measuring the depth of political sophistication among these domestic actives. There are a variety of ways to define ideology, although given contemporary analysis in political science it may be more useful to justify the use of the concept. In this case, we make no assumption that the concept is useless, just because of the broad decline of conflict in American society (even this latter conclusion is questionable). But even if this presumed decline were true, it is not at all applicable to the black American community, where there is continuing conflict about its role in the political structure. This has yielded an enduring ideological component to independent black political efforts. Moreover, in the content of this analysis, mobilization adds strength to the ideological component with the prominent role political education plays in activating citizens. This often meant that interpretations and supporting materials were developed in an ideological manner—i.e.: "integration," "community power," or "cultural nationalism," etc. This pattern of behavior is almost singular to blacks in the American context, for among few others was the denial of "rights" so systematic and widespread.

Therefore, contrary to the general finding about ideology in the political science literature, the hypothesis here is that ideology too is affected by one's experiences in a given political environment. So it is that blacks in general may not express ideological positions on matters not directly in the purview of their experience, but they are critically attuned to matters regarding the denial of political rights. It was expected that this posture would be evident in our sample at all levels of the socioeconomic spectrum. Hence it was hypothesized that we would find the anomalous situation of lower-SES persons with an unusual capability for ideological thinking about the special circumstances of American racial exclusion.

In defining ideology here, Everett Carll Ladd has been used as a guide. His recent analysis is especially useful in highlighting the political components that form the basis of the operational definition.

> Ideology refers to a set of prescriptive positions on matters of government and public policy that are seen as forming a logically or quasi-logically interrelated

system, with the system treating an area of political life that is both broad and significant. This area of political life typically includes such things as the structure of government and the distribution of power, the political objectives that the society should try to realize and how it should go about it, the distribution of resources of the system, and the manner and bases for their allocation. . . . A person sees politics ideologically when he applies some over-arching conceptual dimension to the myriad of policy choices, when he organizes remote and abstract matters in to what for him is a logical or quasi-logical system.[57]

To understand ideology among these respondents, a series of questions were asked about ideas and issues presumed to affect their daily lives as black people. Some of the questions sought to elicit philosophical commitments, while others sought policy perspectives. Along these lines, several themes were selected on integration or the desire to achieve full rights in the society—each respondent was asked to comment on social integration (in public schools) and political integration (in local government). Then, the depth of ideological commitment was tested by also asking several questions (of some ideological import) regarding sentiments toward black Africa. It was assumed that in the presence of strong domestic ideology and particular concern about Africa, there would be a transfer of ideological commitment to the international sphere. The previous finding, however, about the modest effect of domestic information and participation upon that in the international sphere did not bode well for the transfer of ideology.

School integration was used as an issue by which to understand the respondents' commitment to integration as an ideal. In the short history of the Brown decision, school integration and public accommodations came to be symbols of the singularly pursued goal of inclusion.[58] School desegregation has continuously been seen by many whites as a depth of commitment impossible to accept, leading to withdrawal from schools where blacks appeared. (This has been the fate of the schools in and around the three towns.) Blacks, on the other hand, largely see school desegregation as a symbolic step toward the ideal of racial harmony and resource redistribution. Yet even in places where legal challenges were successful in reality the ideal has not been achieved. To this end, therefore, it seems that continuing commitment to this concept may be an adequate test of an underlying principle that guides policy commitments.

Data in Figure 6.4 show the responses to questions on the notion of integration, both in the abstract and in reference to school integration. Each of the questions was posed in such a way that its policy implications were evident, but somewhat removed from topical circumstances. For example, respondents were asked if they supported the ideal of integration in the running of the government, and not to evaluate the present government. On school integration they were asked about the ideal of all children attending the public schools together in the local town, and not to evaluate the present circumstances. As expected, the acceptance of integration was very high in all towns, especially in

Tchula (91 percent) and Mayersville (92 percent).[59] In this instance, far fewer Boltonians (58 percent) found the abstract ideal of integration entirely acceptable. This may be associated with the reality of greater racial division because of complete white withdrawal at the election of Thompson. The duration of the black regime without white cooperation may well have led more blacks to accommodate themselves to less than the ideal.

Figure 6.4   Preferences for Integration.

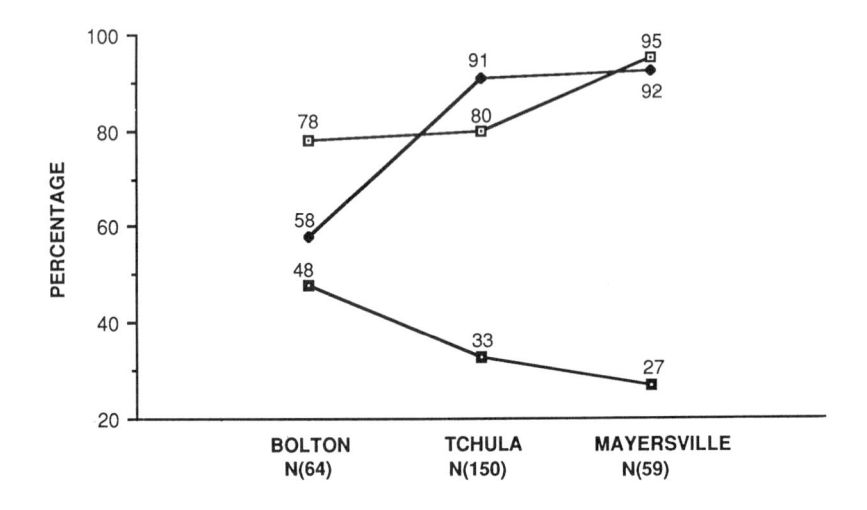

- Prefer integrated schools
- Acceptance of integration in the abstract
- Prefer few or no whites in government offices

In reference to school integration, similar results were found. Fewer respondents found school integration desirable than supported integration in the abstract. Yet the numbers who supported school integration were quite high. Boltonians and Mayersvillians found it easier to accept school integration than what we assumed was the easier proposition (the integration ideal). This difference, however, is only important in Bolton, where proportionally 20 percent more of our respondents found school integration more acceptable.

Later, when respondents were asked to explain their acceptance of the abstract ideal of integration in society and in the schools, interesting results emerged. They revealed that about as many people were concerned about policy implications as were concerned about sheer ideals. As reasons for accepting an integrated society, about 30 percent gave abstract answers, while nearly 30 percent referred to the implications of integration for improving opportunities for blacks. But in regard to schools, there was an overwhelming focus on abstract implications. Fully 65 percent of the respondents in all towns saw school integration as a means of enhancing racial harmony. This sustained our view that school integration is as good or perhaps better measure of the principle of integration in ideological thinking among these respondents. They tended to pin their hopes for the future on the possibility of better relations between children across racial lines. They seemed to believe that ideas would change with greater interaction at this socialization stage. We frequently found respondents who said "maybe our children will grow to teach us how to love each other," or "their possibilities for good relations will be enhanced by getting to know each other before they can be tainted by existing adult ideas."

It was also our expectation that a more radical ideology would be present among these citizens because of the mobilization they had experienced. That is, not only would there be a principle such as integration to guide the policy perspectives of these citizens, but an attitude of progressivism in support of social change, bordering on nationalism, would be present. It is suggested that their experience of power transfer would lead them to have a rather different view of power relationships than support for the principle of abstract integration would lead us to believe. In order to test this proposition, we asked respondents to take a position on the absence or near-absence (as in Tchula) of whites in the government structure—did they see this as a good or bad thing. The intent here was to judge the ability of citizens to make a distinction between different kinds of integration and to see what kind of practical evaluation they made of the black power ideal.[60]

In Figure 6.5 data are presented for respondent preferences about sharing power in the three towns. The results are strikingly different. Clearly, respondents in every town made a sharp distinction between the abstract ideal of togetherness and sharing political power. Not 50 percent in any town wished to share power with whites. Indeed those who were most committed to the integration ideal were less likely to find power sharing acceptable. Twenty-seven percent of those in Mayersville and 33 percent of those in Tchula preferred power sharing. And the most politically sophisticated of the towns—Bolton— found power sharing most palatable (48 percent). In some sense, the responses by town were surprising because those more committed to the philosophical ideal were expected to find power sharing easier. Instead what the findings may reveal is something about the stage of development in the separate towns. That is, although their responses surely represented some degree of nationalist feeling (as over 50 percent of them indicate in explaining their preferences), primordial feelings are also likely to come into play. Therefore, those in more isolated Mayersville were more skeptical, while those more sophisticated and more settled into the experience, as in Bolton, expressed confidence. Nevertheless, there was across the board a greater rejection of the practical prospect of integrated government.

In cross-tabulations of preferences with socioeconomic phenomena, there was modest support for the conclusion that the distinction between abstraction and policy preference was most easily drawn by those who had more education and higher incomes. It was critical to test this dimension, because only on ideological preferences for sharing power were there enough variations for meaningful comparison. From primary education through college and advanced university degrees, a gradual rise in the opposition to power sharing was observed. Only a third of those who completed primary school were opposed, while 67 percent of those with advanced degrees were opposed. This would seem to indicate that as one's level of education rose, there was a greater likelihood that a hard-line nationalist perspective would develop, or that one at least becomes more conscious of the benefits that accrued from the exercise of power. There was a similar pattern for income, where the higher the income the more likely one was to reject power sharing, though the variations were more modest. It is also suspected that as one went up the economic scale, the level of education also increased, yielding a correlation between these two phenomena.

Figure 6.5 Opposition to Power Sharing, by Education and Income.

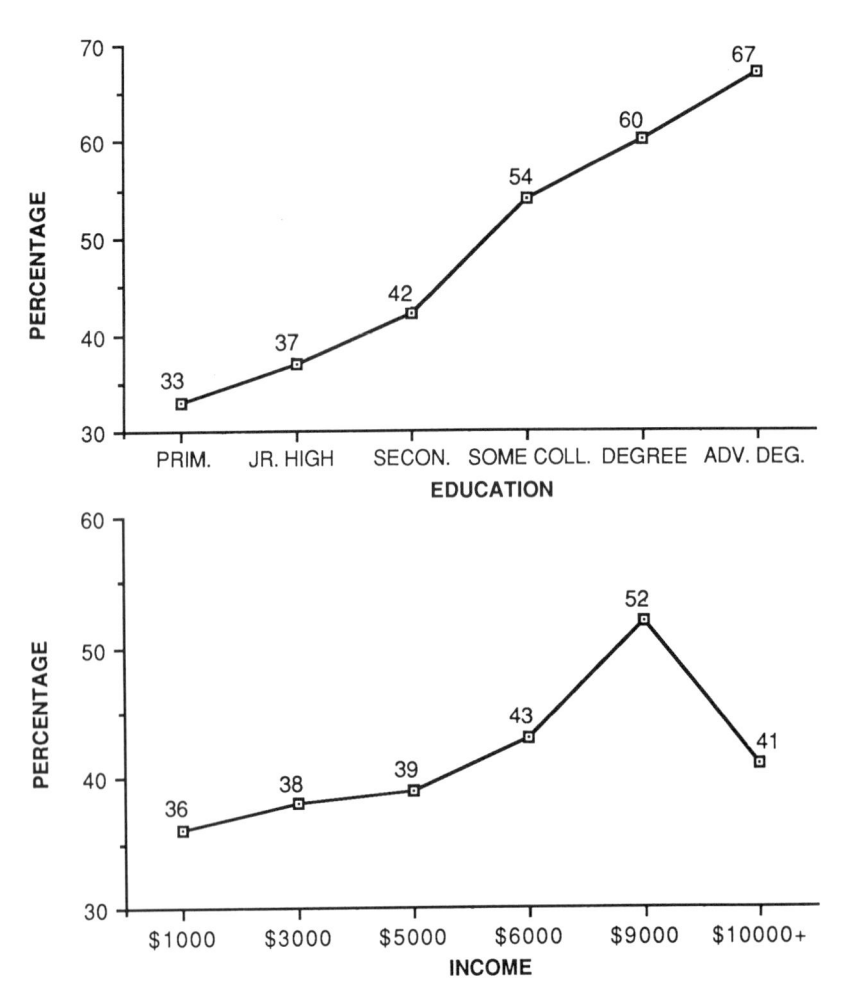

International Issues and Ideology

All told, what this meant was that there was a high degree of ideological thinking in these towns, and that there were also very clear principles that provided a framework for evaluating certain issues and events in the social structure. Did such high levels of sophistication and participation add up to similar results in reference to international issues, particularly in reference to Africa? It will be recalled that information levels on Africa were actually quite low. Nevertheless in further explorations these respondents were again asked to give their attitudes toward issues in contemporary Africa.

The issues selected to tap respondent awareness were all topical and dealt with South Africa. The Soweto riots and the circumstances surrounding apartheid were widely covered by the media and thereby easily met the criteria for topicality.[61] Respondents were asked a series of three questions on the subject "Should the United States stop trading with South Africans who discriminate against blacks?" "Is that something you care a great deal about?" And, "Do you believe black Americans should go over to Africa to fight against the whites who discriminate against black Africans?" The purpose was not only to further examine information levels, but also to understand the difference between activism and sentimental attachment to certain ideals. In these instances, respondents were required to possess less precise information, though the questions were quite specific. For here we provided the information that South Africa was a racist society, and then sought to build on this in seeking philosophical principles.

Since the analysis on the definition of apartheid was not encouraging, some might challenge the utility of further exploration. However this further probing was most revealing about the depth of principles among the respondents. Those who chose to answer these quite specific questions either knew the issue involved or wanted to speak on the philosophical implications of it. The evidence was reasonably clear (see Table 6.18) that while far more individuals recognized the importance of South Africa than were able to define apartheid, it was less than an overwhelming percentage (31 percent). In fact a larger percentage (50 percent) were prepared to bar trade in light of discrimination than expressed concern as a result of philosophical affinity. The number of individuals, however, who responded positively are a marked improvement over the five (2 percent) who could define apartheid. One hundred and thirty-six would support barring trade with South Africa, while 85 were concerned with the discrimination there. In this case it was easier to discuss policy than ideals.

Nevertheless, there was a reverse of this perspective when respondents were asked the more difficult question about warfare. Much more concern was expressed about the specific policy of Afro-Americans in warfare against South Africa—a clear majority of 66 percent (180) did not favor such a policy. A plausible explanation for this is that these respondents, even those who know the South African situation, were unprepared to support warfare. Therefore, it is concluded that while these rural blacks may be somewhat informed about South Africa as a general issue, sentimental attachment is a more probable explanation for the larger number of responses to philosophical ideals and hypothetical policy stances. Moreover, if one were to speculate about the political implications of this conclusion, it could be predicted that if called to do so, these respondents could be mobilized for issues bearing on discrimination against black South Africans. Such activity is widely known among sentimental groups living in diasporic conditions around the world, and would be in keeping with a long black American tradition.

Table 6.18. Opinions on Racism in South Africa.

Opinion	%	N
Bar trade with South Africa	50	136
Expression of concern for South African racist practices	31	85
Afro-Americans should go to South Africa to fight against racism	24	66
Total N = 273		

Table 6.19. Pearson's Correlations (SES) with Africa Opinion Variables.

Issues	Socioeconomic Status			
	Sex	Age	Education	Occupation
Bar Trade	.131[b]	.135[b]	.145	.046
Expression of Concern	.210	.190[a]	−.122	.098[c]
Fight in South Africa	.016[b]	.144	−.115	.109

a = .001
b = .01
c = .05

Because these findings deviated so significantly from those dealing with domestic affairs, additional statistical measures were utilized to ascertain what factors were operating upon those who were knowledgeable or exhibited ideological thinking in reference to continental Africa. In Pearson's correlations shown in Table 6.19, some opinion variables have stronger association with SES than with the information variables; but these are also inconsistent with the prediction of education and income as the best correlates. Age is significant in explaining the desire to bar trade with (.01), and expressions of concern (.001) for South Africa; sex correlates with barring trade, while occupation does so with expression of concern for South Africa.

In zero-order partial correlations, this pattern, opposed to what was hypothesized, continued (see Table 6.20). In this case, each of the SES variables was controlled to determine the independent association of the others upon opinion about Africa. Again, the stronger relationship was on the issue of trade with South Africa. Still, the expected relationships were not strongly sustained. There was one instance when education had an independent impact—when sex was controlled for the variable on barring trade. Otherwise, it was age that was important for all but the variable on "concern for South Africa." In one case, age showed independent strength against at least two SES variables, thereby strengthening its position. Sex and occupation did not make showings of particular significance in this analysis, though sex was the stronger of the two.

Conclusion

The foregoing demonstrates the critical linkage between the mobilization that began in the 1960s, the neo-leadership group, and the constituency in these rural black towns. It had been asserted that the new leadership in Bolton, Tchula and Mayersville was only as good as the constituent community that stood behind them. Yet all of our best knowledge on American politics suggested that factors other than the political ones associated with mobilization were likely to reduce the significance of the independent black constituency. These people were poor, uneducated, and in isolation from the American mainstream. Their mobilization to register was likely to be absent the commitment necessary for translation into real political power. In short, there was likely to be little depth (if history was any guide) to the attitudes and behaviors of these constituents. Our contention was that under these particular circumstances in American history, we would find a constituency of considerable activism and depth in the political sphere. These circumstances had to do with the existence of a black American majority, the experience of a civil rights mobilization campaign, and the emergence out of that campaign of figures with a vision to lead. In large measure this contention has been sustained.

In an empirical analysis of four dependent variables it has been observed that these rural townsmen were as profoundly knowledgeable and active as any generally found in the United States. The variables were participation, political information, efficacy and ideology. These phenomena have all been found to be of significance in identifying political actives in American society. In an analysis of registration and voting in these towns it was found that since the passage of the Voting Rights Act of 1965, virtually everyone was registered. They reported participation at very high levels in national as well as local elections. Moreover,

Table 6.20. Zero-Order Correlations and Opinion Variables.

	Bar Trade					Express Concern/So. Africa					Fight in South Africa			
	Sex	Age	Educ.	Occu.	Sex	Age	Educ.	Occu.	Sex	Age	Educ.	Occu.
Sex	—	.121	.124	.130[b]	—	.199	.205	.208	—	.050	.055	.058
Age	.126[b]	—	.079	.127[b]	.177	—	.152	.168	.140[b]	—	.104	.115
Education	.138[b]	.094	—	.142	.111	.041	—	.117	.111	.056	—	.109
Occupation	.042	.001	.038	—	.093	.037	.091	—	.107	.065	.103	—

a = .001
b = .01
c = .05

their turnout seemed very much related to the perceived political gain from participation. Their greater turnout for Jimmy Carter was very much a product of a campaign that showed the candidate to be attuned to their direct local needs. The domestic knowledge of these individuals was equally striking. While their knowledge did not exceed their participation, it was certainly higher than generally reported for most Americans and especially on local issues and politicians.

That there is depth to their knowledge and participation was observed when an analysis was made of ideology. These respondents made some of the clearest distinctions on issues and principles that have been noted for the most sophisticated political cadres. In the first place they indicate a strong adherence to the principle of integration in the abstract and social senses. But later when they were asked about the dimensions of integration in the political sphere, most were unwilling to accept such a proposition. Hence, the mobilization campaign and the positive experience of black leadership had not been lost on them. They were unprepared, even at the risk (or perhaps in spite) of damaging one of their abstract principles, to share local political power. In this sense we find political communities and new leadership that are operating in some degree of synchrony.

This pattern is only lessened when we attempt to transfer the level of domestic sophistication to the international arena, albeit concerning issues assumed to be of importance to the respondents. These sophisticated domestics do not exhibit anywhere near the expected levels of knowledge of African affairs. Perhaps this is because of the great distance of details of African life from most of our respondents' experiences. Even in the absence of great knowledge, however, their ideological thinking does allow a sizable number of individuals to express expected sentiments about issues that have to do with principles opposed to integration. As predicted, these respondents reject such sentiments.

7

The Political Economy of Rural Black American Mobilization

Much of the preceding analysis has focused on the role of political factors in Afro-American political mobilization. Yet such factors are but one part of a much larger picture. In American politics in particular, economic factors also constitute a very important part of the power equation. To understand this in a common-sense way, one need only note the connection between political elections and campaign financing. Largely, those who are able to mobilize substantial financial resources achieve office.[1] Much of the literature on elitism in American government shows that mobilization of such resources is very much dependent on where one is placed in the economic hierarchy. Those who have wealth, for example, find it much easier to generate the economic resources necessary to achieve power. That is, wealth and power are believed to go hand in hand, without much circulation to those outside the small circle. Michael Parenti and Dolbeare/Edelman have made fairly sophisticated theoretical and empirical arguments about the overwhelming importance of financial interests to control of the political structure. We have already seen that they suggest that power is in the hands of a small number of wealthy elites, who thereby dictate the rules of the political game and dominate its play. They note that this general system has particular disadvantages for blacks in the exercise of political power. In this light, the purpose of this chapter is to evaluate the impact of economic factors upon the political fortunes of blacks in rural towns.[2] That is, in the context of the larger American political system, what are the policy dimensions and outputs for the new leaders and their constituents? Do they sufficiently control economic resources with which to sustain their political programs? What factors impinge upon this process, and what strategies are developed in light of mobilization?

In general, what do we know about the linkage between Afro-American power and the possession of access to economic resources? In the Dolbeare/Edelman analysis, the black situation is treated in the aggregate in making the finding that blacks are largely outside the power elite. Others have attempted to answer the question by analyzing circumstances where blacks have achieved administrative control without gaining critical economic resources or financial control. One of the earliest works in this genre asked rhetorically if such political achievements by blacks did not constitute mere "hollow prizes." Apparently much of what was controlled was beyond the scope of these black politicians.[3] This perspective has continued even as the number of such cases has increased, especially in central cities. Peter Eisinger has asserted that there are severe limits on what political control in the black-controlled urban community can mean because of the agreed-upon rules of the game. These rules dictate that only incremental changes can be made in the reallocation of resources that are at the government's disposal. There are many other resources, however, that the government does not control and cannot afford to appropriate. Such private resources are generally the driving force behind the economy and largely remain as such, notwithstanding election of a black.[4] Mack Jones has considered the economic consequences in Atlanta. He argues that the only advantage blacks had toward the realization of political power was "population distribution." Their general socioeconomic status was too low to put them in a potential position to mobilize for service and technological orientation of the Atlanta economy. Moreover, "the [real] economic wealth of the black community, as determined by median family income and the number of minority enterprises and their gross receipts, [was] not especially significant."[5]

But as we have seen, some analysts of the Afro-American condition have taken this a step further to argue that the success of the elites (almost always whites) has been sustained because of structural conditions of dependency created for blacks. As in colonial society, by this view, blacks were relegated to an instrumental role that made the environment safe for the elite to flourish. A virtual caste system was created that denied blacks mobility as well as the independent development of a cultural community. The indelibility of color and the theory of racial inferiority made it easy for the elites to denigrate distinct cultural patterns, while at the same time denying assimilation to the mainstream. Carmichael and Hamilton[6] and Balandier[7] have referred to this domination by saturation of one's total life experience as the colonial situation. Its present–day consequence is what Kwame Nkrumah termed "neo–colonialism:[8] and Andre Gunder Frank termed dependency.[9] By this they mean that there is a continuance of control by the elites even after so-called independence is achieved. The patterns persist, they argue, because the structural components are so well fixed by historical patterns of elite control that those formerly dominated merely feed into existing networks. For black Americans this would seem to imply that even electoral success without economic power would not mean the exercise of real political power.

Yet, in elaborating the preconditions for electoral success in an earlier chapter, we have seen that control and allocative power of economic resources are required. The purposive welfare program that leaders must have in order to achieve success in these environments can only be sustained by controlling certain economic resources. If the empirical and theoretical contentions are true that black electoral success does not yield commensurate economic control, then is there any ground on which this all-important precondition is being met? For example, does the programmatic effort of the mayors match their success in general political mobilization? In this latter respect it can be argued that considerable success has been realized. Participation levels have gone up remarkably and some measure of improved efficacy is observable. Moreover, these small town electors exhibit broad domestic sophistication and ideological commitment.

Now, in light of apparent economic realities, one is forced to ask whether it is all for naught. With the evidence from these cases in hand, an understanding is sought of how the absence of independent economic resources within the black constituency and the towns generally affect the continuity of the regimes. Or, how do these small town leaders, under circumstances of extreme economic scarcity and only partial and recent political clout, meet the basic human needs and escalating welfare demands of their newly franchised and highly mobilized constituents?

In the course of this chapter the analysis proceeds from this theoretical and general discussion of economics and politics to the local conditions in the three towns. Initially an exploration is made of the local political systems and economic conditions in the towns. It will be illustrated that while a purposive welfare program is demanded by the constituents, the local leaders have little independent capacity for delivering one. (A detailed evaluation of the few economic resources available and who controls them completes this part of the analysis.) In order to compensate for this lack of capacity, these black leaders develop a reliance upon the federal government. We shall see that the latter does indeed provide considerable financial support to modestly sustain three distinct phases of political and economic development in the towns. The first phase is that which meets basic human needs, the second is concerned with infrastructure, while the barely visible third is concerned with institutionalization.

The Local Political Systems and Economics

A basic theoretical assumption in this analysis is that American success and regime maintenance are critically affected by access to certain minimal economic resources. Observations of communities like those in this analysis show that political power has not meant economic power. Most of the rural towns that have elected a black American mayor are poor, have a largely black population, and lack independent bases for revenue. Moreover, the independent revenue that exists is not controlled by the new regime or the new constituency. The economic sector usually consists of a few stores, a declining agricultural sector, and the public payroll. Most gainfully employed residents work outside the town in small factories; others are seasonal workers, or are unemployed. Conditions in the three Mississippi towns were especially indicative of these points. The transfer of political power had yielded no such transfer or redistribution of economic resources.

Therefore, the new leaders had to seek economic resources elsewhere with which to sustain their heavy programs of social welfare. The search for external benefits was complicated because the state government was largely unsupportive. Mississippi remains a poor state, and in any case its strong legislative body was often hostile to these new regimes. Early in their administrations these mayors found federal support for their programs, support which has steadily declined in the last several years. Indeed, without this external support, it was difficult to identify much in the way of independent local programs. In the three towns there was a high correlation between the availability of economic programs and political success. In part this resulted because previous exclusion of blacks from community resources left so many basic human needs unsatisfied. This factor was exaggerated by the many demands of the newly mobilized constituencies that required delivery of specific welfare benefits. In direct response to this challenge the small-town mayors in Mississippi had little choice but to bid in the external marketplace for resources that were unavailable locally.

In this aggressive pursuit of outside resources, the mayors were able to meet some of the most immediate demands of their constituents, without apparent compromise of other requisites for black American leadership (such as civil rights experience and ideology). Some of the demands that were evidently satisfied were in the areas of social services and short-term employment. All of the mayors were relatively successful at expanding health, day-care, nutrition, and facilities for elderly persons. Involvement in such programs vastly increased the towns' status as employer, since a small local bureaucracy was required to operate the programs. Moreover, the modest infrastructure programs became available, though not broad enough to generate other capital investments.

A special relationship developed between the small towns and the federal government in the 1960s and 1970s, continuing a traditional pattern of greater support for black concerns from the federal government.[10] The relationship can be partially described as a convergence between the interests of the ruling coalition in the federal government at the time and the small towns. Blacks, a well-accepted part of the Democratic coalition by this time, had well-articulated demands. In response to these demands, the federal government developed certain programs earmarked for black Americans, simply as a matter of good politics. Also, many elected officials, conscious of the rising numbers of black American electors after 1965, began to respond to these new constituents. The spirit of the "New Frontier" and executive initiatives in proposing the "Great Society" programs were symbolic of the period.[11] The new black American leaders became willing partners in this arrangement because they served as conduits for the federal largesse. It was these resources that satisfied some immediate demands of the constituents and provided symbolic benefits that greatly enhanced the standing of local leaders. Therefore, there was a minimal confluence of goals between local and national politicians that solidified the working relationship—interest in extending tenure in office.

Otherwise, the relationship was partially sustained by the unintended, adaptable functions that certain national policies can always fulfill. This is denoted by many programs that are specifically designed to appeal to certain special interests, but can be adapted to other uses if necessary. Housing programs designed for urban interests are one example. The aggressive pursuit of resources by the mayors led some Washington bureaus to make programs available to rural areas that were designed to meet other needs. Such a process also worked the other way. Oftentimes leaders were forced to devise ways to take advantage of programs that were designed to appeal to other kinds of rural interests. Consider the allotments the Department of Agriculture has traditionally made to farmers for fallow acreage. Normally only the largest (usually white) farmers took advantage of the program. Now modest black farmers were more likely to make requests for such support. Equally relevant were some rural programs perceived as inappropriate by local leaders, but to which the latter had to conform if resources were to be made available. We have seen Bennie Thompson lament about such problems that forced Bolton to meet regulations, clearly meant for a more highly bureaucratic entity, in applying for certain grants.

Meanwhile, reliance upon federal support created certain problems for the institutionalization of these regimes ideologically committed to social change. There are several aspects to this. Little of the federal monies available were specifically designed for the needs of such rural communities. Funds were more often but a part of the package of programs, designed at the federal level, for a coalition of largely urban[12] and bureaucratic interests.[13] Consequently, the programs were subject to shifting political alignments mostly determined by factors outside the control of rural, southern towns. Perhaps the most salient evidence of this was the decline in fortunes of these regimes under the emergent Republican coalition that followed the Johnson administration. The black leaders and new constituents faced a national coalition that included many Southerners bent on maintaining white supremacy. This meant that blacks had found a less favorable environment for pursuit of their independent goals.

Moreover, the policy process for resource allocation to these rural towns was, even in the best of times, characteristically an *ad hoc* one. Rural constituents' needs were often perceived as being extrinsic[14] to the highly organized[15] bargaining process that determines policy. Allocations to rural black American interests, therefore, tended to be short-term and non-institutionalized. In sum, the economic resources available to these black leaders were not designed to boost locally derived or independent sources of revenue for the towns. What emerged was local dependency on the national government to sustain even modest short-term projects.

The political-economic condition of these towns and their dependent relationship to the federal government are of strategic importance in explaining the political economy facing black American leadership. This conclusion is hardly different than ones made by others who have studied the linkage between politics and economics on a general basis. Michael Parenti has said that such relationships result from the "allocation of scarce resources for competing ends, involving conflicts between social classes and among groups and individuals within classes."[16] Simply put, there is a positive correlation beetween the possession of economic resources and success in attaining political power. It is correct, by this view, that power is the ability of "X" to force or significantly influence the actions of "A." It is also important that "X" has the ability to define the terms on which "A" sees the world.[17] Therefore, a variety of resources must be at the disposal of "A" to provide the mechanism for influence. Murray Edelman has shown that in the organizational sphere alone, those who possess disproportionately large amounts of resources are far more successful in pressing their will.[18] In analyzing leadership in the three rural towns in Mississippi, the political and economic relationships that devolve from the understanding of power are of paramount importance. In this way a complete picture of the potential for the institutionalization of social change can be presented.

The Economic Bases of Neo-black Leadership

A variety of factors impinged upon black control of the local economic sector. It has been noted that blacks historically were excluded from the profit side of the economic structure in these towns. Even their labor was commanded and often owned by whites. This was of vital importance to the new black American leaders because it meant that they had little economic support from their natural constituency. Local whites, even under the best circumstances, did not generally provide economic support to sustain mayoral programs. They either withdrew from the political arena, or exhibited overt hostility. This economic divide was obvious in each of these towns. There may not have been a set of railroad tracks to divide the races, but all the same it was clear who owned what. The whites owned almost all lucrative businesses, means of production and most property. Blacks were largely without economic power. The professional class of blacks was almost limited to school teachers, who, as a rule, owned no other income-producing enterprises. The business sector among blacks was small to nonexistent, and in any case was hardly of a level of development to influence economic decisions. In Mayersville, indeed, one was hard put to find business people in the pure sense of the word. In Bolton, blacks owned a café or two that catered to the weekend leisure trade, providing light meals and beverages. The lone black funeral home in the rural county was also located there. Tchula came closest to having an independent and potentially influential business sector during the reign of the mayor. In fact it was the mayor himself who dominated this sector with his various businesses. Yet none of these businesses was in a position to be a mayoral benefactor, or to influence others on the basis of quasi-corporate connections.

The position of blacks was not the only problem. There was an overall decline in the independent economic bases in these rural areas—particularly in human resource capital. If there is no population to sustain economic growth by investment or supply of labor decline is all that can be expected. Data show that there was a continuous decline in such a vital resource in all but Hinds county (Bolton) in the 1970s. But in the 1960s, during the intense social mobilization, all of the counties showed a negative outmigration. This was exceedingly high in small Issaquena County (–37 per cent) and Holmes County (–26 per cent). (See Table 7.1.)

Table 7.1. County Population Migration, 1960-1975

County (1975 Population)	1960-1970	1970-1975
Hinds (228,521)	– 2.6%	1.7%
Holmes (22,835)	–26.3	– 5.0
Issaquena (2,359)	–37.6	–17.4

Source: Mississippi Research and Development Center, *Mississippi County Data Book*, 1976.

There is another, perhaps more critical, impingement on the development of local economic resources for political deployment. Prior to the transfer of power there was a remarkable decline in the mainstay of these economies— agriculture. This was coupled with many demographic changes that affected the very character of life in these towns. Cotton acreage had declined substantially in each of these counties since the 1930s and 1940s, though Holmes County was showing an upswing in the late 1970s. At the same time, in all the counties there was a dramatic decrease in the number of small farm owners (many of whom were black). This moved blacks further away from the productive sector in several ways. They no longer owned as much land, but because of the overall decline in the cotton industry they also lost their major source of employment.

216   BLACK POLITICAL MOBILIZATION

Table 7.2.   County Farm Ownership (A) and Operation (B) among Afro-Americans, 1940-1978, by Number

	Hinds		Holmes		Issaquena	
Year	A	B	A	B	A	B
1940	—	4,849	—	5,274	129	991
1945	621	4,450	839	4,334	159	955
1950	—	3,534	—	3,741	139	545
1954	612	3,100	752	3,121	97	373
1959	553	1,905	593	1,612	72	155
1964	442	1,247	471	1,138	39	63
1969	391	583	455	643	27	51
1974	191	266	253	305	17	42
1978	156	207	127	192	17	31

Source: *U.S. Census of Agriculture* (by year indicated).

Table 7.3.   County Farm Ownership (A) and Operation (B) among Whites, 1940-1978, by Number

	Hinds		Holmes		Issaquena	
Year	A	B	A	B	A	B
1940	—	1,547	—	1,076	79	167
1945	1,118	1,541	667	1,056	158	263
1950	—	1,471	—	1,090	169	256
1954	1,004	1,527	560	981	140	232
1959	794	1,148	433	728	102	158
1964	649	982	362	656	80	132
1969	697	1,056	339	582	54	123
1974	564	870	309	484	32	92
1978	489	807	213	449	35	112

Source: *U.S. Census of Agriculture* (by year indicated).

The severity of the ownership problem through the years is revealed in the relative decline of black farm owners and operators. Data in Table 7.2 show that while the absolute numbers of black owners in two counties actually exceeded those for whites (Table 7.3) in the 1940s, black ownership had declined at a much more rapid rate. White owners and operators exceeded blacks, notwithstanding the continued black majority in two of the counties. It is interesting that the decline was more precipitous in the area of farm operators. In Hinds County, the number of blacks in farm operation declined from 4,800 to 200 in just over 35 years. White decline was from 1,500 to 800 in the same period. In

Holmes and Issaquena counties, the data also show dramatic declines for blacks, indicating the more rapid decline in recruitment due to the increasingly mechanized farm industry. In short, at the time they gained political power, blacks were insignificant in this previously most important sector of the agricultural-based economies. That they were without influence here put their weaknesses in the political institutional sector in bold relief.

At the same time that population resources and the number of farms were declining, the amount of acreage devoted to the major agricultural and food products continued its long-term decline. Census data show that there was an across-the-board drop in acreage being farmed. In Holmes County the number of ten-acre farms dropped from 549 in 1954 to a mere eleven in 1978. Meanwhile, this decline was not being made up by larger-acreage farm plots, for such larger plots also declined. For example, 100-500 acre plots in the same period declined from 582 to 284. Decreases in Issaquena were more dramatic. Ten-acre farms dropped from 157 in 1954 to three in 1978. Declines in Hinds County were less substantial, but no less dramatic. And as market interest in cotton continued to decline, either acreage had to be reduced or the return on yield would be further reduced. Thus Hinds County made out better by reducing cotton acreage by over 50 per cent between 1954 and 1978, from 33,817 acres to 15,506. Holmes County, however, increased cotton acreage from 41,042 acres to 58,770. Acreage in Issaquena was 13,646 in 1954, dropped sharply to 9,975 in 1959, but had rebounded to 13,343 in 1978.[19]

The volume of foodstuffs normally produced for local consumption also declined. Corn, sweet potatoes, Irish potatoes, wheat, peanuts, and sugar cane all declined or disappeared from production after the late 1940s. The decline in corn production was especially notable since the crop was a supplementary human food product and a staple for such farm animals as hogs and cattle. Corn acreage in Holmes County declined from 64,000 in the early 1940s to under 5,000 acres in 1978; other counties showed similar declines. Sweet potatoes, Irish potatoes and sugar cane all but disappeared everywhere. In short, at the time of black American political accession the agricultural sector was almost decimated for all but the wealthiest white farmers, whose absolute numbers were piteously small. As such there was little in the way of an agricultural sector to harness, or from which investments could be exacted.

So much for the modest private sector. What about the public purse, which these new leaders did control? The budget and institutional salience of these small towns were both nonexistent at the election of the black American mayors. Indeed, there was very little in the way of formal public service performed by these units of government. What there was of an institutional sector had been controlled by a class of planters since at least 1875, but in some cases since the early 1800s. Their informal exercise of power had led to the lack of salience of the formal political sector. Despite this, the towns (Mayersville excepted) had a charter for operation that required a mayor and boards of aldermen. None of these officers were regarded as full-time or even part-time; only the mayor received modest compensation. Otherwise the towns had police forces of two or three men, a town clerk, and perhaps one or two part-time persons affiliated with a volunteer fire service. The budget was formed mostly from local property taxes, although some revenue did result from water/sewage taxes, utility taxes, and certain other monies dispensed by the state government on the basis of a derivation formula. In short, local government units in Mississippi at this period did not differ from similar units elsewhere in the country, where the formal institutional base and functional responsibilities were minimal.[20]

An exploration of the financial base, and the socioeconomic profile it shapes in these towns, is best revealed in the tax structure. Though there are numerous taxes, the essential bases for revenue are sales and property in this highly taxed state. A high proportion of revenue results from a tax on sales.[21] In 1980 the state collected over $600 million in such taxes, and returned some $90 million to the municipalities (and some $94 million to state roads and schools).[22]

The balance of about $424 million constituted 44 per cent of the state general fund. State law also provides for the towns to collect taxes from utilities that they own (water), or that operate there (telephones). The other lucrative sources of revenue for the towns are taxes on real and personal property, largely automobiles. Statewide in 1978, these taxes totalled $3,302,042,828. Finally, the municipalities are permitted to raise certain other specialized revenues that are designed to improve public facilities or services (as for roads).[23] In small towns like those under analysis here, such revenue is of little consequence.

In the evaluation that follows of the public sector revenues of the three towns, a caveat is in order. Some of the data from which extrapolations are made presented difficulties because such data was often only reported in the aggregate by county. This was the case for property taxes, which were also only reported by broad sub-categories. And, of course, much of the information that may have been available on town property was not reproduced because the scale of operation was too small to protect the privacy of individual owners. Hence some of the data are presented only by county, which distorts the picture of the towns. The problem was lessened in Mayersville and Tchula because they were much more representative of their essentially rural counties. Bolton, however, was unlike much of urban Hinds county. It should be understood therefore that such data, when useful, will be presented with some qualifications.[24] Finally, since fairly complete budgetary information was only available for Bolton, these data will be evaluated as an illustrative case about the scale of public resource availability and allocation in such political entities.

The bases for corporate and personal incomes gives an immediate profile of these towns. The three towns had virtually no manufacturing sector from which taxes were drawn. This was equally true for at least two of the counties as well. The entire county of Issaquena had no manufacturing sector, and manufactures constituted six percent of the income base for Holmes County. The absense of such a sector means that corporate taxes played no role in the economy; neither would personal income taxes for individuals who might be employed in such corporate or industrial enterprises. Much of the base for income in Holmes and

Issaquena counties (see Table 7.4) was transfer payments: 28 percent in Holmes and 14 percent in Issaquena. This means that a large portion of those benefiting from such arrangements were unavailable to, or outside of, the employment pool. The second major source of income was farms. These were especially important in Issaquena County (where they were 5 percent of the income base). But even here a distortion occurs because the income from farms was concentrated in the hands of a very small number of white farmers, whose contribution to the black regime, beyond taxes, was nil. It is also observed that government employment and property taxes were of some benefit in Holmes County, but not much in Issaquena.

Table 7.4. Sources of Income for Two Counties

Sources of Income	Holmes	Issaquena
Transfers	28%	14%
Farms	17	51
Government	13	8
Property	13	6
Wholesale	9	2
Manufactures	6	0

Sources: *Economic Development Blueprint for Mississippi*, Parts IX and XI, March 1978 and August 1978, respectively (Jackson: Mississippi Research and Development Center).

It is hardly a surprise that estimates put 78 percent of black Holmes Countians and 71 percent of Issaquena Countians below the poverty level. There was very little within these towns at which to employ people. Most who were in the work force at all were concentrated in agriculture, domestic, self-employment or unpaid family work. Even many of these were seasonally idle. A combination of other factors conspired to reduce the economic capability of the towns. Median school years (7.0 in Holmes; 5.8 in Issaquena) were low and restricted employment possibilities in surrounding areas.

Local governments also saw their tax bases limited by the lack of personal and real property ownership. In 1977 it was estimated that over 57 percent of the housing in Holmes County was either dilapidated or deteriorating. About 50 percent of that in Issaquena County was estimated to be in a similar state of disrepair,[25] indicating little tax value.

The latter notwithstanding, it is now possible to evaluate the comparative value of the various classes of personal properties (see Table 7.5). (Data are used from the three counties, though that for Hinds County is used primarily as a standard of well-being against which the other counties are contrasted.) Data were available on the following classes of taxed properties: homes and land, automobiles, mobile homes, airplanes, vending machines and jewelry, gasoline stations and associated equipment, office and store equipment, and merchandise. Hinds County tax revenue surpasses the others by far. In automobile taxes for 1978, Hinds County raised $108 million, compared to $4.2 million and $1

Table 7.5. Taxes on Certain Classes of Personal Property (1978), by County ($ millions)

Classes	Hinds	Holmes	Issaquena
Automobiles	$108.0	4.7	1.0
Mobile Homes	1.0	.175	.64
Airplanes	.647	.004	.0
Vending/Jewelry	.598	.005	.005
Gasoline/Equipment	.503	.030	.004
Office/Equipment	4.0	.018	.0
Merchandise	26.5	.574	.005

Source: *Service Bulletin*, "Property Assessments and Ad Valorem Taxes" (Jackson: Mississippi State Tax Commission, 1977-1978).

million in Holmes and Issaquena counties respectively. The gap between the counties lessened for mobile homes, with the two poorer counties collecting proportionally more taxes on such abodes. Airplanes were insignificant in all but Hinds County, with its airports and landing strips. The situation was similar for vending machines, jewelry and gasoline taxes. Hinds county collected over a million dollars in such taxes, while the other counties combined collected less than $50,000. Issaquena County collected nothing for office and store equipment, compared to $18,000 for Holmes and $4 million for Hinds. Even in merchandise taxes the extremely low scale of activity in Issaquena was glaring. A mere $5,000 was raised. The same sector in Holmes yielded $555,000-plus; Hinds yielded $26.5 million. Moreover in taxes on personal homes, Hinds yielded $583 million, compared to $29 and $9 million for Holmes and Issaquena respectively. It is important, however, to keep in mind that Hinds County is physically larger (876 square miles) than Holmes (769 square miles) or

Issaquena (414 square miles). Even so, the value per acre in Hinds was $1,343, compared to $64 in Holmes and $39 in Issaquena. All told it can be concluded that, at least in Holmes and Issaquena counties, there was very little in the way of personal properties that could sustain an independent and vibrant economy. And in separate data on personal properties in the town of Bolton, the same conclusion could be drawn. Despite its location in relatively wealthy Hinds County, personal property taxes in the town were not grossly out of line for those in the other towns in the period. Though its receipts were higher ($25,147) than those for more populous Tchula ($19,121), or Mayersville ($6,796), the figures were in no way proportionate to those for urban Hinds County.[26]

Data on sales taxes are much more useful for evaluating our individual towns. These taxes are collected exclusively within boundaries of the towns on virtually every sale. In this regard it is expected that the variant demographics of the three towns would have quite an effect upon economic activity. In Table 7.6 data are reported for a twelve-year period beginning in 1969 when the power of the white leaders began to decline. This twelve-year period also provides the opportunity to see if any differences can be observed in economic activity at the advent of a power transfer.

Table 7.6. Sales Taxes in the Towns, 1969-1980 ($thousands)

Year	Bolton	Tchula	Mayersville
1969	$ 7,269	$26,604	$ 2,287
1970	10,780	25,026	2,748
1971	11,592	27,430	2,992
1972	13,447	30,621	3,061
1973	12,551	31,713	3,173
1974	14,003	32,264	3,245
1975	14,988	38,876	4,533
1976	14,857	40,288	3,577
1977	17,300	41,880	3,933
1978	17,071	43,197	2,188
1979	17,583	45,372	3,537
1980	20,143	48,983	3,975

Source: *Service Bulletin*, "Sales Taxes" (Jackson: Mississippi State Tax Commission, July 1, 1979-June 30, 1980).

What is most evident from these data is the extremely low level (comparatively) of sales tax activity in Bolton and Mayersville in the early years. In 1969, Bolton was only collecting $7,000-plus and Mayersville barely over $2,000. Tchula, whose population was over twice that of the others, was collecting over three times as much in sales taxes. Yet in the next several years in Bolton (about the time when blacks first won electoral posts), the volume of activity increased remarkably. In one year (1969-1970) sales tax revenues increased by over $3,000. Though the rate of improvement did not continue as rapidly for the twelve-year period, the volume of activity increased nearly threefold. Improvements were not so rapid in either of the other towns. When Mrs. Blackwell came into office in Mayersville at the end of 1977, sales actually declined for the next year. Moreover, at the end of the twelve-year period in Mayersville, the total taxes did not yet amount to $4,000. In 1975, however, the figure of $4,500 was inexplicably reached, but then a sharp decline occurred and the $4,000 figure has not been reached since. In Tchula taxes did improve, but not by a rate inconsistent with an established pattern. The mayor's election did not spur a decline or any extraordinary leap in activity. To some degree this was surprising in light of the town's conflict, which might have been expected to affect buying habits.

The sources for the taxes were few and so was the volume of revenue generated. Data in Table 7.7 show the small number of categories in which there was activity, as well as the number of such activities or taxpayers. Most taxes resulted from automobiles, food and beverages, apparel/general merchandise and some contract building. It can be seen that while the volume of activity in Bolton was not the largest, there seemed to be modestly more diversification there, at least in the early 1970s. By 1978 some decline was evident as both food and beverage sales and automobile sales began to dominate. Tchula also illustrated diversification, although automobiles were always a more significant entity. Yet there was considerable activity in foods and more in contract building than might ordinarily be expected in a poor county. The position of Mayersville was below that of the other towns. The activity tended to be concentrated in the food and beverage category. Apparel and merchandising, and automobiles, were of the most modest import prior to 1980. In short, there was very little activity of any kind in Mayersville from which these taxes could be earned. Moreover, the volume of activity in each of the other towns indicated less than overwhelming vibrance. When it is said that there was diversification in Bolton, that is only in comparison to the very modest conditions in other places similarly situated. Neither Bolton nor Tchula represented highly mobilized independent economic entities.

In a further analysis of budgetary data available from Bolton it was possible to more clearly establish the rudimentary character of the economic sector in these small towns. These data for the period of fiscal 1970-1971 (August) through fiscal 1975-1976 fell into two distinct periods: before and after the mayoral election of Bennie Thompson. The budgets in the pre-Thompson period (1970-1973) were very modest indeed. In 1970-1971 the total (actual) general fund revenue was $35,942.09, plus $15,650.73 in water utility revenue. Two fiscal years later the general fund figure had only reached $41,000, while water works brought in $15,937.

The second period began with the election of Thompson and was distinguished by two phenomena. In the first place, there were far better reporting procedures that gave a more complete picture of the volume of revenue being

Table 7.7. Gross Sales ($ millions) by Category, 1970, 1974, 1978, 1980

Town and Year	Auto	Food/Beverage	Furniture	Apparel/Merchan.	Contract Building	Total
Bolton						
1970	.216(5)[a]	.866(8)	.003	.222	.009	1.3
1974	.193(5)	.529(15)	.002	.298(3)	.075(2)	1.8
1978	.208(3)	.356(13)	—	.416(2)	—	2.1
1980	.307(3)	.423(10)	—	—	—	4.2
Tchula						
1970	1.5(11)	.950(38)	.100(3)	.303(11)	.331(7)	4.1
1974	1.9(16)	1.2(34)	.095(2)	.200(6)	.360(4)	4.2
1978	2.3(13)	1.4(29)	.096(2)	.226(7)	.274(5)	5.1
1980	2.0(13)	2.3(31)	.183(4)	.187(5)	.288(4)	5.5
Mayersville						
1970	.002(1)	.260(6)	.004	.049	—	.356
1974	.019(1)	.347(6)	—	.006(1)	—	.384
1978	.029(2)	.145(6)	—	—	—	.216
1980	—	.346(8)	—	—	—	.403

Source: *Service Bulletin*, "Sales Taxes" (July 1, 1979-June 30, 1980).

[a]Parentheticals represent the number of local activities until 1974. Thereafter they represent the actual number of taxpayers, some of whom may be engaged in more than one activity.

handled by the town. (It was only in fiscal 1972-1973 that auto license taxes were reported, for example.) But the real differences occurred in the more extensive reporting of 1973-1974 when the categories of *ad valorem* (properties) taxes were separated. (Prior to this a broad category that combined all *ad valorem* taxes was used.) Even in this better data period the modest, though improved, level of revenues was no less notable.

The data in Table 7.8 illustrate the changes that occurred in collections for the general fund and from the water utility over the period 1970-1976. The election of Thompson produced an immediate rise in revenues, especially in the general fund. Even so, these figures did not represent all new monies. For example, they did not include federal grants, a number of which had become available by 1973. (These will be discussed separately later.) Water revenues, however, did not seem to follow any clear pattern as they rose and fell almost from year to year.

Table 7.8. General Fund and Water Utility Revenues, 1970-1976, Bolton

Year	General Fund	Water Utility
1970-1971	$35,942.09	$15,650.73
1971-1972	37,656.62	14,565.39
1972-1973	41,396.70	15,937.24
1973-1974	52,811.93	10,240.25
1974-1975	61,790.47	13,307.76
1975-1976	66,937.00	16,399.00

Source: *Service Bulletin* (1970-1976).

In comparing the pre-and post-Thompson periods, several factors are revealed. The largest tax categories were sales and *ad valorem*. In the first period 34 percent of the general fund revenues came from sales taxes, while 28 percent came from property taxes. The balance resulted from gas and light franchises, and gasoline and oil taxes. It is worth noting that Bolton, having several small oil wells in the town, collected a small amount in oil and oil well severance taxes that were not available to the other towns. In the first period these taxes constituted just under 5 percent of the general fund revenue.

In the second period—post-1973—a slightly different picture began to emerge because of the better reporting procedures, but also because of increased revenues in certain areas. There was evidence for the first time of revenues from real property on a separate line. These revenues improved considerably by the end of fiscal 1974, when $18,075 was collected. In the previous year, as far as can be estimated, such taxes brought in just over half as much. The explanation would appear to be that such increased funds resulted from the tax reassessment which Thompson made just after entering office (under considerable protest from whites). Moreover, when real property and personal property taxes ($3,906) for the same year are compared with sales taxes ($17,761) collected over the period, it is noted that sales taxes declined, relatively, while taxes on properties increased. In short, Thompson made an early effort to shift the burden somewhat from the poor masses, who paid a heavier share in sales taxes and owned less property (see Table 7.9.).

Table 7.9. Chief Sources of Bolton Revenue, Post-1973

Source	1974	1975	1976
Property	$21,981.80	$22,636.33	$20,969.00
Real	18,075.00	18,882.75	17,536.00
Personal	3,906.80	3,753.58	3,433.00
Sales	17,761.47	15,642.27	13,877.00
Oil Severance	3,222.62	3,265.87	284.00
Auto Tag	2,655.41	2,648.50	2,918.00
Pub. Utilities	2,030.28	2,686.51	2,502.00
Franchises	1,980.63	2,595.77	2,859.00
Police Fines	923.00	2,769.00	2,638.00

Totals are not provided, since some categories of revenue are not shown.

Source: Town budgets as specified.

What these data reveal, beyond a modest shift in the tax burden, is that the town continued to be heavily dependent on the usual sources for revenue: property and sales taxes. Yet it is noteworthy that as the real increases occurred, especially in property taxes, modest increases were also recorded for certain other areas. For example, auto taxes, fees from public utilities and franchises, and police fines rose over this period. This means several things. First there was an infusion of new monies at some place in the economy; those who had new money were spending it to provide conveniences or services. Some were buying cars or trading them while others were receiving the benefits of utility services previously unavailable. It seems almost certain that there was a "crackdown" on crime, as the amount collected in fines showed quite remarkable increases.

Excluding external resources, Bolton had a budgeted general fund that had not reached $100,000 by 1976. By any estimation, this is a piteous sum with which to undertake major infrastructure changes in a town. When an analysis was done of expenditures from the general fund, it immediately became clear that hardly any of this money could be made available for non-routine, programmatic efforts. The sheer costs of running the town's affairs and paying the bills virtually depleted the general fund each year. The chief items for which expenditures were made included salaries and supplies. In 1970, over $27,000 out of $35,000 was spent on meeting routine costs such as those above. This yielded a small excess that was carried over to the following year. Such small, but ever-declining balances constituted a pattern until the end of fiscal 1974. In fiscal 1975 the books merely showed a balance between revenues and expenditures. Hence even as small-scale as the operation in Bolton was at the time, like larger entities, Bolton was bordering on public indebtedness. This was all the more critical since the general fund only covered routine bills. There was no consideration in this of using such funds for innovations or new programs. The funds simply were not available, and this forced Thompson to look elsewhere.

The preceding only points out that the resource base in Bolton was mediocre. We can surmise that the base was even worse in the other towns because it is already known that Bolton was considerably better off. We can only go a short distance in illustrating this from a budgetary standpoint, however. The best direct comparative data come from the 1978 fiscal year, and even this is not easy to compare since the data are from town ledgers, not audit reports. At the end of this fiscal year Mayersville received a mere $6,796 from property taxes, compared to $19,121 in Tchula and $25,147 in Bolton. In this same year data were not available for sales and utility taxes in Bolton, but were known for the other towns: sales generated in Mayersville $984 and Tchula $48,224 in taxes; while utilities brought $51 and $8,034, respectively. This was especially significant in two ways. It showed Bolton's position relative to the others—the town was only modestly larger than Mayersville and almost half the size of Tchula. Yet Bolton's property tax revenues were much larger.

A Special Relationship with the Federal Government and the National Democratic Coalition

The mobilization campaign of the new black American leaders was not limited to political factors. Since most constituent demands included requests for additional financial resources, the new leaders immediately sought means of assuaging this desire. A hallmark of a leader's early campaign in Mississippi during this period was demonstrating influence with external sources of power. Largely this was accomplished by showing that one was respected by state leaders in the Democratic coalition, but also by having relationships with national political figures. It has been demonstrated that Thompson and Blackwell were particularly known for their clout with such external resource providers. Therefore, during election campaigning these leaders could bid for support based on a record of some achievement in purposive programming. Both Thompson and Blackwell were instrumental in the receipt of Headstart funding prior to their mayoral accession. As such they were already seen to be providing jobs. Moreover, they and Carthan had made a number of other propositions to the federal government that were being evaluated or did receive funding soon after their election. These efforts formed a pattern by which the individual mayors sought economic resources for their purposive social welfare programs. By such actions these mayors created the most substantial changes the economies of their small-town governments ever experienced.

Precisely how did they do this, in light of the absence or unavailability of indigenous local funds? They began by going to the only source avowedly willing to listen to their claims—the federal government. These mayors, via their already well-established contacts with the national cadre of the Democratic coalition, began to aggressively pursue any funds available with which basic human needs could be satisfied. They were particularly lucky, though none of this was accidental, to be a part of the ruling coalition that perceived the demands as a part of the national drive for civil rights. These new black American leaders merely took advantage of their strategic position in the coalition to seek largesse that would keep them in power, at the same time that a critical component of their ideological program for social change could be sustained. This was seen as a legitimate means of pursuing their goals, because they could do so as bonafide partners in the ruling coalition. Indeed there were no special terms that required the new leaders to compromise or negotiate on less than equal terms. They deemed that their relations with and the receipts of benefits from the federal government were the result of real and institutionalized participation. To engage in such a relationship with an external source, in other words, was not perceived to be in any way damaging to the uncompromising attitude of the new leaders on civil rights matters. For many constituents, in fact, the material advantages that became available seemed to indicate the appropriateness of the strategy. Symbolically it was also of great importance when one's own small-town mayor could be seen rubbing shoulders with Washington "bigwigs."

The election of a black American mayor in light of the preceding signaled a considerable rise in revenues directly managed by the towns. In all three towns there was a vast and rapid increase in funds available to the local budget. Most of these came via intergovernmental transfers from Washington, and not from increased direct local revenue such as property or other local taxes. Growth also occurred in the receipt of resources from state agencies and from the federal government (largely grants). Often the federal grants required no local matching effort.

The town of Bolton was the best example of this trend. Initially, the greatest increases in revenue there occurred in direct grants and intergovernmental transfers. Federal monies constituted most of these resources, though some of the intergovernmental transfers included matching money from the state's general fund. In addition, a few small private grants were received in the first two years. The data show that only in 1973-1974 (the first year of black American leadership) was there a favorable comparison between general revenues and external sources. Then, by 1978, external resources were over eight times greater than local ones (see Table 7.10). The variety of programs for which support was received over a 10-year period was broad. There were traditional programs like education and welfare, but equally prominent was support for youth, elderly, recreation, housing, and health services. In most cases this infusion of funds also vastly expanded the function of the local government as an employer.

Table 7.10. Revenue in Bolton 1973-1974. ($thousands)

Year (fiscal) (October-September)	General Fund Revenue[1]	Intergovernmental Transfers[2]	Direct Grants[3]
1973-1974	$52,811	$ 9,330	$ 57,444
1974-1975	54,488	10,300	146,700
1975-1976	47,000	50,600	180,000
1976-1977	44,900[4]	33,700[4]	350,000
1977-1978	51,018	76,775	363,266[5]

1. Including sales, property, privilege taxes; user fees; fines. Excluding water taxes.
2. Including revenue sharing, state-federal matching grants, direct federal grants to state or other local units of government.
3. Including federal and private sources. Grants to private corporations of several million dollars are excluded.
4. Estimates.
5. All figures are rounded to the dollar.

Data are derived from: Private communication with Frederick Cooper, Mississippi Institute for Small Towns (MIST); Mississippi State Tax Commission; Mississippi Research and Development Center (MSR/D); and the *1970 U.S. Census*.

Though much of the increased activity happened suddenly, it was not random. It formed a part of a well-conceived welfare strategy in consonance with the leaders' ideological commitments and the desires and perceived needs of the black constituency. At this early stage three patterns or phases were observable. Phase one occurred in the early part of the black American administration, and was highly focused on basic human needs and social services. During this period the mayor solicited funds to alter some of the most visible signs of past racial exclusion: inadequate health care and food, as well as symbols of overt racial exclusion such as segregated water fountains, doctors' offices, and schools. The second phase began simultaneously or shortly thereafter, within the first four or five months of administration. It was denoted by pursuit of larger infrastructure projects (roads, sewers, and buildings) designed to achieve more generalized development of the local communities. These projects provided amenities and facilities that increased a town's independence, wealth, and growth potential. There was less focus on the black American constituents in this phase, though they surely benefited from this work. The third phase was hardly discernable in most towns, but was philosophically outlined by many leaders quite early. This may be termed the institutional phase. It was the period when leaders sought resources and other supports to maintain both the spirit of their regime and themselves in office. Because of the focus on social change in these mobilization regimes, the task in the institutional phase was to channel activities in an environment that rapidly became more politicized. Then the leaders could focus on longer-term community projects with investment potential. Such would then be used to stimulate a stronger, more attractive base for generating local revenue. In short, these would provide some means for local system maintenance.

The administration of these towns in each of the phases delimited was critically affected by the special relationship with the federal government. Without the latter the leaders would have been unable to deliver any of the promises made prior to election, or to respond to the high expectations and pressures exerted by constituents for performance. The leaders quickly learned that while ideological rhetoric and a past association with civil rights activity were a *sine qua non*, delivery of certain benefits that devolved from the civil rights program was also required.[27] The leadership realized all too soon that little could be done without external, usually federal, support. In order to survive and meet the increased demands from the dispossessed black American constituents, a dependency on the federal government evolved to supply ideas, programs, and money. Indeed, the funds received from Washington were the major means by which these small governments sustained themselves in the period under discussion.

The more successful the towns were in attracting funds and the longer their mutual relationship existed with the federal government, the more dependent the small towns became. This situation developed for two reasons. First, success was determined by the degree that a town could match its program interests with those of the federal government. And second, the more successful a town was, the more vulnerable it became to the whims of and shifts in the ruling federal coalition. Observations indicate that only at the beginning of the black American administrations, when the scale of demands was low, was there relatively less tradeoff of local interests in the competition for national resources. Later, as the scale of local demands rose, there were greater tradeoffs and less success.

Dependency and the caprice of politics in the larger environment converged with detrimental consequences for the phased pattern of program development attempted in the towns.

The following data descriptively illustrate the nature of programs and the degree of success during the three phases. Descriptive, as opposed to interpretive, analysis was appropriate for several reasons. First, there was a great need for basic descriptive work on these communities, where little had been done before. Second, there was the database problem. Most allocations and activities of federal and state governments occurred at the county level, or for municipalities of 10,000 or more population. Consequently, most data were aggregated and reported for such larger units. Each of the units in this analysis (formally known as municipalities in Mississippi), however, was below 2,000. This presented a considerable problem in locating and verifying data. Few of the myriad data sources were comparable. The problem was complicated by the multiple ways state and county units made local allocations. Therefore, in the absence of aggregate information on towns like these, considerable cross-checking was required in obtaining reasonable accuracy. At this stage, the most sophisticated and reliable analysis is descriptive.

Phase One: The Political Economy of Basic Human Needs

In the first phase (of greatly increased local budgets) the mayors initially gave credibility to many "poverty" programs as activities for local government involvement. They achieved this by openly associating themselves with and by seeking additional financial outlays for existing programs run by private and quasi-private groups. In addition, they increased lobbying efforts on state and county governments for a larger share of transfer funds.

Headstart is the prime example of an existing program that all towns virtually co-opted as a local government enterprise after election. In the first place, all the mayors were involved in this program prior to their election. In many ways this was so because Headstart, while not only for blacks, functioned almost as such in the beginning in Mississippi. In fact, some attempted to paint the entire program as a civil rights venture, as we have seen. The program was indeed a symbol of the social change wrought by the movement, whereby blacks and whites cooperated in the administration of a program primarily designed as a compensatory tool for Mississippi blacks. In this sense it was foremost an educational venture with far-reaching civil rights policy implications. This put the program in an ideological category preferred by the new leaders. But the existence of Headstart also meant the creation of new jobs which would be available to the black constituents. By accepting these programs and maintaining influence in their management, the mayors were allowed to claim them as evidence of mayoral programmatic success.

At the same time lobbying efforts with other state units were undertaken to expand their involvement with federal programs that would provide additional revenue for the towns. In the short run this was less successful, though the new pressures forced the state agencies to adopt more equitable allocation patterns. During this first phase there was also a symbolic dimension that was perceived to be of some economic consequence. This was the physical transfer of power. Though many citizens did not actually know the economic conditions of the towns, they assumed that with the transfer of the trappings of power one acquired the right to manage certain economic goods. With the transfer came the keys to town hall, control of the police force and the collection of taxes, and the assumed allocation of rewards the government was thought to possess. Though there was little that was real in all this, each of the mayors extracted as much as possible from these symbols of transfer. Thompson's first inaugural was a day-long affair of parades, speeches, and joviality. Local and national politicians were present, and so were representatives of government agencies. Similar activities occurred elsewhere. Inauguration in Tchula was perhaps the most elaborate, doubling as a "homecoming" for former town residents. Again, prominent state officials, including the governor, took part. It was obvious to most citizens that the reins of power were being transferred. Most perceived that there was a connection between the symbols and the alleviation of some of the basic human problems that marked everyday life.

There were certain tangible programs in this period that were intended to meet some basic human needs. The mayors developed their own proposals to the federal government and became direct recipients of these grants. The programs that were aggressively sought were designed to give the new constituents some immediate, not necessarily systemic or institutionalized, relief. These projects, too, were also heavily imbued with symbolism. In Bolton one such early program was in law enforcement. Funds were sought and received from the Law Enforcement Assistance Administration (LEAD) to upgrade and equip the local police force. The town received new police cars and assistance with police personnel, both of which were symbolic to the larger constituency and materially beneficial to individual constituents. For the first time in history, the symbol of white authority represented by the police force was absent; the policies were determined and offices staffed by blacks. Meanwhile, the three or four new jobs created in this area indicated the significance of the town as an employer. Many other such employment opportunities were to become available in the first two years of Thompson's tenure (1973-1975). The Comprehensive Employment Training Act (CETA) provided a variety of public employment opportunities (public works and administrative assistance); and ACTION provided several Volunteers in Service to America (VISTA). Similar actions occurred later in Tchula: CETA provided administrative and secretarial assistants, a nutrition site for the elderly received partial support, Mississippi Action for Community Education (MACE) supported programs for seasonal farm workers, and the Youth Employment Training Program (YETP) assisted with youth employment.

The amount of the financial transfers was not abundant. Rather, there were small, short-term grants that made a dent in material circumstances only because conditions were already dire. In the first several years of Thompson's administration, less than $200,000 was collected in direct federal funds. Nevertheless, he easily created, directly or indirectly, more than 25 new jobs. The impact was considerable; previously there were less than 10 jobs on the public payroll. In Tchula the employment benefits were even more dramatic. Mayor Carthan collected $500,000 in direct and indirect grants and created over 40 jobs in the same time frame. Matters moved more slowly in Mayersville, but Mayor Blackwell could easily claim responsibility for 10-15 employees in Headstart, housing, health and programs for elderly person in the county (see Table 7.11).

Table 7.11. Federal Support (by Agency, Type and Town)

Agency	Project	Town
Housing & Urban Development	housing	(B,M,T)[1]
	water lines	(B,M)
	sewers	(B,M)
Agriculture	fire equipment	(B,M)
	parks	(B)
	housing	(B,M)
Health, Education & Welfare (Human Resources)	day care	(B,M,T)
	welfare	(B,M,T)
Interior	parks	(B)
Labor	employment training	(B,T)
Environmental Protection Agency	sewers	(B,T)
Transportation	roads	(B)
Justice	law enforcement	(B,T)

[1]B = Bolton; M = Mayersville; T = Tchula

Phase Two: The Political Economy of Infrastructure Development

The second phase of budgetary increases involved infrastructure developments. This period was marked by conscious and aggressive pursuit of programs that created capital improvements and enhanced the general quality of life.

Examples of these projects were sewage and pollution control facilities, housing, and permanent public facilities. Such programs were often not of immediate and direct personal benefit to citizens, nor did they have a ready symbolic import. Their impact was longer-term and required some degree of planning and then construction time. On the other hand, these projects had broader institutional impact because they ultimately increased the basic level of town assets. This in turn created the minimal conditions whereby the small town could take advantage of technological advances elsewhere. The development of a good water system illustrates this point. A town lacking such a system could hardly develop a clean and efficient sewage system. Therefore, Mayersville was required first to install a municipal water service before eligibility could be established for federal assistance with a sewage program.

This phase, like the first, was overwhelmingly supported by the federal government. Many of the same agencies identified in phase one were active here: Housing and Urban Development (HUD), the departments of Labor, Justice, Transportation (DOT), and Commerce, The phase commenced (at least the outlines of the larger, more costly, infrastructure programs were drawn) as early as four to six months after accession of the new mayor. This seemed to be related to program ideas the mayors developed during their previous involvement in community and civil rights efforts. Consequently, shortly after the mayoral office was assumed (and during the time when the provision of the basic necessities appeared to be paramount), a large number of other requests were presented to many of the same federal agencies. The applications sought construction of roads, recreation facilities and municipal buildings, sewage systems, and housing. The mayors, however, did not do this alone. During the Carter Administration, many mayors had sympathetic friends in high cabinet positions as well as support from a broad Democratic Party coalition. Similarly, technical assistance in preparing requests was available from outside experts with civil rights credentials. These resources were used to identify sources for support and or to conduct feasibility studies to determine how and where available funds could be used.

Judging by examining the receipts for these towns, the second phase was remarkably successful. Each of the towns received its share of big grants that improved the capital standing and broadly affected local quality of life. Bolton was far and away the most successful per capita because of the number of such programs funded. Since coming to office in 1973, Thompson's campaign rhetoric in 1979 boasted of over $8 million in federal programs. Much of his literature said that this support came from HUD, the Labor and Commerce departments. The infrastructure programs from HUD were varied for a town the size of Bolton. Nearly $150,000 was received for the creation of permanent recreational facilities: acquisition of land, landscaping, and equipment installation; $300,000 for housing rehabilitation; and $1,500,000 for new housing (40 units). In addition, $250,000 received for an industrial park, $40,000 for a permanent structure for a fire station, and $250,000 for sewage treatment. The Department of Commerce provided over $360,000 for the construction of a municipal building and a neighborhood center, and the CETA program provided equipment for the recreational facilities.

Tchula and Mayersville had shorter experiences in seeking these infrastructure supports, but each had a degree of success that was equally remarkable. Mayor Carthan of Tchula outlined a program about four to six months after election and rapidly put some longer-range programs in force. HUD provided over $500,000 for housing rehabilitation, street improvement, and a weatherization program. Proposals were also prepared that sought construction of a municipal facility, improved water and sewer facilities, and permanent recreational facilities. In Mayersville, however, Blackwell spent more time on phase one because of the town's impoverished condition and lack of a formal city charter. During our Mayersville survey in 1980, this phase was just beginning, but its direction was the same. The most salient example was Mayersville's receipt of support from the Environmental Protection Agency (EPA) for construction of a municipal water system. When that was completed, the mayor applied for and received additional grants from EPA and HUD for over $400,000 to install a sewer system. Indications were that the next part of Blackwell's program would include some type of public housing. Therefore in both of these towns it was anticipated that this phase of development would be supported by federal resources. As in Bolton, the targeted sources were several offices of HUD, Commerce, and sometimes Labor. By far the heaviest support was received from HUD (see Table 7.12).

While the second phase was, like the first, almost entirely sustained by federal grants, there were significant distinctions. Whereas the funds received in the first phase were often indirect, those in the second were often made directly to the local governments, laying the groundwork for substantial improvements in the general quality of life and the capital position of the towns. Creation of new physical structures and other infrastructure improvements would have major long-term effects, because of their permanence and potential for expanding other industrial and technological options. The prime examples were the building programs in Bolton and improvements to sewage in the other towns.

The towns were not able to independently exploit much of the potential for local expansion provided by the external financial support, however. Little independent financial stimulation emerged from the construction of the municipal buildings or the installation of sewers. There were no local construction industries and few skilled workers to take advantage of the jobs that became available. Subsequently, outside firms and skilled workers were secured to complete most aspects of the work. The installation of the sewer system in Mayersville illustrates this point. A Louisiana firm was awarded the contract and imported virtually all staff and equipment; two to four local workers in unskilled positions were intermittently employed. The effect of this was that Mayersville acquired the sewer system, but little independent economic stimulation; most of the revenue was spent outside the town. Moreover, the sewage system actually increased expenses for the average citizen: household connection charges had to be paid and indoor toilet facilities purchased.

Table 7.12. Phase Two Projects

Project	Agency	Town & Support Level (Combined dollars)		
		Bolton 1973-1979	Tchula 1977-1979	Mayersville 1977-1979
Recreation (Parks/Permanent Equip.)	HUD; Interior Labor, & Agriculture Depts.	$216,000		
Housing (New Construction Rehabilitation)	HUD	877,000	$311,000	$238,000
Sewage/Water	EPA, HUD	187,000	37,000 102,000[a]	494,150
Civic Facilities (Construction)	HUD	402,000	350,000[a]	
Other Services Facilities (e.g., roads)	DOT, HEW	250,000	102,000	

[a]Proposed for funding.

Sources: Local town documents, Mississippi Institute for Smal Towns (Frederick Cooper).

In Bolton, Thompson attempted to compensate for this problem by guaranteeing that some contracts and subcontracts be let to "minority" businesses. These contractors, however, all came from outside the community. And even they faced the same challenge of filling skilled labor needs. Since the local area could not provide such labor, it was imported. Generally, what remained was a small number of unskilled positions to be filled by local personnel. In effect, many of the new projects actually negated the principle that large-scale infusion of capital stimulates economic expansion. The construction of public housing or even a sewer system did not, under local conditions, create sufficient pockets of capital with which to support other capital improvements.

Phase Three: The Political Economy of Institutionalization

The third phase was marked by the solicitation of funds specifically designed to institutionalize the ideology and benefits of the black American regime. The leaders sought to maintain themselves in office and to prolong the ideas of social change that accompanied their initial election. Now the task was not merely provision of basic human needs, but structuring some intrinsic base for development. Here the political economy of black American leadership was clearest because of the broad intersection of politics and economics. The essential question was, once a leader began to think in strategic terms about system maintenance, what resources were available to guarantee continuity? In this more avowedly political phase, which has only begun in Bolton, success depended not on mere delivery of goods, but on the ability to manage and control circumstances in the political-economic sphere. In this period, many of the moral imperatives that propelled the leaders to power no longer existed as such. The old bases for group solidarity were lessened as particularism, class, and other sentiments formed the new bases for alignment. The leaders were required to successfully negotiate and manage events in this environment.

As vital as this phase was to the process of mobilization, it was too early at the time of our survey to see more than the rudiments of institutionalization. Much of this resulted because many of the War on Poverty programs were unsuitable for the longer-term requests now being made by the towns. But more importantly, with shifting interests and political alignments in Washington, federal funds dried up. Even the Democratic coalition was less willing to sponsor the larger projects in the rural areas, where political returns were minimal.[28] Then with the Nixon and succeeding Republican administrations' emphasis on a "new federalism"[29] the towns had little incentive to pursue independent sources in Washington. Funds were now awarded through state institutions, many of which remained hostile to these towns with black leaders.

The best case of modest institutionalization was Bolton, where Thompson was entering his second term as mayor in 1977. By then he already had a track record for securing grant support, a fact that made it easier for him to attract new and larger grants. Returning to the data in Table 7.10 (page 228), steady improvements are observed in both intergovernmental transfers and direct grants for the town over a five-year period. Government grants of slightly more than $50,000 in 1973 increased to over $300,000 in 1977. Moreover, the mayor could also take claim for several million dollars awarded to the Bolton Development Corporation (a private group of citizens under Thompson's leadership) for housing. In short, the mayor had built up substantial capital upon which he could trade in the management of local affairs. The marker of his success was the maintenance of broad solidarity in the local community throughout his tenure.

Even more critical in illustrating the modest success of the institutionalization of the mobilization in Bolton was when Thompson moved to a higher local office, but maintained broad control over the progress of town developments. He became a county supervisor in 1980 with responsibilities for Bolton and several other rural Hinds County towns, an indication of appeal beyond the local base. However, in Bolton his influence appeared to be as great, if not greater. He was able to virtually name his mayoral successor and to maintain a direct role in town affairs. Moreover, in his higher office he could still independently solicit and dispense benefits within the town. This he did with greater success for black constituents than any local politician had, since Charles Caldwell during reconstruction. Hence, even though he was beyond the town officially, he nevertheless remained the chief sponsor and benefactor of the mobilization.

In Mayersville, this period had hardly begun because the town's official status was so new. In addition, there was far less of a basis for strategic political alignment. The broad economic position of the citizenry was still so low that the rudimentary elements for articulating particular interests were hardly present. Consequently there was very little to manage in the way of local cleavages. Mayor Blackwell won a second term in 1981, but even this was not accomplished with any particular concern for institutionalization. To wit, there was little in the way of a campaign since the mayor assumed community-wide acceptance. Indeed, this seemed to be the case since most respondents in interviews discussed little beyond aspects of the mayor's achievements in phases one and two.

The routine, unilinear pattern of phases observed in Bolton and Mayersville did not occur in Tchula. Though apparent black citizen solidarity was achieved for the election of the mayor in 1977, this soon disappeared. Incipient elements of class and other idiosyncratic factors rapidly became prominent features of political life. When the mayor began to solidify a program for aggressive pursuit of outside support for phase two projects, a split arose in the town's board of five aldermen. These alignments aborted group solidarity— solidarity which proved especially important in the other towns in the first stages of development. Instead, the political blocs in Tchula became diametrically opposed.

Political activity in this town, therefore, showed aspects of the three phases simultaneously. Strategic alignments appeared at such an early stage in the regime that stability and longevity were hardly possible: the principal task became mere survival. Much of the activity occurred at the leadership level where two social class types were represented. The mayoral bloc consisted of townspeople from traditionally higher social and economic positions, in competition with others from rural plantation backgrounds. The other critical dimension we have seen was the presence of the white alderman in support of the latter bloc. These patterns accounted for divergent political sentiments, and conflict that led to the mayor's downfall. Beyond these dynamics, however, was also the presence of a variety of idiosyncratic social and political elements that figured in the affairs of the town and regime—incidents of political and quasi-political violence and exaggerated routine social problems. In a town this size, these factors combined to restrict the potential for institutionalization of the spirit or person of the regime.

Conclusion

The analytical question that remains is the extent to which mobilization reached its natural culmination with the realization of institutional power for these towns, given economic resources. Did the extension of the economic sector (seen as the infusion of federal money) contribute to the independent growth and institutional capacity of the current regimes to meet the political demands of local constituents? There are two answers to this. The first is that in the short term, there was a kind of political and economic growth, though not institutionalization. Insofar as the new political leaders were able to make financial assistance available for basic human needs, certain gains were made. Such gains appeared to far outdistance the long-term ones. This analysis showed that in the first two phases all of the towns enjoyed relative success in securing funds for the short-term human needs of the communities. There was a sizable amount of federal largesse to dispense, including some jobs in the administration of grant programs. At the same time the new leaders acquired all the symbolic trappings of power: they ran city hall on a daily basis and did so in the face of former white leaders, who exhibited varying degrees of hostility. Therefore, in the short run, the new leaders appeared to be providing all things necessary to maintain credibility and influence with their highly mobilized constituents who demanded the "spoils" of rule never before available. But even here the close connection between numerous material demands and the absence of independent economic resources posed a question about the future of such regimes.

The mayors resorted to what seemed to be a willing partner to answer this dilemma, for what can only be regarded as partial short-term relief. In the long term there were far more problems with the federal relationship for Afro-American leadership than direct benefits. The problems resulted from a combination of structural, environmental and racial factors that undergirded the position of dependency. In any case they critically affected the possibility of institutionalization of such regimes.

First, there was the problem of representativeness. Could the rural towns justifiably make claims upon a group of national politicians as their "representatives? Theoretically, according to the "rules of the game," the black American bloc can rarely determine the outcome of political bargaining at the national level without a coalescence of some kind. Usually it is only a few urban districts that can do this since there are few such direct representatives at the national executive and legislative levels.[30] Even perceived indirect representation—the Congressional Black Caucus (CBC)[31] and high-level bureaucrats[32]—is too insignificant to exert sufficient influence to protect rural black American interests. Though blacks are often spoken for generally by the CBC, the electoral base for most of its members is urban. Caucus power, therefore, is most effectively exerted in collusion with other urban representatives.[33] This process of alignment by "expanding conflict" was not available to the small towns. They had very little to trade and could expect a minimum of support for their claims from national representatives. Independence for the towns was thereby thwarted because of the problem of representativeness. Gains were made insofar as the towns were instrumental to the maintenance of national power; independent influence upon national agenda setting was minuscule.[34]

The inability to effectively "expand conflict" in Schattschneider's terms [35] was evident even when there was an apparent convergence of interests between the small towns and the federal government. The weak position of the small towns was especially obvious. In phase one, for example, the initial need of the towns to solicit to meet basic human needs led the leaders to opt for the quickest supports and symbols available. At the time certain apparently appropriate projects were available from the federal government under the War on Poverty programs. This appeared to represent a degree of convergence between the interest of the towns and Washington. But many of these federal projects were designed to respond to other problems (such as urban riots)[36] and were only later made available to the rural towns. In fact the federal government could make some of these funds available to rural blacks at little cost. The awards were relatively small and the political fallout was minimal. Indeed certain political gains could be made because these rural constituents could be considered a part of the new presidential coalition, if need be. Yet the towns had little or no influence upon the design, the amount of money available, or the length of these programs.

Another important dimension of the problem was efforts of the leaders to fundamentally alter local political arrangements. Oftentimes these new political leaders asserted that they would institute quite revolutionary changes, one of which was the redistribution of local resources. However, few of the instituted programs have had such an effect. The early programs were all relatively small and temporary. They were not designed to alter the structure of the social institutions as would be necessary to sustain long-term change. The immediate effects of these social welfare programs were, therefore, short-term and superficial. Subsequent proposals for larger infrastructure capital investment projects were far less successful in Washington. Yet even the larger projects were not designed to create the basis for independent local operation. Though more money was forthcoming for each individual infrastructure project, the money was not allocated so as to stimulate other independent enterprises. To wit, very little stimulation could be provided by a new sewer system where few complementary resources were available. Moreover, at this level there was little convergence between the interests of the two entities, and it was the small towns that lost most.

Then there were certain environmental circumstances that negatively affected the independence and institutionalization of the regimes. Some of these were certain patterns of interest articulation. The intense and continuous mobilization of the community for exacting benefits from the political system was a case in point. Group mobilization was the process by which most of these new leaders were elected. This pattern remained a prominent feature of local politics. In its early stages mobilization was especially useful because it inspired solidarity against southern racial exclusion. But after the transfer of power, solidarity was less easily maintained; newer, sophisticated interests were soon articulated. As these interests grew and were refined, demands often exceeded the capacity of the young leaders to respond. The difficulty increased when the newly articulated interests required infrastructure projects or when fundamental structural change to the system was sought.

Largely, the excess demands were two types. First, a plethora of particularistic interests emerged. They did damage not because they required large capital outlays, but because they diverted the leadership as it attempted to manage the political environment and its consequences. In Mayersville, some of this was inevitable because general need levels were so high. Those who wanted housing rehabilitation were seeking assistance; so were those needing sewage, water, medical assistance, etc. Each of these groups found its needs worth pressing, and the mayor was seen as the provider in all these circumstances. But because the resources were so scarce and virtually no independent resources could be marshalled from local enterprises, effectiveness could be expected to gradually decrease.

Ultimately many of the intra-group cleavages resulted in incipient elements of social and economic class, with equally negative consequences. This factor was denoted by an increasing cleavage in some towns between economic groups and/or leadership groups. The economic cleavage usually included higher-salaried professionals against unskilled workers, while the leadership cleavage usually pitted social change-oriented leaders against status quo types. In Tchula this reached a high level, albeit mostly within the leadership group. This pattern thrived as the leadership polarized the community on the ideological contentions of two classes about the distribution of resources. Ironically, a liberal, higher-status group was representative of social change in this context. The conflict circulated around the appropriateness of alignment with whites in local government, and how broadly the responsibilities of the government should be expanded to meet the needs of blacks. The polarization virtually halted the town's development program.

The final constant strain on the process of institutionalization was local white racism. In one manner or another the significance of racial exclusion in the past affected current race relations. Economic power and control of other nonelective positions remained in the hands of local whites. The latter still espouse the theory of black inferiority and largely had not accepted the new regimes as legitimate. Usually this meant that whites entirely withdrew from public life. They ignored the new regimes or tolerated them until such time as they could be overthrown. Each of the three cases was subject to this problem, though Mayersville was somewhat less hampered because there was no previously entrenched white power structure. Bolton and Tchula, on the other hand, were critically affected by the behavior of whites in public affairs. In Bolton the whites withdrew from participation in the formal institutions of government, thereby rejecting any degree of interracial interaction about political organization. This put Thompson and the succeeding mayor in the ultimate position of being leaders to only blacks. But the whites maintained control of most local income-producing entities and endeavored to further exclude black Americans from such enterprises. This lack of independent control of resources by blacks contributed to the dependent federal resource relationship. In Tchula, while whites did not withdraw, their activities to thwart the new regime's programs were evident. The lone white alderman took issue with the philosophical and practical aspects of the mayor's development program, and aligned with other black opponents against Carthan's rule. In the process, local institutions of government became meaningless; the exercise of power occurred elsewhere. Here, as in Bolton, the continuing white belief in racial exclusion almost always destroyed the potential for institutionalization by forcing leaders to seek economic resources from external sources.

8

Conclusion

Much of the effort of black Americans to achieve power has been expended in a struggle against the vagaries of white racism—a product and vestige of the enslavement era. As noted in a survey of Mississippi history herein, nowhere else was this system more virulently practiced. In this analysis of contemporary Mississippi politics, continuing aspects of this struggle were explored as they affected the assumption of power by blacks. Under circumstances where many of the basic human rights were still denied blacks, with little possibility for political expression, this analysis has revealed a process of change in motion. In three Mississippi towns we have followed the emergence of a pattern of responses designed to fundamentally alter the human status of black people via the assumption of political power. In the end this culminated in what is analytically denoted mobilization. This process of mobilization, it was argued, was the most useful means of accounting for this continuing struggle, especially as it was revealed in the civil rights movement well in force by the mid-1960s. But how far can we go in concluding that this process of mobilization is indeed the most revelatory about black southern politics, and what are the implications for the future of blacks in the American political process?

Many theories have been advanced to account for how displaced groups (including blacks) have acquired a foothold in the American political system. However, mobilization was particularly attractive because of its attributes that accommodated the complex ideational and activist nature of the contemporary black struggle. That is there were unconventional aspects to this drive for power among blacks, at least in the context of routine American party politics. Blacks had the unyielding ideal of equal acceptance of their human quality in the society; and they usually were inexorably cast by negative racial stereotypes that spurred activist solidarity for group betterment. Mobilization theory as defined here captured this complex dimension of social change in the black community. It will be recalled that mobilization is understood as the collective activation and application of community or group resources to the acquisition of social and political goods.

In discussing the process of mobilization it was revealed that certain factors are of particular importance in stimulating change. There first had to be a will for action or a desire for change. In the black community, as noted, historical circumstances had created an unyielding will to change from the inception of enslavement. However, true mobilization was seen also to require a critical combination of will with commitment, loyalty, and opportunity for activism. There had to be change or power to seek, and agreed-upon means for seeking it. In the United States, the absence of power among blacks meant that there was much to be sought. How it was to be sought was a question with implications for mobilization. Among southern blacks, as among many of the previously decolonized peoples of the third world, a highly organized, mostly indigenous effort was mounted to pursue the desired goals of change and resource acquisition. All over the South in small communities like the Mississippi towns, buttressed by a highly visible and effective new class of leaders, protest ensued on the strength of local community resources and the ideal of equality and power acquisition. This made for the opportunities for mobilization in Bolton, Tchula and Mayersville.

In the analysis of the three towns, an exploration was made of how far the mobilization campaigns went toward the goals of community activation and acquisition of political resources. This problem was explored by a broad investigation of two vital indigenous elements to the mobilization process: leadership and the constituency. In separate chapters an exploration was made of leaders in Bolton, Mayersville and Tchula, followed by an investigation of the ideals and behavior of the black constituents in these towns. It was revealed that at the base level a degree of mobilization was put in process that at least achieved the transfer of power from white to black. In other instances much more was achieved.

In Bolton the process that culminated in the election of Bennie Thompson started much earlier with salient and highly organized indigenous black efforts in Hinds County. The citizens in this small town near the capital had been directly engaged since the early 1960s in a process of political education that sustained revitalized ideals for equality and participation. Many had already gone time and again to the white town clerk to be denied voter registration. Later all eligible would acquire this privilege. By 1969 these new citizens were ready to exercise their franchise for one of their own running for a leadership position—Bennie Thompson. The Thompson era began modestly in 1969 when he was elected as town alderman, along with two other blacks. The black voting majority, however, was rendered useless by a new rule requiring a three-fourths majority in council voting, but at the very next mayoral contest (1973) Thompson and a full slate of black contenders won all local electoral posts. In the span of eight years in the administration of local government Thompson acquired a reputation for successful and creative management of political resources in Bolton. He worked with a sophisticated and demanding constituency that was highly mobilized.

Thompson's commitment was not unlike that of his constituents. Indeed his work and style of operation served to bring together the community groups and marshall their efforts to the goal of obtaining local community power. The terms on which he did this were as a radical populist. His experiences and particular ideas gained at college and from his own intellectual bent gave him an abiding interest in grassroots politics and how abstract ideas could be utilized to serve his constituency. Full and absolute participation was the ultimate goal, especially for the blacks who were previously excluded. For him there was a particular virtue in these "little people" in a system that made it possible for their will to flourish.

Unita Blackwell, the heroine/inventor, was much more of a factor in the mobilization effort in Mayersville. The analysis revealed that she was of vital importance in establishing the terms of intensified resistance to racial exclusion in the early 1960s. Long before she focused on acquiring political power, Mrs. Blackwell was in the forefront of organized citizen efforts for the recognition of basic human rights. She was an initial sponsor of the move to develop new loyalties, commitments and activation among blacks in Mayersville. She was a factor in all of the organizing efforts in the town that created black solidarity, leading many of them—voter registration, freedom schools, and legal court challenges. And most of the institutional civil rights groups that had Mayersville branches (NAACP, SNCC, COFO, MFDP) were spearheaded by Mrs. Blackwell. In short, she was the embodiment of the early activation process that became prominent among the local black citizenry.

Mrs. Blackwell later occupied the central position in the stage of mobilization that focused on power acquisition. Unlike Thompson or Carthan, she had no institutional base at which to direct the energies of the mobilized citizens. There was no formal town office to seek. She therefore turned her attention to the issue of town incorporation as a means for full realization of power. Again, consummate skill was utilized in organizing her constituents to accept this proposition as a logical stage in the process of change. That she succeeded so rapidly and eventually occupied the chief administrative office was a testament to the commitment and loyalty that had been built up in the indigenous community.

In terms of activation of the citizenry and the development of leadership to capture the spirit of the time, Tchula was no different than Bolton or Mayersville—indeed, the move to activation may have even been more intense. The civil rights movement began early in this town and spawned a cadre of indigenous leadership that organized and exacted a variety of commitment and activism befitting mobilization. The organizational effort was very visible and perhaps even more intense because of the heated denial of rights by local whites and their subsequent backlash campaign, once the move for social change was discerned.

Eddie Carthan came onto this scene and sought to focus the existing movement on the goal of power transfer. Since Tchula was a larger town and because of its earlier intensified campaign, Carthan's task was broader than that in the other towns. In the first place there was a perceptible town sector and a rural one. He had to be an agrarian and a townsman to succeed. Then he had to match the intensity of the organized effort that created the activism of the early civil rights forces. Carthan was very conscious of both of these problems and orchestrated a campaign that ultimately rose above them. The appelation of agrarian/townsman is one that he may have easily applied to himself. In seeking to continue the local mobilization he made much of his mixed background on the farm and in town. He asserted that he was cosmopolitan, but also a commoner who knew farming and farm ways. As for an ability to match the activism of the past, Carthan had little problem. He very much associated himself with this earlier group and its sentiments, and had their support.

Though success did not last long, Carthan did oversee the transfer of power in Tchula. To a degree this represented the culmination of the process of mobilization seen as resource acquisition, wrought from the commitment displayed by constituents. The will to change was certainly evident and acted upon by the citizens when Carthan was easily elected. In short, he appeared to embody the ideals of this diverse black community. That he ultimately failed seemed to have less to do with the electorate *per se*, a matter to which we shall return.

The vital role of the black citizenry as a stimulus to mobilization and as its driving force was evident in the early 1960s in each of these towns. It has been demonstrated what their broad commitments were and the risks they took in acting upon their commitments in pursuit of something as simple as voter registration. Then we observed the critical function of leaders in channeling these efforts to institutional power acquisition. But the vital function of the citizenry did not end there. The constituents' support and definition of the social and political order were still required; without these the mobilization was little more than a facade. An empirical investigation of their continued role in the process revealed a singular level of importance.

The investigation explored two distinct parts of this process. First, an effort was made to account for activist behavior by measuring citizen participation and beliefs about such. Second, an effort was made to understand the principles that guided their behavior and attitudes. Much of the information sought on the measures of participation and beliefs were for the period after these blacks became voters, as their previous participation was obviously naught. Moreover, their most recent participation gave a clue to their support for the black leaders that took up office at the transfer of power. This investigation also considered data from the separate towns so that comparisons could be made where required, even though results were expected to be quite similar.

The results on both behavior and beliefs were supportive of the proposition that mobilization was sustained by an active, demanding and sophisticated black population. These average citizens—poor and previously disfranchised—revealed a clear sense of goals and indicated a pattern of behaviors consistent with achievement of those goals. In spite of all expectation that modern political science would lead us to have about them, these citizens exhibited some of the most participant behavior in all of contemporary America. Their voter registration levels were extraordinarily high, and so was their participation in all levels of public elections. Moreover they had considerable faith in the abilities of the new governments to meet some of their needs. In this their activism appeared to continue beyond the mere election of one set of officers as a novelty. Their high participation in different types of elections, in multiple instances, indicated depth.

The most revealing aspects of these findings were those about citizen principles for action. The high levels of participation in all of the towns were sustained by strong principles on issues regarding the status of blacks in society. For the most part our investigation centered on various aspects of integration. There was very broad support for the philosophical concept of integration seen as interactions between the races on equal terms. The respondents accepted a variety of social and educational opportunities as a desired and reasonable means toward the integration ideal. Much hope and potential, for example, was seen in the policies requiring school integration; such was deemed to be enhancing for both black and white children. But this policy regarding schools was of particular importance to the principles of blacks, insofar as it was the culmination of a long and fierce battle between the races in each of the towns.

On the other hand, a sharp distinction was made when it came to questions of power-sharing as an aspect of integration. When the respondents were asked about their principles for "integration" of the institutional government sector, they were much less supportive. They found much less reason to trust whites as equal partners in the exercise of public power, out of an apparent belief that past modes of white discrimination would reemerge. Their new-found power, in short, was much more jealously guarded. Its acquisition was seen as the culmination of another aspect of the long struggle to overthrow and replace the chief arbiters of racial exclusion.

Consequently there was a direct, vital linkage between the leaders who directed the political mobilization effort and their constituents. The strong principles and high participation levels of the citizens provided motivation and sustenance for the work of the leaders. Indeed, in the mobilization drive one could hardly separate these two entities.

One can return to the preconditions that sustain leadership in substantiating this critical point. It was argued that leaders were all but required to have a political office, to have a youthful and charismatic presence, to have inculcated the values of the civil rights movement, and to have a program for responding to the welfare needs of their constituents. On every one of these counts it can be seen how the citizen presence dictated a certain level of performance for leader success. Once the citizens assumed their responsibilities as voters, it was inevitable that they would show concern on how to exercise the franchise. Leaders who most attracted voters were those who spoke in the idioms of the people, with an appealing plan of action for the rural poor and race-conscious blacks. Thompson, Carthan and Blackwell easily met this challenge in demonstrating their unities with the will of their communities. Moreover they were prepared to move forward on the local ideals with practical programs. In large measure, there was little disjuncture between the communities and their leaders (later circumstances in Tchula excepted). This provided the advantage of substantive activation with which new political resources could be assumed and exercised.

The ends of mobilization as defined here were, however, not met merely because of the transfer of power. Another vital part of the process was what benefits accrued after the assumption of power. In other words, of what value was occupation of this political kingdom of which constituents were so protective? In large measure this was a political economy or resource benefit question. In the analysis it was investigated by identifying the specified aims of the leaders for satisfying the welfare demands of their constituents, and then by measuring their level of success. The evidence revealed a mixed picture of the mobilization process at this juncture that showed some limits on the process.

All of the leaders well understood at their election that they had to rapidly attend to problems of basic human need among their black constituents. The only problem was how to generate sufficient resources. The most that the indigenous black community could provide in this regard was human capital; economic capital was scarce. Even the local institutional government sector was bereft of resources as the obvious physical impoverishment of the towns illustrated. Most indigenous economic resources were controlled by whites, whose resolve to maintain segregation caused withdrawal from a black-controlled public sector. As a result, the mobilization effort had to be directed beyond the local communities. At the time and for certain obvious reasons (notably that of accessibility), it was directed at the federal government, not without success. For a time the simultaneous challenges presented by blacks in urban areas yielded a substantial short-term resource response from the federal government. Many of the basic needs claims of rural residents could be met by these programs, thereby creating the impression of a sustained economic mobilization. Our analysis revealed a flourishing sector of small government programs in virtually all of the towns that produced services, jobs and a host of symbols of economic vibrance immediately after the black mayors were elected. In the one town where the mayor had served two terms by 1979, available data showed remarkable annual increases in the local budget. Mobilization did appear to be complemented by growth in economic and political power.

This apparently complete realization of mobilization was nevertheless stymied at the critical stage of institutionalization of the new values and resource opportunities. Though some short-term resources did become available, considerable difficulties characterized efforts to acquire longer-term, more costly programs. Given the poverty and size of these communities and continued white racism, there was no local means of generating independent resources. Therefore, the towns' resorting to the federal government rapidly became a dependence. This, coupled with their lack of clout in the ruling national coalition, left their proposals at the whims of the national government. And with subsequent changes in Washington, there was a rapid decline in the ability of the towns to get support. This was particularly evident for the larger, infrastructure-type programs that became a staple of mayoral ideas after some time in office. This lack of support seriously affected the mobilization drive for direct economic benefits. The mayors found their programs stagnating, even at a time when their demanding constituents were likely to become more highly focused in their requests. This seemed to indicate that at least one strong constraint on the full realization of mobilization was this absence of an independent base for generating economic benefits, coupled with insufficient influence upon the external sources that can provide such benefits.

Hence it can be said that mobilization has produced significant change in the lives of these blacks in rural Mississippi. It has been demonstrated how their resource level increased remarkably in a fairly short period of time. Yet all of the changes have not produced uniformly beneficial results or even long-term ones. There was a critical difference in the abilities of the mayors to deliver benefits that could institutionalize the new and quite radical values introduced with the transfer of power. All this raises the inevitable question of what implications there are in a mobilization campaign such as was inspired by the civil rights movement and the particular circumstances under which such might occur. Moreover, of what importance are the particular circumstances of black people mobilizing within the American political system?

In assessing the appropriateness of mobilization and ultimately its importance, one must go back to the beginning. Though American society has long since claimed democracy, that hardly applied to black Americans in the South. They, like many pre-World War II colonized peoples, had been completely barred from the exercise of free expression and political rights. For blacks a long portion of their disfranchisement had occurred in enslavement, followed by a system of institutionalized exclusion that was equally as definitive. This was a position never accepted, however, especially in a context where the principle of democracy was otherwise so strong. Thus the critical contradiction between racial exclusion and the dictates of democracy created conditions for mobilization.

In large measure the conditions for mobilization or broad activation were so easily met because of the almost complete isolation of southern blacks (like colonized people) from freely organized participation in aspects of society. They were denied not merely political rights, but the base rights of humanity, including the exercise of cultural traits. Culture was denigrated so as to sustain the instrumental function of the excluded. Thus any effort to alter such practices, and the principles that undergirded them, required the total absorption of those seeking change. In this context mobilization flourished. Consistent with the emergence of the process elsewhere, we saw black Americans first adapting a new set of definitions for themselves that resulted in new commitments and the will to act. But actions occurred on all fronts, leaving little differentiation between the personal and the public. After all, it was no safer for blacks to drink from "white" water fountains than it was to vote at the polls on election day. The investment was entirely different from that of a group of highly organized and powerful whites who "mobilized" for the acquisition of new resources. The latter organized in the context of known and accepted rules in the system. The blacks who mobilized did so on the basis of new commitment for the assumption of goods never possessed.

The implication here is that mobilization was partially successful because of the particular circumstances of exclusion of blacks from the benefits of the political system. Thus it may be assumed that the depth of oppression was a defining quality in this context. If blacks had already been an institutionalized part of the system, then likely a whole set of different rules would have been in order for seeking change. As it was, however, the absence of any regularized mechanisms for inclusion required blacks to develop independent sources within virtually every aspect of their existence. Subsequently it would be expected that other similar circumstances would also yield mobilization.

There are other positive implications for mobilization that seem to be a product of local environmental circumstances. The first of these is in the sheer impoverishment of these places. All were desperately poor, and their lack of basic human resources made for an easily convincing argument for support. Though we already know that no economic transformation took place in the towns, leaders did find a ready response to appeals for food and shelter in the early parts of their administrations. It was not politically astute, for example, for the federal government to deny food to hungry children, or medical attention. As a result, the towns received fairly handsome returns for the welfare program proposals that characterized their early administrations. Such short-term outlays were regarded as almost charitable, though they made a material dent in lives and inspired more intensified activation.

The ruralness of these communities was even more of a factor in the success of mobilization. The small size of the towns and the simpleness of life severely constrained the variety of problems and issues that arose. For the most part there was uniformity in the fundamental needs of a large number of these constituents. Thus it was easier to find agreement on the new commitments necessary for activation, and to define tasks. This set of factors was of considerable importance in driving the voter registration campaigns and in structuring the debate about general welfare needs. All this was combined by the leaders in targeting the institutional sector of public affairs for the takeover. In short, they did little more than build on and channel the will of already well-consolidated constituencies.

It would be expected that under such circumstances, mobilization would indeed flourish. The expectations for such among blacks in the South is, therefore, fairly high. There are innumerable such rural places where mobilization could flourish. Indeed, the rapid and broad growth in the number of elected black officials in such places would seem to confirm this outlook.

In another sense the very political nature of the process of mobilization as it occurred in the rural, black-belt South had positive implications. There were two parts to this. On the one hand mobilization required new commitments and definitions. With the complete isolation of blacks from the existing institutional arrangements, the new definitions had to be devised in a completely new context. Cooperation with local whites, for example, was impossible. Blacks had to devise independent means. This placed a premium on racial organization, an act that was to politicize and reverse the very factor that sustained past isolation. In the end the politicization of race as a factor of mobilization served to reduce the negative effects other attributes were supposed to have on black interest and activism. For example, highly focused political campaigns obliterated the importance of low socioeconomic status in vitiating participation. Politics was such a strong animating feature that it inspired a broadly based effort among constituents to create and seize opportunities for diminishing the power of whites.

The second all-important part of this was the presence of a black majority in each of these towns. This was of singular importance in steering the leaders to the institutional political sector. They saw that the numbers were right for winning the ultimate local political prize—they could take over the entire government structure. In every case the leaders could make a convincing argument to their constituents that this was the most important use of the vote. If whites refused to be cooperative, then the true democratic majority (blacks) could finally legitimately determine policies in the political community. There was everything to be gained, given the assumed routine hostility of whites with their ideals of racial supremacy. True to form, this factor did serve as the base for electoral success in the Mississippi towns. As a rule blacks voted solidly for the black candidates and whites voted for whites, or not at all. Only in Tchula did a white receive considerable black support, but only as a product of his perceived deviation from the policies of white supremacy.

Politics in the Mississippi towns is similar to other places where some mobilizational success has occurred. In the first place, political factors have come to outweigh the great mass of other variables that we know to be important for behavior in public affairs. Moreover, the full realization of such political goals is repeatedly achieved on the strength of having a sufficient electoral majority. It is still a rare phenomenon for significant numbers of whites to vote across racial lines. This would seem to suggest that the distinction rural Mississippi residents make between the philosophy of integration and its practical use in interracial power sharing is based on empirical reality.

There are limits to mobilization that were revealed in this analysis, and they occur at a very critical stage of the process. Insofar as mobilization as we defined it was about resource acquisition, that is where the most serious challenge still remains for the Mississippi towns. Though real measurable resources were acquired, these were incomplete, short-term and some merely symbolic. Ironically, some of these difficulties result from the very factors that made for successful mobilization, and they all have serious implications for participatory democracy.

The poverty of these areas that made it relatively easy for the acquisition of base economic resources, is at another turn one of the most serious impediments to complete mobilization or rearrangement of resource allocations. The baseline financial commitments made to the towns at the initial election of the black mayors had virtually no effect on the institutionalization and expansion of a new economic base. The essential impoverishment of the towns remained. Hardly anything fundamentally new, with independent generative power, was added. There was little indigenous capacity to be corralled by the new leaders. The previous driving force of these economies, agriculture, was in great decline. Moreover, what wealth there was belonged to whites, who used it as a weapon against the black community. So what blacks really gained in measurable power was limited and of a short-term effect, without access to some economic means with which to drive needed welfare programs.

The way that the mobilization leaders got around this problem had its own disadvantages, despite many attractions. The political climate made it feasible to approach the federal government, with some favorable results. In the process the approach to the federal government became a dependency. Indeed, it was the only sector of government willing and able to provide substantial support. By some measure it was also seen as the last resort, having an obligation to protect and uplift depressed sectors of the political community. But even this was limited by resource availability and, more importantly, politics. As the political environment changed it became more and more difficult to maintain federal support, especially as costs escalated. Beyond grants for modest infrastructure improvements, most of which could not even be considered capital assets, government support remained welfare-oriented and short-term. Thus the towns were unable to institutionalize the new resources with which to sustain the political change. There were fits and starts, but hardly a way to regularize benefits given escalating claims and expectations.

The long-term implications of this have to do with the nature of political alignments and the dictates of democracy—factors somewhat contradictory to each other. Much of the failure to sustain the dependency on the federal government was because these rural political entities were always located on the fringes of the national ruling coalition. There was never an ability to exert true independent clout upon the federal government to guarantee support. These areas came closest when they could team up with urban black interests during the northern conflagration, but ultimately direct policy interests were much more successful when fronted by the urban interests. It is already known that racial division obviated a coalition with other southern rural peoples whose interests were more similar. This left the small towns floundering, receiving support mostly based on goodwill as opposed to direct influence.

This conflicted with a well-earned and jealously guarded principle of participatory democracy. The mayors and the citizens sincerely believed that their acquisition of power represented the quintessence of an American ideal and equally well satisfied the dictates of mobilization. In a sense they were correct. Nevertheless what they had not necessarily gained was a more legitimate standing in the broader community where the principle of democracy was redefined. Converting their local majority as they bid in the national political community meant expanding their goals or trading on advantages for support. It was not easy to do either. Expanding goals was tried by Thompson and Blackwell as they sought to convince a national audience of the importance of the rural areas to national goals. They made their arguments eloquently, but larger interest groups made such arguments more persuasively. Trading on distinct local advantages with others was even more difficult as the towns had little to trade, due to the scale of their operations and the localized influence patterns of their leaders.

Moreover internal dynamics can have a restraining effect upon full mobilization. It is quite normal under circumstances like these for constituents to become more differentiated in time. As citizens begin to develop greater expectations, they more precisely refine their goals. To a degree this was already occuring in Bolton where base needs were gradually converted to concerns about the quality of performance (as in housing rehabilitation). In this case, however, the greater differentiation of claims did not fundamentally alter the solidarity in the community or the responsiveness of the leadership. However, when such differentiation occurs too rapidly there will be few mechanisms for aborption. The lack of leadership agreement in Tchula is an example of the consequences of this. Since there was basic disagreement about how to satisfy mobilization goals, the whole system broke down. Though this was largely a leadership problem, it illustrated the fragility of small-scale communities for handling internal conflict amidst weakness and uncertainty. Mobilization was only beginning to bear fruit when conflict broke open. The result was that the already dependent town had virtually no independent base for resolution of issues. The fierce competition between leadership forces was subsequently exploited by whites and the entire administration was obliterated by legal challenges. This shows that one of the greatest dangers to success is internal. If solidarity of both leadership and constituents cannot be maintained, then all other constraints are merely exacerbated. In Tchula we saw that when the leadership could not present a united front, the federal government withdrew virtually all of its support. This made it safe for the whites to return to power in the face of a completely incapicitated leadership, notwithstanding the presence of a black population majority.

The future for black mobilization, however, is not entirely bleak given these drawbacks. The extent of the mobilization as measured by both leadership and constituents is sufficiently broad to be self-driving and to create new patterns and relationships for resource acquisition. Except for Tchula, leadership confidence and singularity of purpose has been an advantage in the growth and development of a strong political program and certain strategic actions for resource acquisition. This is much strengthened by what appears to be a continuously strong commitment and activism toward the new ideals by constituents. The ideological principles, sophistication and participation of the citizens do not appear to be fleeting or without direction. It was noted that while the local political arena inspired the greatest participation, there was remarkably high participation in the national political scene. Voters seemed to know quite well who presidential candidates were and which of them were more supportive of black community interests. In the long run it is expected that these aspects will enhance prospects for broader participation in the political community, and to lay the groundwork for expanding local interests to a point where useful coalitions with others can be sustained.

Notes

Preface

1. Everett Carll Ladd, *Negro Political Leadership in the South* (Ithaca, N.Y.: Cornell, 1966), pp. 1–3.
2. Robert Brisbane, *Black Activism* (Valley Forge: Judson, 1974), p. 43.
3. Voter Education Project, Press Release, "What Happened in the South?," Atlanta, Nov. 15, 1964, p. 2.
4. *Ibid*.
5. Mack Jones, "Black Political Officeholding and Political Development in the Rural South," *The Review of Black Political Economy* (Summer 1976), pp. 375–407.
6. Voter Education Project, "Voter Registration in the South," Atlanta, Summer 1968, unpaged.
7. K.C. Morrison and Joe C. Huang, "The Transfer of Power in A Mississippi Town," *Growth and Change*, 4:2, (April 1973), p. 25.

Chapter 1

1. James Madison, "The Union as a Safeguard Against Domestic Faction," in Hellman Bishop and Samuel Hendel, eds., *Basic Issues of American Democracy*, 6th ed. (New York: Appleton-Century-Crofts, 1965), pp. 47–53.
2. David B. Truman, *The Governmental Process* (New York: Alfred A. Knopf, 1951).
3. Robert Dahl, *Who Governs* (New Haven: Yale University Press, 1961), p. 228.
4. Kenneth Dolbeare and Murray Edelman, *American Politics*, 3rd ed. (Lexington, Mass.: D.C. Heath, 1979), p. 232.
5. Dolbeare and Edelman, p. 232.
6. Dolbeare and Edelman, pp. 25–28.
7. Floyd Hunter, *Community Power Structure* (Chapel Hill, N.C.: University of North Carolina, 1953), pp. 112–113.
8. Michael Parenti, *Power and the Powerless* (New York: St. Martins Press, 1978), p. 29.
9. Marguerite Ross Barnett, "A Theoretical Perspective on American Public Policy," in M.R. Barnett and James Hefner, eds., *Public Policy for the Black Community: Strategies and Perspectives* (Port Washington, N.Y.: Alfred, 1976), p. 9.
10. *Ibid.*, p. 16.

11. Mack Jones, "A Frame of Reference for Black Politics," in Lenneal J. Henderson, Jr., ed., *Black Political Life in the United States* (San Francisco: Chandler, 1972), pp. 7–20.
12. Dolbeare and Edelman, p. 29.
13. Milton Morris, *The Politics of Black America* (New York: Harper & Row, 1975), pp. 49–50.
14. Lucius Barker and Jesse McCorry, *Black Americans and the Political System* (Boston: Little, Brown, 1980), p. 26.
15. Milton Morris, *The Politics of Black America*, p. 19.
16. Stokely Carmichael and Charles Hamilton, *Black Power* (New York: Random House, 1967), pp. 3, 5.
17. Herbert Blauner, "Internal Colonialism and Ghetto Revolt," in Gary Marx, ed., *Racial Conflict* (Boston: Little, Brown, 1971), p. 54.
18. Milton Morris, *The Politics of Black America*, p. 22.
19. Karl Deutsch, "Social Mobilization and Political Development," *American Political Science Review*, 55:3 (1961), p. 493.
20. David Apter, *The Politics of Modernization* (Chicago: University of Chicago Press, 1965), p. VII.
21. Karl Deutsch, pp. 494–495.
22. David Apter, pp. 51–52.
23. Robert Kearney, "Political Mobilization in South Asia," in Robert Crane, ed., *Aspects of Political Mobilization in South Asia* (Syracuse University: Foreign and Comparative Studies Series, 1976), p. 1.
24. J.P. Nettl, *Political Mobilization* (New York: Basic Books, 1967), p. 32.
25. *Ibid.*, p. 33.
26. Lloyd Rudolph and Susanne Rudolph, *The Modernity of Tradition* (Chicago: University of Chicago Press, 1967), pp. 25–26.
27. Much of this criticism has been presented by the dependency theorists. See Walter Rodney, *How Europe Underdeveloped Africa* (Washington, D.C.: Howard University Press, 1974), pp. 3–29; James Cockcroft, et al., *Dependence and Underdevelopment* (New York: Anchor, 1972).
28. William Nelson and Philip Meranto, *Electing Black Mayors* (Columbus, Ohio: Ohio State University Press, 1977), p. 27.
29. Karl Deutsch, p. 495.
30. Quoted in Charles Tilly, *From Mobilization to Revolution* (Reading, Mass: Addison-Wesley, 1978), p. 69.
31. *Ibid.*, p. 78.
32. *Ibid.*, p. 73.
33. Doug McAdam, *Political Process and the Development of Black Insurgency* (Chicago: University of Chicago Press, 1985), p. 15.
34. *Ibid.*, p. 2.
35. William Gamson, *The Strategy of Social Protest* (Homewood, Ill.: Dorsey, 1975) p. 15.
36. Anthony Oberschall, *Social Conflict and Social Movements* (Englewood Cliffs, N.J.: Prentice-Hall, 1973), p. 102.
37. *Ibid.*, p. 124.
38. Doug McAdam, *Political Process . . .* , p. 15.
39. William Gamson, *The Strategy . . .* , p. 15.
40. Quoted in Charles Tilly, *From Mobilization . . .* , p. 72.

41. *Ibid.*, p. 73.
42. Anthony Oberschall, *Social Conflict* . . . , p. 119.
43. Doug McAdam, *Political Process.* . . . pp. 41–44.
44. Everett Carll Ladd, *Negro Political Leadership in the South* (Ithaca: Cornell University Press, 1966), pp. 48–109.
45. Donald Matthews and James Prothro, *Negroes and the New Southern Politics* (New York: Harcourt Brace & World, 1966), pp. 61–98.
46. Stokely Carmichael and Charles Hamilton, p. 39.
47. William J. Wilson, *The Declining Significance of Race* (Chicago: University of Chicago Press, 1978), p. 137.
48. *Ibid.*, p. 138.
49. Robert Brisbane, *Black Activism* (Valley Forge, Pa.: Judson Press, 1974), p. 11.
50. Doug McAdam, *Political Process* . . ., *passim*.
51. Aldon Morris, *The Origins of The Civil Rights Movement* (New York: Free Press, 1984), p. XII.
52. *Ibid.*, pp. 4–11.
53. *Ibid.*, *Passim*.
54. The state capital, Jackson, is just over twenty miles away and has a metropolitan population of over 300,000.
55. U.S. Bureau of the Census, *1970 Census of Population* (Mississippi) (Wash. D.C.: Government Printing Office, 1973), p. 37.
56. Initially, a survey was made of public positions available in the towns and the individuals holding those positions. Then public and private organizations operating in the towns were identified, together with individual leaders. Local and regional media were also consulted to determine the frequency of notice given the activities of individuals from the particular towns. From the survey a list of those with the most prominent reputations resulted. The importance of these as leaders was confirmed by interviews with those on the list and a random group of non-influentials in each town. These lists were then compared with the results of a systematic survey of each town's population regarding who were local leaders.
57. Lester Salamon, "Leadership and Modernization," *Journal of Politics*, 35; (1973), p. 623.
58. Max Weber, *The Theory of Social and Economic Organization* (Glencoe: The Free Press, 1947), p. 358.
59. John Friedland, "For a Sociological Concept of Charisma," in Marion Doro and Newell Stultz, eds., *Governing in Black Africa* (Englewood Cliffs, N.J.: Prentice Hall, 1970), p. 61.
60. Irvine Schiffer, *Charisma* (Toronto: University of Toronto Press, 1973), p. 19.
61. Geneva Smitherman, *Talkin' and Testifyin* (Boston, Houghton-Mifflin, 1977), pp. 76–77.
62. Nathan Huggins, "Afro-Americans" in John Higham, ed., *Ethnic Leadership in America* (Baltimore: Johns Hopkins University Press, 1978), p. 100.
63. Minion K.C. Morrison, "The Impact of Federal Resource Provision on the Development of Afro-American Leadership" forthcoming in *Publius* (1987).
64. Everett Carll Ladd, *Negro Politcal Leadership* . . ., p. 176.
65. Daniel Thompson, *The Negro Leadership Class* (Englewood Cliffs: Prentice Hall, 1963), p. 71.

Chapter 2

1. Eugene Genovese, *The Political Economy of Slavery* (New York: Pantheon, 1967), p. 28.
2. W.I. Newman. *The Politics of Aristotle*, Vol, I (New York: Arno Press, 1973), pp. 144–47.
3. Nathaniel Weyl and William Marina, *American Statesmen on Slavery and the Negro* (New York: Arlington House, 1971), pp. 146–48.
4. *Ibid.*, 152. "At the time of Pericles, Athens had 43,000 (voting) citizens, 28,500 . . . aliens, and 115,000 slaves. A century and half later [there were] 21,000 citizens, 10,000 (aliens), and 400,000 slaves."
5. *Ibid.*, pp. 149–50.
6. Winthrop Jordan, *White Over Black* (Chapel Hill: University of North Carolina Press, 1968).
7. John van Evrie, "A Scientific Proof of the Biological Inferiority of the Negro," in Gilbert Osofsky, *The Burden of Race* (New York: Harper and Row, 1967), pp. 104–109.
8. Leslie Owens, *This Species of Property* (New York: Oxford, 1976), p. 3.
9. Philip Foner, *History of the United States*, vol. 3 (New York: International Publishers, 1962), p. 260.
10. *Ibid.*, pp. 259–60.
11. Herbert Aptheker, *The Labor Movement in the South During Slavery* (New York: International Publishers, 1955), p. 17.
12. E. Genovese, pp. 221–235.
13. V.O. Key, *Southern Politics in State and Nation* (New York: Alfred A. Knopf, 1950), pp. 11–16.
14. *Ibid.*, pp. 46–52.
15. *Ibid.*, pp. 131–32, 232–39.
16. Percy Lee Rainwater, *Mississippi: Storm Center for Secession 1856–1861* (New York: Dá Capo, 1938), pp. 2–3.
17. Wilbur J. Cash, *The Mind of the South* (New York: Alfred A. Knopt, 1941), p. 23.
18. V.O. Key, p. 233.
19. *Ibid.*, p. 236.
20. *Ibid.*, p. 231.
21. P.L. Rainwater, p. 5.
22. Cash, pp. 68–78.
23. P.L. Rainwater, p. 5.
24. Paul Levinson, *Race, Class and Party* (New York: Oxford, 1932) pp. 7–8.
25. Cash, p. 37.
26. Rainwater, pp. 164 ff.
27. Albert Kirwan, *The Revolt of the Rednecks* (Lexington: University of Kentucky Press, 1951), p. 42.
28. V.O. Key, p. 232.
29. James Loewen and Charles Sallis, eds., *Mississippi: Conflict and Change* (New York: Pantheon Books, 1974), p. 192.
30. William Holmes, *The White Chief* (Baton Rouge: LSU Press, 1970), pp. 96–7.
31. V.O. Key, p. 243.
32. Aptheker, *The Labor Movement in the South*, p. 17.

33. C. Vann Woodward, *Origins of the New South* (Baton Rouge: LSU Press, 1951), p. 278.
34. William Holmes, pp. 77–78.
35. *Ibid.*, p. 36.
36. Adwin Wigfall Green, *The Man Bilbo* (Baton Rouge: LSU Press, 1963), p. 100.
37. *The Congressional Record*, 75th Congress, 3rd Session, vol. 83 (1938), *passim*.
38. Green, p. 100.
39. Charles Sydnor, *Slavery in Mississippi* (New York: Appleton-Century, 1933), pp. 185–86.
40. *Ibid.*, p. VIII.
41. Owens, *This Species of Property*, pp. 3–18.
42. Vernon Wharton, *The Negro in Mississippi 1865–1890* (Chapel Hill: University of North Carolina, 1947), pp. 11–13.
43. William K. Scarborough, "Heartland of the Cotton Kingdom," in R. A. McLemore, ed., *A History of Mississippi*, vol I (Jackson: University and College Press, 1973), pp. 329–30. Many have speculated that this is due to the size of the black population, which exceeded that for the whites as early as 1840. "The presence of [such] a large population of [slaves] in Mississippi *obviously* (emphasis mine) required the imposition of [these] strong police measures by state authorities."
44. Sydnor, p. 78.
45. Sydnor, pp. 86–101.
46. Wharton, p. 12.
47. Eugene Genovese, *Roll, Jordan, Roll* (New York: Pantheon Books, 1974), p. 406; cf. Wharton, p. 13.
48. John Blassingame, *The Slave Community* (New York: Oxford, 1979), pp. 3–48.
49. Lawrence Levine, *Black Culture and Black Consciousness* (New York: Oxford, 1977), p. 4.
50. L. Owens, pp. 172, 171.
51. Vincent Harding, *There Is A River* (New York: Harcourt, Brace, Jovanovich, 1981).
52. The literary medium has been used to illustrate the strength of such patterns with great effort. Margaret Walker, *Jubilee* (New York: Bantam Books, 1966).
53. Genovese, *The Political Economy*, pp. 43–67.
54. Herbert Aptheker, *American Negro Slave Revolts* (New York: International Publications, 1970), p. 14.
55. Arna Bontemps, *Black Thunder* (Boston: Beacon, 1968).
56. Herbert Aptheker, *Nat Turner's Slave Rebellion* (New York: Humanities, 1966).
57. Aptheker, *American Negro Slave Revolts*, pp. 11–17.
58. John Gwaltney, *Drylongso* (New York: Random House, 1980), XXII–XXX.
59. Aptheker, *American Negro Slave Revolts*, pp. 24–25, 253–54 and 363.
60. Clement Eaton, *The Freedom-of-Thought Struggle in the Old South* (New York: Harper Torchbooks, 1964), pp. 97–98.
61. Wharton, p. 146.
62. *Ibid.*, p. 164.

63. William C. Harris, "The Reconstruction of the Commonwealth 1865–1870," in Richard McLemore, ed., *A History of Mississippi*, p. 559.

64. *Ibid.*, p. 561.

65. Buford Satcher, *Blacks in Mississippi Politics* (Washington, D.C.: University Press of America, 1978), p. 25.

66. John R. Lynch, *The Facts of Reconstruction* (Indianapolis: Bobbs-Merrill, 1970), p. 44; Wharton, p. 173.

67. Wharton, pp. 173, 176. These increased numbers were tempered by the lessened solidarity of the Republican majority, however. Moreover, a few blacks later chose or were forced to align themselves with the emerging Democratic Party, as political fortunes shifted.

68. *Ibid.*, pp. 157–63; George Sewell, *Mississippi Black History Makers* (Jackson: Univesity Press of Mississippi, 1977), pp. 15–66, *passim*.

69. Wharton, p. 167.

70. *Ibid.*, p. 167.

71. "Their importance was due chiefly to the work of rebuilding or repairing bridges, public buildings, etc. destroyed by the war, and to the vast majority of petty offenses over which the justices exercised jurisdiction. In the southern type of government . . . [i]t assesses and disburses the taxes, has supervision of roads, highways, selects juries, awards county contracts, examines and determines upon the sufficiency of official bonds, negotiates loans, and in the river counties appoints the levee commissioners. John Garner, *Reconstruction in Mississippi* (Baton Rouge: LSU Press, 1968), p. 307.

72. Satcher, p. 39. Many scholars believe that this office even exceeded that of supervisor in power. "He controlled to a large extent the selection of trial juries, appointed one of the three election registrars, and collected the state and county taxes. Much of his compensation consisted of fees and perquisites for services, which were numerous during the reconstruction period." Garner, p. 305.

73. Wharton, p. 203.

74. *Ibid.*, p. 203.

75. Lynch, p. 118.

76. Sewell, p. 27.

77. William Harris, "Introduction," in Lynch, pp. XXIV-V.

78. Lynch, p. 92–3.

79. Lynch, p. 107.

80. Wharton, p. 173.

81. *Ibid.*, pp. 182–84.

82. *Ibid.*, p. 219.

83. Kirwan, pp. 23–25.

84. Here is just one example. Four whites who had been jailed in protective custody, after being accused of collusion with blacks during recent electoral violence, were forced out (in a style usually reserved for blacks) and murdered. They were killed by a white mob before any trial. Yet three influential newspapers, "[t]he Meridian *Mercury*, Jackson *Clarion*, and Vicksburg *Herald* openly approved [the] liquidation, and other papers were half-hearted in their criticism." Kirwan, p. 25.

85. Wharton, p. 202. There were still some elected officials and vestiges as late as 1890, when six blacks remained in the state legislature.

86. *Ibid.*, p. 211.

87. Kirwan, p. 71.

88. U.S. Commission on Civil Rights, *Voting In Mississippi* (Washington, D.C.: 1965), p. 7.
89. Kirwan, p. 72.
90. Congressional Quarterly, *Guide to U.S. Elections* (Washington, 1975), sections on Mississippi, *passim*.
91. Hanes Walton, *Black Republicans* (Metuchen: Scarecrow, 1975), p. 135.
92. Loewen and Sallis, p. 237.
93. Wharton, p. 221.
94. Loewen and Sallis, p. 155 ff.
95. Aldon Morris, *The Origins of the Civil Rights Movement* (New York: Free Press, 1984), p. X.
96. Aldon Morris has defined this as "an established group or organization that is only partially integrated into the larger society because its participants are actively involved in efforts to bring about a desired change in society. . . . [They have no] base . . . [but] develop a battery of social resources such as skilled activists, tactical knowledge, media contacts, workshops, knowledge of past movements, and a vision of a future society."Aldon Morris, p. 140.
97. "A local movement center is a social organization within a community of a subordinate group. (It is denoted by) an interrelated set of protest leaders, organizations and followers who collectively define the common ends of the group, devise necessary tactics and strategies along with training for their implementation, and engage in actions designed to attain the goals of the group." Morris, p. 40.
98. Loewen and Sallis, pp. 244–46.
99. Charles C. Mosely (Mrs.), *The Negro in Mississippi History* (Jackson: Hederman Bros., 1950), p. 131.
100. Doug McAdam, *Political Process and the Development of Black Insurgency* (Chicago: University of Chicago Press, 1982), pp. 103–06.
101. *Smith V. Allwright*, 321 U.S. 649 (1944); *Brown v. Board of Education of Topeka*, 347 U.S. 497 (1954).
102. Loewen and Sallis, pp. 252–3.
103. *Ibid.*, p. 247.
104. Robert Brisbane, *Black Activism* (Valley Forge: Judson, 1974), pp. 21–41.
105. John Salter, Jr., *Jackson, Mississippi* (New York: Exposition Press, 1979), pp. 185 ff.
106. William B. Huie, *Three Lives for Mississippi* (New York: New American Library, 1969).
107. K.C. Morrison, "Electoral Politics in the South," paper presented at the National Conference of Black Political Scientists (NCOBPS), (Washington, D.C.: April 1970).
108. Morris, pp. 40–76.
109. Elizabeth Sutherland, ed., *Letters from Mississippi* (New York: McGraw-Hill, 1965); Debbie Louis, *And We Are Not Saved* (New York: Doubleday, 1970).
110. For more complete discussion of the concepts of "vulnerability," "opportunity," and "interactional networks" see D. McAdam, pp. 2–3.
111. Clayborne Carson, *In Struggle* (Cambridge: Harvard, 1981), pp. 45–55.
112. Stokely Carmichael and Charles Hamilton, *Black Power* (New York: Vintage, 1967), p. 88.
113. Robert Brisbane, *Black Activism* (Valley Forge: Judson, 1974), pp. 73–104.

114. Loewen and Sallis, p. 282.
115. K.C. Morrison and Joe C. Huang, "The Transfer of Power in a Mississippi Town," *Growth and Change*, 4:2, (April 1973), pp. 25–29.
116. Mack Jones, "Black Officeholding and Political Development in the South," *Review of Black Political Economy*, 6:4, (Summer 1976), pp. 375–407.
117. Kenneth S. Colburn, *Southern Black Mayors* (Washington, D.C.: Joint Center for Political Studies, 1974), pp. V, and 33.
118. Jones, "Black Officeholding. . .," p. 389.
119. Morrison and Huang, "Transfer of Power. . .," p. 25.

Chapter 3

1. Sidney Lens, *Radicalism in America* (New York: Crowell, 1966), p. 3.
2. Margaret Carnovan, *Populism* (New York: Harcourt, Brace, Jovanovich, 1981), p. 9.
3. Nell Irvin Painter, *Exodusters* (New York: Alfred A. Knopf, 1977).
4. Charles M. Bacon, "A History of Hinds County, Mississippi," M.A. Thesis (History), Mississippi College (Aug. 1959), p. 63.
5. Buford Satcher, *Blacks in Mississippi Politics, 1865–1900* (Washington, D.C.: University Press of America, 1978), p. 205.
6. Dunbar Rowland, *History of Mississippi, vol. II* (Jackson: S.J. Clarke Publishing Co., 1925), p. 143.
7. Vernon Wharton, *The Negro in Mississippi* (Chapel Hill: University of North Carolina, 1947), p. 149.
8. Since the board controlled county finances and was the state administrative arm, Caldwell was exceedingly powerful. His success in the position is still recalled today. For example the Thompson administration publicly honored Caldwell and celebrated his contributions. *Muhammad Speaks*, Nov. 7, 1975, p. 2.
9. Herbert Aptheker, "Mississippi Reconstruction and the Negro Leader Charles Caldwell," *Science and Society*, 2:4 (Fall, 1947), pp. 340–71.
10. *Ibid.*, p. 340.
11. *Ibid.*, p. 351.
12. The problem was that Democratic Party stalwarts, who had never accepted the post-Civil War peace, were gaining political strength with legal and extra-legal means. Black leaders were being eliminated from office by violence and co-optation, while white Republicans were being forced to join the Democrats. Caldwell led the troops deputized by the governor to protect the electoral process in Hinds County. Herbert Aptheker, pp. 364–365.
13. Albion Yourgee, in Lerone Bennett, *Black Power, USA* (Chicago: Johnson, 1967), p. 329. "There was little respect for laws that could not be enforced; personal vengeance, the 'fair fight,' and the duel still held their place in the minds of the people, if not in the books of the law." Wharton, p. 216. At Clinton, months before Caldwell was murdered, over a four-day period there was "unbridled, systematic slaughter of Negro and white radical leaders [amounting] to somewhere between thirty-five and fifty [deaths]. This was accomplished by about two hundred local 'citizen soldiery' . . . and a train-load of expertly trained and fuly armed [other white] men . . . from Vicksburg." Aptheker, "Mississippi Reconstruction," p. 360.

14. Albert Kirwan, *Revolt of the Rednecks* (Lexington Ky.: University of Kentucky, 1951), p. 16.

15. Hanes Walton, *Black Republicans* (Metuchen, N.J.: Scarecrow, 1975), pp. 131-35.

16. Everett Carll Ladd, Jr., *Negro Political Leadership in the South* (Ithaca: Cornell, 1966), pp. 42-45.

17. Daniel C. Thompson, *Negro Leadership Class* (Englewood Cliffs, N.J.: Prentice-Hall, 1963), p. 166; E.C. Ladd, Jr., pp. 42-3.

18. Charles Hamilton has said that on the one hand, the preacher was "always propelled . . . up front. He was always given a seat on the platform. He was sought after by whites who wanted to reach the Black community, either to receive or to give information." On the other hand, "He has been a natural leader in the Black community. He has a fixed base, the church; he has a perpetual constituency, the congregation, which he sees assembled for at least one to two hours each week." Charles Hamilton, *The Black Preacher in America* (New York: Morrow, 1972), pp. 14 and 12, respectively: John Blassingame, *Slave Community* (New York: Oxford, 1972), pp. 49-104.

19. E.C. Ladd, Jr., p. 141.

20. James Loewen and Charles Sallis, *Mississippi: Conflict and Change* (New York: Pantheon, 1974), p. 252.

21. The council started in 1968 at Tougaloo College. It modestly pledged to "work for freedom of speech and assembly, equal enforcement of the law, voter registration reforms, fair employment, voluntary end to segregation laws, integration of schools, and the appointment of Blacks to local and state boards of education." John Salter, Jr., *Jackson, Mississippi* (New York: Exposition Press, 1979), p. 38.

22. John Salter, Jr., pp. 31-2; James Meredith, *Three Years in Mississippi* (Bloomington, Ind.: Indiana University, 1965).

23. *Ibid.*, p. 8.

24. Clayborne Carson, *In Sruggle* (Cambridge, Mass.: Harvard, 1981), p. 37.

25. *Ibid.*, pp. 36-37.

26. John Salter, Jr., p. 32 ff.

27. Since Jackson's television media have always been (and remain) the media of Bolton, these events were available on a daily basis and had an equally mobilizing effect, especially on students in the county.

28. U.S. Civil Rights Commission, *Hearings on Voting, VI* (1965), p. 182.

29. *Ibid.*, pp. 264-68.

30. His mother died in 1986.

31. Donald Matthews and James Prothro, *Negroes and the New Southern Politics* (New York: Harcourt, Brace and World, 1966), pp. 407-16.

32. *Ibid.*, p. 412.

33. *Ibid.*, pp. 412-13.

34. *Ibid.*, pp. 416-19.

35. In Bolton two separate lists of leaders were generated—those before the election of Thompson and those after. Pre-Thompson lists mentioned 16 leaders, five of them mutiple times. On the post-Thompson lists there were 21 names, six with multiple mentions. That the two lists are very different is striking. The most prominent name of the pre-Thompson list does not appear at all on the Thompson list. And, only two of those with multiple showings on the pre-Thompson list appear on the post-Thompson list. The group of old-line annointed leaders (preachers, teachers, businessmen, etc.) does not show up here. Matthews and Prothro, p. 176.

36. The educational level of the leadership class in Bolton was and remains strikingly high. The mayor, however, possessed at the time of election a college degree in political science and was pursuing a Master's degree in education. Later he was to pursue a doctorate. And a disproportionally high number of those in the first black administration in the town was highly educated. Only one (the older member) of the five did not have at least some college.

37. Many of the aldermen at the beginning of his tenure were similarly situated, insofar as having employment and commanding more than average material resources and property.

38. The high school at Utica was about 40 miles from such actions in Jackson.

39. C. Vann Woodward, *Tom Watson* (2nd ed.) (Savannah Ga.: Beehive Press, 1973).

40. Margaret Carnovan, *Populism*, p. 9.

41. Sidney Lens, *Radicalism in America*, p. 3.

42. Staughton Lynd, *Intellectual Origins of the American Revolution* (Cambridge, Mass.: Harvard, 1982), p. VI.

43. Richard Flacks, "The Liberated Generation," in James McEvoy and Abraham Miller, *Black Power and Student Rebellion* (Belmont, Calif.: Wadsworth, 1969), pp. 354–78.

44. James Silver, *Mississippi: The Closed Society* (New York: Harcourt,, Brace and World, 1964), p. 33.

45. The Human Relations Council was an integrated group formed in 1962 and President A.D. Beittel of Tougaloo College was made president of the group. Just how radical this move was is seen in the behavior of the local authorities at the initial meeting at Tougaloo. "Police were thick at the college gate and the Sovereignty Commission investigators were everywhere—at the gate and on the campus, taking photographs of people and copying down license numbers," John Salter, Jr. p. 38.

46. This fact is notably unlike that found in Matthews and Prothro, where students in the humanities and the pure sciences tended to be more activist. Matthews and Prothro explain this as a product of class variations among students and the quality of arts and sciences programs in the black colleges they surveyed. Matthews and Prothro, pp. 430–32.

47. Stokely Carmichael and Charles Hamilton, *Black Power* (New York: Random House, 1967), pp. 164–77.

48. Frantz Fanon, *The Wretched of the Earth* (New York: Grove, 1965), pp. 35–106.

49. Lucius Barker and Jesse McCorry, *Black Americans and the Political System* (Cambridge, Mass.: Winthrop, 1976), p. 175.

50. *Ibid.*, p. 187.

51. Carmichael and Hamilton, pp. 3–34.

52. *Ibid.*, p. 35.

53. *Ibid.*, p. 54.

54. *Ibid.*, p. 44.

55. Early on this young group resisted affiliation with the Southern Christian Leadership Conference, its benefactor for an organizational conference. Their reasoning was that they did not wish to be considered just another group interested in the abstract principles of human rights. Cleveland Sellers, *The River of No Return* (New York: Morrow, 1973).

56. Howard Zinn, *SNCC* (Boston: Beacon, 1964), p. 11.

57. *Ibid.*, p. 8.
58. *Ibid.*, p. 12.
59. *Ibid.*, p. 62 ff.
60. Lester Salamon and Stephen Van Evera, "Fear, Apathy, and Discrimination," *American Political Science Review*, 67:4 (Dec. 1973), pp. 1288–1306.
61. Douglas St. Angelo and Paul Puryear, "Fear, Apathy and Other Dimensions of Black Voting," in Michael Preston, et. al., eds., *The New Black Politics* (New York: Longman, 1982), pp. 109–130.
62. Murray Jacob Edelman, *The Symbolic Uses of Politics* (Urbana, Ill.: University of Illinois, 1964), pp. 2–3.
63. Bennie Thompson, Testimony at the Conference of Full Employment, Atlanta, Ga. (1977), pp. 22–43.
64. *Ibid.*, pp. 8–9.
65. Lynd, pp. 17–63.
66. Julian Foster and Durward Long, ed., *Protest! Student Activism in America* (New York: Morrow, 1970), pp. 225–361.
67. G. Louis Heath, ed., *Vandals in the Bomb Factory* (Metuchen, N.J.: Scarecrow, 1976).
68. G. Louis Heath, ed., *Mutiny Does Not Happen Lightly* (Metuchen, N.J.: Scarecrow 1976), pp. 3–8; George Vickers, *The Formation of the New Left* (Lexington, Mass.: Lexington, 1975), pp. 99–100.
69. Matthews and Prothro, p. 407 ff.
70. Durward Long's data also sustain the view that black colleges were more active, at least through 1963—60% of them experienced some protest, compared to 43% for other institutions. Durward Long, "Black Protest," in J. Foster and D. Long, eds., *Protest!*, pp. 62, 471.
71. It is noted that these assumed conservatives were more responsive to student claims than non-black institutions. Lawrence B. de Graaf, "Howard: The Evolution of a Black Student Revolt," in Foster and Long, pp. 321–23.
72. Patricia Gurin and Edgar Epps, *Black Consciousness, Identity and Achievement* (New York: Wiley, 1975), p. 204.
73. Harry Edwards, *Black Students* (New York: Free Press, 1970), p. 62.
74. Howard University is but one example, "having been designed along the lines of white colleges, imitating their curricular emphasis and striving to match their academic standards. . . . Aside from its graduate programs in African Studies, there was little in the Howard curriculum or organization to meet the peculiar needs or desires of Negroes." de Graaf. p. 320.
75. Cited in Gurin and Epps, p. 206.
76. *Ibid.*, p. 209 ff.
77. Clarice Campbell and Oscar Rogers, Jr., *Mississippi: The View From Tougaloo* (Jackson, Miss.: University Press of Mississippi, 1979), pp. 215–17.
78. *Ibid.*, p. 215. Meanwhile, the Owens administration had other problems. The college was in dispute with the state legislature about the expansion of the school charter. An old statute was resurrected that limited the value of the college's physical plant to $500,000, a figure already exceeded. And while it seemed doubtful that the legislature could sustain its threats to close the institution, the matter caused uncertainty. As negotiations went along, therefore, it was of considerable advantage to the Owens administration that a defense of its students in public demonstrations was not required; such past actions in this regard were already the cause of legislative anger.

79. This broad street merged with a major artery from downtown and carried westbound traffic to State Highway 80 and Interstate 20. The street bisected the heart of the campus, separating a row of dormitories from classroom complexes and dining quarters. The voluminous pedestrian and auto traffic had long since caused student concerns for safety.

80. See variously the *Jackson Daily News* (May 11–12, 1967), Sec. 1, p. 1.

81. The *Jackson Daily News* (May 11, 1967), p. 1.

82. Thompson approached the status of the classical "bad nigger" who not only violates taboos but flaunts the behavior because his clout otherwise makes him immune from certain risks. Al-Tony Gilmore, *Bad Nigger! The National Impact of Jack Johnson* (Port Washington: Kennikat Press, 1975), pp. 11–18.

83. These new code requirements had enlarged the committee, changed its voting rules, and added property qualifications for membership.

84. *Bennie G. Thompson, et al. vs. William G. Brown, et al.* Brief for appellants to U.S. Court of Appeals, 5th Circuit. #29087, p. 4.

85. This was one of several legal groups established in the 1960s and staffed by northern lawyers. They provided much needed resources to supplement the civil rights work of black lawyers. Frank Parker, a Harvard-trained lawyer, headed the Lawyer's Committee, and was already known for his deft, efficient and usually successful presentation of such cases.

86. *Bennie G. Thompson, et al. vs. William C. Brown, et al.*, p. 2.

87. *Ibid.*, p. 14.

88. *Allen vs. Johnson*, 413 F.2d 1218 (5th Circuit., 1969).

89. *Thompson vs. Brown*, pp. 28–29.

90. The District panel upheld the black petitioners by asking "is ownership of real estate a fair and reasonable requirement of a candidate for or holder of public office, or is it an irrelevant requirement and an invidious discrimination? We think the latter," they answered. The court referred to *Harper vs. Virginia Board of Elections*, 383 U.S. 663, 672, in which it was concluded that "wealth or fee paying has, in our view, no relation to voting qualifications; the right to vote is too precious, too fundamental to be so burdened or conditioned." *Bennie G. Thompson vs. William C. Brown, et al.*, Brief appendix, pp. A–9 and 10.

91. *Ibid.*, pp. 26–31.

92. *Ibid.*, pp. 29–30.

93. Frank Parker, memorandum on "Bolton Election Contest Litigation," (Sept. 17, 1973), p. 1.

94. *Douglas Beard, Jr., vs. Bennie Thompson*, before Democratic Executive Committee of the Municipality of Bolton, Mississippi, n.d.

95. The succeeding paragraphs on these disputes rely heavily upon Frank Parker's Memorandum on "Bolton Election Contest Litigation."

96. *Ibid.*, p. 5.

97. *Ibid.*, p. 6.

98. *Graham vs. Daniel*, #6514, Hinds County Chancery Court.

99. *Mashburn vs. Daniel*, #6518, Hinds County Chancery Court.

100. *Mashburn vs. Daniel*, #73 J-138 (R) (Southern District of Mississippi).

101. The petitioners claimed that the committee's actions "were, and continued to be arbitrary, intentional, designed to prejudice the rights of Plaintiffs in their pursuit of elective offices and are intended to cause plaintiffs much worry, inconvenience and monetary loss." *Beard vs. Daniel*, #3682, Hinds County Circuit Court.

102. *Mashburn vs. Thompson*, #3683, Hinds County Circuit Court.
103. Frank Parker, p. 14.

Chapter 4

1. In 1970, 64% of its developed area was residential, 28% of other developed places were "rights-of-way." And between 1960 and 1970 its farm laboring class dropped from over 400 to about 250. Mississippi Research and Development Center (R&D Center), "Community Development Plan" Mayersville, 1978, unpaged.
2. The county's southernmost tip is at the confluence of the Yazoo and Sunflower Rivers, that wash into the Mississippi River. Mayersville and the entire western side of the county is fronted by the Mississippi.
3. John Gonzales, "Flush Times, Depression, War and Compromise," in Richard Aubrey McLemore, *History of Mississippi* (Hattiesburg, Miss.: University Press of Mississippi, 1973), p. 285. The old Natchez district began settlement as early as 1800. Percy Lee Rainwater, *Mississippi: Storm Center of Secession 1856–1861* (New York: DaCapo, 1938), pp. 8–9.
4. Wade Hampton, a South Carolinian, developed a tract of some 2,700 acres. William Scarborough, in McLemore, p. 349.
5. William Scarborough, in McLemore, p. 348.
6. Unlike landlords in the Caribbean, these only oversaw a segment of a planter's holdings. The stringency of the system could thereby be maintained. John Gonzales, in McLemore, p. 235.
7. Lewis C. Gray, *History of Agriculture in the Southern United States to 1960* (Washington, D.C.: The Carnegie Institution of Washington, 1933), p. 531. Between 1850 and 1860 six absentee planters owned 300–720 blacks. J.K. Menn, "The Large Slaveholders of the Deep South, 1860" (Unpublished Ph.D. Dissertation, U. of Texas, 1964), Vols. I and II, *passim*.
8. "This compares to the bulk of the slaveowners (who) were small farmers. . . . More than 200,000 owners in 1860 had five slaves or less. Fully 338,000 owners, or 88 percent of all the owners of slaves in 1860, held less than twenty slaves." John Hope Franklin, *From Slavery to Freedom*, 5th ed. (New York: Alfred A. Knopf, 1980), p. 133.
9. Charles Sydnor, *Slavery in Mississippi* (New York: Appleton-Century, 1933), p. 69.
10. James Garner, *Reconstruction in Mississippi* (Baton Rouge, La: Louisiana State University, 1968, reprint of 1901), p. 308.
11. At the state level, there were five members of the lower house of the legislature. The earliest appeared in the 1870 session (Len Moore), followed by Richard Griggs (later a cabinet member), W.H. Jones, S.B. Blackwell (grandfather of Mayor Unita Blackwell's former husband), and C.J. Jones. Vernon Wharton, *The Negro in Mississippi* (Chapel Hill: University of North Carolina, 1947), p. 103.
12. In Washington County there was something on the order of a political machine dominated by two blacks. James Garner, p. 311.
13. The sheriff, both on account of the large emoluments which he received and the political powers which he wielded, was the most important county official. He controlled to a large extent the selection of the trial juries, appointed one of the three

election registrars, and collected the state and county taxes. Much of his compensation consisted of fees of the office [and] amounted to as much as $20,000 per year in some of the counties, in others $15,000, while perhaps the average was not far below $5,000 . . . Issaquena in 1876 had a negro [sic] sheriff who [estimated] fees . . . amounted to $3,000 per year. James Garner, pp. 305–306.

14. U.S. Senate Report, 527, V. I. Boutwell Report, 44th Congress 1st Session (Dec. 6, 1875-Aug. 15, 1876), pp. 589–596.

15. *Ibid.*, pp. 601–610.

16. *Ibid.*, pp. 589–596.

17. *Ibid.*, pp 589–604.

18. Vernon Wharton, p. 202.

19. Buford Satcher, p. 206.

20. In local parlance this means brash, outspoken, sassy.

21. Kent L. Steckmesser, *The Western Hero in History and Legend* (Norman: University of Oklahoma, 1975), p. 254.

22. Sidney Hook, *The Hero and History* (New York: John Day, 1942), p. 15.

23. Malcolm Little, *The Autobiography of Malcolm X* (New York: Grove Press, 1966), pp. 1–22.

24. Mayor Blackwell speaks of her in-law, Saul Blackwell, the Reconstruction legislator, as a brilliant black historical figure. With keen awareness of the local history when "blacks controlled the entire county," Mrs. Blackwell sees this period as a symbol of what she aspires for in this new era. Saul Blackwell is seen as especially responsible for policy decisions that positively affected black people's lives. She is especially proud of his reputed role in setting aside land for the creation of schools for black children.

A survey of Mr. Blackwell's role in the Reconstruction legislatures shows that he was active. He offered legislation on a wide range of issues, including those specifically related to Issaquena County. He was especially active in the 1882 session, where it appears that he introduced eight or more bills and commented on many others. In this session he also served on the Committee for Public Roads. In 1886, however, he was much less active, no doubt owing to the much reduced influence of blacks. *Journal of the House of Representatives*, State of Mississippi, Regular Session, Jan. 3, 1882; and January 1886.

25. Personal interview, 1982.

26. For these sentiments see Clayborne Carson, *In Struggle: SNCC and the Black Awakening of the 1960s* (Cambridge, Mass.: Harvard University Press, 1981), *passim*.

27. Personal interview, 1982.

28. Included in this group was Mrs. Minnie Ripley, then over 60. She was a bonafide leader of this period, widely respected for her energy, generosity and wisdom in fighting segregation.

29. U.S. Civil Rights Commission, Hearings on "Voting," Vol. I, at Jackson, Mississippi, Feb. 16-20, 1965, pp. 28–31. The questioner was William Taylor, general counsel.

30. Her sacrifices were not complete, however, as the SNCC position provided a meager eleven dollars every two weeks to help defray the costs of food. Personal interview, 1982.

31. K.C. Morrison, "Electoral Politics in the South: A Report On Mississippi," paper presented at the National Conference of Black Political Scientists (Washington, D.C., 1970), pp. 1–20.

32. U.S. Civil Rights Commission, p. 32. (Ervin Griswold ws the questioner.)

33. *Ibid.*, p. 46.
34. *Ibid.*, pp. 47–51, *passim*.
35. Morrison, "Electoral Politics in the South: . . ." pp. 1–20.
36. "Lady Mayor of Mayersville," *Ebony* (Dec. 1977), pp. 55–56.
37. Personal interview, 1982.
38. Unita Blackwell, personal biographical data, undated.
39. USCPFA membership brochure, n.d.
40. Joseph Spengler, "Theory, Ideology, Non-Economic Values, and Politico-Economic Development," in Ralph Braibanti and Joseph Spengler, ed., *Tradition, Values, and Socio-Economic Development* (Durham: Duke University Press, 1961), pp. 34–35.
41. Geneva Smitherman, *Talkin and Testifyin: The Language of Black America* (Boston: Houghton Mifflin, 1977), pp. 1–15.
42. He goes on to equate the verbal pyrotechnics with a kind of game—not unlike the dozens—where one-upmanship is the rule. Matthew Holden, *The Politics of the Black "Nation"* (San Francisco: Chandler, 1973), pp. 21–22.
43. Holden, pp. 18–20, 23–24.
44. Personal interview, 1982.
45. Quoted in Kenneth Smith and Ira Zepp, *Search For the Beloved Community* (Valley, Forge, Pa.: Judson, 1974), pp. 120, 121, and 126.
46. Personal interview, 1982.
47. Personal interview, 1982.
48. Vincent Harding, *There is A River: The Black Struggle for Freedom in America*, 1st ed. (New York: Harcourt Brace Jovanovich, 1981).
49. Personal interview, 1982.
50. Personal interview, 1982.
51. Stokely Carmichael and Charles Hamilton, *Black Power: The Politics of Liberation in America* (New York: Random House, 1967), pp. 2–34. Stokely Carmichael, *Stokely Speaks* (New York: Vintage Press, 1971), pp. 182–227.
52. In Clayborne Carson, p. 151.
53. *Ebony*, pp. 55–56.
54. Len Holt, *The Summer That Didn't End* (New York: William Morrow, 1965), pp. 98–99.
55. *Ibid.*, p. 98.
56. *Ibid.*, p. 98.
57. Clayborne Carson, p. 109.
58. Len Holt, p. 103.
59. Pat Watters, "Their Text is Civil Rights Primer," in August Meier and Elliott Rudwick, eds., *Black Protest in Sixties* (Chicago: Quadrangle, 1970), p. 80.
60. Howard Zinn, "Schools in Context," *The Nation* (Nov. 23, 1–64), p. 371.
61. Elizabeth Sutherland, ed., *Letters from Mississippi* (New York: McGraw-Hill, 1965), p. 1.
62. Pat Watters, pp. 79–80.
63. Clayborne Carson, p. 109.
64. Len Holt, p. 113, lists these ideas that guided teaching: (1) Comparison of the student's reality with that of others (the way the students live and the way others live); (2) North to Freedom? (The Negro and the North); (3) Examining the apparent reality (the "better lives" that whites live); (4) Introducing the *power structure*; (5) The poor Negro and the poor white; (6) Material things versus soul things; (7) The Movement.

65. Frederick Heinze, "The Freedom Libraries," *Library Journal* (April 15, 1965), pp. 37–39.
66. Miriam Braverman, "Mississippi Summer," *Library Journal* (Nov. 15, 1965), pp. 31–3.
67. SNCC Papers. Reel 65, #s 197-198.
68. SNCC Papers, Reel 38, #128; and Reel 65, #s 197 and 198.
69. Jerry DeMuth, "Summer in Mississippi," *Nation* (Sept. 14, 1964), pp. 104–105.
70. *Burnside, et al. vs. James Byars* (363 F 2d 744, 1966), p. 745.
71. *Blackwell vs. Issaquena Co. Bd. of Ed.* (363 F 2d 749, 1966), p. 751.
72. *Ibid.*, p. 751.
73. *Ibid.*, p. 751.
74. *Adams vs. Mathews* (403 F 2d 181, 1968), p. 181.
75. Personal interview, 1982.
76. The regulations in this regard state:

> When a territory desires to be incorporated as a municpality at least two-thirds of its qualifed electors must file a petition in the chancery court of the county in which the territory is located. The petition will define the proposed boundaries, the name, population, assessed valuation, aims of the petitioners in seeking incorporation, the public services to be rendered, the necessity for incorporation, the names of those the petitioners would desire as municipal officers; and the petition must be sworn to by at least one of the petitioners.

Edward Hobbs and Donald Vaughan *A Manual of Mississippi Municipal Government*, 2nd ed. (Oxford: University of Mississippi Press, 1962), p. 11.

77. Personal interview, 1982.
78. Personal interview, 1982.
79. Personal interview, 1982.
80. Personal interview, 1982.

Chapter 5

1. *Holmes County Herald*, "Bicentennial Special," (July 1, 1976), p. 22.
2. In more agricultural Tchula, however, blacks were the overwhelming majority, constituting 86 percent in 1860 and 79 percent in 1870. *U.S. Census of Population*, 1860 and 1870.
3. This entire paragraph is based on data from the *U.S. Census of Agriculture* 1850, 1860, 1870.
4. Vernon Wharton, *The Negro in Mississippi* (Chapel Hill, N.C.: University of North Carolina, 1947), p. 80.
5. *Ibid.*, p. 169.
6. *Ibid.*, p. 173.
7. U.S. Senate Report, 527, V. 1 (Boutwell Report), 44th congress, 1st Session (Dec. 6, 1875-Aug. 15, 1876), pp. 572-588.
8. Carlton J. Corliss, *Main Line of Mid-America* (New York: Creative Age Press, 1950), p. 241.
9. Daniel Berman, *A Bill Becomes a Law*, 2nd ed. (New York: Macmillan, 1966), pp. 33–42. Eastland had already organized "a number of other segregationist associ-

ations . . . States Rights Councils, the National Association for the Advancement of White People, Southern Gentlemen, Inc., the Pro-Southerners, and the Tennessee Society to Maintain Segregation." Their aim was a "united movement for the preservation of America under a constitutional form of government." Robert Brisbane, *Black Activism: Racial Revolution in the United States, 1954-1970* (Valley Forge, Pa.: Judson Press, 1974), p. 25.

10. Governor Hugh White had instituted a "school equalization" program in 1953, calling for "equal salaries for Negro teachers and equal educational opportunities for Negro students, as well as equal transportation facilities and physical plants for Negro schools" to try and delay school integration. Neil R. McMillen, *Citizens' Councils* (Urbana, Ill.: University of Illinois, 1971), pp. 15–16.

11. For this reason "such epithets as 'white-collar Klan,' 'uptown Klan,' 'button-down Klan,' and 'Country Club Klan,' have been used to describe them." Francis M. Wilhoit, *The Politics of Massive Resistance* (New York: George Braziller, 1973), p. 111.

12. Numan Bartley, *The Rise of Massive Resistance* (Baton Rouge, La.: Louisiana State University, 1969), p. 85.

13. Neil McMillen, "Development of Civil Rights, 1956-1970," in Richard McLemore, *A History of Mississippi*, Vol. II, (Jackson, Miss.: University Press of Mississippi, 1973), pp. 159–160.

14. Hodding Carter, III, *The South Strikes Back* (New York: Doubleday, 1959), pp. 26–31.

15. Hodding Carter, *First Person Rural* (New York: Doubleday, 1963), pp. 217, *passim*.

16. Carter, III, *The South Strikes Back*, p. 220.

17. Carter, *First Person Rural*, p. 221.

18. James Silver, *Mississippi: The Closed Society* (New York: Harcourt, Brace, and World, 1963), p. 38.

19. Carter, *First Person Rural*, p. 223.

20. Carter, III, *The South Strikes Back*, p. 153.

21. John Salter, Jr., *Jackson, Mississippi* (New York: Exposition, 1979), pp. 29–31.

22. *U.S. Civil Rights Commission Hearings at Jackson Mississippi*, 2 vols., 1965.

23. James Silver, p. 38.

24. James Silver, p. 37.

25. Carter, *First Person Rural*, p. 223.

26. According to one reporter: "William Moses, a local businessman, [was] head of the Lexington chapter, and State Representative-elect J.T. Love [was] head of the Tchula chapter. Others later identified included Wilburn Hooker, a state representative; T.M. Williams, a state senator; and Edwin White, a former state representative. Carter, III, *The South Strikes Back*, pp. 150–155.

27. Carter, III, *The South Strikes Back*, p. 153.

28. Previous legislation called for transaction of such business only in the local county. Silver, p. 39.

29. *Ibid.*, p. 37.

30. Carter, III, *The South Strikes Back*, p. 149.

31. James Silver, p. 37.

32. In 1962, out of a black voting age population of 8757, only eight were registered in the county. U.S. Civil Rights Commission, *Voting in Mississippi* (Washington, D.C.: Government Printing Office, 1965).

33. SNCC Papers. Reel 65, #184, pp. 631, 638.
34. *Ibid.*, p. 632.
35. *Ibid.*, pp. 621–629.
36. *Ibid.*, pp. 633–635.
37. Elizabeth Sutherland, ed., *Letters from Mississippi* (New York: McGraw-Hill, 1965), pp. 41, 47–49.
38. Certainly the number of white outsiders was ample to create these situations. In various reports over a one-year period, references were made to over 15 workers who could be identified as white. There could have been others of whom no such reference was made. SNCC Papers, Reel 65, #184, p. 636.
39. Howell Raines, *My Soul Is Rested* (New York: Penguin, 1983), pp. 260–267.
40. James Silver, p. 95.
41. SNCC Papers, Reel 65, #184, p. 636.
42. Still others were arrested for taking part in a boycott of businesses in Lexington. SNCC Papers, Reel 65, #185, pp. 640–642.
43. SNCC Papers, Reel 65, #187, p. 656.
44. Stokely Carmichael and Charles Hamilton, *Black Power: The Politics of Liberation in America* (New York: Random House, 1967), p. 88.
45. U.S. Civil Rights Commission, *Political Participation* (Washington, D.C.: U.S. Government Printing Office, 1968), p. 109.
46. *Ibid.*, pp. 108–110.
47. *Ibid.*, pp. 90–91.
48. *Ibid.*, p. 11.
49. *Ibid.*, pp. 73–74.
50. James Q. Wilson, *The Amateur Democrat* (Chicago: University of Chicago Press, 1962), p. 2.
51. Robert Merton, *Social Theory and Social Structure* (Glencoe, Ill.: Free Press, 1957), pp. 387-420.
52. Personal interview with Elijah McGee, MVSU Student Leader, July 1981.
53. *Delta-Democrat Times* (Greenville, Miss.), February 11, 1969, p. 1.
54. *Greenwood Commonwealth* (Greenwood, Miss.), February 10, 1969, p. 1.
55. Some charge that this occurred only after the president met with the governor and secured approval for what should have been a local decision. *Delta-Democrat Times*, February 11, 1969, p. 1.
56. United Press International Wire Service (UPI) (Itta Bena, Mississippi), February 9, 1984, p. 1.
57. Tyrone Gettis was born and reared in Mississippi, unlike Wilhelm Joseph (the previous leader) who was Trinidadian and often looked upon as an "outside agitator."
58. *Clarion-Ledger* (Jackson, Miss.), February 10, 1970, p. 1.
59. These "go for bad" types usually exhibit some aspect of aggression in pursuit of their goals. Al Tony Gilmore, *Bad Nigger!* (Port Washington, (New York: Kennikat, 1975), p. 13.
60. Personal interviews, 1980–1981.
61. In this respect Carthan espoused a variety of nationalism akin to DuBois' "common suffering." "Blacks have a strong, hereditary cultural unity born of slavery, of common suffering, prolonged proscription, and curtailment of political and civil rights.... Prolonged policies of segregation and discrimination have involuntarily welded the mass almost into a nation within a nation." Eric Lincoln, *The Black Muslims in America* (Boston: Beacon, 1961), p. 45.

62. Both declined to be interviewed for this study, and one of them exhibited great hostility when approached.

63. "The house Negroes—lived in the house with master, they dressed pretty good, they ate good because they ate his food—what he left. . . . They loved the master more than the master loved himself. . . . If the master said, 'We got a good house here,' the house Negro would say, 'Yeah, we got a good house here' . . . whenever the master said 'we,' he said 'we'. That's how you can tell a house Negro." "Message to the Grassroots," in George Breitman, ed., *Malcolm X Speaks* (New York: Grove Press, 1966), pp. 10–11. James Silver, pp. 107–140.

64. John Wahlke, Heinz Eulau, William Buchanan, and LeRoy Ferguson, *The Legislative Process* (New York: John Wiley & Sons, 1962), pp. 267–286.

65. Walter Rodney, *How Europe Underdeveloped Africa* (Washington, D.C.: Howard University, 1974), pp. 93–146.

66. Personal interviews, December 1980.
67. Personal interview, December 1980.
68. Personal interview, 1980.
69. *Clarion-Ledger* (Jackson, Miss.), May 2, 1980, p. 3-A.
70. *Holmes County Herald* (Lexington, Miss), July 12, 1979, p. 1.
71. *Clarion-Ledger*, October 16, 1980, p. 3-A.
72. *Holmes County Herald*, March 20, 1980, p. 1.
73. *Clarion-Ledger*, May 2, 1980, p. 3-A.
74. *Jackson Advocate*, May 7-13, 1981, p. 1.
75. *Jackson Advocate*, April 28-May 4, p. 1.
76. *Tchula Times* (Tchula, Miss.), November 22, 1980, p. 1.
77. *Tchua Times*, May 30, 1981, p. 4.
78. "Editorial Notes," *Tchula Times*, April, 1982, p. 3.
79. "Editorial Notes," *Tchula Times*, April 1982, p. 3.
80. *Clarion-Ledger*, November 5, 1982, p. 14.
81. Meuchy was subsequently given a three-month prison term, three years probation, a fine of $2,500 on false claims. *Clarion-Ledger*, October 16, 1980, p. 3.
82. *Clarion-Ledger*, October 15, 1983, p. 1.
83. *Clarion-Ledger*, (October 28, 1980, p. 1; September 30, 1981, p. 1; October 28, 1980, p. 3.
84. By government estimate, the prices offered by Foreman's company were often three or four times above market.
85. *Clarion-Ledger*, October 28, 1980, p. 1; September 30, 1981, p. 1; October 1, 1981, p. 3.
86. At his trial for assault on the police officer it was observed that he had a bulge in his clothes. *Holmes County Herald*, May 15, 1980, p. 1.
87. *Clarion-Ledger/Jackson Daily News*, July 4, 1981, p. 3.
88. *Clarion-Ledger*, April 17, 1982, p. 8.
89. *Clarion-Ledger*, April 23, 1983, p. 3-A.
90. *Tchula Times*, April 1982, p. 3.
91. *Clarion-Ledger*, April 23, 1983, p. 3–8.
92. M. Pinsky, "American Gulag," *Progressive*, Vol. 41, (Nov. 1977), p. 9.
93. *Jackson Daily News*, Nov. 4, 1982, p. 1.
94. *Jackson Daily News*, Nov. 4, 1982, p. 1.
95. This group of nearly 20 members in 1981 sought to establish relationships

between newly elected officials for the exchange of ideas, and to function as a kind of lobby for black political interests.

96. *Clarion-Ledger*, May 16, 1981, p. 3-A.
97. Elmer Schattschneider, *The Semi-Sovereign People* (New York: Holt, Rinehart & Winston, 1960).
98. This group had been founded in 1976 in Chicago and was self-described as an umbrella civil rights and labor organization.
99. Personal interview, Ted Quant, Equal Rights Congress (New Orleans, 1984).
100. *Clarion-Ledger*, July 31, 1981, p. 3.
101. "National News Update," October 16th Rally Committee, Help Us To Make A Nation, Inc. (Dayton, Ohio), October 7, 1982, unpaged.
102. "National News Update," unpaged, n.d.
103. "National News Update," unpaged n.d.
104. But the picture many of these organizations sought to portray was that of more generalized political repression in America. For them the Carthan trials provided another standard by which to measure the deterioration of democratic values.
105. Both of these donations were criticized by church people in Mississippi, including one group which sought to have the contributions disavowed. In the case of the Presbyterians it was argued that the contribution was liable to affect the upcoming merger plan between the northern and southern denominations. Fallout among the Methodists, however, was of major consequence. Local churches noted that notwithstanding Carthan's problems, church funds were never made available to a region without local consultation. Eventually they succeeded in exacting censures and reassignments for those who had made the decisions to support Carthan.
106. "National News Update, " unpaged, n.d.
107. *Clarion-Ledger*, April 23, 1983, p. 3–8.

Chapter 6

1. Richard Niemi and Herbert Weisberg, ed., *Controversies In American Voting Behavior* (San Francisco: W.H. Freeman, 1976), pp. 11–13.
2. Angus Campbell, Philip E. Converse, Warren E. Miller, and Donald Stokes, *The American Voter* (New York: John Wiley & Sons, 1960), pp. 270–279. It was reported in a 1968 analysis (that has since been revised) that "almost half of the habitual nonvoters live in the South . . .; one-fourth are Negro."
3. It was also indicated that they "also appear to be more seriously handicapped by the legal restrictions on the franchise in their districts." Angus Campbell, et al., p. 282.
4. William Flanigan, *Political Behavior of the American Electorate* (Boston: Allyn & Bacon, 1968), pp. 20–23. "Not all agreed with this interpretation. Downs is one example. There are two reasons to suspect that the proportion of low-income citizens who abstain is usually higher than the proportion of high-income citizens who do so. First, the cost of voting is harder for low-income citizens to bear; therefore, even if returns among high and low income groups are the same, fewer of the latter vote. Second, the cost of information. Since uncertainty reduces the returns from voting, a lower proportion of low-income groups would vote even if voting costs were equally difficult for everyone to bear." Anthony Downs, "The Causes and Effects of Rational Abstention" in Niemi and Weisberg, eds., p. 42.

5. Sidney Verba and Norman Nie, "The Rationality of Political Activity," in Niemi and Weisberg, ed., pp. 62–63.
6. Dwaine Marvick, "The Political Socialization of the American Negro," in Harry Bailey, ed., *Negro Politics in America* (Columbus, Ohio: Charles Merrill Co., 1967), p. 35.
7. Milton D. Morris, *The Politics of Black America* (New York: Harper & Row, 1975), p. 125.
8. Paul Abramson, *The Political Socialization of Black Americans* (New York: Free Press, 1977), p. 3.
9. Campbell, et al., p. 479.
10. Abramson, pp. 80–81.
11. Dwaine Marvick, "The Political Socialization of the American Negro," p. 41.
12. Abramson, pp. 82–83.
13. Abramson has summarized the various ways scholars have sought to explain these phenomena. (1) Education explanation: Since teachers are less effective in imparting democratic values of participation to blacks, the latter have lower levels of efficacy and trust. (2) Social Deprivation explanation: Environmental conditions of poverty and exclusion from systemic channels of society yield attitudes of non-participation, etc. (3) Intelligence explanation: since blacks are less intelligent than whites, patterns of non-participation are inevitable. (4) Political/Reality explanation: black attitudes and behavior inconsistent with democratic values are due to the objective situation of powerlessness that they endure in the system. Paul Abramson, pp. 27–97, *passim*.
14. Angus Campbell, et al., pp. 192–193.
15. Philip E. Converse, "The Nature of Belief Systems in Mass Publics," in David Apter, ed., *Ideology and Discontent* (New York: Free Press, 1964), p. 207.
16. Seymour Martin Lipset, *Political Man* (New York: Anchor Press, 1963), p. 443.
17. Daniel Bell, *The End of Ideology* (New York: Free Press, 1960).
18. "For the truly involved citizen, development of political sophistication means the absorption of contextual information that makes clear to him the connections of the policy area of his initial interest with policy differences in other areas; and that these broader configurations of policy positions are describable quite economically in the basic abstractions of ideology. Most members of the mass public, however, fail to proceed so far. Certain rather concrete issues may capture their respective individual attentions and lead to some politically relevant opinion formation. . . . The common citizen fails to develop more global points of view about politics." Philip E. Converse, in David Apter, ed., p. 213.
19. *Ibid.*, p. 213.
20. Kerner Report, National Advisory Committee on Civil Disorders (Washington, D.C.: Government Printing Office, 1968), p. 240.
21. Nancy Weiss, *Farewell to the Party of Lincoln* (Princeton N.J.: Princeton University Press, 1983), p. 210.
22. Lucius J. Barker and Jesse McCorry, *Black Americans and the Political System* (Cambridge, Mass.: Winthrop, 1976), pp. 233–244.
23. Aldon Morris, *The Origins of the Civil Rights Movement* (New York: Free Press, 1984), pp. 40–76.
24. Weiss, p. 210.
25. Rex Campbell, et al, "Return Migration of Black People to the South," *Rural Sociology*, vol. 39 (Winter 1974), pp. 514–527.

26. Allan Spear, "The Origins of the Urban Ghetto, 1870-1915," in Nathan Huggins, et al., eds., *Key Issues in the Afro-American Experience*, Vol. II (New York: Harcourt, Brace, Jovanovich, 1971), pp. 153–166; Hanes Walton, *Black Politics* (Philadelphia: Lippincott, 1972), p. 44.

27. Barker and McCorry, pp. 239–240; Donald R. Matthews and James Prothro, *Negroes and the New Southern Politics* (New York: Harcourt, Brace and World, 1966), p. 115.

29. Martin Kilson, "Political Change in the Negro Ghetto, 1900-1940s," in Nathan Huggins, et al., ed., p. 175; Marcus Jones, *Black Migration in the U.S. with An Emphasis on Selected Cities* (Saratoga, Calif.: Century Twenty-One Publication, 1980), p. 37.

30. Steven Lawson, *Black Ballots* (New York: Columbia, 1976); Pat Watters and Reese Cleghorn, *Climbing Jacob's Ladder* (New York: Harcourt, Brace and World, 1967).

31. Kenneth Smith and Ira Zepp, *Search for the Beloved Community* (Valley Forge, Pa.: Judson, 1974), pp. 11–20.

32. U.S. Commission on Civil Rights, *Hearings on Voting*, Vol. I (February 16-20, 1965), p. 23.

33. McGovern forces had also sought to more effectively integrate blacks into the "new" Democratic coalition by reforming the national party structure. Commission on Party Structure and Delegate Selection, *Mandate For Reform* (Washington, D.C.: Democratic National Committee, 1970).

34. The Democratic candidate was a North Mississippi lawyer, Cliff Finch, who used a lunch pail as he made well-orchestrated appearances at laborer work sites. The Republican was Gil Carmichael, a wealthy car dealer, who sought to reform state government.

35. Numan Bartley and Hugh Graham, *Southern Elections* (Baton Rouge, La.: Louisiana State University, 1978), pp. 141–144.

36. *World Almanac* (New York: Newspaper Enterprise Association, 1982), p. 286.

37. Austin Ranney and Hugh Bone, *Politics and Voters* (New York: McGraw-Hill, 1976), p. 32 ff.; William Flanigan, p. 22.

38. In the 1972 presidential election, while the number of participants was comparatively high for Mississippi, there clearly was less interest than in 1976.

39. Richard Shingles, "Black Consciousness and Political Participation," *American Political Science Review*, 75:1 (March 1981); pp. 76–91; Richard Engstrom and Michael McDonald, "The Election of Blacks to City Councils," *American Political Science Review*, 75:2 (June 1981), pp. 34–54.

40. Flanigan has indicated some of the varying circumstances under which such increased participation might be evident: (1) differences in media coverage, (2) perceived significance of the office, (3) issues, and (4) candidates attractiveness. Flanigan, p. 23.

41. *Ibid.*, p. 21.

42. Donald R. Matthews and James Prothro, p. 271.

43. These questions sought information about the presidency, the name of the governor and his term of office, and the local county seat. Other questions were about the terms of Senators, number of Supreme Court justices, and an historical question on the admission of states to the union. Donald R. Matthews and James Prothro, p. 271.

44. *Ibid.*, pp. 272–273.

45. Barbara Hinckley, et al., "Information and the Vote," in Richard Niemi and Herbert Weisberg, eds., pp. 274–296, *passim*.

46. Flanigan, p. 117.
47. Melville Herskovits, *The Myth of the Negro Past* (Boston: Beacon, 1958), p. 7.
48. Mary Berry and John Blassingame, *Long Memory* (New York: Oxford, 1982), p. 389.
49. Robert Brisbane, *Black Activism: Racial Revolution in the United States, 1954-1970* (Valley Forge, Pa.: Judson, 1974), p. 175.
50. Gordon Henderson, *In Introduction to Political Parties* (New York: Harper and Row, 1976), p. 105.
51. *Ibid., passim*.
52. Anthony Lake, *The "Tar Baby" Option* (New York: Columbia University, 1976), p. 123 ff.
53. Minion K.C. Morrison, "Afro-Americans and Africa: Grassroots Afro-American opinion and attitudes toward Africa," in *Comparative Studies In Society and History*, vol. 29, #2 (April 1987).
54. *New York Times*, October 3, 1975; and *Amsterdam News*, May 7, 1977, p. B-3.
55. The intent was to isolate those who know racial segregation generally from those who could identify the policy by its particular South African name. The ability to define the word apartheid was taken as evidence that fairly direct knowledge of the South Africa situation existed.
56. Mayersville was excluded because it had no previous local administration.
57. Everett Carll Ladd, *Ideology in America* (New York: Norton, 1972), pp. 7–8.
58. For our purposes school integration is the better continuing symbol because overt segregration in other public accommodations disappeared fairly early during mobilization, while schools became an enduringly contentious issue.
59. In this instance data for the towns have been separated since there were some notable distinctions between the various populations, especially in Bolton.
60. It must be noted that at the time of our survey there was but one white serving in these governments. The lone white alderman was at Tchula. Moreover, there had never been a white to serve in the administration at Bolton, though there had been an integrated board of aldermen just prior to Thompson's election as mayor. In the first part of Mayor Blackwell's tenure, there had also been whites on the board, but none served at the time of the survey.
61. In an analysis of *New York Times* articles on South Africa throughout the mid-1970s and early 1980s, very few materials do not deal with the question of race. Over 200 pieces concern human rights (individual cases and/or philosophical problems of apartheid); another 200+ explore South African involvement in the Zimbabwe and Namibia disputes, and/or involvement with Western powers over the latter two problems.

Chapter 7

1. Herbert Alexander, *Money In Politics* (Washington, D.C.: Public Affairs Press, 1972), pp. 39–59.
2. Michael Parenti, *Democracy For the Few*, 2nd ed. (New York: St. Martin's, 1977) pp. 9–32; Kenneth Dolbeare and Murray Edelman, *American Politics*, 3rd ed. (Lexington, Mass.: Heath, 1971), pp. 21–37.
3. Harold Baron, "Black Powerlessness in Chicago," in Edward Greenberg, et al., eds., *Black Politics* (New York: Holt, Rinehart & Winston, 1971), pp. 105–117.

4. Peter Eisinger, *The Politics of Displacement: Racial and Ethnic Transition in Three American Cities* (New York: Academic Press, 1980), pp. 112–127; 192–199.

5. Mack Jones, "Black Political Empowerment in Atlanta: Myth and Reality," *Annals of the American Academy of Political and Social Science*, Vol. 439 (Sept. 1978), p. 97.

6. Stokely Carmichael and Charles Hamilton, *Black Power: The Politics of Liberation in America* (New York: Random House, (1967), pp. 2–34.

7. Georges Balandier, "The Colonial Situation," in Pierre van den Berghe, ed., *Africa* (San Francisco: Chandler, 1965), pp. 36–57.

8. Kwame Nkrumah, *Neocolonialism* (New York: International, 1965), p. IX.

9. Andre Gunder Frank, "The Sociology of Development and the Underdevelopment of Sociology," in *Latin America* (New York: Monthly Review, 1969), pp. 21–94.

10. Samuel Krislov, *The Negro and Federal Employment* (Minneapolis: University of Minnesota, 1967); Franklin P. Kilpatrick et al., *The Image of the Federal Service* (Washington, D.C.: Brookings, 1964), pp. 93 and 225.

11. John C. Donovan, *The Politics of Poverty*, 2nd ed. (New York: Pegasus, 1973), pp. 27–38.

12. E.E. Schattschneider, *The Semi-Sovereign People* (New York: Holt, Rinehart & Winston, 1960), pp. 78–96.

13. Matthew Holden, " 'Imperialism' in Bureaucracy," *American Political Science Review* 60:4 (1966), pp. 943–951; Guy Benveniste, *The Politics of Expertise* (Berkeley: Glendessary Press, 1972), pp. 3–21.

14. Gideon Sjoberg, Richard A. Brymer, and Buford Farris, "Bureaucracy and the Lower Class," *Sociology and Social Research*, Vol. 50:1 (1966), pp. 325–337.

15. Murray Edelman, *Politics as Symbolic Action* (Chicago: Markham, 1971), pp. 116–141.

16. Parenti, p. 4.

17. Robert Dahl, "The Concept of Power," *Behavioral Science*, Vol. 2 (July 1957), pp. 201–215.

18. Murray Edelman, *The Symbolic Uses of Politics* (Urbana: University of Illinois, 1964), pp. 22–43.

19. Data in this and the following paragraph are derived from the *U.S. Census of Agriculture*, as specified by year.

20. Ira Sharkansky, *The politics of Taxing and Spending* (Indianapolis: Bobbs-Merrill, 1969), pp. 171–172.

21. Because of the generally regressive nature of the state's tax systems, a heavier burden falls on the poor and especially blacks in the three counties under discussion. The state was one of the first to institute a broad state sales tax which raises considerable revenue, a portion of which is returned directly to the municipalities. Ira Sharkansky, p. 171.

22. *Service Bulletin*, Mississippi State Tax Commission, 1980, p. 5.

23. Edward Hobbs and Donald Vaughan, *A Manual Of Mississippi Municipal Government* (Oxford, Miss.: University of Mississippi, 1962), pp. 66–95, *passim*.

24. Sales taxes, on the other hand, were much easier. Data were readily available by town and will be presented as such.

25. Mississippi Research and Development Center, *Economic Development Blueprint*, parts IX, XI.

26. Town Budget Ledgers, Fiscal 1978, for Bolton, Mayersville and Tchula.

27. Minion K.C. Morrison, "Preconditions for Afro-American Leadership in the Rural South," *Polity*, Vol. XVII:3, Spring 1985, pp. 504–29.

28. Robert Havemen, ed., *A Decade of Federal Antipoverty Programs* (New York: Academic Press, 1977), pp. 1–19.

29. Michael Reagan, *The New Federalism* (New York: Oxford, 1972), pp. 3–53.

30. Murray Edelman, *The Symbolic Uses of Politics*, pp. 172–187.

31. Arthur Levy and Susan Standinger, "The Black Caucus in the 92nd Congress," *Phylon*, Vol. 39 (December 1978), pp. 322–332.

32. Milton Morris, *The Politics of Black America* (New York: Harper & Row, 1975), pp. 277–302.

33. Arthur Levy and Susan Standinger, p. 330.

34. James Cockcroft, et al., *Dependence and Underdevelopment* (New York: Anchor Press, 1972), pp. 3–45, *passim*.

35. E.E. Schattschneider, *The Semi-Sovereign People*.

36. James W. Button, *Political Violence* (Princeton, N.J.: Princeton University Press, 1978).

Selected Bibliography

Abramson. Paul. *The Political Socialization of Black Americans*. New York: Free Press, 1977.

Alexander, Herbert. *Money In Politics*. Washington, D.C.: Public Affairs Press, 1972.

Apter, David. *The Politics of Modernization*. Chicago: University of Chicago Press, 1965.

Aptheker, Herbert. *American Negro Slave Revolts*. New York: International Publishers, 1970.

Aptheker, Herbert. *The Labor Movement in the South During Slavery*. New York: International Publishers, 1955.

Aptheker, Herbert. Mississippi Reconstruction and the Negro Leader Charles Caldwell. *Science and Society*, 2:4 Fall 1947. 340–71.

Aptheker, Herbert. *Nat Turner's Slave Rebellion*. New York: Humanities Press, 1966.

Bacon, Charles M. A History of Hinds County, Mississippi. M.A. Thesis (History). Mississippi College. 1959.

Balandier, Georges. The Colonial Situation. In Pierre van den Berghe, ed. *Africa*. San Francisco: Chandler, 1965. 36–57.

Barker, Lucius and McCorry, Jesse. *Black Americans and the Political System*. Boston: Little Brown, 1980.

Barnett, Marguerite Ross. A Theoretical Perspective on American Public Policy. In Marguerite Ross Barnett and James Hefner, eds. *Public Policy for the Black Community*. Port Washington, New York: Alfred Publishing Company, 1976. 3–53.

Baron, Harold. Black Powerlessness in Chicago. In Edward Greenberg; Milner, Neal; and, Olson, David; eds. *Black Politics*. New York: Holt, Rinehart and Winston, 1971. 105–117.

Bartley, Numan. *The Rise of Massive Resistance*. Baton Rouge, Louisiana: Louisiana State University Press, 1969.

Bartley, Numan and Graham, Hugh. *Southern Elections*. Baton Rouge, Louisiana: Louisiana State University, 1978.

Bell, Daniel. *The End of Ideology*. New York: Free Press, 1960.

Bennett, Lerone. *Black Power U.S.A*. Chicago: Johnson Publishing Company, 1967.

Benveniste, Guy. *The Politics of Expertise*. Berkeley: Glendessary Press, 1972.

Berman, Daniel. *A Bill Becomes a Law*. 2nd. Ed. New York: Macmillan, 1966.

Berry, Mary and Blassingame, John. *Long Memory*. New York: Oxford University Press, 1982.

Blassingame, John. *The Slave Community*. New York: Oxford University Press, 1979.

Blauner, Herbert. Internal Colonialism and Ghetto Revolt. In Gary Marx, ed. *Racial Conflict*. Boston: Little, Brown and Company, 1971. 52–61.

Bontemps, Arna. *Black Thunder*. Boston: Beacon, 1968.

Braverman, Miriam. Mississippi Summer. *Library Journal* November 15, 1965. 31–33.

Brisbane, Robert. *Black Activism*. Valley Forge, Pennsylvania: Judson Press, 1974.

Burnside et al. vs. James Byers, 363 F.2d 744 (1966).

Button, James. *Political Violence*. Princeton: Princeton University Press, 1978.

Campbell, Angus; Converse, Philip; Miller, Warren; and Stokes, Donald, eds. *The American Voter*. New York: Wiley and Sons, 1960.

Campbell, Clarice and Rogers, Oscar, Jr. *Mississippi: The View From Tougaloo*. Jackson, Mississippi: University Press of Mississippi, 1979.

Campbell, Rex; Johnson, Daniel; and Stangler, Gary. Return Migration of Black People to the South. *Rural Sociology*. 39 (Winter 1974). 514–27.

Carmichael, Stokely and Hamilton, Charles. *Black Power*. New York: Random House, 1967.

Carnovan, Margaret. *Populism*. New York: Harcourt, Brace, Jovanovich, 1981.

Clarion-Ledger Newspaper. Jackson, Mississippi.

Carson, Clayborne. *In Struggle*. Cambridge: Harvard University Press, 1981.

Carter, Hodding. *First Person Rural*. New York: Doubleday, 1963.

Carter, Hodding, III. *The South Strikes Back*. New York: Doubleday, 1959.

Cash, Wilbur. *The Mind of the South*. New York: Knopf, 1941.

Cockcroft, James; Frank, Andre Gunder; and, Johnson, Dale, eds. *Dependence and Underdevelopment*. New York: Anchor, 1972.

Colburn, Kenneth. *Southern Black Mayors*. Washington, D.C.: Joint Center for Political Studies, 1974.

Congressional Quarterly. *Guide to U.S. Elections*. Washington: 1975.

Converse, Philip. The Nature of Belief Systems in Mass Publics. In David Apter, ed. *Ideology and Discontent*. New York: Free Press, 1964.

Corliss, Carlton. *Main Line of Mid-America*. New York: Creative Age Press, 1950.

Dahl, Robert. The Concept of Power. *Behavioral Scientist*. 2 (July 1957). 201–215.

Dahl, Robert. *Who Governs*. New Haven: Yale, 1961.

de Graff, Lawrence. Howard: The Evolution of a Black Student Revolt. In Julian Foster and Durward Long, eds. *Protest! Student Activism in America*. New York: Morrow, 1979. 319–344.

Delta-Democrat Times Newspaper. Greenville, Mississippi.

De Muth, Jerry. Summer in Mississippi. *Nation*. September 14, 1964. 104–105.

Deutsch, Karl. Social Mobilization and Political Development. *American Political Science Review*. LV:3 (September 1961), 493–514.

Dolbeare, Kenneth and Edelman, Murray. *American Politics*. 3rd. ed. Lexington, Massachusetts: D.C. Heath Company, 1979.

Donovan, John. *The Politics of Poverty*. 2nd. ed. New York: Pegasus, 1973.

Downs, Anthony. The Causes and Effects of Rational Abstention. In Richard Niemi and Herbert Weisberg, ed. *Controversies in American Voting Behavior*. San Francisco: W.H. Freeman, 1976. 32–44.

Eaton, Clement. *The Fredom of Thought Struggle in the Old South*. New York: Torchbooks, 1964.

Edelman. Murray. *Politics as Symbolic Action*. Chicago: Markham. 1971

Edelman, Murray. *The Symbolic Uses of Politics*. Urbana, Illinois: University of Illinois Press, 1964.

Edwards, Harry. *Black Students*. New York: Free Press, 1970.

Eisinger, Peter. *The Politics of Displacement*. New York: Academic Press, 1980.

Engstrom, Richard and McDonald, Michael. The Election of Blacks to City Councils. *American Political Science Review*. 75:2 (June 1981). 344–54.

Fanon, Frantz. *The Wretched of the Earth*. New York: Grove Press, 1965.

Flacks, Richard. The Liberated Generation. In James McEvoy and Abraham Miller, eds. *Black Power and Student Rebellion*. Belmont, California: Wadsworth, 1969. 354–78.

Flanigan, William. *Political Behavior of the American Electorate*. Boston: Allyn and Bacon, 1968.

Foner, Philip. *History of the United States*. Vol. 3 New York: International Publishers, 1962.

Foster, Julian and Long, Durward, eds. *Protest! Student Activism in America*. New York: Morrow, 1970.

Frank, Andre Gunder. The Sociology of Development and the Underdevelopment of Sociology. In Andre Gunder Frank, ed. *Latin America*. New York: Monthly Review Press, 1969. 21–94.

Franklin, John Hope. *From Slavery to Freedom*. 5th. ed. New York: Knopf, 1980.

Friedland, John. For A Sociological Concept of Charisma. In Marion Doro and Newell Stultz, eds. *Governing in Black Africa*. Englewood Cliffs, New Jersey: Prentice-Hall, 1970. 58–68.

Gamson, William. *The Strategy of Social Protest*. Homewood, Illinois: Dorsey, 1975.

Garner, John. *Reconstruction in Mississippi*. Baton Rouge, Louisiana: Louisiana State University Press, 1968.

Genovese, Eugene. *The Political Economy of Slavery*. New York: Pantheon, 1967.

Genovese, Eugene. *Roll, Jordan, Roll*. New York: Pantheon, 1974.

Gilmore, Al-Tony. *Bad Nigger! The National Impact of Jack Johnson*. Port Washington, New York: Kennikat Press, 1975.

Gonzales, John. Flush Times, Depression, War and Compromise. In Richard A. McLemore, ed. *History of Mississippi*. Vol. I. Hattiesburg, Mississippi: University Press of Mississippi, 1973. 284–309.

Graham vs. Daniel. 6514. Hinds County Chancery Court (1973).

Gray, Lewis. *History of Agriculture In The Southern United States to 1960*. Washington, D.C.: The Carnegie Institution of Washington, 1933.

Green, Adwin Wigfall. *The Man Bilbo*. Baton Rouge, Louisiana: Louisiana State University Press, 1963.

Greenwood Commonwealth Newspaper. Greenwood, Mississippi.

Gurin, Patricia and Epps, Edgar. *Black Consciousness, Identity and Achievement*. New York: Wiley and Sons, 1975.

Gwaltney, John. *Drylongso*. New York: Random House, 1980.

Hamilton, Charles. *The Black Preacher in America*. New York: Morrow, 1972.

Harding, Vincent. *There is A River*. New York: Harcourt, Brace Jovanovich, 1981.

Harris, William. The Reconstruction of the Commonwealth 1865-1870. In Richard McLemore, ed. *A History of Mississippi*. Vol. I. Hattiesburg, Mississippi: University Press of Mississippi, 1973. 542-570.

Havemen, Robert, ed. *A Decade of Federal Antipoverty Programs*. New York: Academic Press, 1977.

Heath, G. Louis, ed. *Mutiny Does Not Happen Lightly*. Metuchen, New Jersey: Scarecrow, 1976.

Heath, G. Louis, ed. *Vandals in the Bomb Factory*. Metuchen, New Jersey: Scarecrow, 1976.

Heinze, Frederick. The Freedom Libraries. *Library Journal*. April 15, 1965. 37-39.

Henderson, Gordon. *An Introduction to Political Parties*. New York: Harper and Row, 1976.

Herskovits, Melville. *The Myth of the Negro Past*. Boston: Beacon Press, 1958.

Hinckley, Barbara; Hofstetter, C. Richard; and Kessel, John. Information and the Vote. In Richard Niemi and Herbet Weisberg, eds. *Controversies in Amercian Voting Behavior*. San Francisco: W.H. Freeman Press, 1976. 274-96.

Hobbs, Edward and Vaughn, Donald. *A Manual of Mississippi Municipal Government*, 2nd. ed. Oxford, Mississippi: University of Mississippi Press, 1962.

Holden, Matthew. 'Imperialism' In Bureaucracy. *American Political Science Review*. 60:4. (1966). 943-951.

Holden, Matthew. *The Politics of the Black Nation*. New York: Chandler, 1973.

Holmes County Herald Newspaper. Lexington, Mississippi.

Holmes, William. *The White Chief*. Baton Rouge, Louisiana: Louisiana State University Press, 1970.

Holt, Len. *The Summer That Didn't End*. New York: Morrow, 1965.

Hook, Sidney. *The Hero in History*. New York: John Day, 1942.

Huggins, Nathan. Afro-Americans. In John Higham, ed. *Ethnic Leadership in America*. Baltimore: Johns Hopkins University Press, 1978. 91-118.

Huie, William. *Three Lives for Mississippi*. New York: New American Library, 1969.

Hunter, Floyd. *Community Power Structure*. Chapel Hill, North Carolina: University of North Carolina Press, 1953.

Jackson Advocate Newspaper. Jackson, Mississippi.

Jackson Daily Newes Newspaper. Jackson, Mississippi.

Jones, Mack. A Frame of Reference for Black Politics. In Lenneal Henderson, Jr., ed. *Black Political Life in the United States*. San Francisco: Chandler, 1972. 7-20.

Jones, Mack. Black Political Empowerment in Atlanta. *Annals of the American Academy of Political and Social Science*. 439 (September 1978). 90–117.

Jones, Mack. Black Political Officeholding and Political Development in the Rural South. *The Review of Black Political Economy*. 6:4 (Summer 1976). 375–407.

Jones, Marcus. *Black Migration in the U.S. With an Emphasis on Selected Cities*. Saratoga, California: Century Twenty-One Publishers, 1980.

Jordan, Winthrop. *White Over Black*. Chapel Hill, North Carolina: University of North Carolina Press, 1968.

Kearney, Robert. Political Mobilization in South Asia. In Robert Crane, ed. *Aspects of Political Mobilization in South Asia*. (Syracuse: Syracuse University Foreign and Comparative Studies Series, 1976. 1–6.

Kerner Report. National Advisory Committee on Civil Disorders. Washingotn, D.C. Government Printing Office, 1968.

Key, V.O. *Southern Politics in State and Nation*. New York: Knopf, 1950.

Kilson, Martin. Political Change in the Negro Ghetto, 1900-1940s. In Nathan Huggins, Martin Kilson, and Daniel Fox, eds. *Key Issues in the Afro-American Experience*, Volume II. New York: Harcourt, Brace, Jovanovich, 1971. 167–92.

Kilpatrick, Franklin et al. *The Image of the Federal Service*. Washington, D.C.: Brookings Institution, 1964.

Kirwan, Albert. *The Revolt of the Rednecks*. Lexington: University of Kentucky, 1951.

Krislov, Samuel. *The Negro and Federal Employment*. Minneapolis: University of Minnesota, 1967.

Ladd, Everett Carll. *Ideology in America*. New York: Norton, 1972.

Ladd, Everett Carll. *Negro Political Leadership in the South*. Ithaca, New York: Cornell University Press, 1966.

Lady Mayor of Mayersville. *Ebony* (December 1977). 52–56.

Lake, Anthony. *The "Tar Baby" Option*. New York: Columbia University Press, 1976.

Lawson, Steven. *Black Ballots*. New York: Columbia University Press, 1976.

Lens, Sidney. *Radicalism in America*. New York: Crowell, 1966.

Levine, Lawrence. *Black Culture and Black Consciousness*. New York: Oxford, 1977.

Levinson, Paul. *Race, Class and Party*. New York: Oxford, 1932.

Levy, Arthur and Standinger, Susan. The Black Caucus in the 92nd Congress. *Phylon*. 39 (December 1978). 322–332.

Lincoln, Eric. *The Black Muslims in America*. Boston: Beacon, 1961.

Lipset, Seymour Martin. *Political Man*. New York: Anchor, 1963.

Little, Malcolm. *The Autobiography of Malcolm X*. New York: Grove Press, 1966.

Loewen, James and Sallis, Charles, eds. *Mississippi: Conflict and Change*. New York: Pantheon, 1974.

Louis, Debbie. *And We Are Not Saved*. New York: Doubleday, 1970.

Lynch, John. *The Facts of Reconstruction*. Indianapolis: Bobbs-Merrill, 1970.

Lynd, Staughton. *Intellectual Origins of the American Revolution*. Cambridge: Harvard, 1982.

Madison, James. The Union as a Safeguard Against Domestic Faction. In Hellman Bishop and Samuel Hendel, eds. *Basic Issues of American Democracy*, 6th. ed. New York: Appleton-Century-Crofts, 1965. 47–53.

Marvick, Dwaine. The Political Socialization of the American Negro. In Harry Bailey, ed. *Negro Politics in America*. Columbus, Ohio: Charles Merrill Co., 1967.

Mashburn vs. Daniel. #6514. Hinds County Chancery Court. (1973).

Matthews, Donald, and Prothro, James. *Negroes and the New Southern Politics*. New York: Harcourt, Brace & World, 1966.

McAdam, Doug. *Political Process and the Development of Black Insurgency*. Chicago: University of Chicago, 1982.

McMillen, Neil. Development of Civil Rights, 1956-1970. In Richard McLemore, *A History of Mississippi* ed. Vol. II. Jackson, University Press of Mississippi, 1973. 154–76.

McMillen, Neil. *Citizens' Councils*. Urbana: University of Illinois Press, 1971.

Menn, J.K. The Large Slaveholders of the Deep South, 1860. Vols. I and II. Unpublished Ph.D. Dissertation. University of Texas, 1964.

Meredith, James. *Three Years in Mississippi*. Bloomington: Indiana University Press, 1965.

Mississippi Research and Development Center (R&D Center). Community Development Plan. Mayersville, 1978.

Mississippi Research and Development Center. *Economic Development Blueprint*. Parts IX and XI.

Morris, Aldon. *The Origins of the Civil Rights Movement*. New York: Free Press, 1984.

Morris, Milton. *The Politics of Black America*. New York: Harper and Row, 1975.

Morrison, K.C. and Huang, Joe, C. The Transfer of Power in a Mississippi Town. *Growth and Change* 4:2. (April 1973). 25–29.

Morrison, Minion K.C. Afro-Americans and Africa: Grassroots Afro-American Opinion and Attitudes Toward Africa. *Comparative Studies in Society and History.* 29:2 (April 1987) 1–42.

Morrison, Minion K.C. Electoral Politics in the South. Paper presented at the National Conference of Black Political Scientists (NCOBPS). (Washington, D.C., April 1970). 1–20.

Morrison, Minion K.C. The Impact of Federal Resource Provision on the Development of Afro-American Leadership. Forthcoming in *Publius* (1987). 1–25.

Morrison, Minion K.C. Preconditions for Afro-American Leadership in the South. *Polity.* 17:3 (Spring 1985). 504–29.

Mosley, Charles (Mrs.). *The Negro in Mississippi History.* Jackson: Hederman Bros., 1950.

Nelson, William and Meranto, Phillip. *Electing Black Mayors.* Columbus, Ohio: Ohio State University Press, 1977.

Netl, J.P. *Political Mobilization.* New York: Basic Books, 1977.

Newman, W.I. *The Politics of Aristotle,* Vol. I. New York: Arno, 1973.

New York Times.

Niemi, Richard and Weisberg, Herbert, ed. *Controversies In American Voting Behavior.* San Francisco: W.H. Freeman, 1976.

Nkrumah, Kwame. *Neocolonialism.* New York: International, 1965.

Oberschall, Anthony. *Social Conflict and Social Movements.* Englewood Cliffs, N.J.: Prentice-Hall, 1973.

Owens, Leslie. *This Species of Property.* New York: Oxford, 1976.

Parenti, Michael. *Power and the Powerless.* New York: St. Martins Press, 1978.

Painter, Nell Irvin. *Exodusters.* New York: Knopf, 1977.

Parker, Frank. "Memorandum on Bolton Election Contest Litigation." September 17, 1973.

Rainwater, Percy Lee. *Mississippi: Storm Center for Succession 1856-1861.* New York: Da Capo, 1938.

Ranney, Austin and Bone, Hugh. *Politics and Voters.* New York: McGraw-Hill, 1976.

Reagan, Michael. *The New Federalism*. New York: Oxford, 1972.

Rodney, Walter. *How Europe Underdeveloped Africa*. Washington, D.C.: Howard University, 1974.

Rowland, Dunbar. *A History of Mississippi*, Vol. II. Jackson: S.J. Clarke Pub. Co., 1925.

Rudolph, Lloyd and Rudolph, Susanne. *The Modernity of Tradition*. Chicago: University of Chicago Press, 1967.

Salamon, Lester. Leadership and Modernization. *Journal of Politics*, 35:3 (1973). 615–646.

Salamon, Lester and Van Evera, Stephen. Fear, Apathy, and Discrimination. *American Political Science Review*. 67:4 (December, 1973). 1288–1306.

Salter, John Jr. *Jackson, Mississippi*. New York: Exposition, 1979.

Satcher, Buford. *Blacks in Mississippi Politics, 1865-1900*. Washington: University Press of America, 1978.

Scarborough, William K. Heartland of the Cotton Kingdom. In R.A. McLemore, ed. *A History of Mississippi*, Vol. I. Jackson: University and College Press, 1973. 310–351.

Schattschneider, E.E. *The Semi-Sovereign People*. New York: Holt, Rinehart Winston, 1960.

Schiffer, Irvine. *Charisma*. Toronto: University of Toronto Press 1973.

Sellers, Cleveland. *The River of No Return*. New York: Morrow, 1973.

Sewell, George. *Mississippi Black History Makers*. Jackson, Mississippi: University Press of Mississippi, 1977.

Sharkansky, Ira. *The Politics of Taxing and Spending*. Indianapolis: Bobbs-Merrill, 1969.

Shingles, Richard. Black Consciousness and Political Participation. *American Political Science Review*. 75:1 (March 1981). 76–91.

Silver, James. *Mississippi: The Closed Society*. Harcourt, Brace and World, 1964.

Sjoberg, Gideon, Brymer, Richard and Buford Farris. Bureaucracy and the Lower Class. *Sociology and Social Research*. 50. (1966).

Smith, Kenneth and Zepp, Ira. *Search for the Beloved Community*. Valley Forge, Pa.: Judson, 1974.

SNCC Papers. Sanford, N. Carolina: Microfilming Corporation of America, 1982. Microform, #4663. Reels 38 and 65.

Spear, Allan. The Origins of the Urban Ghetto, 1870-1915. In Nathan Huggins, Martin Kilson and Daniel Fox eds. *Key Issues in the Afro-American Experience*. Vol. II. New York: Harcourt, Brace & Jovanovich, 1971. 153–166.

Spengler, Joseph. Theory, Ideology, Non-Economic Values, and Politico-Economic Development. In Ralph Braibanti and Joseph Spengler, ed. *Tradition, Values, and Socio-Economic Development*. Durham: Duke University Press, 1961.

St. Angelo, Douglas and Puryear, Paul. Fear, Apathy and Other Dimensions of Black Voting. In Michael Preston, Lenneal Henderson, Jr. and Paul Puryear eds., *The New Black Politics*. New York: Longman, 1982. 109–130.

Steckmesser, Kent L. *The Western Hero in History and Legend*. Norman, Oklahoma: University of Oklahoma, 1965.

Thompson, Daniel C. *Negro Leadership Class*. Englewood Cliffs, N.J.: Prentice-Hall, 1963.

Tilly, Charles. *From Mobilization to Revolution*. Reading, Mass.: Addison-Wesley, 1977.

Truman, Daniel. *The Governmental Process*. New York: Knopf, 1951.

van Evrie, John. A Scientific Proof of the Biological Inferiority of the Negro. In Gilbert Osofsky, ed. *The Burden of Race*. New York: Harper and Row, 1967. 104–109.

Verba, Sidney and Nie, Norman. The Rationality and Political Activity. In Richard Niemi and Herbert Weisberg, eds. *Controversies in American Voting Behavior*. San Francisco: W.H. Freeman, 1976. 45–65.

Walton, Hanes. *Black Politics*. Philadelphia: Lippincott, 1972.

Walton, Hanes. *Black Republicans*. Metuchen, N.J.: Scarecrow, 1975.

Walker, Margaret. *Jubilee*. New York: Bantam, 1966.

Watters, Pat. Their Text is a Civil Rights Primer. In August Meier and Elliot Rudwick, eds. *Black Protest in the Sixties*. Chicago: Quadrangle 1970. 79–88.

Weber, Max. *The Theory of Social and Economic Organization*. Glencoe: The Free Press, 1973.

Weiss, Nancy. *Farewell to the Party of Lincoln*. Princeton: Princeton University Press, 1983.

Weyl, Nathaniel and Marina, William. *American Statesmen on Slavery and the Negro*. New York: Arlington House, 1971.

Wharton, Vernon. *The Negro in Mississippi 1865-1890*. Chapel Hill: University of North Carolina, 1947.

Wilhoit, Francis M. *The Politics of Massive Resistance*. New York: George Braziller, 1973.

Wilson, William J. *The Declining Significance of Race*. Chicago: University of Chicago, 1978.

Woodward, C. Vann *Origins of the New South*. Baton Rouge: LSU Press, 1951.

Woodward, C. Vann. *Tom Watson*. 2nd ed. Savannah, Georgia: Beehive Press, 1973.

Zinn, Howard. *SNCC*. Boston: Beacon, 1964.

Index

A

Abramson, Paul, 196
ACTION, 231
Advisory Committee of the Civil Rights Commission (Miss.), 178
Africa, constituents' knowledge of, 184, 190-93, 194, 203-5, 206
Allen vs. State Board of Elections, 86
American Indian Evironmental Council, 158
American Missionary Association (AMA), 68
Amin, Idi, constituents' knowledge of, 190-91, 193, 194
Amnesty International, 157, 159
Andrews, Jim, 147, 148, 159
Apartheid, constituents' knowledge of, 190, 191-92, 193, 194
Apter, David, 7
Aptheker, Herbert, 34, 35
Aristotle, 25
Atlanta, Ga., 4

B

Balandier, Georges, 210
Banks, Fred, 188
Barker, Lucius, 5, 165
Barnett, Marguerite Ross, 5
Barnett, Ross, 127
Beittel, Adam, 78
Bilbo, Theodore, 31-32, 46

Black and Tan Party, 44-45, 58
Black political history. *See* Civil rights movement; Disfranchisement of blacks; Mobilization of 1940-1970; Reconstruction-era mobilization; Slavery
Black Power (Carmichael and Hamilton), 69-70, 71
Blackwell, Jeremiah, 101
Blackwell, Saul, 111
Blackwell, Unita
  assessment of, 122, 245
  change priorities, 99-100
  charisma of, 109-10
  childhood, 99, 100-101
  civil rights background, 18
  constituents' knowledge of, 188
  economic reprisals against, 106, 116
  as external resource provider, 227, 232, 234
  "freedom buttons" episode, 116-19
  freedom school activities, 114-16
  as heroine inventor, 19, 95-97
  ideology of
    Chinese experience, interpretation of, 113
    integration concerns, 110-11
    rural values, 112-13
    sacrifice, 111-12
    social change focus, 100, 111
    Third World perspective, 113
  incorporation of Mayersville, 119-22
  individualism of, 100
  mayor, selection as, 121-22
  mobilization campaign
    church, role of, 102-3

civil rights movement as inspiration for, 18, 102-3
moral/philosophical bases of, 102
older leaders in, 101
organizations, links with, 108
voter registration, 103-6, 107-8
national recognition for, 108
personal risks, acceptance of, 106
social status, 17
speaking talents, 109-10
as youthful leader, 17, 101
Bolden, R. L., 149, 150
Bolden, Vincent, 151-52
Bolton, Miss. (Hinds County), 53
constituent political behavior data, 176-77, 181-82, 191, 195-97, 200, 201
demographics, 14-15
disfranchisement of blacks, 56-59
election challenges by whites
1969, 84-87
1973, 88-92
formal leaders, 16
infrastructure projects, 233-34, 235
institutionalization of black regime, 236-37, 240-41
map of, 54
mobilization in, 244-45
  civil rights movement and, 59-61
  radical populist leaders and, 64-67
  students, role of, 62, 63-64
  voter registration, 61
  youths, role of, 67
"out-group based" leaders, 58-59
political economy, 215
  external funding, 227-28, 231
  tax base, 218-22, 224-26
political isolation of, 74-76
population history, 55
prosperity of, 15
reconstruction-era mobilization, 55-56
see also Thompson, Bennie
Bolton Development Corporation, 236
Bond, Julian, 158
Brady, Tom, 127
Brisbane, Robert, 12
Brown vs. Board of Education, 46
Bruce, B. K., 38
Bryant vs. Blunt, 86

C

Caldwell, Charles, 36, 38, 56, 58
Calhoun, John C., 25, 26
Campaign financing, 209
Campbell, Angus, 165, 166
Carmichael, Stokely, 12, 69, 71, 210
Carnovan, Margaret, 65
Carter, Hodding, 129
Carter, Jimmy, 179, 184, 207
Carthan, Eddie
  as agrarian townsman, 20, 135, 140-41
  assault, trial and conviction for, 147-49, 155-56, 159
  assessment of, 160-61, 246
  business successes, 138
  campaign approach, 140
  civil rights movement, influence of, 136, 140
  college education, 16, 136-38
  conspiracy against, alleged, 147-49, 153-54
  constituents, attitude toward, 135
  as external resource provider, 227, 232, 234
  "independence from whites" ideology, 144-45
  mayoral election, 125, 134-35
  "misuse of funds" charges against, 146, 149-50, 153-54, 159
  murder trial, 151-53, 154, 159
  political beginnings, 138-39
  political conflicts
    appointments and, 145, 146-47
    black opposition, 141-42
    business expenses and, 145
    coalition of white and black opponents, 143-44
    lock-out from town hall, 145-46
    modernization program, cutoff of, 146
    police chief issue, 146-47
    white opposition, 142-43
  as political prisoner
    campaign against black politicians, symbol of, 156
    Carthan's rationale re, 153-54
    defense committees and support groups, 149, 155-57, 158

INDEX 295

legal defenses, 159
publicity activities, 157-58
racial aspects, 155
supporters' beliefs re, 154-55
voting rights issue, 156-57
popularity of, 139-40
prison term, 159
"public interest" focus, 135-36
socioeconomic status, 17
"solidarity of blacks" ideology, 140-41, 142
teaching career, 138
violence following convictions, 150-51
as youthful leader, 17, 136
Catholic Committee of the South, 158
Center for Constitutional Rights, 158
Charisma of leaders, 17-18
langauge usage, 109-10
religion and, 110
speaking abilities, 109
China, People's Republic of, 113
the Church and mobilization, 13, 102-3
Civil rights movement
Blackwell's mobilization campaign, inspiration for, 18, 102-3
Bolton mobilization and, 59-61
constituent political behavior, influence on, 168-69, 173-74, 175
economic discrimination, focus on, 61
leaders, influence on, 18
political empowerment through, 12-13
public demonstrations, 60, 61
in reconstruction era, 41
student protests, 63
Tchula mobilization and, 130-32
white reaction to, 60, 61
Civil War, 30
Clark, Robert, xv, xvi, 50, 125, 133
Clark, Tom, 159
Coalition of Black Trade Unionists, 158
COFO. *See* Council of Federated Organizations
Collective attribution, 13
Commerce, U.S. Department of, 233
Committee of One Hundred for the General Improvement of the Condition of the Colored People of Mississippi, 45

Committee to Defend the Tchula 7, 156
Comparativists, 8-9
Comprehensive Employment Training Act (CETA), 231
Conflict model mobilization, 10
Congressional Black Caucus (CBC), 238
Congress of Racial Equality (CORE), 11-12
Constituent political behavior, 163-64
civil rights movement, influence of, 168-69, 173-74, 175
conclusions re, 205, 207, 246-48
Democratic Party's appeal to blacks and, 169-70
efficacy variable
conventional wisdom on, 195
definition of, 175
growth in efficacy, 196-97
"interaction with city hall" measure, 195-96
political changes, relation to, 197-98
election participation, findings on, 164-66, 179-81
gubernatorial elections, participation in, 179, 180-81
ideology variable
definition of, 175
integration issue, 199-201
political power sharing issue, 201-2
questions for measurement of, 199
relevance of, 198
socioeconomic status and, 201-2
transfer of ideology to international sphere, 203-5, 206
King's influence on, 173-74
knowledge variable
candidate/office visibility and, 183
conventional wisdom on, 182-83
definition of, 175
improvement of knowledge, 184, 185
information sophistication, domestic, 183, 184-85
information sophistication, international, 183-84, 190-93, 194
mayors, knowledge of, 184
organizations and indirect local leaders, 188-90
participation, relation to, 183

socioeconomic status and, 185-87, 192-93, 194
participation variable, 177-78
  definition of, 175
  intensity of campaign and, 181-82
  knowledge, relation to, 183
  leader influence and, 181
  socioeconomic status and, 185-87
  voter registration and, 178-82
political socialization and, 166-68
presidential elections, participation in, 165-66, 179-81
racial experience, impact of, 172-73
study sample, 175-77
Constituents
  African affairs, interest in, 184, 190-93, 194, 203-5, 206
  isolation from American mainstream, 168
  leaders, relations with, 14, 20, 247-48
  mobilization process, role in, 20, 246-47
  political education programs for, 72
  politicians, distrust of, 167
  population figures, 170, 171
  principled commitment among, 167
  radical populists' focus on, 66-67
  school desegregation, attitudes toward, 199-201
  voter registration data, 170, 172
Cooper, Frederick, 228
CORE. *See* Congress of Racial Equality
Corporate political influence, 4
Council of Federated Organizations (COFO), 45, 47, 49, 61
Cox, Eugene, 129, 130

D

Dahl, Robert, 3
Davis, Ossie, 157
Deliberate political acts, 8
Dellums, Ronald, 158
Delta Ministry of the National Council of Churches, 157
Democratic Party, 50
  appeal to blacks (1930s), 168, 169-70
  blacks barred from, 43, 49
  civil rights plank (1948), 46
  external resources accessed through (1970s), 226, 227
  in reconstruction era, 39, 42-43
Deutsch, Karl, 7, 10
Disfranchisement of blacks
  in Bolton, 56-59
  era of disfranchisement, 43-45
  in Mayersville, 98-99
  process of, 39-40, 41-43
Dolbeare, Kenneth, 4, 5, 209, 210
Dunn, Jim, 157
Dymally, Mervyn, 158

E

Eastland, James, 44, 127
Economic aspects of mobilization. *See* Political economy of mobilization
Edelmen, Murray, 4, 5, 209, 210, 214
Eisenhower, Dwight D., 170
Eisinger, Peter, 210
Electorates. *See* Constituent *headings*
Elitist theory of politics, 4-5
  black political life, application to, 5
  political economy and, 209-11
English, Mrs. Luetishie, 107
Environmental Protection Agency (EPA), 234
Epps, Edgar, 78
Equal Rights Congress of New Orleans, 156-57
Etzioni, Emitai, 9
Evers, Charles, xiv, xvi, 50, 137
Evers, Medgar, 46, 47, 51, 61, 155

F

Fanon, Frantz, 70
Farmers Home Administration (Miss.), 75, 76
Federal government-small town relationship. *See under* Political economy of mobilization
Ford, Sharkey, 146
Foreman, Harold "Hap", 149, 150
Framers of the Constitution, 3, 4

Frank, Andre Gunder, 211
Freedom buttons, 115, 116-19
Freedom rides, 60
Freedom schools, 114-16, 131
Freedom Summers of 1964 and 1965, 48, 115-16, 130-31
Friedland, John, 17
Frye, Henry, xiii

G

Gamson, William, 10
Genovese, Eugene, 25, 34
Gibson, Jacyne, 141-42, 143, 145
Gleed, Robert, 38
Granderson, Roosevelt, 141-42, 143, 145-46, 150
 murder of, 151-52
Gregory, Dick, 157
Griggs, Richard, 98
Gubernatorial elections, black participation in, 179, 180-81
Gurin, Patricia, 78
Gwaltney, John, 35

H

Halfway homes, 46
Hamilton, Charles, 12, 69, 71, 210
Harris, James, 147-48
Hatcher, Richard, 158
Hayes, Ralthus, 132-33, 139
Hays, John Edgar, 142-43, 145
Headstart programs, 73, 227, 230
Heggies Scouts (terror group), 126
Henry, Aaron, 46, 51, 188
Henry Weathers High School, 117
Hero(ine) inventors, 19. *see also* Blackwell, Unita
Hester, David, 151-52
Hinds County. *See* Bolton, Miss. (Hinds County)
Hine, Darlene, 173
History of Mississippi and the south
 anti-democratic foundations, 25
 black history. *See* Disfranchisement of blacks; Mobilization of 1940-1970; Reconstruction-era mobilization; Slavery
 poor whites, 26
 populist political leaders (white), 30-32, 65
 white aristocratic regime, 24-26
 white intragroup factionalism (hills *vs* delta), 26-28
 political conflicts, 30-32
 slavery and, 28-30
 white political hegemony, 31-32
Holmes County. *See* Tchula, Miss. (Holmes County)
Holmes County Herald, 129
Holmes County United League, 156
Holt, Len, 114
Hook, Sidney, 100
Housing and Urban Development, U.S. Department of (HUD), 233, 234
Housing programs, 213
Howard University student protests, 77, 78
Humphrey, Hubert, 46
Humpstone, Charles, 108
Hunter, Floyd, 4

I

Indigenous perspective, 13
Infrastructure projects, 212, 229, 232-35, 239
Institutionalization of political regimes, 213-14, 229, 235-37, 240-41, 249
Institutionalized racism, 6
Interstate Commerce Commission, 60
Issaquena County. *See* Mayersville, Miss. (Issaquena County)

J

Jackson, Jesse, 158
Jackson, Miss., civil rights movement in, 59-61, 79-80
Jackson State College, 79-80
Jefferson, Thomas, 25
Jim Crow laws, 11
Johnson, Leroy, xiii

Johnson, Mrs. Elra, 133-34
Joint Center for Political Studies (JCPS), xvi
Jones, Mack, xiv, 5, 210
Jones, Marcus, 169
Jordan, Vernon, 158
Justice, U.S. Department of, 233

K

Kanter, 10
Kearney, Robert, 8
Kennedy, John F., 48
Key, V. O., 27, 28, 170
King, Martin Luther, Jr., 48, 102, 169
  constituent political behavior, impact on, 173-74
  on integration, 110
  as leader, xiii, 12, 13-14, 173-74
Kirksey, Henry, 188
Kirwan, Albert, 30
Kissinger, Henry, constituents' knowledge of, 190, 191, 193, 194
Ku Klux Klan, 43, 116
  constituents' knowledge of, 188

L

Labor, U.S. Department of, 233
Ladd, Everett Carll, xiv, 12, 198
Lamb, Hazel, 118
Law Enforcement Assistance Administration (LEAD), 231
Law enforcement projects, 231
Lawson, Steven, 173
Lawyers' Committee for Civil Rights Under Law, 85
Leaders
  agrarian townsmen, 19-20. *see also* Carthan, Eddie
  characteristics of, 15, 248
  charisma of, 17-18, 109-10
  civil rights ideology, 18
  constituent political behavior, influence on, 181
  constituents, relations with, 14, 20, 247-48

cooperation with whites, promotion of, 141-42
  deliberate political acts by, 8
  education levels, 16
  elected officials, 15-16
  as external resource providers, 212-13, 226-27, 230-35
  hero(ine) inventors, 19. *see also* Blackwell, Unita
  institutionalization of regimes, 213-14, 229, 235-37, 240-41
  interventionist political programs, 18
  King's leadership, xiii, 12, 13-14, 173-74
  of mobilization of 1940-1970, 46, 47, 51-52
  NAACP, influence on, 46
  "out-group based" leaders, 58-59
  radical populists, 18-19, 64-67. *see also* Thompson, Bennie
  of reconstruction-era mobilization, 38-39, 40-41, 56
  regional affiliations, 16
  situational factors, impact of, 18
  socioeconomic status, 16-17
  speaking powers, 17, 109-10
  as symbols of success, xvi
  youth of, 17-18, 63, 101
Lens, Sideny, 66
Levine, Lawrence, 34
Lexington *Advertiser*, 128
Lincoln, Abraham, 111
Literacy tests, 43
  administration of, 107-8
  testimony on, 103-6, 107
Loewen, James, 45
Lowery, Joseph, 157
Loyal Leagues, 36, 56
Lynch, James, 38, 40-41, 56
Lynch, John R., 38, 40, 41-42, 56, 58
Lynchings, 31-32
Lynd, Staughton, 66, 76
Lyon, Lester, 159

M

McAdam, Doug, 10, 11, 12-13, 14
McCorry, Jesse, 5, 165

McGovern, George, 179
Manifold organizations, 13
Marvick, Dwaine, 167
Matthews, Donald, 12, 63, 64, 179, 182, 184
Mayersville, Miss. (Issaquena County)
 constituent political behavior data, 176-77, 188, 200, 201
 disfranchisement of blacks, 98-99
 formal leaders, 16
 incorporation of Mayersville, 119-22
 infrastructure projects, 233, 234, 235
 institutionalization of black regime, 237
 map of, 96
 political economy, 215, 218-22
 profile of, 14-15, 95
 reconstruction-era mobilization, 98
 slaveocracy history, 97-99
 see also Blackwell, Unita
May 2nd Movement, 77
Meredith, James, 59
Merton, Robert, 135
Meuchy, Koai, 149
MFDP. See Mississippi Freedom Democratic Party
Minter, David, 129, 130
Mississippi Action for Community Education (MACE), 231
Mississippi Conference of Black Mayors, 155
Mississippi counties, map of, 2
Mississippi Freedom Democratic Party (MFDP), 49, 50, 108
 Tchula mobilization, role in, 132-33
Mississippi Free Press, 128
Mississippi Human Relations Council, 59
Mississippi Regional Council of Negro Leadership, 46
Mississippi Valley State University (MVSU), 136-37
 student protests at, 137-38
Mobilization, definition of, 3
Mobilization of 1940-1970, 11-12
 elected officials, 50-51
 halfway homes and, 46
 leaders, role of, 46, 47, 51-52
 local actions, focus on, 46-47, 50
 NAACP, role of, 46-47, 48
 organizational solidarity, 47-49
 voter registration efforts, 45-46, 48-49, 50, 51
 white reaction to, 47, 49
 white students, involvement of, 48
Mobilization process
 black majorities and, 251
 black political empowerment, appropriateness for, 249-54
 change-stimulating factors, 244
 the church, role of, 13, 102-3
 "collective activation" aspect, 10, 11
 commitments and definitions required by, 251
 comparativist perspective, 8-9
 constituents, role of, 20, 246-47. see also Constituent political behavior
 creation of community, 10
 defensive mobilization, 11
 dependency on federal government and, 252-53
 differential mobilization, 8
 future mobilization, prospects for, 253-54
 horizontal mobilization, 8
 internal dynamics, restraining effect of, 253
 leader-constituent relations and, 14, 20
 limits of, 251-52
 modernization process and, 7, 9
 oppressor class replaced through, xvii
 organizations, importance of, 13-14
 preconditions for, xvii
 protest activity and, 11
 racism as catalyst, 6, 9, 11
 resource control as goal of, 1, 3, 9-10
 social mobilization and, 6-7, 9
 studies on, 12-13
 successes of, 250-51
 symbols and language of, 12
 Third World decolonization and, 6-9
 see also Leaders; mobilization subheadings under Blackwell, Unita; Bolton, Miss.; Tchula, Miss.
Mobilization theory, black political empowerment best described by, 244
Modernization process, 7, 9
Montgomery, Ala. boycott, xiii, xiv

Moore, Amzie, 46
Morris, Aldon, 12-13, 14, 45, 47, 169
Mosley, Mrs. C. C., 46
MVSU. *See* Mississippi Valley State University

N

NAACP. See National Association for the Advancement of Colored People
National Association for the Advancement of Colored People (NAACP), 13
  Blackwell, work with, 108
  constituents' knowledge of, 188-90
  legal activities, 59, 108, 169, 170
  mobilization of 1940-1970, role in, 11, 46-47, 48
  public demonstrations, 60, 61
  students' rights activities, 117, 137
National Campaign to Free Mayor Eddie J. Carthan and the Tchula 7 and to preserve Black Political Rights, 149, 157
National Committee for SANE Nuclear Policy, 77
National Conference of Black Mayors, 158
National Council of Churches, 157, 158
Nationalism of black students, 77-78
National Urban League, 158
Neo-colonialism, 210-11
Nettl, J. P., 8
New federalism, 236
New Haven, Conn., 3
Niemi, Richard, 164
Nkrumah, Kwame, 211

O

Oberschall, Anthony, 10
Operation Push, 158
Owens, George, 79, 82, 83
Owens, Leslie, 34

P

Parenti, Michael, 4, 209, 214
Parker, Frank, 85, 86, 89, 90, 91, 92

Plato, 25
Plessy vs. Ferguson, 58
Pluralist theory of politics
  black political life, application to, 3, 5
  characteristics of, 3-4
Political behaviors, models for measurement of, 164
Political economy of mobilization
  agricultural declines, 215-17
  conclusions re, 237-41, 248
  dependency, structural conditions of (neo-colonialism), 210-11
  economic division, black and white, 214-15
  elitist theory re, 209-11
  external funding
    allocation to rural constituents, 214
    excess demands for funds, 239-40
    human needs focus, 212, 228-29, 230-32, 238, 239, 248
    infrastructure projects, 212, 229, 232-35, 239
    institutionalization of regimes and, 213-14, 229, 235-37, 240-41, 249
    intra-group cleavages and, 240
    local expansion through, 234-35
    problems fostered by, 238-40
    rise in revenues through, 227-28
    sources of, 226-27
    transfer of power through, 231
  federal grovernment–small town relationship, 212-14, 226-27, 236
  dependency on federal government, 229-30, 252-53
  labor, outmigration of, 215
  private resources outside the reach of blacks, 210
  public treasury upon election of blacks, 217-18
  tax structure, 218
    black mayors, impact of, 222, 224-26
    income taxes, 218-19
    property taxes, 219-21
    sales taxes, 221-22
    volume of revenue generated, 222, 223, 224-26
  white racism, impact of, 240-41
"Political kingdom" for blacks, xvi
Poll taxes, 43
Poll watchers 133-34

Populist political leaders (white), 30-32, 65
Presidential elections, black participation in, 165-66, 179-81
Progressive Voters League, 45
Prothro, James, 12, 63, 64, 179, 182, 184
Providence Cooperative, 129-30

R

Racism
  black political development, impact on, 9, 11
  colonial roots, 6
  constituent political behavior, impact on, 172-73
  elitist theory of politics and, 5
  as mobilization catalyst, 6, 9, 11
  pervasiveness in the political system, 5-6
  philosophical roots, 25
  political economy of mobilization, impact on, 240-41
  slavery, relation to, xv, 25-26, 29
  white female virtue and, 31-32
  of white populist leaders, 31-32
  see also White Citizens' Council
Radical populist leaders, 18-19
  backgrounds of, 64-65
  constituents, focus on, 66-67
  ideology of, 66
  strategy for the community, 67
  white populists and, 65
  see also Thompson, Bennie
Rainwater, Percy Lee, 28
Reconstruction-era mobilization
  black majority in Mississippi, 35
  briefness of, 41
  Cooperationist stage, 35-36
  cooperation with whites, blacks' beliefs re, 41-42
  fusion (disfranchisement) stage, 39-40, 41-43, 58, 98-99
  leaders of, 38-39, 40-41, 56
  power base for blacks, 55-56, 57
  Republicanism stage, 36, 38-39
  state constitution, reconstruction of, 35-36
  successes and failures of, 40-42
Republican Party
  black control of, 44, 58
  decline of, 43-44
  in reconstruction era, 36, 42
Revels, Hiram, 38
Roosevelt, Franklin D., 168, 169-70
Rose Hill Baptist Church Center, 115
Russell, Dan, 92

S

Sallis, Charles, 45
Sample ballots, 134
Schattschneider, E. E., 156, 239
School desegregation
  constituents' attitudes toward, 199-201
  local action for, 119
  white resistance to, 127
SCLC. *See* Southern Christian Leadership Conference
Scott, H. P., 98
SES. *See* Socioeconomic status
Slaughter, Constance, 80, 81
Slaveocracy, 97-99
Slavery
  cotton production and, 33
  distribution of slaves by soil areas, 37
  "independent" lives of slaves, 34-35
  music of slaves, 34
  as political experience, 32-35
  poor whites' dilemma re, 28-29
  racism, relation to, xv, 25-26, 29
  revolts by slaves, 34-35
  rules and regulations of, 33
  white aristocrats' attitudes toward, 25-26, 29-30
Smith, Hazel Brannon, 128-29, 130
Smith vs. Allwright, 46
SNCC. *See* Student Non-Violent Coordinating Committee
Social mobilization, 6-7, 9
Socioeconomic status (SES)
  constituents' ideology and, 201-2
  constituents' knowledge and, 185-87, 192-93, 194
  constituents' participation and, 185-87
  definition of, 164
  of leaders, 16-17

"Solidarity of blacks" ideology, 140-41, 142
South Africa, constituents' attitudes toward, 203-5, 206
Southern Christian Leadership Conference (SCLC), 13-14, 173
Southern Regional Council, 45, 46
Stokes, Carl, xv
Strauder vs. West Virginia, 86
Stringer, Thomas, 36, 38, 56
Student Non-Violent Coordinating Committee (SNCC), 47, 69, 77
  Blackwell, work with, 102-3 106
  freedom schools, 114, 115
  goals and strategy of, 48, 70-72
Student protests
  in Bolton mobilization, 62, 63-64
  motivations for, 77-78
  at MVSU, 137-38
  see also under Tougaloo College
Students for a Democratic Society, 77
Supreme Court, 170
Sydnor, Charles, 98

T

Tax structures. *See under* Political economy of mobilization
Taylor, Mrs. Deane, 148
Tchula, Miss. (Holmes County)
  constituent political behavior data, 176-77, 188-90, 195-97, 200, 201
  formal leaders, 16
  infrastructure projects, 234, 235
  institutionalization of black regime, 237, 240
  map of, 124
  mobilization in
    assessment of, 160-61, 246
    black political fragmentation, 141-44, 160
    civil rights movement and, 130-32
    community center, 131
    election activities, 133-34
    MFDP, role of, 132-33
    political organizations, 132-33
    white opposition, 131-32, 133, 142-44, 160
    young leaders for, 134-35
  political and economic development, 125-26
  political economy, 215, 218-22
  profile of, 14-15, 123, 125
  white supremacists in, 127-30
  see also Carthan, Eddie
Tchula Times, 147, 152
Third World decolonization, 6-9
Third World perspective, 113
Thompson, Bennie, 3, 53
  aldermanic elections, 72-73, 84-87
  assertiveness of, 76-77
  assessment of, 93, 245
  blacks, unity with, 69
  childhood, 62
  civil rights background, 65
  college education, 16, 68, 69-70
  community-sense of, 70
  as external resource provider, 227, 231, 232, 235
  grassroots power base, 72-73
  Headstart programs, 73
  housing efforts, 74-76
  institutionalization efforts, 236-37, 240
  leadership at Tougaloo, 82-83
  mayoral election, 88-92, 182
  policy proposals, 73
  political education, 67-72
  as radical populist, 19, 54-55, 65-67
  small town powerlessness, focus on, 74-76
  SNCC, influence of, 70-72
  socioeconomic status, 16, 65
  speeches and interviews, 74
  student protests, influence of, 62-63
  student protests, involvement in, 80-83
  tax revenues, impact on, 222, 224-26
  white challenges to electoral victories, 84-85, 88-89
  legal actions in response to, 85-87, 89-92
  whites, political isolation from, 73-74
  as youthful leader, 17
Thompson vs. Bolton Municipal Democratic Executive Committee, 90-92
Tilly, Charles, 10, 11
Tougaloo College, 62

business boycott, 61
  as community, 70
  history of, 68
  progressive philosophy, 68-69
  public library incident, 60
  student protests against the administration, 78-79
    boycotts, 81
    civil rights focus, 79
    faculty support, 82
    Jackson State riot and, 79-80
    negotiations, 81
    president's reaction, 82
    "self determination for blacks" issue, 81
    Thompson's leadership, 82-83
    trial of Slaughter and Thompson, 80-81
  Thompson's education at, 69-70
Transportation, U.S. Department of (DOT), 233
Truman, David B., 3
Turnbow, Hartman, 132
Turner, Nat, 34

U

U.S./China People's Friendship Association, 108
United Methodist Voluntary Services, 158
United Negro College Fund (UNCF), 68
University of Mississippi, integration of, 59

V

Vardaman, John, 31
Vesey, Denmark, 34
Virginia vs. Rivers, 86
Volunteers in Service to America (VISTA), 231
Voter Education Project (VEP), xiv
Voter registration, xiv
  in Blackwell's mobilization campaign, 103-6, 107-8

  in Bolton, 61
  constituent political behavior and, 178-82
  constitutent registration data, 170, 172
  elections, impact on, xiv
  in mobilization of 1940-1970, 45-46, 48-49, 50, 51
  personal involvement for constituents through, 51
Voting Rights Act of 1965, xiv, 48, 85-86, 156, 179

W

War on Poverty, 12
Water systems, development of, 233
Watters, Pat, 173
Weber, Max, 17
Weisberg, Herbert, 164
Welfare programs, 212, 228-29, 230-32
Wharton, Vernon, 33, 34, 36, 45
White, Dan, 118
White Citizens' Council, 125
  organization of, 47
  political power, 127-28
  progressive elements, campaign against, 128-30
  school desegregation, resistance to, 127

W

Williams vs. Reed, 86
Wilmington 10, 153
Wilson, James Q., 135
Wilson, William J., 12
Wood, Robert, 38
The Wretched of the Earth (Fanon), 70

Y

Young, Andrew, constituents' knowledge of, 190, 191, 193, 194
Youth Employment Training Program (YETP), 231